EVOLUTION OF THE
AIRLINER

British Air Liner. 2o062 5B

EVOLUTION OF THE
AIRLINER

Ray Whitford

THE CROWOOD PRESS

First published in 2007 by
The Crowood Press Ltd
Ramsbury, Marlborough
Wiltshire SN8 2HR

www.crowood.com

British Library Cataloguing-in-Publication Data
A catalogue record for this book is available from the British Library.

ISBN   978 1 86126 870 9

Typeset by Servis Filmsetting Ltd, Manchester

Printed and bound in Great Britain by Biddles Ltd, King's Lynn

Contents

Contents

Contents

Preface

The period 1914–18 saw the aeroplane develop from a device useful in a general's bag of tricks in waging war to something that could conduct war over long distances. Some enlightened enthusiasts saw that, if aeroplanes could do that with bombs, there was a possibility of carrying passengers. With the ending of the First World War several visionaries turned their attention to the possibilities of commercial aviation. Their attempts were hesitant, largely because of the necessary reliance on aircraft drawn from the existing pool of military equipment.

It was not until the mid-1920s, as the world economy improved, that any progress was made with aircraft designed specifically as airliners. Even then, operations had to be subsidized by governments requiring the transport of airmail. As related in this book, the major improvements originated in the late 1920s and early 1930s, when designers at last grasped the opportunities offered by a combination of technological innovations. Thus the wooden biplane was transformed into a streamlined monoplane capable of competing with existing modes of transport, namely overnight trains and, more notably, a product from the USA.

The advances that made the airliner commercially viable came from the USA around 1930, and not from Europe, where the aircraft industry had until then been the biggest and strongest. Despite the pioneering work of the Wright brothers, the US industry had less of a past than Europe's, and this helped it to innovate. In addition, the USA had a proportionately greater commercial business, with a large continental market that accounted for nearly half of civilian aircraft sales between 1927 and 1937. Another crucial factor may have been that many of its designers were men who had started their careers after 1918, and so did not have the traditions of the war, and of the biplane, to forget. Whatever the reasons, the USA produced aircraft in the early 1930s that incorporated all the features that led to the 'modern airliner'; low-wing monoplanes built from aluminium alloys, with retractable undercarriages, wing flaps, and variable-pitch propellers driven by cowled engines. A relatively small group of people provided the ideas or inspirations for the key developments, and their enthusiasm

for ideas, not always of immediate value, accelerated progress.

Over more than twenty years airliners got bigger, faster and more powerful, with pressurized cabins to allow them to fly higher, but basically they remained like the Douglas DC-3. The advent of the Second World War and preparations for it concentrated effort on military aircraft, and once again produced rapid progress. This time, however, it also helped stimulate a more fundamental innovation in technology, the jet engine. By 1945 the British and German air forces were using jet-propelled aircraft, Germany also incorporating the swept wing. Within a decade these developments were adopted by the commercial aircraft industry to enhance the fundamental benefit of air travel, speed.

The costs of carrying passengers fell, in four distinct periods. Firstly in the 1930s, when the shape of the airliner was revolutionized by metal monoplanes, well ahead of contemporary military aircraft; secondly in the 1950s, as piston-engine pressurized airliners grew larger, with double the number of seats; thirdly in the late 1950s with the introduction of the first jet airliners, with a further doubling of seats; and, finally, in the early 1970s with the introduction of high-bypass-ratio turbofan-powered widebodies with up to 450 seats. The picture of the commercial aircraft industry was thus not one of steady technical progress, but of widely spaced jumps. More recently, progress has become more evolutionary than revolutionary. Speed, albeit with an excursion into the supersonic regime, has remained the same as in the late 1950s. However, electronic entertainment systems have at least reduced the boredom for the average passenger, and nowadays there are beds for those in first class. Today the 1,000-seat airliner is within sight.

With increasing emphasis on safety, economics and reliability, allowing twin-engine aircraft almost unlimited range, the industry has witnessed large-scale rationalization, and now there are only two major airframe and three major engine companies. The future of airliners will be governed inevitably by the demand for even lower seat-mile costs, though constrained by higher fuel bills together with reduced environmental impact.

Chapter 1

Airline Growth and Economics

This chapter deals with the origins of air transport and the development of commercial aviation. It was the remarkable technological progress, especially in the early 1930s, that enabled aircraft recognized today as the first 'modern airliners' to appear. In the 1950s airlines embraced the jet engine and swept wing to pursue the demand for speed and greater capacity, causing traffic to grow rapidly. The demand for lower operating costs in the 1960s inevitably gave rise to widebody airliners and the 'jumbo jet'.

Handley Page H.P.42s served Imperial Airways for ten years without a fatal accident. The UK was the first major world power to sponsor its own national airline. At the time of the formation of Imperial Airways the USA possessed no civil airlines at all.
(*AIR International* Collection)

The earliest commercial operations

During the early years after the Wright brothers' first powered flights in 1903, aeroplanes were regarded as vehicles best suited for entertainment. By 1910, however, the thought had occurred to a few experimenters that light commercial loads could be carried. Although the world's first official airmail flight (on February 18, 1911) is credited to India, a series of such flights were made in England later that year by the Grahame-White Aviation Company between London and Windsor, using French aircraft. This narrowly bettered similar ventures in the USA and Italy. Between April and November 1918 two converted Handley Page O/400 bombers carried more than 1,800 passengers between Marquise, near Calais in France, and Lympe, Kent, in the UK. Although regularity was poor, here was evidence that scheduled operations, as distinct from a spasmodic series of flights, were a practical possibility.

The immediate post-war period was a troubled time for the adventurous spirits trying to launch British air transport. The cause was simple economics: high costs and inadequate revenues. Whereas in France the government gave generous assistance to its fledgling airlines, and the German States helped aviation to survive by subsidizing air services, the British policy was that the airlines should 'fly by themselves'. Fortunately there was sufficient outcry and parliamentary lobbying to produce action so that services were sustained, backed by a modest contribution of government money. Despite the complex problems yet to be solved for flying on a commercial scale, many were convinced that the future would be for aircraft dominating

the world's great transport routes. The rate of technical advance made during the war could not continue in peace, and the progress in flying was bound to decrease in the face of the demands of peacetime. The first transatlantic landplane flight (from Newfoundland to Ireland) was made by Alcock and Brown in 1919. It was a hazardous experience and yet a prophetic one, because it demonstrated that large multi-engine aircraft were the future for long-distance flight. However, twenty years were to pass before many of the dreams of 1919 came to fruition.

Imperial Airways

During 1922 the route structure of British companies was rationalized so that Handley Page Transport concentrated on Paris, Instone Air Line on Brussels and Daimler Airway on Amsterdam. Once again, though, subsidies were inadequate to carry the airlines though the winter months. More government money was injected to form the Imperial Air Transport Company Ltd (taking over the existing airlines) in 1924, with the caveat that only British aircraft and engines would be used. Provided it met an agreed mileage each year, the company would receive a total subsidy of £1m over ten years. Thus the UK was the first major world power to sponsor its own national airline. At the time of the formation of Imperial Airways the USA had no airlines at all.

This photograph of Boeing's 247 and 777 gives an illustration of how airliner technology has advanced. The Boeing 247 made its first flight in February 1933, carried ten passengers and cruised at 155mph. By comparison the 777, first flying in 1994, carries up to 550 passengers and cruises at Mach 0.87.
(Boeing)

The First World War had left Britain with political commitments in the Middle East. To forge a speedy communications link across inhospitable territory devoid of surface transport, the Royal Air Force (RAF) had organized some squadrons of Airco D.H.9As to provide airmail and courier services between Cairo and Baghdad in 1921. Imperial Airways had set its sights eastwards, ranging through India to Singapore, Hong Kong and Australia. While this trailblazing was going on, steady progress was being made, though the number of ways by which the airline reached India was quite bewildering in terms of routes and the combination of air and rail links. A journey time of seven-and-a-half days was commendable, bearing in mind the performance of the aircraft used, the nature of the terrain covered and the absence of navigation aids.

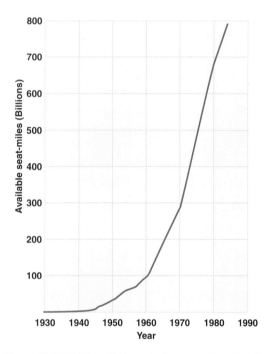

Traffic growth (1919–90): available seat-miles versus time. There have been six main reasons for the growth in traffic: increase in speed, increase in frequency, more direct routes, growth in GNP, growth in discretionary income and fare reductions. Nobody in the 1930s could have anticipated that commercial air transportation would far exceed that of surface carriers between the major cities of the world. When the public's fear of flying was overcome, and time-saving, comfort and reliability had been amply demonstrated, most travellers accepted the airliner as the most reasonable mode of long-distance transportation. Traffic growth really started to climb following the Second World War.
(*AIR International*)

US commercial operations

Established air transportation in the USA started in the mid-1920s and, like that in the UK, owes its beginnings to unfettered private enterprise. The industry, such as it was, was run by rugged individualists, many of whom were barnstorming pilots, though few were sound businessmen or engineers, since there appeared to be little engineering background or stability to the enterprise. There were many financially minded promoters, more interested in Wall Street than the development of the industry, and numerous enthusiasts and visionaries, some of whom truly saw the ultimate commercial possibilities of air transport. More of them were just afraid they would miss out on the excitement

of this new adventure. They were all motivated to fly at any cost, which they did. One slogan of air transportation in those days was: 'The more you fly, the more you lose'. With such a background there was a wide variety of transport aircraft types, materials and methods of construction. There was still a preponderance of small, mail-only type aircraft, as the origins of commercial aviation lay in the carriage of mail. A few somewhat larger types carried mail and tolerated a few passengers.

The importance of airmail

The British government's *laissez-faire* attitude was in direct contrast to that of the US Airmail, the principal instrument of US governmental support of aviation from 1911. By 1915 a small group of enthusiasts had obtained appropriations through the US Congress for a Post Office experiment with airmail. The First World War delayed the experiment until 1918, when the first true US airmail flights were made by Army pilots.

The US Post Office created navigation/communication stations and emergency landing fields. By 1923 the first stretch of 'lighted airway' was completed between Chicago, Illinois, and Cheyenne, Wyoming. Regular overnight airmail delivery was instituted between New York and Chicago in 1924. With the impetus of the more advanced European air transport background, use had begun to be made of larger aircraft, designed to carry passengers in some degree of comfort, as well as mail and cargo. US governments consistently used airmail contracts to support development of commercial aviation. This, however, was at the expense of the hundreds of small independent carriers who had struggled with minimal resources and poor equipment to fly unenviable routes. It was seen with undeniable logic that a national airline business needed a critical mass of capital resources and superior equipment. To achieve this, a series of mergers were forged in which only the fittest or most politically adept survived. The period 1925–38 saw the emergence of four major US domestic carriers: American, Eastern, Trans World Airlines and United Airlines, unofficially known as the 'Big Four', to whom airmail routes were allocated. After 1930 the Postmaster General could contract with airlines on a space-available rather than piece-rate basis, permitting the government to subsidize the purchase of larger, more advanced, aircraft. For the period 1931–39 airmail constituted a large proportion of US airline revenue: $134m (£74m at the current exchange rate), versus $144m (£80m) in passenger revenue, which helped create a viable self-supporting commercial aviation system.

Early aircraft

The one class of aircraft left undeveloped in the First World War was the transport. In May 1917 the Civil Air Transport Committee (CATC) was formed in the UK and forecast post-war air transport needs shrewdly, but recommended that commercial aircraft should also be effective for military purposes. When the war ended, commercial aviation had to make do with converted military aircraft. In 1918 Lord Northcliffe, then the CATC's chairman, stated: 'Cost what it may, this country must lead the world in civil air transport'. For a number of years the UK did indeed lead the world, but its advance in aircraft design was retarded by the slow growth of reliable, high-powered aero engines, coupled with

Period	Characteristic	Leading equipment
1920s	Beginning of commercial operations	Junkers G.24, F.VIIb/3M, Ford 5-AT
1930s	Introduction of the 'modern' airliner, USA takes the lead	B 247, DC-3, Fw 200, M-130, B 314, B 307
1940s	World War Two (US gains in large airliner technology)	DC-4, L.049, DC-6
1950s	Consolidation of large propeller airliners, introduction of gas-turbine propulsion and swept wings	DC-7, B 377, L.1049, Viscount, Britannia, Tu-104, Comet I, Caravelle, B 707, DC-8
1960s	Introduction of turbofans and stretching of basic designs	B 707-320, DC-8-60, VC10, Il-62
1970s	Introduction of wide-bodies and high BPR turbofans	B 747, L-1011, DC-10, A300
1980s	Derivatives, introduction of glass cockpits and fly-by-wire	A310, B 767, MD-11, B 747-400, A320
1990s	Rationalization of manufacturers: Boeing versus Airbus	A330/340, B 777

Chronology of major airliner development

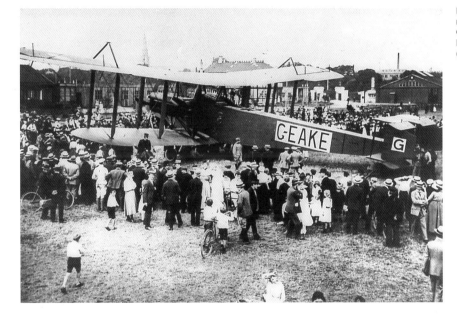

Many of the early post-war airliners were converted military aircraft. One example is Handley Page O/400 G-EAKE, ex-J2252, photographed in Norway.
(Gordon Swanborough Collection)

an unwavering preference for the biplane. Then, starting in 1927, and for twenty years thereafter, US enterprise acquired and retained the leadership in both quantity and quality of air transport.

Great strides were being made towards improving the world economy in the early 1920s. An important factor was the increasingly intensive operation of transport aircraft. Immediately after the First World War the highest aircraft utilization rates attained in practice were usually in the range of 500–800hr/year. Often they were a great deal less than this. In the late 1920s, however, rates rose towards 1,000hr and, in the 1930s, still further, to between 1,000 and 2,000hr. The actual values varied between operators.

Speed, range and operating altitude crept upward slowly. Sir Roy Fedden, head of Bristol Engines, on a trip to the USA in 1926, had several meetings about the future outlook for civil airline business. Almost everywhere he was assured that the USA was not likely to embrace air transport fully in the foreseeable future, since the country had a good network of overnight train services. He was unconvinced, and found Curtiss-Wright, Ford and Lockheed all working on new airliner projects, but without much encouragement. Hardly

had he returned to UK when the whole outlook changed. Charles Lindbergh made his historic solo non-stop flight from New York to Paris in 33hr and, as a consequence, the USA suddenly became enthusiastic about air transport. After the setback of the 1929–31 recession, by the mid-1930s it was building up rapidly.

Air transport in the 1930s

Bill Stout, designer of the Ford Trimotor (known as the 'Tin Goose'), defined an airliner in 1925 as 'a machine capable of supporting itself financially and aerodynamically at the same time'. In 1928 the Boeing Company introduced its Model 80 trimotor biplane to compete with the all-metal Ford-Stout 5-AT and the Fokker F.VIIb3/m with its plywood wing structure, (both monoplane trimotors). These aircraft demonstrated that the traveller preferred embarking upon his journey without the necessity of donning helmet, goggles and flying suit. Public acceptance of these three-engine, enclosed-cabin aircraft, plus some smaller single-engine ones, gave sufficient encouragement to the manufacturers to proceed with new designs. In 1930 the Boeing Air Transport

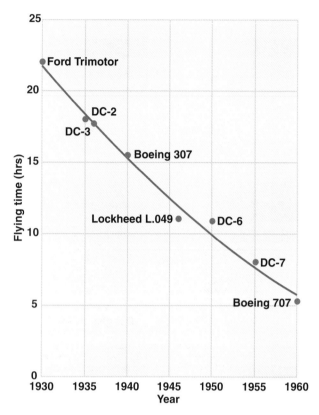

Flight times across the USA, New York–Los Angeles. On average, the DC-3 covered the 2,930 miles (4,720km) from New York to Los Angeles (Newark–Chicago–Kansas City–Albuquerque–Los Angeles) in 16–17 flying hours, and made the return trip in 14hr. The total elapsed time for the one-way journey was usually about 24hr. This compares with the 8hr non-stop schedule achieved later by those descendants of the DC-3, the DC-7 and Super Constellation, and 5½hr by today's jet airliners (no faster than the first-generation jets).
(*AIR International*)

When it was introduced in 1928 the Ford Trimotor represented the state of the art in transport aircraft of the time, with its steel-frame construction, aluminium alloy skin and a cruising speed of 105mph. Renowned as a pioneer of the development of modern air travel, the 'Tin Goose', as it became affectionately known, offered comfort and convenience not found previously on passenger-carrying aircraft. Within a decade, however, the dramatic increase in performance and capacity of the ubiquitous DC-3 rendered the Trimotor obsolete. In addition to the standard landplane variant, the Trimotor was also produced as a floatplane, as evidenced here by NC414H, in Ford house colours.
(*AIR International* Collection)

De Havilland D.H.50J VH-ULG *Hippomenes* and a D.H.61 opened up the first regular Australia/England mail and charter service on 10 December 1934. The D.H.50J was capable of carrying a pilot and four passengers at a cruising speed of 105mph.
(*AIR International* Collection)

Company introduced the first flight attendants, who were trained nurses. The Boeing Model 80A on which they served carried up to eighteen passengers at no more than 125mph (200km/h), and the flights were often rough. The Boeing Model 40A, cruising at best at 105mph (170km/h), carried two passengers and mail bags. The contest between nature and machine was not yet won; as an aircraft crested a ridge in the Rockies it often met a headwind greater than its airspeed and was literally blown backwards, unable to continue.

That same year Boeing Air Transport was also operating single-engine Model 40 biplanes used primarily for carrying mail, but they could also accommodate either two or four passengers in very crowded seating. National Air Transport was using Ford Trimotors, Curtiss Carrier Pigeon mailplanes and Travel Air two-passenger monoplanes. There were fifteen scheduled stops on the transcontinental routes that originated in Oakland on the West Coast and in Newark on the East Coast. The eastbound flight required 27hr, while the westbound flight was scheduled to take 32hr. The fare was $258 (£143) or 8.2¢ (4.6p) per mile (5¢/km).

European air routes expanded as special aircraft were built for them, including the Armstrong Whitworth Argosy and de Havilland D.H.66 Hercules, both trimotors, and the four-engine Handley Page H.P.42, which served Imperial Airways for ten years without a fatal accident.

International competition

American participation in international competition after 1926 was directly keyed to commercial aviation development. The year 1934 was marked by the MacRobertson England-Australia Air Race. This scratch event was a brilliant success for de Havilland engines and aircraft. The de Havilland D.H.88 Comet, a very clean twin-engine low-wing monoplane designed especially for the race, reached Melbourne in just over 70hr at an average speed of about 210mph (338km/h). This was a striking performance, being about 40mph (65km/h) better than current Service fighters.

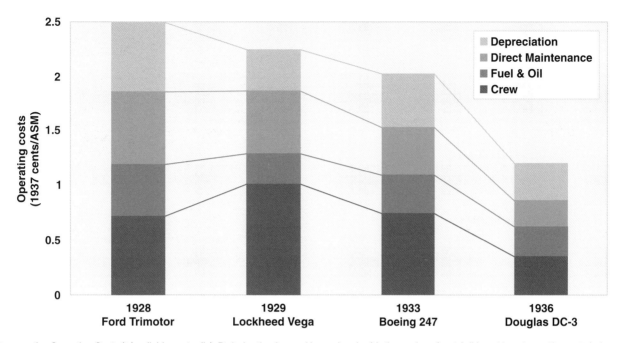

Comparative Operating Costs (¢/available seat-mile). Reducing the drag and increasing size (via the number of seats) did most to cut operating costs between the Ford 5-AT Trimotor and the Douglas DC-3. Despite its increased speed, the cost of fuel per seat-mile was 40 per cent less for the DC-3 than for the Ford. Improved engine design (with the more expensive higher-octane fuels used), helped by the use of variable-pitch propellers, probably accounted for about a third of this reduction in fuel costs, reduced drag doing the rest. By making possible the higher cruise speed, the reduction in drag also helped to reduce crew, maintenance and depreciation costs per seat-mile by increasing the amount of revenue earned in a given time. The greater seating capacity also meant more passengers per crew. The maintenance costs of the DC-3 were over 60 per cent lower than those of the Ford. Other features that reduced costs were the use of two (more durable) engines rather than three, and the superior design of the airframe. Although the DC-3 had an unexpectedly long service life because more modern designs were uncompetitive, depreciation charges on it were unnecessarily high, even though they were roughly half those of the Ford. As the Boeing 247 and DC-2 had rendered the Ford obsolete, so the DC-3 rendered them obsolete in turn.

This aircraft, designed and built in six months, foreshadowed the wartime Mosquito. Nevertheless, the air transport world could talk of nothing but KLM's remarkable feat in coming second using the Douglas DC-2. Carrying three passengers and 180kg (400lb) of mail, it completed the journey to Melbourne in less than four days. This performance outclassed all current schedules on the route, and awoke Europe to the fact that the USA, slow off the mark in air transport, was now outpacing the world. The DC-2 was an extremely clean low-wing monoplane with a retractable undercarriage and very neat National Advisory Committee for Aeronautics (NACA) cowlings, and flew with a uniformed crew and genuine passengers. Roy Fedden wrote: 'I had seen and photographed one of these machines in America in June 1934, but when I showed my picture to a member of the UK Government's Directorate of Technical Development staff he refused to believe it was a real machine!'. However, the DC-2 and Boeing's 247 made a profound impression on British aircraft designers, several of whom had new designs of biplanes on their drawing boards but quickly changed them to monoplane configuration after seeing the US products.

Introduction of the 'modern' airliner

The new transports introduced in the 1930s provided revolutionary gains in performance compared with previous aircraft. The first all-metal commercial monoplane, with all the features characteristic of the modern airliner except the variable-pitch propeller, was the Boeing 300 Monomail of 1930, a single-engine mailplane. Boeing used the experience gained in semi-monocoque and stressed-skin construction on

the Monomail to design a prototype bomber, the YB-9, in 1931.

Boeing 247

By 1932 Boeing was giving serious thought (in conjunction with its associate company United Air Lines (UAL), just formed out of an amalgamation of a number of earlier operators, including Boeing Air Transport) to a smaller civil outgrowth of the B-9 configuration. The result was the famous Boeing 247, the world's first truly modern airliner, which made its first flight in February 1933 and started in UAL service less than two months later. United had ordered it 'off the drawing board', and eventually had a fleet of sixty. Although the 247 carried only ten passengers, fewer than the Ford Trimotor, it cruised 30mph (50km/h) faster at 155mph (250km/h), which gave it an immediate competitive advantage with the elapsed cross-country time cut to 19.5hr. The scale of US aircraft production, even at this early date, is shown by the fact that thirty 247s had been delivered to UAL by the end of June 1933. By placing its large order for 247s, UAL ensured that no spare aircraft would be available for any competitors.

However, the 247's superiority was to be of short duration. In August 1932 Transcontinental and Western Air (TWA) wrote to Douglas Aircraft, expressing an interest in purchasing 'ten or more all-metal tri-motor 12-passenger aircraft, with a top speed of 185mph [300km/h] and a range of 1,080 miles [1,740km]'. Douglas responded, proposing to TWA a twin-engine aircraft of similar general configuration to the Boeing 247 but incorporating several advanced features. TWA had asked for an aircraft with unusually good performance with one engine failed, so in going for a twin-engine design

Aircraft	Introduction	Passengers	Cruising speed @ 50 per cent take-off power/max speed (mph)
Junkers G.24 (monoplane)	1925	10	100/118
Armstrong Whitworth Argosy (biplane)	1926	18	95/110
Fokker F.VIIb/3M (monoplane)	1928	8	105/115
Ford 5-AT Trimotor (monoplane)	1928	13–15	120/135
Handley Page H.P.42 (biplane)	1931	38	105/115
Junkers Ju 52/3M (monoplane)	1932	15–17	125/150
Boeing 247 (monoplane)	1933	10	155/200
Douglas DC-2 (monoplane)	1934	14	200 at 10,000ft/213
Boeing 247D (monoplane)	1934	10	160 (189) at 7,500ft/202
Douglas DC-3 (monoplane)	1936	21	192 at 10,000ft/212

Chronology of major transports of 1920s and 1930s. If the Ford Trimotor monoplane (steel frame and corrugated aluminium skin) with its 105mph (170km/h) cruising speed is taken as representative of transport performance in 1928 (it was one of the best available), then the performance gain provided by the larger DC-3, with its cruising speed of 192mph (310km/h), is striking.

Douglas had set itself a much more difficult task. It won the contract in September 1932, and the DC-1 was born. 'It was the challenge of the 247 that put us into the transport business,' Donald Douglas said later.

Douglas DC-2

The possibility of improving the DC-1 was obvious by the time the one and only example was built. Even before it had completed its flight trials the Wright Company had produced a more powerful R-1820 engine to replace the one used on the DC-1. With the new powerplant, and on the strength of the order from TWA for twenty-six aircraft (later increased to forty-one), Douglas developed the DC-2.

The DC-1 was appreciably larger than the 247, and the DC-2 even more so, with passenger accommodation up from twelve to fourteen. The first DC-2 first flew in May 1934 and was certificated and put into TWA service in July, sixteen months after the Boeing 247 entered service with UAL. On the Newark – Pittsburgh – Chicago run TWA's DC-2s made the trip in 5hr, rather than the 5.5hr taken by the 247. In an effort to regain the upper hand, in 1934 UAL undertook conversion of its fleet to 247Ds, an improved version with new and more powerful engines and several interior refinements. The DC-2 was still about 10mph (16km/h) faster than the Boeing 247D. It was also longer-ranged, offering a maximum practical stage-length of about 1,000 miles (1,600km), compared with 750 miles (1,200km) for the 247. The DC-2 could carry its maximum payload for about 500 miles (800km), the only parameter where it showed no improvement over the 247.

As soon as the DC-2 was established in service its outstanding qualities became apparent. The type sold quickly, and American Airlines and five other US domestic operators followed TWA's lead, along with KLM and Swissair. By the end of 1934 Douglas was producing ten DC-2s a month, and the 100th was delivered to American Airlines in June 1935. The Boeing design was eclipsed: while Boeing built 75 247s, Douglas sold 220 DC-2s, many of them abroad.

Douglas DC-3

Early in 1935 discussions started between Douglas and one of its leading customers, American Airlines, about a scaled-up version of the DC-2. This was to be used as an overnight coast-to-coast sleeper transport to succeed the Curtiss Condor biplanes then in service. While the sleeper idea was popular with passengers, the Condor was not; it was slow. The new aircraft for American was to provide sleeping accommodation for fourteen passengers. Work on the first Douglas Sleeper Transport (DST), later to become famous as the DC-3, started in mid-1935, and the prototype flew for the first time in December of that year.

The widened and lengthened fuselage could accommodate twenty-one day passengers in a wider fuselage that gave a fortuitous improvement in efficiency, for the fatter shape was better streamlined and the 50 per cent increase in capacity caused little increase in drag. The result was an aircraft that had no contemporary rival, and which established new standards of operation wherever it was used. With a seating capacity now 110 per cent higher than that of its Boeing rival, its operating cost per seat-mile was 25 per cent less that of the 247D, making it the most economical passenger carrier in existence. Compared even with the DC-2, the DC-3, usually having 50 per cent more seats, was only 10–12 per cent more expensive per mile flown.

While the sales success of the DC-2 had been outstanding, that of the DC-3 was phenomenal. The aircraft soon came to be accepted as the universal standard, both abroad and on US domestic routes. The latter were now expanding so vigorously that their proportion of traffic was equal to that of the rest of the world's airlines put together. Most of the USA's domestic airlines eventually adopted the DC-3, and by 1939 it was carrying about 75 per cent of US traffic. Douglas now had a monopoly position in the supply of airliners up to the outbreak of war, apart from Lockheed's smaller and faster aircraft and a few bigger ones from Boeing. The success of the DC-2 and DC-3 allowed Douglas to grow from sales of $2,294,000 (£1,274,000) in 1933 to $20,950,000 (£11,639,000) in 1937, 60 per cent of which came from civil sales.

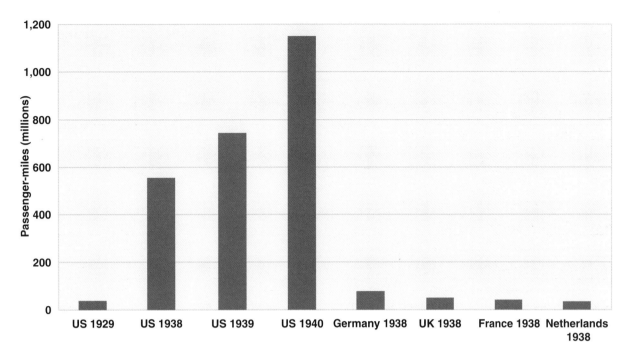

Airline traffic growth in the 1930s. The 1930s saw a creation of modern commercial aviation. In 1929 airlines flew a total of 96 million passenger miles, whereas, by 1939, they flew a total of 1,395 million passenger miles, a better than thirteen-fold increase. The growth of commercial aviation was geo-politically biased. Whereas, in 1929, all of Europe accounted for 48.9 million passenger miles, the USA accounted for 38.1 million. By 1939 European airlines flew 434.4 million passenger miles, while all US airlines flew 745.5 million passenger miles. The single most highly developed European national airline system, that of Germany, flew 79.5 million passenger miles in 1938, the last complete pre-war year. In contrast, US airlines flew 554.2 million passenger miles in 1938, almost seven times the German total. Between 1938 and 1940 US passenger miles doubled to 1,150.3 million. The US lead in commercial aviation was reflected in every other dimension by which it could be measured: total aircraft-miles flown, total number or capacity of commercial aircraft, and quality and frequency of service.

The main reasons for the USA's lead

The USA unquestionably developed the world's largest and best commercial aviation system, led by the 'Big Four'. In the international arena a single airline, Pan American World Airways, rose to dominance on Latin American routes. There was no transatlantic airline service in 1938; only a small experimental transpacific service launched by Pan American in 1936 (*see* Flying-Boats chapter).

The USA's lead in commercial aviation resulted from the interaction of a variety of historical factors. These included private enthusiasm and entrepreneurial commitment to aviation, governmental support (both in terms of direct subsidy and in terms of research and development (R&D) support), general economic affluence, geography, and effective transportation systems, notably railways. Ironically, the very excellence of US passenger train services, combined with the great distances within the USA, seems to have provided a niche ideally suited to the potential of the first modern transport aircraft. The railways provided just enough competitive pressure to demand the best that aircraft manufacturers could provide.

Three other circumstances enhanced the hospitality of the US aeronautical environment. Firstly, no question of international boundaries arose. Secondly, the entire flight was over land, on routes with navigational aids, both high-intensity visual and radio beacons, plus a series of emergency landing fields and weather reporting stations. Thirdly, the US population was large enough, rich enough and diverse enough to provide sufficient demand for frequent airmail and passenger services.

The USA was the classic continental market. More specifically, because great overland distances separated large and wealthy population centres, speed was clearly more of a premium on the 1,860-mile (3,000km) run between Chicago and San Francisco than on the 210-mile (340km) flight between London and Paris. Over 210 miles the difference in flight time for a 200mph (320km/h) versus 140mph (225km/h) average block speed is less than half an hour. However, such moderate speed differentials also matter less over large distances requiring many stops, especially when the competing modes of transport are very slow. For example, the Imperial Airways service to India, via Cairo, Basra and Karachi, used relatively slow Short Calcutta flying-boats and D.H.66 biplanes in 1929. This was a lot better than 2–3 weeks on a ship. Even though it was further from San Francisco to New York than from London to Cairo, the political and geographical conditions in the USA were incomparably more favourable. In February 1934 a TWA DC-2 set a Los Angeles–New York record of 13hr 4min, compared with 90hr by rail, and the flight was made at night.

European growth

The development of commercial aviation in the UK and Germany highlights the unique conditions in the USA. Britain, with its compact geography, poor weather and excellent railway system, had little need for a domestic air service. Except for a few major routes, Britain ignored Continental service, partly by choice, partly because of the rampant nationalism in Europe. Britain's principal interest in commercial aviation was as an instrument of Imperial policy, a means of binding its empire together. British airlines were semi-nationalized, generously subsidized 'chosen instruments' of foreign policy. This circumstance does much to

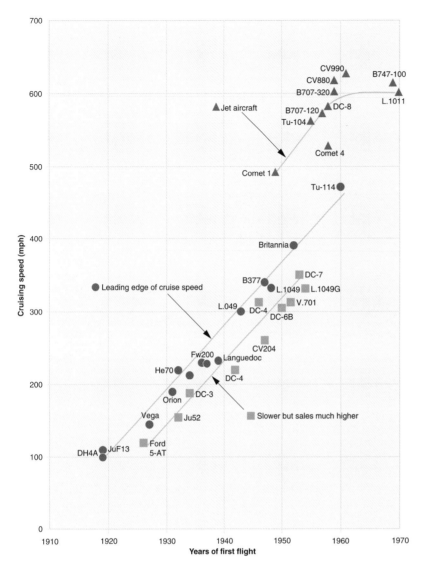

Rise in cruising speed. British airliners were often not the fastest, because of the UK's reluctance to dispense with the biplane and Imperial Airways' emphasis on 'luxury'. That said, high speed did not necessarily make a successful transport, although it was a useful ingredient. Success is won by a combination of many factors, not least of which is timing. This figure demonstrates that in many circumstances high speed alone was insufficient to produce volume sales, especially during the 1930s. Less than a year after BOAC eventually began transatlantic service with the Britannia (1957), PanAm Boeing 707s were outflying it. The cruising speeds of current airliners is restricted by compressibility, and they fly no faster than the first generation of jet transports.

explain the character of British commercial aircraft during the 1930s. Imperial Airways' routes were long distances over water and through underdeveloped colonial routes. Traffic was, to say the least, sparse, and emphasis was placed on large reliable, sturdy, easily maintained aircraft. Because of the lack of navigation/communication aids, flying could only be done in daylight, and distances were so great that speed lost some of its urgency. Lack of traffic precluded the purchase of large numbers of aircraft, so that economies of scale like those in the USA, especially with respect to development costs, were not possible. Thus the character of British commercial aircraft was determined by considerations less scientific and technical than political and economic.

In contrast, Germany in 1939 had the most highly developed commercial aviation system in Europe. Lufthansa, however, was purely an instrument of political and military policy, and was totally under governmental control. The structure of the German economy and its excellent railway system limited the domestic airline market; emphasis was therefore placed on fast mailplanes carrying a few passengers. Later, with the Junkers Ju 90 and Focke-Wulf Fw 200, Germany used its airlines to facilitate political penetration of the Balkans and South America. By 1939 German objectives in Europe had altered from political and economic hegemony to outright military conquest. Every German transport aircraft from the Heinkel He 70 onwards was either designed or later developed as a bomber. Certainly Germany had the technical and scientific capability to equal, if not surpass, US achievements in commercial aviation. Its government was otherwise inclined.

US versus European design philosophies

While US manufacturers developed the world's best commercial aircraft, they were the product of conscious development choices and quickly established a developmental lead, and were not the result of any intrinsic or unique US technological capability. Practitioners in the USA had full access to contemporary aerodynamics, and their empirical methods were second to none. However, sharp differences characterized European and US technology. That of the USA tended to be functional, cheap, rugged and energy-intensive. The quest for technical excellence at the expense of utility was quite foreign to most US technological practice. European craftsmen and manufacturers were more comfortable with small-volume, very expensive, and often not very practical aircraft. The basic technology used for the US transports of the 1930s was based on an international pool of technology. The evolution of the essential

Although the USA clearly held the lead in development of commercial transport aircraft in the 1930s, it had no technical monopoly. Heinkel's He70 of 1932, for example, was technically superior to the Boeing Monomail. Featuring an oval duralumin semi-monocoque fuselage, with seating for four passengers and a retractable undercarriage, the He70 had a maximum speed of 224mph.
(*AIR International* Collection)

When Douglas proposed its definitive DC-4 to American, Eastern and United Air Lines the carriers were enthusiastic and, after a change in powerplant to the higher-powered 1,450hp Pratt & Whitney R02000 Twin Wasp, orders began to flow. However, by the time the aircraft first flew, in February 1942, America had entered World War Two and, as the C-54, the new Douglas aircraft was produced in large numbers as a military transport. Consequently, it was not until 1946 that the DC-4 entered airline service. American Airline's service between New York and Los Angeles made just one stop en route, against three stops for the DC-3, and cut the flying time westbound from 17.5 hours to 13.25 hours.
(*AIR International* Collection)

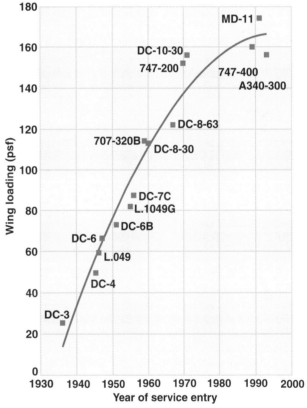

Trend in wing loading (maximum take-of weight/wing area) for leading long-haul aircraft. The provision of more-powerful and more-efficient engines has always played the major part in the development of air transport, but the aerodynamicist has ensured that wings have become increasingly capable of carrying more load per unit area. (Note: 160psf (lb/ft^2) is the weight of the average adult UK male spread over a square foot or 780kg/m^2).

components of the modern airliner (stressed-skin all-metal wing and fuselage structures, variable-pitch propellers, retractable undercarriages, high-lift devices) was international, with German, British and US practitioners making approximately equal contributions.

Although the USA clearly held the lead in development of commercial transport aircraft, it had no technical monopoly. Heinkel's He 70 of 1932 was technically superior to the Boeing Monomail. Similarly, the Junkers Ju 86 and Ju 90, Heinkel He 111, Dornier Do 17 and the Focke-Wulf Fw 200 were in no sense technically inferior to US contemporaries. The German aircraft generally carried fewer passengers at higher speeds and less economically, but that was a matter of choice, not of technical deficiency.

British commercial aircraft during the 1930s were markedly inferior to German and US types, though the UK certainly had access to, and had indeed helped create, the technology for the more-modern machines. Likewise, the other European nations, while they did not develop competitive aircraft, had the ability to do so. Neither the USA's lag in aeronautical science, which did exist, nor any peculiarly US technical advantage, which did not, accounts for the supremacy of its commercial aviation. The USA had adequate science and, at most, only slightly more than equal access to technology.

Air transport at the end of the 1930s

British attempts to keep up with the USA at this time can be viewed in retrospect as a chapter of accidents with no one party, airline, government or aircraft manufacturer, completely blameworthy or blameless. Air travel was still an adventure; the British aircraft symbolized romance, prestige and technical achievement, but was seldom an economic load carrier. Thus, while the press became excited by the latest Schneider Trophy contest or world speed record, or an impractical pick-a-back idea for carrying mail across the Atlantic, the Armstrong Whitworth Ensign four-engine forty-seat airliner ordered by Imperial Airways in 1934 was delayed by other priorities on the manufacturer. When it did eventually go into service, on the London–Paris route in October 1938, it was hopelessly underpowered. Equally one of the great tragedies of British air transport was the wooden de Havilland D.H.91 Albatross; its superiority over other foreign types was, at best, of short duration. At this time every US manufacturer was forging ahead with all-metal airliners of ever-increasing efficiency. Only eighteen months after the Albatross's debut, TWA put the Boeing 307 Stratoliner four-engine pressurized airliner into service.

By this time, British efforts to improve the competitive impact of both airline and airliner within Europe had been frustrated by the dire necessity to modernize the RAF in time to face the growing German challenge that Allied strategists now saw as inevitable. The Second World War put an end to the development of promising new airliners of all-metal construction, incorporating the major design features that had become standard practice in the USA.

Post-war Britain

As Britain emerged from the Second World War its ability to produce transport aircraft was very limited, because its experience in this sector had stagnated for over six years. Promising designs were cancelled in favour of heavy-bomber developments or conversions, such as the Avro Lancastrian, based on the Lancaster, and the Handley Page Halton, based on the Halifax. When conditions permitted, the British flag airline, British Overseas Airways Corporation (BOAC), resumed its direct England–Australia service. In May 1945 a Lancastrian left England and reached Sydney in less than three days. This was a speedy service, but it was a trial of endurance for those who shared the nine seats arranged along the starboard side of the narrow bomber fuselage. It was unreliable, and was withdrawn after less than a year.

In 1946 there were fifty-five British aircraft at the Society of British Aircraft Companies' (SBAC) Radlett airshow (later to move to Farnborough), twenty-two aimed at the civil market, with far too many airframe and engine manufacturers. It was inevitable that, in such a situation, the products of both sections of the industry would duplicate one another. This was the time for the industry to rationalize, rather than have nationalization forced upon it in later years. Yet, once again, pre-war attitudes predominated. Aircraft manufacture was still 'fun', and it was believed that UK manufacturers could afford to compete not only with the USA, but also with themselves. This resulted in a glut of unwanted prototypes.

Britain had the Avro York, a civilianized development of the Lancaster. The first BOAC service using this slow,

cumbersome and noisy aircraft began in 1944, but its performance fell well below that of the unpressurized Douglas DC-4 or the pressurized Lockheed L.049 Constellation. It even lacked many of the qualities of the pre-war Focke-Wulf Fw 200. If this was not bad enough, Britain embarked upon a programme of interim types of doubtful ancestry, such as the Avro Tudor and Handley Page Hermes, which failed to provide competitive standards, giving it little chance of survival in the hard world of competition that was to characterize post-war air transport. Inevitably, BOAC, which in 1947 operated 175 aircraft of eighteen different types, of which only six could be described as long-haul, had to turn to the USA for competitive equipment. Indeed, without US equipment it could not have survived. It started its significant post-war operations with forty-four-seat Lockheed Constellations, the design of which had started in 1939 to meet a TWA requirement for its transcontinental services.

The Brabazon Committee

In 1942 the British government had set up the Brabazon Committee to advise on what civil aircraft types should be developed, provided the war effort was not impaired. This was a brave move at a time when there was little sign of victory. However, some of the ambitious British post-war types, stemming partly from the Brabazon Committee recommendations, were no help. The ill-fated Bristol Brabazon and the ten-engine Saunders-Roe Princess flying-boat were examples of projects that were magnificent in concept and technically feasible, but commercially impracticable. The Brabazon embraced the view that a small number of people (fifty) would be carried in extreme comfort over long distances (London to New York). Nevertheless, by the time it flew in 1949 the aircraft had the 'great white elephant' tag firmly attached to it.

Post-war USA

Manufacturers in the USA had developed four-engine transports sufficiently during the Second World War to be ready for civilian use following the end of hostilities. This was to give the USA a dominant advantage in post-war civil aviation, since they were easily converted and the accumulated design expertise was of untold value. There was a widespread impression that the US advantage sprang from a wartime agreement among the Allies that the USA should be responsible for production of transport aircraft for all the allied air forces. There was no such agreement. Because Britain did not have the spare capacity to build transport aircraft, the USA had to take responsibility for providing all forms of military transport aircraft required by the Allies. So the USA, with its superb technical facilities for R&D, combined with the knowledge and capacity at its command, could easily re-establish its pre-eminence. The USA had a much bigger home market, and had 50 per cent of world air traffic. This was the suction pump that was sucking aircraft out of its factories, whereas the British were trying to apply a pressure pump to push them out.

The airliner scene at the beginning of the 1950s

The war had brought about three major changes in air transport: the design and construction of higher-capacity, long-range aircraft capable of transoceanic operations; the

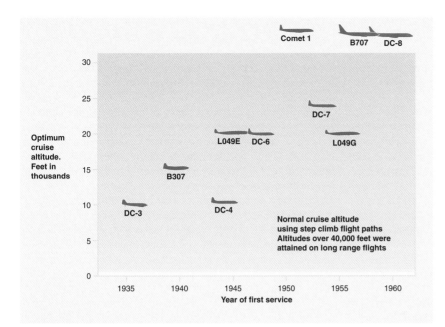

The passenger appeal of pressure cabins, that enabled airliners to fly above much more of the weather, also allowed higher speed and an improvement in productivity for an airline. Until the Boeing 307 of 1938, transports were limited to 10,000ft (3,000m). The 2.5lb/in^2 (17.2kN/m^2) cabin differential of the 307 allowed it another 5,000ft (1,500m) in cruising altitude. Even when flying at 42,000ft (12,800m) the modern airliner has to maintain a cabin pressure altitude of 8,000ft (2,400m) for passenger comfort.
(Pete West/*AIR International*)

Even while the Second World War was still being fought, Sergei Ilyushin's Design Bureau began work on the USSR's first post-war transport aircraft, the Il-12. Seating 21–32 passengers, the type was introduced by Aeroflot in August 1947. It was superseded by the longer Il-14, seen here at Zhukovsky test centre outside Moscow in 1999.
(Ray Whitford)

large-scale construction of land airports; and worldwide operations by US aircraft. At the beginning of the 1950s the medium- to long-haul requirement was fulfilled by the Douglas DC-6, Lockheed Constellation and Boeing Stratocruiser. It had been evident that cabin pressurization, to permit passenger aircraft to operate at higher altitudes of 15,000–20,000ft (4,500–6,000m), thus avoiding much of the turbulence prevalent lower down, was essential. This had been first been demonstrated with the Boeing 307 Stratoliner of 1938, introduced by TWA in 1940. The obvious advantages of cabin pressurization meant that, when the Constellation entered service with TWA in 1946 on its New York–Paris and New York–Los Angeles routes, Douglas had to match it with its pressurized DC-6. Both aircraft, along with the Stratocruiser, which entered service in 1949, stimulated long-haul travel with a much higher degree of comfort.

Introduction of gas turbines

By the late 1940s realization was just dawning that reasonable increases in size, coupled with the economic benefits to be achieved from high-altitude, high-speed operations, could permit the early development of civil aircraft powered by adequately proved and efficient turbojets. During the war de Havilland had looked into the merits of jet propulsion instead of propellers. Although this meant some sacrifice in productivity/fuel burn, it was seen that a small improvement in efficiency would restore the upward path that had been uninterrupted since 1918.

Compressibility drag rise characteristics directly influence maximum speeds, the selection of wing thickness ratio and sweepback, and the selection of engine location and arrangement. For de Havilland, its Vampire jet fighter and subsequent D.H.108 tailless aircraft seemed to supply a broad enough base on which to start the world's first jet airliner, the

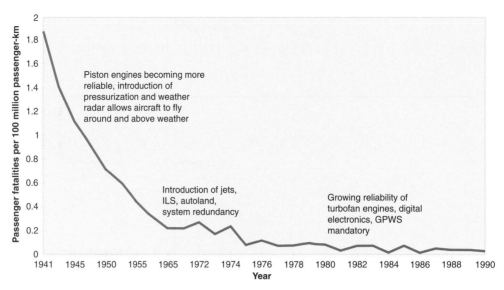

Piston engines becoming more reliable, introduction of pressurization and weather radar allows aircraft to fly around and above weather

Introduction of jets, ILS, autoland, system redundancy

Growing reliability of turbofan engines, digital electronics, GPWS mandatory

Improving safety of world's major airlines. The above figure for scheduled airline safety is based on data from the US Air Transport Association. Reasons for the dramatic improvement in safety during the period from 1941 to 1959 are numerous. There was the continuing development of additional safety features in the aircraft itself: pressure cabins permitted more over-weather flights, and thunderstorm avoidance radar, first tested by United Airlines, increased safety and comfort. With the introduction of jet aircraft in 1959 the improvement in safety continued, despite the fact that a great many people had doubts over whether the continued decrease in the accident rate could be maintained. From 1969 through 1975 scheduled US carriers were on the same level of safety as that achieved by bus and rail transportation. For example, in 1964 the US airline accident rate (fatalities per 100 million passenger-km) was at 0.087, while that of buses was 0.081 and trains 0.031. An airline pilot in 1964 had a 200 times greater chance of 'surviving on the job' than in 1930. Note: It is the *number* of accidents not the *rate* that affects public opinion on safety of airline travel. The greatest threat to a favourable public perception would be the growth in the number of accidents in line with industry expansion.

The first of the turboprop-powered airliners, the Vickers Viscount went into operation with British European Airways in April 1953. The aircraft was an immediate success and went from strength to strength, leading to the Series 800. During the early 1990s British Air Ferries was the world's largest Viscount operator; G-AOYN was photographed at Glasgow Airport in 1993.
(Malcolm English/*AIR International*)

D.H.106 Comet 1. This was a dramatic technical advance made by a British manufacturer that, within the space of a few years in the early 1950s, not only gave the UK at long last some competitive aircraft, but made it the envy of the world. By the early 1950s Britain had a lead over the USA in the use of gas turbines for high-speed commercial aircraft (such as the Vickers Viscount, Comet, and in Canada, the Avro Jetliner). In 1953 there was just one US gas-turbine-powered transport, a Convair CV240 tested with Allison T38 turboprops.

Thus Britain took the risk of being first in the turbine age with airliners. In the case of turboprops, it attained worldwide success with the Viscount, achieving export sales never equalled before or since. But in the case of pure jets it paid a crippling penalty. The Comet 1 entered BOAC service on the South African route in 1952. Its thirty-six seats were not enough for profitable operations by normal airline standard, but the Comet was not normal. Revenue from its high load

factors offset high operating costs, and the aviation world recognized immediately that a new dimension had been added to airline operations; jet speed. The Comet cut journey times almost in half, and de Havilland had a fast-growing queue of customers. The aircraft seemed to reflect the image of the new Britain, as it moved from the grey dullness of the war years into an exciting future.

However, the Comet accidents of 1954, when two were lost with everybody on board after the type had been in service for two years and had built up 30,000 flight hours, were a shattering blow to de Havilland, BOAC and the UK. The Court of Inquiry found that the instantaneous decompression of the cabin (due to metal fatigue) that caused the crashes was unforeseeable. The UK industry had explored beyond the frontiers of knowledge and had paid the price. Years of patient pioneering work was undone and, in the time that elapsed before the new Comet 4s appeared, the

At the time this photograph was taken (before the Comet 1 accidents in 1954), Britain was three years ahead of its jet-airliner competitors. From front to rear: G-ALYP (first production Comet 1), G-ALVG (first prototype Comet) and G-ALZK (second prototype Comet).
(*AIR International* Collection)

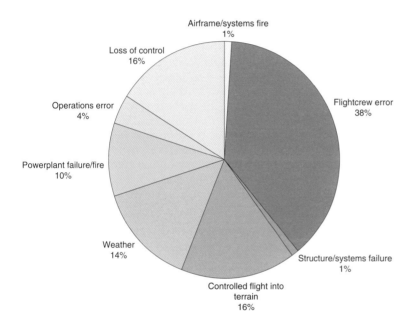

Airframe/systems fire 1%
Loss of control 16%
Operations error 4%
Powerplant failure/fire 10%
Weather 14%
Controlled flight into terrain 16%
Flightcrew error 38%
Structure/systems failure 1%

Causes of fatal accidents. Most accidents have more than one causal factor. Those shown are the principal apparent ones, though they may be subject to revision following a full inquiry.

UK industry had to accept that the USA had been given a totally unexpected chance to overtake, with the additional advantage of profiting by hard-won British experience. Again, BOAC had to turn to the USA for additional aircraft, and it regressed to the piston-engine age with the Boeing 377 Stratocruiser and Douglas DC-7C. Then, just as Britain had made up some of the lost ground, the Soviet Union took a great leap forward, stepping straight from piston-engine standards to begin the world's first sustained jet service in September 1956 with the fifty-seat Tupolev Tu-104.

US thoughts on jet transports

To Boeing the Comet was no persuader. It carried far fewer passengers than the Stratocruiser and had a much more limited range. Nevertheless, though its design was modest, the British aircraft did show how jet propulsion would transform airline travel, cruising at nearly 500mph (800km/h) above 30,000ft (9,100m). At the time there was much discussion in the USA about the real need for a civil jet. Moreover, the Comet's problems raised questions in the

minds of many people about the safety of jet transports. Fortunately the metal fatigue problem of the Comet was discovered in time, so that it could be avoided in US aircraft. Despite its uniqueness as an airliner, the Comet represented a more cautious design philosophy than Boeing's. In 1947 Boeing had flown its B-47 Stratojet bomber, with six podded engines spread across its highly-swept wings. When Sir George Edwards (head of Vickers-Armstrongs) was shown it, he is reported to have commented: 'Only Boeing would have the guts to design a ' plane like that'. By comparison the Comet had negligible sweepback, with four engines buried in the wing roots.

By 1956, when the new Comet 4 was ready, potential customers had withdrawn. There was now another, newer shape in the sky, namely the Boeing 367-80, which had flown less than a month after the Comet had been grounded. Its design had emerged as a sketch by Boeing engineers in 1949, but was shelved for two years, during which the Comet was gaining momentum. However, by 1951 Boeing realized that the United States Air Force (USAF) would probably need a jet tanker able to refuel its B-52 Stratofortress bomber, due to

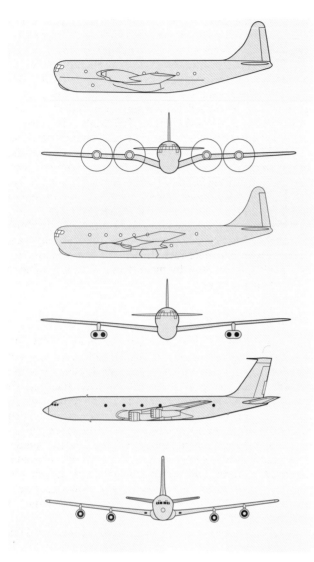

Jet transport evolution. Some of the concepts studied by Boeing that led to the Model 367-80 'Stratoliner'. Top to bottom: 367-60 (1950), a gull-winged turboprop version of the C-97 Stratofreighter; 367-64 (1951) retained the double-bubble fuselage but was to be powered by turbojets in twin pods mounted on a 25-degree swept wing; and the almost definitive 367-80 with individual pods, oval-section fuselage and increased sweep (35 degrees) that permitted a thicker wing/greater fuel volume, which flew in 1954. On 22 April 1952 Boeing president William Allen took the proposal of the Stratoliner to the company board. Allen made one change, illustrating the gravity given to model numbers. He withdrew the number 707 and renumbered it the 367-80. Model 367 was the series number for the military freighter version of the Stratocruiser. To try to throw competitors such as Douglas off the scent, Allen added the -80, suggesting nothing more than an extension of the Stratocruiser genus. (Pete West/*AIR International*)

enter service in 1955. The company agreed in 1952 to sanction the construction of a prototype that would fly as a transport at the then unheard of speed of 600mph (970km/h). It was a decision that was to have a profound effect on the future of aviation.

US reluctance to embrace jets

No airline had shown more than a passing curiosity in the 'Dash 80', as it became known, and since it was a single-copy prototype they were not being asked to order it. Passengers who were regularly flying around the world in piston-engine airliners scarcely imagined they could fly in more elegant style. The leisurely cruising speeds, seldom more than 300mph (480km/h), and the restricted ranges of the aircraft were not seen as a hindrance to the experience, since on the one hand they allowed for gastronomic pampering in the air and the other for exotic vistas during refuelling stops at Athens, Cairo, Tehran and Bombay. It was a well-mannered kind of travelling that set its adherents apart from ordinary mortals. Flying this way, without trepidation, was very chic. It would be some years before this community of comforts would be undermined and then eradicated by an urgent spreading egalitarianism of movement. Nevertheless, the first flight of the new Boeing jet in 1954 was without fanfare, but it heralded the beginning of the end for piston-engine airliners. Lord Hives, head of Rolls-Royce, saw that the Dash 80 was the writing on the wall for every airliner then flying. As far as he was concerned this signalled the demise of British aviation. Because of the Comet crashes the British were not investing in jets, but were concentrating instead on turboprops, though for long-haul flights they would lead nowhere. The future belonged to big jets.

Douglas's response

In 1954 the Douglas production line was so busy filling orders for piston-engine airliners that, to Donald Douglas, a jet seemed a distraction from the business of making money. He would never have sanctioned a programme as risky as the B-47, and was under pressure from American Airlines to produce the DC-7. An added disincentive was Douglas's lack of an adequate high-speed wind tunnel for testing a swept-wing transport. Yet the evolution of the Boeing 367-80 into the 707 was leading to the first viable jetliner, and it was evident that the Seattle company had become far more responsive to what the airlines were seeking. Every airliner Douglas was building was obsolete. It had to face the unpalatable prospect of having to spend hundreds of millions of dollars to catch up with Boeing and develop its own jet transport urgently.

Developed to meet PanAm's requirement for an aircraft fully capable of scheduled non-stop transatlantic service in either direction and even against prevailing winds (the DC-7B could not fly westbound against average winds), the Douglas DC-7C became the world's first truly long-range commercial transport. The aircraft seen here, N5901, was in service with Braniff Airways. (*AIR International* Collection)

Boeing had no patent on its basic formula: the swept wing and podded engines, nor the engine pod and pylon design. Douglas did have access to the latest aerodynamic data, and was the world leader in the construction of large airliners. Moreover, it had one salient advantage: the respect the company enjoyed with virtually all the world's major airlines. In spite of its lack of experience in building large jet aircraft, Douglas elected to forego a prototype. It put its DC-8 design, which looked remarkably like the 707, directly into production to avoid trailing too far behind Boeing. Despite being second, there were advantages for Douglas. It was able to build into its design an ability to accommodate more easily any changes to meet airlines' individual requirements. In October 1955 Pan American ordered twenty 707s *and* twenty-five DC-8s.

Big jets in service

The USA's first jet airliner, the Boeing 707, was at the forefront of the jet air travel revolution. The 707-320C was the definitive commercial variant, with 337 delivered to forty-six civil operators and eight governments or air forces. This aircraft, N375WA, was one of nine 707-320Cs operated by World Airways. The suffix 'C' indicated 'convertible'; a 'combined passenger/cargo variant'. (*AIR International* Collection)

The 707 could carry 80 per cent more passengers than a Stratocruiser and cruise 70 per cent faster. In the subsequent decade the jet airliner transformed not just air travel, but the attitude of people towards travel. Eventually jets would introduce a new class to advertise Western prosperity. That said, by the end of the 1960s there were fewer than 1,300 of the new jets. Boeing delivered just over 700 of all civil versions of the 707, and Douglas 556 DC-8s; there were a handful of other jets, but nothing of equal consequence. Each jet carried on average between 150 and 180 passengers and, on the whole, did it dependably, safely and with relentless frequency. This was a US-led revolution and, as such, had little patience with elitism. The economics of the jet favoured a levelling equality; the more seats the more the profit. After a debut with five-abreast seating the 707 swiftly regressed to six-abreast. Moreover, with the lengthened fuselage and slightly larger and more fuel-efficient turbofans of the 707-320, payload-range rose by more than a third to produce a really profitable vehicle.

Vickers V.1000 and VC10

Although the US jet transports clearly eclipsed the Comet 4 in both capacity and speed, the British had hoped to match the new US airliners with the Vickers VC7. This was a civil version of the company's V.1000, an RAF transport for which Vickers had an order for a prototype and six production aircraft. It had a wing area 34 per cent greater than that of the 707, fuselage dimensions about the same, and had the range to fly the Atlantic (though at lower speed). This at a time when the DC-8 had yet to fly and the 707 only existed in its prototype form, with a sub-standard fuselage and sub-standard range. It was not to be; BOAC was reluctant to invest in the VC7, and the V.1000 was cancelled by the UK government in 1955.

Of this development, Sir George Edwards commented that

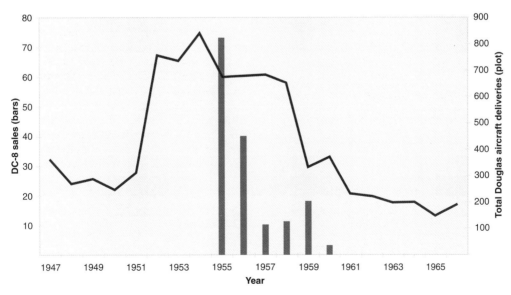

The decline of Douglas. At the height of the boom in airliner sales in the mid-1950s, Douglas, with its DC-6 and DC-7 variants, was outselling all other rivals. The Santa Monica company was showing no signs of giving up on the propeller, but Donald Douglas Snr was finally forced to recognize the threat from Boeing. The evolution of the 'Dash 80' into the 707 produced the first viable jetliner, and it was evident that Boeing had become far more responsive to what the airlines were seeking. Every airliner Douglas was building was obsolete, and it had to face the unpalatable prospect of having to spend hundreds of millions of dollars to catch up. Boeing's eleven-month lead of getting the 707 into service meant that, between 1957 and 1961, Douglas sold only forty-seven DC-8s, whereas Boeing sold 172 707s. The fight was not yet out of Douglas, but for the first time it was behind.
(Ray Whitford/*AIR International*)

if he 'had to find one single significant point in the history of the British aircraft industry since World War Two, it would be the cancellation of the V.1000. I think that if we had got on with the V.1000 and with developments of it, we could have carved out a place in the long-range business that was as good as we had in short-range business. From the moment it was cancelled we were behind all the time.'

Ironically, with the late arrival of the turboprop-powered Bristol Britannia, BOAC became desperate to compete with its rivals' larger and faster equipment across the North Atlantic. It had no option but to buy American, and ordered 707-420s with, as a consolation, Rolls-Royce Conway turbofans instead of turbojets. The order came with a government warning that no more money would be forthcoming for US equipment.

After so many stop-go, on-off decisions since the Second World War, the UK industry bounced back with its eyes fixed on a potential order for BOAC's Far East and African routes with their restricted runways, using Vickers VC10s. It was an uphill battle. The VC10 sprang from the stillborn VC7, and by early 1957 it was emerging as a firm concept. What appeared to be the seal of approval was the BOAC order for thirty-five, with options on another twenty. An even greater boost came when BOAC decided that it would fly the VC10 across the Atlantic if Vickers could provide longer range. Accordingly, it was stretched 13ft (4m) into the Super VC10, with 163 seats.

At that point it looked well set for success. It was the right size for the time, its rear-engine layout had the appeal to airlines and passengers of producing a quiet ride, and it looked different when other airliners were looking much the same. Then came disaster. The UK Government told BOAC that its choice of equipment was to be a matter for the airline's judgement. This implied that the state airline need not slavishly support British industry. Previous experience had involved BOAC in more expenditure with British types than American. As a result Vickers sold only fifty-four VC10s; half the number of Comets. While the VC10 had higher operating costs than the 707 (BOAC reported costs of

£465 per flying hour in 1968–69, compared with £421 for its 707-420s), so popular was the aircraft that it consistently had higher load factors than most of its competitors on the North Atlantic. As a result the airliner's cost per passenger was probably no higher than the 707's. That said, the VC10 was behind its time, first flying in 1962, over four years after the 707 entered service.

'Jumbo jet'

In the 1960s international air travel grew by 15 per cent per year. If it continued at that rate the airlines would soon face problems of capacity, and Pan American Airways (PanAm) for one was concerned about how to catch the tide at full flood. The dilemma facing Boeing was whether it was worthwhile to sink any more money into the 707 for what could only be relatively small gains. The 707 had outperformed and outsold the DC-8, but Boeing had seen very little return on its investment in nearly a decade, after the delivery of over 400 aircraft.

By 1965 Boeing had defined the concept for a very large airliner on the basis of work it had done trying to win the order for the CX airlifter (eventually to become the Lockheed C-5A Galaxy). Because of its size and fuel-efficient high-bypass-ratio (BPR) turbofans then under development, the Boeing aircraft offered a quantum leap in airline economics. It was to be a truly transforming machine, an aircraft so much cheaper to operate that it would bring air travel within the means of millions; a real people-carrier. The aircraft, similar in profile to the 707, was of a wholly different order of scale. With its 747 Boeing was addressing the replacement of one of its products, the 707, that had run out of time.

From the outset the 747 was designed for combined passenger and cargo services, because Boeing believed that much of future long-haul traffic might lie with supersonic transports (SSTs), and that 747s would then be pensioned off as freighters. A single-deck fuselage was decided upon that could accommodate two standard road/rail 8ft × 8ft × 10ft or 20ft (2.4m × 2.4m × 3m or 6m) containers side by side.

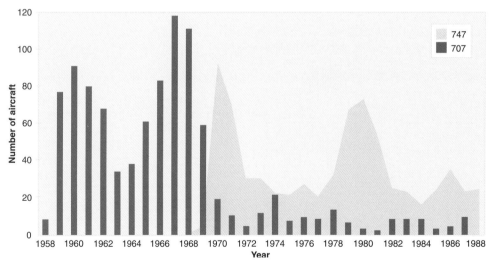

Production cycles of Boeing 707 and 747. At the start of 1968 Boeing had orders for 328 aircraft, but at the beginning of 1969 the figure was down to 164. With the 747, Boeing was addressing the replacement of one of its products that had run out of time, the 707. When the 747 programme was launched, US domestic traffic was growing at an annual rate of 15 per cent, and international trends looked even more promising. In the event, the growth of passenger traffic between 1969 and 1975 was less than 4 per cent. At first the 747 sold well, but then came a period of three years when not a single order was taken and production dropped from seven aircraft per month to less than two, and Boeing laid off 60 per cent of its workforce. The situation only began to recover in 1977, the first year when orders regained their 1967 level.
(Ray Whitford/*AIR International*)

	707-100	747-100
Take-off weight (kg) [lb]	117,800 [260,000]	321,600 [710,000]
Empty weight (kg) [lb]	56,600 [125,000]	167,600 [370,000]
Economy seating	175	500
At average load factor (pax)	87	250
Fuel burn/trip (kg) [lb]	36,200 [80,000]	72,500 [160,000]
Fuel burn/passenger (kg) [lb]	410 [910]	290 [640]

1967 Comparative operating cost prediction

Loading would be through the nose, so the flight deck was placed above the cabin. The cabin was 80ft (24.4m) longer and twice as wide as the 707's, giving accommodation for nearly 500 passengers, nearly three times as many as the 707-120. This meant ten-abreast seating with two aisles, making it the first of the widebody airliners. The benchmark set for operating costs of a third less than the 707 was in time well exceeded; the 747-400 of 1989 had seat-mile costs 45 per cent better than the 707-120's.

PanAm was guaranteed the first five aircraft from each of the first four batches, five of each of the first three batches of ten, and five of the next fifteen, despite Boeing's reluctance to go this far for fear of disaffecting other customers. Though PanAm was well ahead of most airlines in its passion for the 747, most were hoping that nothing would happen, but in April 1966 its board approved the purchase of the 747 at a unit cost of $18m.

Widebodies

Boeing was to enjoy a very short monopoly of the market for the revolution it had initiated: the widebody aircraft. It was neglecting a high-growth market that it had so far cornered with its 727: the main domestic routes. The 727 had failed to grow with the market, and it was by no means sure that the smaller 737 would ever curtail, let alone topple, Douglas's grip on the feeder routes with its DC-9. The domestic carriers were frustrated that Boeing seemed unable to upgrade the aircraft they loved, the 727, but had grasped the appeal of the widebody. Immediately on the horizon were the responses of its rivals, Lockheed and Douglas. Both had seen Boeing's exposed flank; the 747 was too big for most US trunk routes. Although some airlines, such as American and United, had ordered 747s, they had done this simply to offer a widebody, not because they thought it was the right widebody. American Airlines wanted an aircraft tailored for transcontinental, not intercontinental, routes. It liked the widebody cabin, and because the new high-BPR turbofans delivered so much thrust there need be only two to make the 'widebody twin' of irresistible utility.

When it came to sizing an aircraft for the US domestic routes, one number transcended all others, the number of 'city-pair' routes. These are the most densely travelled lines, routes such as New York–Chicago and San Francisco–Kansas City. American Airlines saw an alternative use for the widebody; an aircraft that need only carry 250 passengers, with a range of around 2,500 miles (4,000km). The initial American Airlines specification of March 1966 reflected this, as shown in the box on the right.

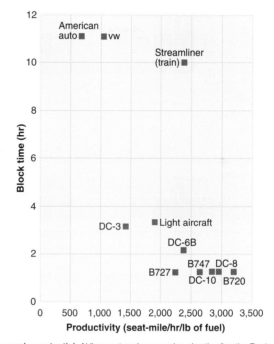

Time-saving potential. Airlines entered a recession shortly after the Boeing 747 entered service in the early 1970s, so there was an oversupply of capacity. There was insufficient traffic to maintain high load factors, and utilizations, even over long hauls, were poor. Many thought that the aircraft was too big anyway. It was disastrous to use the 747 on short distances, and for that reason a number of them were mothballed. Short trips greatly decrease the block speed of even the fastest aircraft, so the time saving becomes increasingly less important, emphasizing the value of matching the aircraft to the route. For the 500-mile (800km) trip shown it would have saved only 50min taking a Boeing 727 rather than a DC-6B, while the older aircraft delivers about the same productivity. Modern propeller-driven aircraft would do better in terms of fuel usage. The Boeing 747 can achieve better than 60 miles/gal/passenger, which is good mileage for a car, and it goes ten times as fast.

American Airlines 'jumbo twin' requirements (March 1966)
Two high-BPR turbofan engines
250 passengers, one-class configuration
1,850nm with 250 passengers and 5,000lb cargo
Mach 0.8 cruising speed
96kt 1g stalling speed at normal landing weight
Operations from New York La Guardia to Chicago

The future of such an aircraft rested on one advance, the high-BPR engine, which promised to redefine airline markets through economies of scale. Although proven in principle, the engine yet had to show that it could meet the same standards of reliability as the first generation of turbofans. The manner in which designers sized their aircraft at this point was bound to be cautious. Doubts were raised concerning the wisdom, from a safety standpoint, of using only two engines for an aircraft carrying 250 passengers. What would be the effect on take-off of the sudden loss of 50 per cent of the thrust on one side? Moreover, opinion swung against big twin-engine airliners largely because of the operating requirements for services from hot and high airports such as Denver and Mexico City. American Airlines became unconvinced about the safety of a large twin so early in the development of the high-BPR turbofan that in July 1967 the specification became that for a tri-jet:

American Airlines 'jumbo trijet' requirements (July 1967)
Three high-BPR turbofans
Range hot day: New York–San Francisco with full passengers and baggage
New York–Chicago with full passengers and baggage plus 5,000lb cargo
New York–San Francisco within 5min of B 747 (Mach 0.85)
35,000ft initial cruise altitude
Economics: Substantially better than B 727-200 New York–Chicago   Equal to B 747 New York – San Francisco
Approach speed lower than B 727-100
Dual-aisles, six-abreast first class, eight-abreast coach

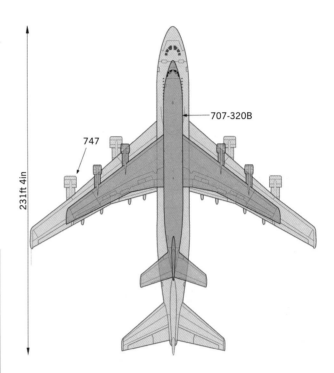

Size comparison of Boeing 747 and 707. The consensus of the airlines at the time of the 747's launch was that it was a bigger aircraft than anyone wanted, apart from PanAm. The new 747 was so large that no existing Boeing plant could accommodate it. Construction of the plant on the land adjoining Paine Field at Everett was paced by the same manic schedule that Boeing had accepted for the aircraft. Development of the 747 was not one programme, but three simultaneous programmes: designing the aircraft, developing the engine, and building the plant. The first fifty 747s were built with a force of 27,500 workers. By 1978, when the 400th 747 was completed (the break-even point), it had been built with 7,500 workers and Boeing was reaching its productivity target, defined as one man-hour/lb of aircraft.
(Pete West/*AIR International*)

The 747 was a bigger aircraft than anyone other than Pan American wanted, and a three-engine 747 configured by Boeing would not have been acceptable. Although more tentative than Boeing, Douglas decided to go where it thought the market was: a tri-jet widebody. The other potential contender, Lockheed, had its hands full with the C-5A and its SST design. In the latter case it was competing against Boeing in the Federal Aviation Administration (FAA)-funded contest. In the event the divergence in the philosophies of the three US companies came down to Douglas (and later Lockheed) deciding to satisfy a proclaimed market and Boeing deciding, far more speculatively, to create a market that could only be met by the 747 itself. By the autumn of 1967 Douglas and Lockheed proposed almost identical three-engine designs sized for domestic carriers, the DC-10 and the L.1011 TriStar. Although it flew within seven weeks of the DC-10, severe problems with the Rolls-Royce RB.211 engines for the L.1011 meant that in April 1972 Lockheed was eight months behind Douglas in getting its aircraft into service.

Widebody twins and the birth of Airbus

More distant and unheeded as a challenge to all three US manufacturers was the original idea of the widebody twin that had been rejected by American Airlines. Its rejection

was an untypically reactionary view from the airline that had sponsored the replacement of the Ford Trimotor by the DC-3. In the short term this might have been justified, but in the time that it would take to develop a widebody twin the new turbofans would mature. Nevertheless, American had very accurately described an aircraft that would be of enormous appeal. While nobody was yet ready to risk a widebody aircraft with only two engines, this would, within a decade, prove to be an extremely profitable formula. The logic of this concept was perceived and pursued rapidly by the Airbus consortium of European manufacturers as the A300, which it launched in 1969. Eventually, Boeing saw that the DC-10 and L.1011 were 'too much airplane for the job', and that the way ahead was via its 757 and 767.

Similar but earlier studies for widebody twins were under way during the 1960s at de Havilland and British Aircraft Corporation (BAC) (with its BAC 211) as larger and attractive alternatives to the Boeing 727 that would be less noisy and have lower operating costs. In the prevailing international climate Hawker Siddeley Aviation (HSA) formed a group with Breguet and Nord that offered a design with a 20ft (6m)-diameter fuselage, 300 seats and two wing-mounted RB.207 turbofans. This closely resembled US designs prepared in response to the original American

Some twenty years after the Comet made its maiden flight, Europe's most successful post-war airliner manufacturer, Airbus Industrie, launched its first model, the A300B. The world's first widebody twin-engined airliner, it became a commercial success in its own right. The first two A300Bs are seen here in 1973.

Airlines specification. Government representatives from Britain, France and Germany met to discuss formal arrangements for collaboration. It was agreed that three national partners work on an extended design study. This was the position when the appropriate ministers agreed that the development costs should be shared 37.5 per cent for UK and France and 25 per cent for Germany. The British Government felt that the A300 could only go ahead given firm commitments for seventy-five aircraft (twenty-five each) from the airlines of the three partner nations, British European Airways (BEA), Air France and Lufthansa.

Eventually the British government would have no part in this new industrial group, since it planned to use the same engine for the A300 (now to carry 250 passengers) as on the DC-10, the General Electric CF6, rather than one from Rolls-Royce. Moreover, there was no commitment on behalf of a national carrier. Despite this the French and German governments agreed to go ahead with construction of a prototype. With great courage and confidence, HSA decided to continue as a partner, with liabilities reduced from 37.5 to 20 per cent. Germany then took equal shares with France, while Spain joined in with a 5 per cent share. The first prototype A300B flew in October 1972, and Certificates of Airworthiness (C of A) were awarded in 1974. For an uncomfortable period Air France was the sole A300 customer. Indeed, there were no other operators for two years, but the aircraft was proving very reliable and popular.

In the late-1970s, however, the consortium, now called Airbus Industrie, began penetrating both the world and the large US jet airliner market with the A300. It would be some time before Boeing realized that its most formidable international competitor had been born, and would expand its range into a complete family of aircraft to equal the US giant.

Chapter 2
Economics

In the 1960s, Jack Steiner of Boeing said: 'An airliner is only as good as its economics: its cost per seat-mile, its passenger appeal and resultant load factor, and its return on investment to its airline owner'.

Development costs have risen enormously with time. Those for the Airbus A380, for example, have been quoted at between $12–15 billion. (Airbus Industrie)

Productivity

An airliner's productivity may be defined as its capability to produce useful transportation, when used in a specific operational situation. That productivity can be revenue

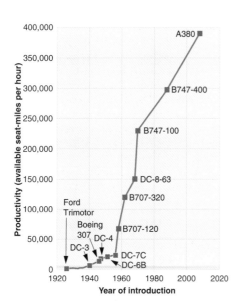

dollars, seat-km, passenger-km, ton-km, etc, produced per hour, day, year, etc. The formula is written as:

Productivity =

Payload (Revenue) × Block Speed × Block Hours

(where block speed is the average speed for the block distance). Since each of the three factors is a multiplier in the above formula, they each affect the other two. It is therefore necessary to consider the combined effect when determining productivity. An adjacent chart shows how productivity has been increased over the years by the leading long-haul aircraft. However, there is difficulty in getting high productivity when aircraft are limited to short-haul operations, where the block speed becomes a smaller fraction of the aircraft's cruising speed. Common experience is that load factors also tend to fall as the distances are shortened within the range limit of the aircraft. It then becomes evident why the total decrease in productivity can be dramatic for short

Productivity = Payload (revenue) × Block speed × Block hours. This chart shows how the productivity of the leading long-range aircraft has improved over the years owing to increased accommodation and speed. Aircraft prices increased by a factor of approximately 500 from the Ford Trimotor of 1926 to the 747-100 of 1970, the relative productivity of the 747 to the Ford being greater by a factor of approximately 140. When inflation is taken into account, the productivity bought per constant dollar of investment was about the same for both aircraft.
(Ray Whitford/AIR International)

Whenever possible, aircraft programmes are sequenced so that one risk is eliminated before the next one is taken. However, when Boeing launched its 727 in 1959 it was still $200 million in the red with the 707. Note the appropriate registration, N727AA, on this American Airlines 727-227. (Key-Malcolm English)

flights, when each of the three factors suffers as stage lengths become shorter. This applies to any airliner, for example, the McDonnell Douglas DC-10, for which the productivity on average for 750-mile (1,200km) flights was only about a third of that achieved on 1,750-mile (2,800km) flights, and this is typical of actual airline experience.

Utilization

Utilization refers to the time that an aircraft is engaged in revenue flights. It does not have anything to do with how well the capacity of the aircraft is being exploited by filling it with revenue passengers (i.e. load factor). Aircraft utilization and load factor (*see* next section) are two different things, but there is a relationship between them that is important in running an airline. It can be poor management to achieve high aircraft usage by having numerous flights, but all with low load factors. That said, sometimes load factors will be low because an aircraft has to get to the right place even with few passengers. Flight scheduling plays a central role in the optimal use of an airline's resources. For each segment to be flown the scheduler must consider how large a market is expected and how it will fluctuate by day of the week and by hour of the day. At some airports the scheduler must adapt to the shortage of slots for landings and departures. At others, curfews may shorten the flying day. Aircraft must be scheduled to end their day's flying at the point of origin of the next day's pattern, and that pattern must bring the aircraft into maintenance shops on a predetermined schedule.

With today's expensive aircraft, the utilization rate is a figure over which managements brood constantly. Depreciation charges are severe, and they apply whether the aircraft is working or idle. At the end of a route it may lay over, but for how long? Passengers want departures and arrivals during certain periods of the day. Experience has shown that 9–10hr utilization per day (over the 25-year lifetime of a long-haul aircraft) is good, though this will vary with the airline, type of route and the type of aircraft. Time on the ground comprises that spent for loading and unloading, fuelling, maintenance and layover.

Load factor

The measure of an operator's skill (for example, choice of aircraft, pricing, scheduling and general comfort of service) is the passenger load factor. This is the percentage of available seat-kilometres converted to revenue paying passenger-kilometres. In terms of cost, the standard international unit of operating cost is the US cent/seat-km. This cost comprises direct and indirect expenses. An economic airline is not necessarily the one with the lowest operating cost. The revenue that an airline earns is obviously the other important quantity. It can be seen that load factor affects both quantities, and is the index of financial success. The break-even load factor must be exceeded at the end of the year if the aircraft is to be profitable. The level of profit aimed at is usually decided before an operating period, and gives a target load factor that must be used when fares are calculated. If the load factor drops below the budget level, when traffic falls too short of capacity, urgent measures must be taken to increase it. A number of steps can be taken in the short term:

- Reduce capacity by using smaller aircraft and cutting routes. This raises load factor, but then equipment and staff are idle. Thus there is a small saving in costs (fuel, landing fees and maintenance), but this amounts to little more than half the total.

- Reduce fares, though this cannot be done by management alone as it requires government approval on an international scale via the International Air Transport Association (IATA).
- Hard sell, to boost seat sales without increasing the promotion costs too much.

Generally, the achievement of a profit-making load factor is not enough. Commercial airliners normally carry some cargo and/or mail, so the total unit of production is best described in terms of capacity tonne-km. This becomes more important the larger the aircraft and the more freight it carries. The major component for most airlines is the passenger revenue, but all productive capacity of an airliner should be fully used. The full economics of air transport are related to cost per capacity tonne-km and to revenue per load tonne-km.

Fares

The factors that enter into determining a rate, whether domestic or international, may be divided into two broad concepts; the cost of the service and the value of the service. The latter is a polite way of saying that a carrier should charge what the traffic will bear. The 'value' of the service on a long trip is greater than on a short one. Air travel saves several days and the tedium of a transcontinental trip by rail or highway, so the time spent going to and from the airports, waiting for baggage and so on is of relatively minor consequence. The value to the business traveller is often greater than to a tourist, as is evident from the fact that business travel is far less sensitive to fare changes (and, indeed, the price of the ticket) than is vacation travel.

Initially there was only one class of passenger service, and the air mode was an expensive way to travel. The competing passenger trains had first-class and considerably cheaper second- and third-class service, but the airlines set their rates in the late 1930s at the level of first-class rail. Juan Trippe, president of PanAm, fought IATA's fare regime from 1945, when he tried to introduce tourist-class fare from New York to London. PanAm cut the round-trip fare by more than a half to $275 (£153), but the British closed their airports to the airline's flights with tourist seats, forcing the aircraft to land at Shannon in Ireland. It was not until 1948 that US scheduled airlines began to introduce a second-class service

in a separate section of the aircraft. Called 'air coach', this offered a fare about one-third less than the regular fare, which then became 'first class'. Initially the coach fares had their own off-peak characteristic, being designed for overnight flights, and were characterized by crowded seating and little, if any, food service. Nevertheless, it was not until 1952 that PanAm's incessant bombardment of IATA forced all the airlines to accept that the age of the tourist fare had arrived, whereupon it introduced a round-trip fare between London and New York of $486 (£270). This was still hardly within reach of many, but it compares strikingly with what it cost to travel on the air-rail coast-to-coast service of Transcontinental Air Transport in 1929. Westbound passengers left New York by train and travelled overnight to Ohio. From there they flew to Oklahoma, then transferred to a train to New Mexico, then flew to Los Angeles. The trip took 48hr, and the fare ranged between $337–$403 (£187–£224).

When PanAm introduced a tourist class, other members of the tight-knit international airline cartel fought it bitterly. It offended their notion that international air travel should be the privilege of an élite, with prices to match. By the 1960s, with the introduction of various discounts, it was common to find passengers sitting side-by-side in the coach section receiving the same service all at different rates. No one was paying the list price any more.

Operating costs

Productivity can be calculated in terms of payload generated per unit time, but in the final analysis of an airline's financial situation it must be converted to the actual revenue required to overcome the airline's operating costs. A major contribution to the better understanding and assessment of aircraft operating costs came in the late 1930s. It was recognized that there was a need for a uniform and comprehensive method of computing and comparing operating costs of airliners. This became the basis for subsequent analyses.

The commonly used breakdown of operating costs into direct operating costs (DOC) and indirect operating costs (IOC) is shown in the table opposite. In general, DOCs (typically 50 per cent of total) that are incurred depend on the operation of the aircraft (the variable element), though some do not vary with the amount of flying (the fixed element).

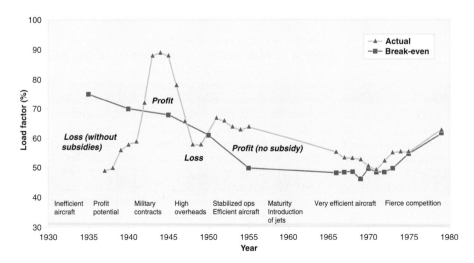

Variation of load factor with time. History of load factors and break-even line
Before 1937 US domestic airlines had trouble breaking even. Indeed, they were covering, on average, less than two-thirds of their total costs. This was raised by the Douglas DC-3 to more than 80 per cent. By the time the USA entered the Second World War, airlines had an aircraft with operating costs sufficiently low that money could be made from carrying passengers without undue dependence on the revenue from government airmail contracts. Load factors averaging about 55 per cent through the mid-1970s had risen to 63 per cent by 1979, but levelled off into the 59–61 per cent range for several years, and have been in the range of about 62–64 per cent since then.
(Ray Whitford/AIR International)

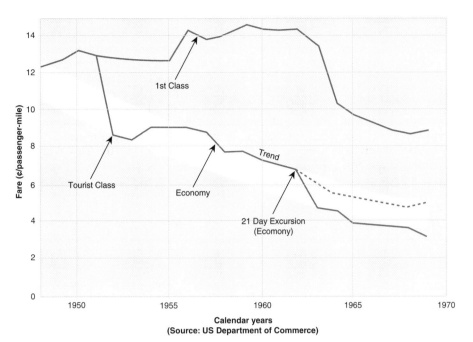

North Atlantic fare history (1948–69).
It was not until 1952, long before jets were in service, that the incessant bombardment of IATA by PanAm's Juan Trippe forced all the airlines to accept the age of the tourist fare. That summer, PanAm introduced a round-trip fare between London and New York of $486. This was still hardly within reach of the man in the street, but it compares strikingly with what it cost to fly on the first Boeing 247 transcontinental service in 1933: $160 one way, equivalent to about $2,000 in the early 1990s, and taking around 30hr.
(Ray Whitford/*AIR International*)

Calendar years
(Source: US Department of Commerce)

Total operating costs (TOC)

Direct operating costs (DOC)		Indirect operating costs (IOC)
Fixed	**Variable**	*Airports*
Interest	*Fuel*	*Baggage handling*
Depreciation	*Crew*	*Passengers services*
Insurance	*Maintenance & overhaul*	*Ticketing, sales, etc.*
	Landing and navigation fees	*Administration*

Profit = Revenue − (IOC + DOC) and, substituting 'typical' percentage points: 10 per cent = 110 per cent − (50 per cent + 50 per cent). So to compare the various investment options in relation to potential returns:
1 per cent change in DOC gives 5 per cent change in operator's profit
1 per cent change in IOC gives 5 per cent change in operator's profit
1 per cent change in TOC gives 10 per cent change in operator's profit
1 per cent change in load factor gives 11 per cent change in operator's profit

Direct operating costs

Fixed portion
Interest on loans has to be paid whether an aircraft flies or not. An airline may not need to pay interest, but because of the high price of aircraft very few operators, if any, can buy aircraft outright (and it is uneconomic to do so anyway). Governments may decide to reduce interest on the capital they supply to flag carriers, and this is a common form of subsidy that is rarely clear in the public accounts.

Depreciation is most important, and depends on aircraft price. Capital equipment must be replaced because of general wear and tear, or because competition has rendered it obsolete. Though not a cash cost, it is an operating cost because it is the means whereby an airline provides for the replacement of equipment and keeps its capital intact. The

amount charged for depreciation is up to the commercial judgement of the airline. Ideally it is the value the equipment would fetch on the open market (sometimes as scrap). Some airlines find leasing more convenient than buying (*see* later). Then depreciation and insurance are replaced by rental charges. Whether leasing is desirable depends a lot on the tax system of the airline's home country.

Insurance is a condition of most loans for the financing of aircraft, in that the borrower has to insure the hull against normal operating risk. Big, well-established airlines with a good safety record pay insurance premiums that in the 1970s averaged between 1–2 per cent of the replacement value of their fleet. Those whose records are not so good pay up to 5 per cent.

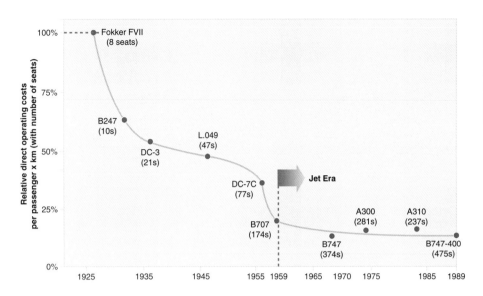

Relative DOC per passenger-mile. There have been two significant drops in DOCs; that in the 1930s with the introduction of the Boeing 247 and DC-3, and then in the late-1950s, when jet services began. Although cost reductions still occur, they are not on the same scale as those resulting from these two revolutionary innovations.
(Ray Whitford/*AIR International*)

Variable portion

Flight operations are easily the biggest item of airline expenditure, comprising crew, fuel, landing fees and en route charges.

Crew costs include wages and training of flight-deck and cabin staff. Reductions in these costs can be achieved by reducing the number of crew, but in the case of the flight deck, only by the increased use of automation. Beyond conforming to minimum safety requirements mandated by airworthiness authorities and trades union agreements, cabin crew number is limited by comfort levels offered by the airline. Training costs could be reduced, but there is the limit of safety requirements. Airlines with the best safety records have traditionally spent up to 2 per cent of their total yearly expenditure on crew training, including refreshers, checking and type conversion. Costs increase to 5 per cent when a new aircraft type is introduced. The economics of training are best summed up by the air safety motto that 'an airline's best investment is a well trained pilot'.

Fuel costs are heavily dependent on range, but account for almost half the total flight operations bill for short-haul twin- and tri-jets. Fuel costs trebled after the oil crisis of 1973–74, and several fuel-saving schemes were considered, including towing aircraft to a point near the runway before starting the

engines, taxiing on fewer engines (now common practice) and powered undercarriages. By 1980 the cost of fuel had returned to that of the mid-1950s at around 50¢ (1975)/gal (*see* accompanying figure). Moreover, big fuel savings have been achieved by technological advances such as the introduction of high-BPR turbofans operating at increasingly higher pressure ratios and turbine entry temperatures. Between 1973 (when fuel represented 20–25 per cent DOC of long-range airliners) and 1983 (when fuel took 50–55 per cent of DOC) there was an increase of about 73 per cent in passenger-km, while total fuel consumption actually dropped, albeit slightly. Unfortunately this impressive gain in efficiency was dwarfed by the astonishing rise in fuel prices during that decade.

As range increases, so the fuel component of DOC increases up to 30 per cent, so that even small economies matter. Prudent pilots and flight-operations staff will plan a flight to achieve best fuel economy. In general the aim is to get to the most efficient cruise condition as soon as possible. Even such small details as getting take-off clearance before engine start can make a significant difference in yearly fuel costs. Safety considerations limit changes in operating procedures to reduce fuel costs, such as reduced fuel reserves to reduce weight, and therefore lift and drag, and hence fuel burn. Over the last few decades, and particularly since the

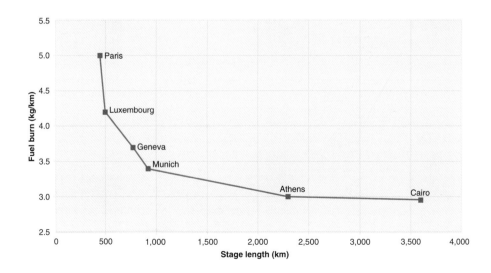

Impact of stage length on fuel burn (A320-200 from London Heathrow). As the distance for flights increases within the range capability of an aircraft, the block speed comes closer to the cruising speed of the aircraft. Consequently more time is spent at the most efficient condition, leading to reduced fuel burn.
(Ray Whitford/*AIR International*)

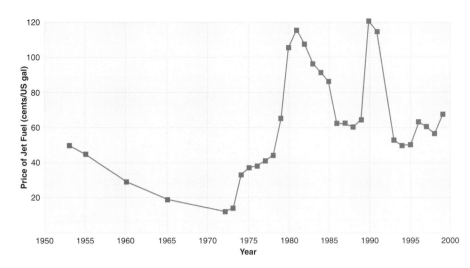

Variation in the price of jet fuel. In 1972 the average price paid by US scheduled airlines for jet fuel was 11.5¢/USgal, but by the end of 1980 it was approaching $1/USgal; a nearly nine-fold increase. Peaking at $1.09 in 1981, a year when fuel represented an average 31 per cent of operating costs, it dropped gradually over a five-year period to about 60¢/gal. The price remained reasonably stable except during the Gulf War, when it reached $1.20/gal. The future course of oil prices is difficult to predict, but since oil is a finite resource the ultimate trend must be upward. As of 1998 US airlines were burning approximately 18 billion gallons of Jet A fuel per year, and every 1-cent rise in the price over a year meant that the airlines would have to spend an extra $180 million. (Ray Whitford/*AIR International*)

Airport fees vary considerably: although landing fees depend upon a number of factors such as the time of day, the carrier and aircraft weight, there is a factor of three between the cheapest and most expensive airports.
(Key – Chris Penney)

1970s, all civil aircraft manufacturers have made great efforts to reduce drag. The long-term aim to reduce fuel consumption by 10 per cent by this means would represent savings of millions of dollars for the airlines (*see* table below).

Another way to improve fuel efficiency is to seek higher load factors by devices such as curtailing the number of flights in leaner markets, but especially by developing effective hub-and-spoke networks. This was a direct consequence of the deregulation that started in the USA in the 1980s. Reducing fuel costs remains a severe challenge to the airlines.

Landing and en-route charges are levied by governments or airport authorities to pay for airport upkeep (such as runways, lighting, air traffic control services and other airport operating facilities). Some countries provide these services to their national airlines free of charge, another hidden subsidy. Landing and en-route charges account for around 11 per cent of DOC for short-haul aircraft, compared with about 7 per cent for long-haul types, although airport fees vary considerably.

Maintenance and overhaul costs take about 15 per cent of an airline's operations budget. The objective is to keep aircraft utilization high at revenue-earning times while fulfilling the safety requirements of maintenance schedules. This is part of the C of A that lays down checks that have to be made and the life of each component according to its reliability in service. Up to the mid-1950s component changes had to be done at set intervals, requiring the airliner to be out of service for some days' duration after every 1,600hr flying. The increased expense of aircraft made the economic need for higher utilization so great that the philosophy of progressive maintenance or 'condition monitored reliability' (little and often) was introduced to keep fleets flying with as little out-of-service maintenance as possible. Such maintenance requires a highly organized and costly engineering department with advanced inspection and data analysis facilities.

At the time of the Boeing 747's first flight in 1969, the company was estimating its DOC compared with its 707-321B as shown in the table overleaf.

Aircraft	Range (nm)	Flights/year	Fuel saving/aircraft/year (tonnes)	Saving ($)
A320	500	2,175	70	23,300
	2,000	802	84	28,000
A340	3,000	657	220	73,300
	6,000	400	310	104,000

Influence of only 1 per cent fuel-burn saving by just one aircraft at $1/USgal

At 3,000nm	707-321B	747-100
Direct cost (¢/statute mile)	1.807	3.714
Direct cost (¢/seat-mile)	1.264	1.026
Seats	143	362
Assumed utilization (hr)	11.35	10.0

707/747 DOC

Indirect costs

Indirect costs are far less sensitive to the type of aircraft used.

Airport costs (baggage handling and general customer services) are up to 20 per cent of total expenses for short-haul airlines, but lower for long-haul.

Passenger services. All staff and facilities directly concerned with passengers (in-flight food, hotels and transport when delayed), 10 per cent of total.

Ticketing, sales and advertising 15 per cent of total.

Administration (accounting, purchasing, office equipment and buildings, etc.) 5 per cent of total.

The US scheduled airlines employed about 537,000 persons as of 1993, of whom 52,000 were pilots/copilots. In the 20 years between 1970 and 1990, while passenger-km grew nearly 250 per cent, total airline employment rose by only about 84 per cent. The remarkable increase in output per employee in the 1970s was largely due to the efficiencies of larger aircraft and computerized reservation systems. In the 1980s and 1990s increased output was achieved due to efficiencies of hub-and-spoke networks and changes in work rules owing to the weaker position of labour unions after deregulation.

Impact of technological advances on costs

Advances in technology have enabled airlines to achieve lower available seat-km costs as a basic trend. The Douglas DC-3, though revolutionary in the 1930s, had very high seat-km costs compared with now, as shown in the figure on page 32. The advent of larger piston-engine aircraft caused seat-km costs to drop, as did the arrival of turboprop aircraft. The introduction of turbojets on even larger aircraft caused a major drop, and the arrival of the widebody airliners even more so. The lowering of seat-km costs, however, has been counteracted to some extent by inflation.

When a new type of aircraft is introduced, the savings in seat-km costs (to whatever extent they may be cancelled out by inflation) may only slowly be reflected in reduced fares. There are various break-in costs, such as training of personnel on the new model. In the past, new aircraft technologies (such as pressurization giving longer range, higher speed and lack of vibration) attracted passengers. Thus, when an airline's fleet consists of a new type and some of the old, the airline will certainly not cut its fares for flights on the new ones that attract passengers. This was particularly noticeable when jet aircraft first began to replace piston-engine aircraft. Some airlines even imposed a jet surcharge based on superior passenger appeal, even though the seat-km cost was lower.

Since the appearance in the late 1950s of the jet transport, the impact of technological advance on costs has come not from faster aircraft but, above all, from fuel efficiency gained from increase in aircraft size and higher-BPR turbofans.

There has also been considerable help from maintenance savings. Improvements in airframe and engine technology can lengthen the period between both routine maintenance operations and long-term overhauls. Other advances helping to lower costs need not be confined to the aircraft itself: improved maintenance equipment, for example, or more efficient equipment for processing passengers, baggage and air cargo. The elaborate computerization of reservation procedures is an example of technological advance that, although requiring a large initial investment, provided a long-term saving in labour expense as well as vastly improved service to the passenger.

Cost inflation

Aircraft prices increased by a factor of approximately 500 from the Ford Trimotor to the Boeing 747. Between 1935 and 1975 the average first cost/kg of all-up weight (AUW) of leading aircraft increased by an overall factor of about 15. This was even greater than the inflationary trends due to what has be described as the 'concentrated complexity per kg of hardware' in current designs. Based on inflationary trends in the USA, it might be concluded that the two effects were each roughly equal to four. In the UK the corresponding factors would be inflation × 8 and complexity × 2, assuming that cost/weight increased by the same factor of 15. Offsetting this, the average productivity (seat-km/hr) increased over the same period by a factor of over eight (*see* the figure on page 28). In the mid-1930s aircraft costs of $10/kg ($4.5/lb) AUW were frequently quoted (at 1975 values this would have been

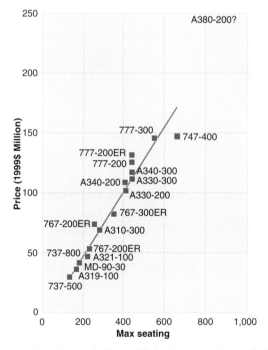

The growth in unit cost of airliners. This has in the main been justified economically in terms of airline operating cost (10¢/available seat-mile of the Ford Trimotor to 1¢/available seat-mile of the 747). It is noteworthy that the economic viability of the airliner has been maintained over the years by the constant increase in size, leading to so-called economies of scale. This in turn depended on ever-growing markets. The quoted price (source: Avmark) of current airliners is shown versus maximum seating (to give, for 1999, $270,000 per seat) with an extrapolation towards the 1,000-seat airliner. This produces a figure of $270 million, which is significantly higher than that suggested by press reports for the price of an A380-200.
(Avmark/Ray Whitford/*AIR International*)

$45/kg ($20/lb)). By 1975 aircraft prices were $90–100/kg ($40–45/lb) AUW, and today that figure stands at around $440–480/kg ($200–215/lb).

Manufacturer's difficulties with the launch of a new aircraft

Launch costs can be reduced by various means, including designing the aircraft with a family of derivatives in mind. This was the case with the Airbus A320 (A318-A321) family.
(Airbus Industrie)

A general measure of financial strength of a manufacturer is its net worth (i.e. the difference between assets and liabilities). It is unusual for an individual to risk all of his/her net worth on a single investment, yet the aircraft industry has repeatedly done just that. There are some significant reservations that must be resolved before a manufacturer will launch a new aircraft:

1. Very large investment is necessary to launch any new programme. For example, the 707 launch nominally cost Boeing $16m (though this was offset by outstanding tax liabilities due to the US Government) to build the first prototype (367-80), representing 20 per cent of Boeing total assets. In the case of the 747 launch costs were 90 per cent of total assets, with no prototype.

2. The relatively limited world market for an aircraft in any particular size and range category while making allowance for the balancing effect of traffic growth and increasing aircraft size. At the launch of the Lockheed L.1011 and Douglas DC-10 great doubts persisted regarding the market's ability to support two very similar aircraft. Likewise, Boeing, recognizing the limited market for an airliner larger than its 747, has left the field open to Airbus and its A380.

3. The very long period that must elapse before any return on investment can be expected under even the most favourable conditions. At the moment of programme launch, based these days on firm orders (though not in the past, for example the 707), very large risk is immediately assumed since the programme has guaranteed to deliver a number of aircraft at a given price, with given performance by a given time. Additionally, there is the total cost, both non-recurring and recurring, of designing, tooling and building those committed aircraft. It also includes an obligation to suppliers if the programme is cancelled. In many cases individual programme risks have been sequenced such that one risk was not eliminated before the next one was taken. Thus cumulative risk at any given time was frequently far greater than the individual risk. When Boeing launched its 727 in 1959 it was still $200m in the red

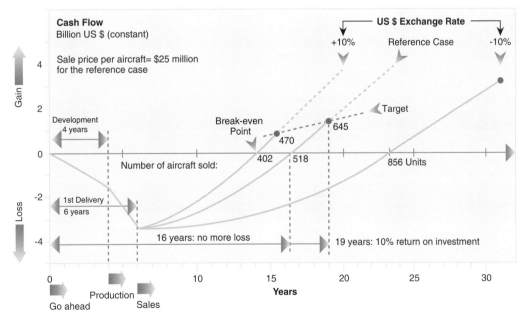

Cash flow versus time. A very long period must elapse before any return on investment can be expected by a manufacturer, even under the most favourable conditions. This figure shows the rapid rate of loss in the early years of a new aircraft programme, followed by an even steeper decline when production starts. This is only arrested by the first sales, which may be no sooner than six years after programme launch. The slow recovery towards the break-even point is heavily dependent on monetary exchange rates, and for this hypothetical case break-even may be as early as 402 aircraft (after 14 years), or 856 aircraft (after 23 years). This highly risky business is obviously compounded not only when derivative models are introduced in a rapidly changing competitive world, but when a new aircraft is launched before the first has stopped losing money.
(Ray Whitford/AIR International)

with the 707. To finance a new project out of revenue from existing projects is hazardous unless the company has a number of successful projects in hand. For the first two years both Boeing and Douglas lost money on 707 and DC-8 production.

4. The wide variation in market demand during the manufacturing phase. For example, when the 747 began service in 1970 the airlines were entering a recession.

5. Significant in the assessment of investment risk is the question of a prototype. In the 1950s a new aircraft was rarely attempted without first hand-building a prototype demonstration model. This was regarded as a reasonable financial burden compared with the investment risk associated with a production programme. The first 747 was retained by Boeing, but most modern 'production prototypes' are used for testing and certification purposes, then refurbished and sold on to airlines.

At the end of the 1970s it was clear to observers that there would be fewer aircraft types, more improved derivatives

Development time-scales (from first firm project studies to entry into service) were little more than 12 months in the 1920s, and still only two years for the DC-3 of 1935 (top). By the late 1940s this had become three to four years, depending on aircraft size. For the Boeing 777 of the 1990s (bottom) it had risen to over six years.
(Key – Duncan Cubitt, Tony Dixon)

and more international collaboration. This has been borne out in practice.

Launching costs

The initial development of the whole DC-1/2/3 series is reputed to have cost only $1.5 million (£0.83m) in the mid-1930s, or $5.8 million at 1975 values. Ten years later even the original L.049 Constellation programme took around $6m ($18m at 1975 values). Current programmes cost billions of dollars (for example, Airbus A380 development is reportedly costed at $12–15 billion). Development time-scales (from first firm project studies to entry into service) were little more than twelve months in the 1920s, and still only two years for the DC-3 of 1935. In the late-1940s this had become three to four years, depending on aircraft size. For the Boeing 777 of the 1990s this had risen to just over six years, after the company became convinced by the airlines that a 767 derivative was not an option.

An approximate estimate of the 1975 launch cost per kg AUW was $6,000 (£3,330), whereas in 1935 the figure was $120/kg ($54/lb). The factor of 50 is built up from: 4 for US inflation and 12 for technological complexity. Development costs for 1980 were four to five times those of 1960 in real terms. On the basis of the widely quoted figure above, the development of the A380 at 540 tonnes (1,190,000lb) AUW will cost roughly $20,400/kg ($11,330/lb), about three times that of the 747 in 1970, without accounting for inflation. High launch costs may be effectively defrayed by spreading them over a greater production run. Apart from the effect of increasing the production run, the launch cost can be reduced by:

1. Using parts (such as fuselage sections) of existing aircraft;
2. Giving the new design the potential for a family of aircraft such that some of the launch cost can be spread over a variety of longer/shorter and re-engined aircraft derivatives (as with the DC-8, DC-9, 737, A320 (A318-A321));
3. Refurbishing and selling prototypes;
4. Constraining certification costs by shortest possible flight-test schedules and modern data analysis methods;
5. Vigilance against 'Parkinsonian' effects in design,

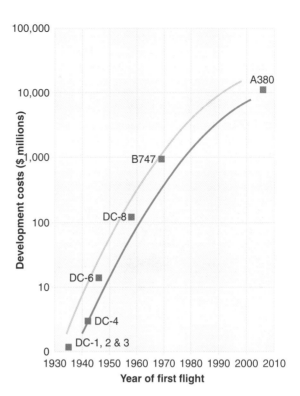

Airliner development costs. Following the Second World War there was a dramatic rise in development costs that was only partly explained by greater weight and higher speed. It was British industry-wide experience through the 1950s that perceived that estimates of development cost allowing for these elements were too low by a factor of around three. Bristol Aircraft adopted a refinement by using a factor of 3.1416 (π). (Note the logarithmic vertical scale, and the fact that no attempt has been made to allow for inflation.)
(Ray Whitford/*AIR International*)

production and certification. In other words, does this proposed design feature or tooling investment give real value for money? In the 1970s the rate of increase in development costs for subsonic transports (five-fold every ten years) was exceeding that for fighters. That trend, combined with the growing technical and economic risk associated with aircraft development, has made each new programme an increasingly hazardous venture.

With its DC-9 the Douglas Aircraft Company found a niche that Boeing had neglected; the short-haul intercity airliner. However, mismanagement and underpricing of the DC-9 resulted in the company's decline and eventual takeover by the McDonnell Aircraft Company in 1967. McDD subsequently developed newer variants of the DC-9 in the form of the MD-80 and MD-82.
(Crossair)

Financing and leasing

Despite a shaky start, the 1970s was a decade of strong growth for the airline industry worldwide. A regulated environment sheltered many operators from truly competitive pressures, and strong resale values of aircraft provided additional comfort to lenders faced with financing the ambitious expansion plans of airlines. The sources of finance available to the industry were diverse, and included access to the equity markets and US institutional funds, together with subsidized export credit and commercial bank loans. The situation in the 1980s proved to be very different. The world was in the grip of recession, traffic growth stagnated, secondhand aircraft values were very depressed, reflecting overcapacity, and markets became far less regulated, leading to discounting in many parts of the world and a virtual free-for-all in the USA. With more and more financial markets closed to the airlines, they had to turn to increasingly innovative financing to meet existing requirements and commitments. The substantial debt obligations assumed in the heady days of the 1970s of relatively easy credit became millstones around the necks of many carriers.

An airline will very rarely acquire an aircraft simply by buying it entirely with its own funds. It is far more likely to obtain financing via a secured debt comparable with a mortgage on a home, only in this case the aircraft is the collateral. Nowadays it is also very common for an airline to lease the aircraft, perhaps by a simple rental or by a long-term lease. Leasing has become increasingly popular with airlines. In 1990 it was estimated that as much as half of the US scheduled airline fleets were leased, with the proportion predicted to rise during the decade. By leasing, an airline conserves its own capital but loses the residual value of the aircraft when it is turned back to the lessor, unless an option to purchase has been included in the lease. Leasing may also help an airline keep its capacity closely tailored to its traffic.

One disadvantage of leasing is its effect on an airline's cash flow. In recent years this has changed dramatically. Whereas, in 1961, 3 per cent of aircraft were leased, by 1988 42 per cent were leased. With an aircraft lease the airline does not lay out cash up front when the aircraft is acquired. Instead, cash is laid out throughout the aircraft's lifetime. With the adoption of leasing by airlines, carriers began to find that required annual cash outlays roughly equalled their cash inflows. As a result, in difficult times, such as a recession or a fuel crisis, carriers can experience negative cash flows and may face bankruptcy. With the great expansion of aircraft leasing by airlines throughout the world, several large companies have become major lessors, with worldwide operations.

Aircraft selection

Nowhere is airline management more severely tested than in making decisions on the types and number of aircraft it will have in its fleet. Beyond the burden of carrying the huge investment that an airline fleet represents, there is the even greater cost consideration of the operating efficiency of the fleet. In approaching the decision on aircraft purchase, many factors must be considered, and the choice has historically been based on the same five: price, performance, after-sales support, residual value and transition costs. Firstly there is the price of the aircraft, which is a matter for negotiation with the manufacturer, especially if there is to be a single commitment to purchase a substantial number of aircraft. Commitments must be made for delivery dates many years into the future, with all the uncertainties that implies, and large sums of money must be obligated. For example, in 1990 United Airlines placed an order with Boeing for sixty-four aircraft, with options on sixty-four more, but with four years before the first delivery. The total bill if all options were exercised was reckoned to be $22 billion (£12.2 billion).

With the coming of the jet transport, airlines found themselves running up ancillary costs they had never dreamed of. Vast new heated overhaul hangers had to be constructed, big storerooms were needed for a new generation of spare parts, engineering staff had to be trained in a completely fresh technology, and clean rooms with the air constantly filtered and with workers wearing dustproof clothing had to be established for servicing the delicate instruments with which the new aircraft were fitted. Out on the apron, trucks, steps, servicing ladders, refuelling equipment and all the other paraphernalia needed if the jets were to be turned around quickly for a new service, an essential matter if their lower operating costs were to be exploited, were all needed afresh. There was no question of trying to adapt the equipment made for the previous generation to suit the new one. Once an airline had made the decision in favour of one aircraft manufacturer and its product, it was unlikely (and remains so) that it would switch to another for anything but very fundamental reasons when the time came to buy the next-generation or upgraded model.

Performance characteristics must be matched against the carrier's existing and proposed routes, the stage lengths and the flow of traffic now and in the future. What is the seating capacity and potential productivity of the aircraft? What is its range; that is, what distance can it fly without having to

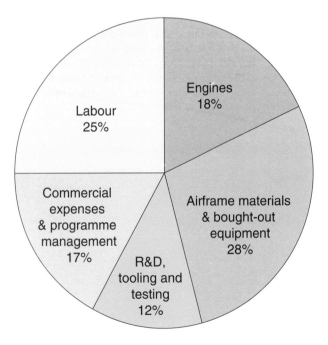

Breakdown of aircraft sale price for a new aircraft. This can only be approximate, but the chart is indicative of a medium-sized twin-engine aircraft. Proportions will vary according to how costs are allocated, and in particular the launch cost spread will be very much a function of the number of aircraft built. Even so, total aircraft production costs are likely to be of the order of 70 per cent of the aircraft selling price.
(Ray Whitford/*AIR International*)

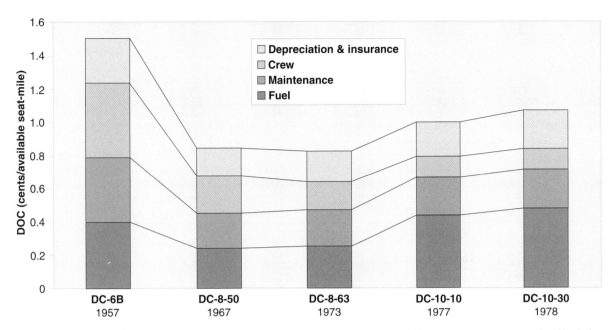

Direct operating cost (1975 cents) comparisons for a range of aircraft in their 'mid-life'. Of particular note is the significant reduction achieved by the jet-powered Douglas DC-8 compared with the prop-driven DC-6B.
(Ray Whitford/*AIR International*)

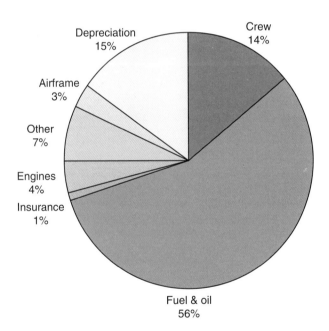

Direct operating costs for the range of widebody airliners in 1983, showing the large influence of fuel costs based on: mean price of fuel 90¢/US gal, mean stage length 3,475km, mean block time 4.66hr, mean number of seats 265, mean direct cost/seat-km 5.5 cents.
(Ray Whitford/*AIR International*)

curtail payload? What is the effective speed for different lengths of haul? What maintenance costs may be anticipated over the lifetime? What crew size is required? Now perhaps the most important question is: how many seat-km will it deliver per kg of fuel? From all this, an attempt is made to calculate the cost per available seat-km (or available tonne-km) at foreseeable load factors. The aircraft must of course meet airworthiness standards with respect to safety, noise and air pollution, and should have passenger appeal. Fleet planning models, with elaborate mathematical balancing of goals and constraints, are prepared by the airlines' research personnel (often with the assistance of the manufacturer). However, the final decision, fraught as it is with the possibilities for profit or calamity, is made by management in a manner that applies a delicate art to a great deal of science.

Chapter 3

Aerodynamics

The period immediately following the First World War saw very little improvement in aerodynamic design. By the late 1920s, however, there were stirrings among designers to clean up their products. With the development of aerodynamic engine cowlings, the cantilever monoplane, retractable undercarriages, attention to smoothness of surfaces and the use of wing flaps to allow higher wing loadings, airliners at the dawn of the jet age were about three times cleaner than those which started operations in the early 1920s. Although the introduction of the swept wing and turbojet brought into view new horizons in aerodynamics, it was accompanied by a host of new problems that needed to be solved if the jet transport was to be made economical. The 1950s saw the origins of the airliner configuration that still endures.

Progress in computational methods has made it possible to address efficiently many more aircraft design objectives than was previously possible, and concurrently reduce the design-cycle time. These advances, leading to the development of supercritical aerofoils, have revolutionized the transonic wing design process. Together with the influence of rising fuel prices, the resulting transport wings designed in the recent past look (from close inspection) quite different from those of the 1960s.

Glossary

Drag equation: Drag $= C_D \times$ dynamic pressure $\times$ wing area

$$= [C_{D_0} + (C_L^2 / \pi Ae)] \times \frac{1}{2}\rho V^2 \rho V^2 \times S$$

where: C_{D_0} is the zero lift drag coefficient (comprising skin friction drag and pressure drag) and $(C_L^2 / \pi Ae)$ is the lift induced drag

C_L is the lift coefficient: (lift force $\div \frac{1}{2}\rho V^2 \rho V^2 S$)
ρ is the air density
V is the velocity
S is the wing area
b is the wing span
A is the aspect ratio (b^2 / S)
e is the wing planform efficiency factor

Drag can be alternatively expressed using the above to give:

$$\text{Drag} = \frac{1}{2}\rho V^2 \rho V^2 S C_{D_0} + \frac{2\left(\dfrac{W}{b}\right)^2}{\rho V^2 \pi e} \text{ where W is aircraft weight}$$

The second term on the RHS shows clearly the dependence of lift induced drag on span loading squared $(W / b)^2$.

Aspect ratio: Wing span squared/wing area.

Boundary layers: The orderly state of affairs within the very thin layer of air adjacent to the skin of an aircraft, where the layers of air slide smoothly over each other as the velocity changes from zero at the surface to flight speed, is known as laminar flow. This occurs near the leading edge of a wing, whereas, further downstream, through a transition region (dependent on the Reynolds number and surface condition) the boundary-layer flow becomes turbulent. In this much more common flow there is a chaotic exchange of air particles within the layer's depth, which becomes thicker, and the drag greater.

Critical Mach number (Mcrit): This is the flight Mach number at which sonic flow first appears (usually on the upper surface of the wing).

Drag divergence Mach number (Mdiv): Also known as the drag rise Mach number. It has various definitions, a common one being the Mach number at which the rate of change of drag with speed is 5 per cent (i.e. $dD/dM = 0.05$).

Lift coefficient: Lift force $\div \frac{1}{2}\rho V^2 \rho V^2 S$, where S is the wing area.

Drag coefficient: Drag force $\div \frac{1}{2}\rho V^2 \rho V^2 S$

Lift/Drag ratio (L/D): An important measure of aerodynamic efficiency.

Mach number (M): Flight speed divided by speed of sound.

ML/D (Mach number times Lift/Drag ratio): This is the classical parameter that measures aerodynamic efficiency, since it is proportional to range, in maximizing 'air miles per pound of fuel', and indicates the speed for maximum range.

Reynolds number (Re = [Z]Vl/[X]): The ratio of inertia forces to viscous forces, where: [Z] is the air density, V is the airspeed, l is a typical length (e.g. wing chord), and [X] is the viscosity (stickiness) of the air. This relationship, discovered by Osborne Reynolds in 1883, between the flow conditions over a scale model used in windtunnel testing, needs to be made as close to that of the full-scale aircraft as possible in order to achieve reliable results. The importance of Reynolds number similarity was recognized as early as 1910, though contemporary aerodynamicists were sceptical of the effect of viscosity, and used only the *Vl* part of the Reynolds number.

Profile drag: The sum of skin friction drag and pressure drag.

Pressure drag (also known in the past as form drag): Pressure drag is the drag caused by flow separation that causes a wake to be formed. An everyday example is a bluff (non-streamlined) object, when the flow is unable to follow the surface due to insufficient kinetic energy in the boundary layer to proceed far into a region where the pressure is rising 'behind' the object. For bluff shapes such as bracing wires (as used on biplanes) the pressure drag may be 95 per cent of the total drag of the wire. Even with streamlined shapes a wake is formed in which the pressure and velocity do not recover to the values in the freestream flow. The loss of momentum shows up as a drag force. For a wing of 15 per cent thickness/chord ratio the pressure drag may be as much as one-third of the skin-friction drag.

Skin-friction drag: Caused by the shearing action within the boundary layer; contributes most of the drag of streamlined bodies.

Span loading (aircraft weight $\div$ span (W/b)): The cost in terms of drag for producing lift becomes less as the wing

This comparison of the Douglas DC-4 and Junkers Ju-52/3m epitomizes the changes in aerodynamic cleanliness in airliner design over just ten years. The Ju-52/3m made its first flight in 1932 and the DC-4 in 1942. Improvements to the Junkers aircraft increased its performance over the years. The engines were cowled, 'particularly smooth' paint was applied and low-drag spats were fitted to the undercarriage. A flat fuselage surface could have improved performance further, but was not deemed cost-effective.
(Key – Duncan Cubitt)

span is increased. Unfortunately, large span means increased weight, which calls for greater lifting power. For a wing of a given planform, induced drag is proportional to the span loading squared $(W/b)^2$ and inversely proportional to air density and square of the speed. In other words, the lower the span loading and the faster and higher the aircraft flies, the lower the induced drag. This had been predicted by Lanchester and Prandtl, but it was Max Munk, who left Germany for the USA in the 1920s, who gave the name 'induced drag' to that caused by trailing vortices.

Trailing vortex drag (also known as lift dependent drag, lift-induced drag): *See* the figure on page 43.

Wing loading [aircraft weight ÷ wing area (W/S)]: One of the main parameters in aircraft design, and to which stalling speed is closely related.

Aerofoil sections

By the time commercial aircraft operations can sensibly be considered to have started, in 1919, German pre-eminence in aerodynamics was beginning to be established. Before Ludwig Prandtl conducted a series of wind tunnel tests in 1915 at the University of Göettingen, the only available aerofoil data was for Reynolds numbers much lower than those for full-scale flight. These showed that maximum lift and L/D both increased as the aerofoil was made thinner and its leading-edge radius was reduced. This confirmed the mistaken notion that thin aerofoils would have less drag than thick ones. Consequently, almost all of the pre-1919 generation of aircraft had very thin wings (thickness/chord <6 per cent) with relatively sharp leading edges.

At the low Reynolds numbers achievable in small low-speed wind tunnels of the time, boundary-layer transition might be delayed to far back on the model wing (so that laminar flow would dominate the flow), while on the full-scale aircraft it might be near the leading edge. Laminar boundary layers are much more liable to separate early,

causing premature stall at misleadingly low angles of attack (AoA). Prandtl's research was revolutionary, since it showed that, as the Reynolds number approached the full-scale value, a thicker aerofoil with a blunt leading edge was much better, especially in delaying stall to higher AoA. This led to a German family of sections of distinctly new form, having much greater thickness than hitherto. There were two further major benefits: sufficient room within the wing to enclose the structure without the need for so much wire bracing, consequently leading to a reduction in overall aircraft drag.

Aerodynamics in Europe and the USA

Continental Europe and the USA were quicker than Britain in exploiting the thicker sections. Tests made at higher speeds with larger models confirmed that much thicker profiles, such as the Göettingen 387, USA 35 and Clark Y (created by simply flattening the underside of one of the best Göettingen forms), were superior. Many of the aircraft designs of the 1920s simply took advantage of this by substituting a single-bay biplane structure with thicker wings for the older, two-bay construction. An apparently outstanding design of the period was the Alexander Eaglerock Bullet, a very clean, low-wing monoplane with a retractable undercarriage and an advertised ability to carry 'four people and a dog'. It did not enter production because flight tests disclosed a much-dreaded phenomenon, the 'flat spin', from which recovery was evidently impossible. Thick sections were used in the contemporary monoplane airliners of the 1920s, such as the Fokker and Ford trimotors.

Beginning in 1920, the National Advisory Committee for Aeronautics (NACA, now known as NASA) began collecting and disseminating, in a uniform notation, the aerodynamic characteristics of aerofoils from wind tunnels around the world. Unfortunately the data varied rather wildly owing to different testing conditions. In terms of maximum lift (near the stall), Reynolds number effects from small-scale-model tests were especially misleading. The desirability of testing at the full-scale Reynolds number became increasingly apparent as examples of discrepancies between model and full-scale results accumulated. Indeed, it was easy to reach the conclusion that, though existing tunnels were invaluable, there was (and still is) always a case for bigger and better ones. By 1922 the variable-density tunnel promoted by Max Munk, who had recently arrived from Germany, had become operational at NACA's Langley Laboratory. This was pressurized up to 25 atmospheres to raise the air density, so that tests could be run at Reynolds number very close to full-scale. Between 1929 and 1934 NACA designed and tested more than 100 different aerofoil sections. A large database was created and was used by designers, who selected their sections from the NACA handbook first published in 1933. The 'four-digit' series proved instantly popular, being used, for example, on the Douglas DC-1 (NACA 2215). The subsequent 'five-digit' series, of which the NACA 23012 is most well known, was very widely used throughout the world. Its maximum lift coefficient was about 8 per cent higher and its minimum drag nearly 20 per cent lower than that of the Clark Y aerofoil used extensively in the 1920s.

Aerodynamics in Britain

When, in 1918, the British captured their first German aircraft having the thicker type of wing section, they tested a scale model of it in a wind tunnel. However, due to the scale effects at the low Reynolds number (70,000) of the tests, the benefits of its thickness and bluntness remained undiscovered. Since the British tendency was to favour the biplane for structural reasons, continued use was made of the relatively thin RAF15 section. It was only the potential for increased speed that forced the UK's development of thicker aerofoils such as the RAF28 (1927) and, as a result of tests using the compressed-air tunnel at the Royal Aircraft Establishment (RAE) at Farnborough, opened in 1933, the RAF32 (1939) for monoplanes.

In addition to reservations regarding structural integrity, early development work on the monoplane in the UK was held back because of the misleading wind tunnel data. High drag coefficients were found from tests because all of the available wind tunnels had much higher turbulence than the atmosphere in which an aircraft flew, although this was not

realized at the time. It was concluded that, for a monoplane to be more aerodynamically efficient than a biplane, it would have to have a smaller wing area (i.e. higher wing loading). It was later realized that the drag of the bracing struts and wires and the interference of the biplane structure had been underestimated, and that the drag of the wing itself had been overestimated, thus giving a quite misleading picture of full-scale drag. In many cases it was taken to prove that the monoplane, especially with a low wing, had no advantage over the biplane. However, it was discovered in the 1930s that much of the monoplane's 'extra' drag was caused by interference at the wing/fuselage junction (*see* later).

If the wing area was made such that the top speed occurred at the AoA for maximum L/D, then the minimum permissible flight speed would be high, making landings very hazardous. It would also result in longer take-off and landing runs and thereby limit the aircraft's usability. Thus designers were forced to use a greater wing area for the sake of landing, and caused high-speed flight to occur at much smaller AoA that that for the maximum L/D.

Lift-induced drag

Lanchester evolved his vortex theory of lift in 1894, but owing to his opaque language and lack of rigorous mathematics his work was not accepted. Eventually, Prandtl evolved a clear mathematical theory showing that the drag coefficient due to lift was proportional to the square of the lift coefficient and inversely proportional to the aspect ratio. It also showed that, for a given aspect ratio, the induced drag was minimized if the spanwise distribution of lift was elliptical. This was a major breakthrough, but because, at the time, induced drag was only around 5 per cent of the total drag, the emphasis that Lanchester and Prandtl put on high aspect ratio was neglected. Inevitably however, the Lanchester-Prandtl vortex theory gained acceptance, initially in Germany, where it was applied to the Heinkel He 70, and then more widely in the USA and UK.

High-lift devices

Leading-edge slots

A crucial development in aerodynamics was the slotted wing. The slot effect was discovered independently in quite different ways between 1917 and 1919 by Handley Page in the UK and Lachmann in Germany. Tests, carried out on

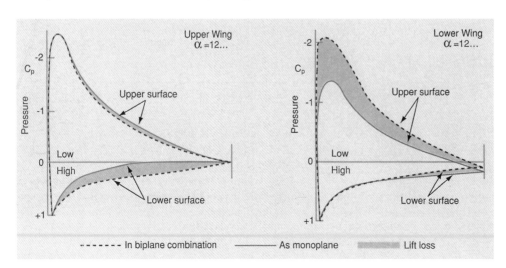

Comparison of biplane and monoplane pressure distributions. The biplane arrangement of having two wings disposed one above the other carries an inherent handicap. In simple terms, the lower wing is flying in the deflected downwash of the upper, so that not only is its lift much reduced, but it is inclined backwards. An ideal monoplane wing would produce much the same lift but with much less area, and, with greater span, that lift would be inclined less to the rear.

Lift-induced drag. As shown, because of the pressure difference between upper and lower wing surfaces the air tries to flow around the wingtip. Because this happens across the whole wingspan, a vortex sheet of rotating flows streams off the trailing edge and eventually rolls up into two big trailing vortices, one from each wing. These induce a downwash behind the wing, acting to reduce the wing's effective AoA, and tilt the lift vector back, as shown in the lower figure. The lift-induced drag can be thought of as the aft component of the deflected lift vector. (Key – Pete West)

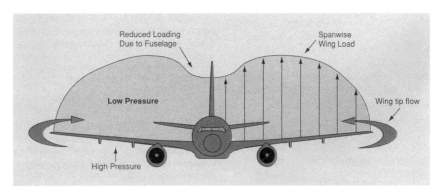

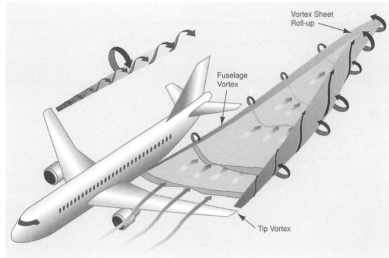

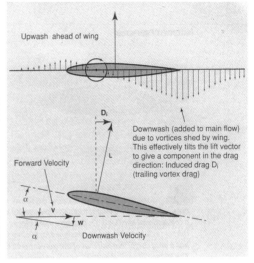

wings with a spanwise slit near the leading edge through which air could flow from the lower surface to the upper surface, gave results that were very encouraging. The slot reduced the severity of the highly adverse pressure gradient (pressure rising in the direction of flow) just aft of the wing leading edge. This helped the airflow cling to the surface, delaying stall to a higher AoA while increasing maximum lift by 50–60 per cent.

The slot was produced by the use of a slat, attached at the front of the wing. At first, a control mechanism was needed to move the slat forward. With improved design, automatic opening and closing could be achieved via the resultant aerodynamic force on the slat, which changed with AoA in such a way that the suction on the slat could open the slot by pulling the slat forward. Though the slotted slat received appreciative notice from many quarters during the 1920s, its adoption (by other than its inventors) was neither immediate nor widespread. However, during the 1930s many British

Appreciating the aerodynamic benefits of high-aspect-ratio wings, Frenchman Maurice Hurel designed and built the Hurel-Dubois series of aircraft in the early 1950s. Although they did not enter civil transport service, ten were completed, including the H.D.34 shown here, eight of which were built for France's Geographique National as photographic survey aircraft. A modified version of the wing was subsequently adopted by Short Brothers for its Skyvan. (Key – Dave Allport)

Handley Page developed the slotted slat, an example of which can be seen on the outer wing leading edge of this H.P.42. This gave a significant increase in lift with only a small increment in drag, and was a good safety feature.
(Key – Gordon Swanborough Collection)

and foreign designers adopted the Handley Page device for thin-winged biplanes, though not for thick-winged monoplanes, since the stall characteristics of the latter were generally more gentle, showing their tendency to trailing-edge stall. Moreover, the use of washout (downward twist of the aerofoil section) towards the wingtips could help retain aileron control to low speeds.

Trailing-edge flaps

As a means of increasing lift for landing and take-off, trailing-edge flaps were first used during the First World War. Flight tests in 1926 on a Bristol F2B Fighter fitted with Fairey 'variable-camber' wings showed that 20 per cent extra lift was generated for only 16 degrees of flap/aileron deflection. Using a trailing-edge flap increases the leading-edge suction peak and thereby increases the tendency to leading-edge flow separation. It was because of these undesirable characteristics that biplane pilots of the day were often reluctant to use their flaps. For thicker wings flaps work much better, though, because contemporary speeds were low and landing distances short, there was no great incentive to use them.

However, with the rise of the monoplane's popularity in the 1930s, trailing-edge flaps became more commonly used to allow a rise in wing loading. Attention turned to perfecting the slotted flap, which, compared with the contemporary split flap, had lower drag at medium deflection angles and therefore could be used to improve take-off. By using either a linkage between flap and main wing or a curved track sliding on rollers, the drag increase due to the gap between flap/main wing and external flap pivots could be limited.

The great virtue of flaps is that they allow a reduction in wing area and weight (for a given landing speed) which, in cruising flight, reduces drag and required lift. That said, the better an aircraft is made from the point of view of low drag and high speed, the more difficult it is to land. The reason for this is twofold. Firstly, the gliding angle is reduced by the low drag, so the aircraft comes in on a less-inclined flightpath and travels further over the ground before it touches down. Secondly, the low drag means less deceleration during the ground run. Aircraft of the 1920s were easy to land because their low wing loadings gave low stalling speeds and high drag. The need for 1930s aircraft was to make them temporarily as inefficient as those of the previous decade. Trailing-edge flaps, though designers were initially reluctant to incorporate them for reasons of added complexity, were very effective on thick wings, for not only did they produce high maximum lift at large deflections, so that landing speeds could be reduced, but they also increased drag.

Another difficulty was that of take-off. High drag is a hindrance to acceleration, whereas lift increase is advantageous because it reduces the take-off speed. The split flap (invented by Orville Wright in 1920) was used at deflection angles of about 15 degrees to give appreciable extra lift without excessive drag. Its disadvantage was its high drag at greater deflections. However, the slotted flap developed by Handley Page was better because it gave much more lift with little increase in drag, and was still as effective as the split flap for landing when deflected to 60 degrees. A similar development was the Fowler flap, which not only increased camber but, by extending rearwards, increased wing area.

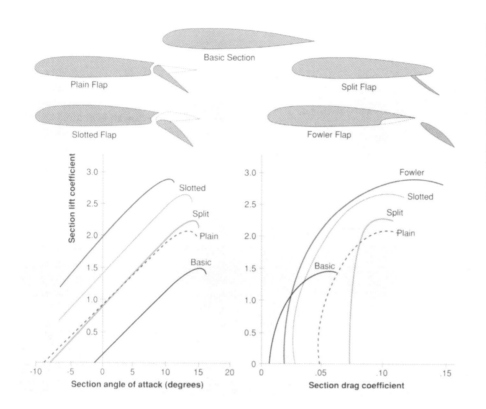

Aerodynamic characteristics of flaps (25 per cent chord, 30 degrees deflection). The split flap, invented by Orville Wright in 1920, was used at deflection angles of about 15 degrees to give appreciable extra lift without excessive drag. Its disadvantage was its high drag at greater deflections. However, the slotted flap, as developed by Handley Page, was better because it gave much more lift with little increase in drag, and was still as effective as the split flap for landing when deflected to 60 degrees. A similar development was the Fowler flap, which not only increased camber but, by extending rearwards, also increased wing area.
(Ray Whitford/(*AIR International*))

Trailing-edge flap type	Split	Slotted	Fowler	Double-slotted
Increment in lift coefficient	1.11	1.15	1.40	1.62
Maximum lift coefficient	2.48	2.53	2.77	2.94

Relative merits of trailing edge flaps (*c*.1950).

The figures above are based on two-dimensional wind tunnel tests for a wing of aspect ratio of 10, thickness/chord ratio 15 per cent, flap chord 30 per cent of wing chord over 70 per cent span. Doctor Hugo Junkers had proposed single- and double-slotted flaps in 1921. By 1939 two-dimensional wind tunnel tests at RAE Farnborough produced a maximum lift coefficient of 3.5 for a double-slotted Fowler flap, and the addition of a leading-edge slat increased this to almost 4.5. However, this overstated the true benefits to an aircraft because of limited flap span and the difficulties of maintaining the trim (balance) of the aircraft.

Aerodynamic cleanliness

In terms of aerodynamic efficiency, as measured by L/D, the best that had been achieved by the late-1920s was an L/D of about 10:1 (or a glide of 1 in 10), typical for an aircraft with a water-cooled engine. Those with air-cooled engines were slightly worse. At the time it was popular to equate the high drag of aircraft to that of more common forms of vehicle, namely the rolling resistance of a motor vehicle that required a slope of only 1 in 50 for motion under gravity alone, so the slope for an aircraft to descend steadily seemed very steep. The rise in cruising speed from 70mph (110km/h) in 1919 (HP O/400) to 120mph (190km/h) in 1929 (Ford 5-AT Trimotor) was due more to increase (80 per cent) in available engine power than to cleaner aerodynamic design (as can be seen from the adjacent figure of zero lift drag). It is evident that very little attention, if any, was paid to aerodynamic cleanliness. However, there were notable exceptions, as demonstrated by the Schneider Trophy series of racing aircraft.

In 1928 Prof Melville Jones of Cambridge University computed the performance of an ideal streamlined aircraft in which the drag was equal only to the sum of the induced drag corresponding to the span loading of the aircraft (as predicted by Lanchester and Prandtl) and the skin friction drag. He was able to show that many contemporary aircraft had two to three times more drag than his ideal aircraft. Furthermore, the best aircraft had an efficiency (defined as: (Power to overcome skin friction and induced drag))/Total installed

Improvement (mph) [km/h]	Speed increase (mph) [km/h]
Reduced drag (-29 per cent)	37 [60]
Increased engine power	20 [32]
Increased propeller efficiency	9 [14]
Increased landing speed	4 [6]
Total	70 [112]

Improvements made during one year (1928–29) to the performance of the Supermarine S.6 that gained the world air speed record at 357.7mph (687.7km/h)

A feature of early airliners was the parasitic drag contributed by struts and wires, upstanding windscreens and open cockpits, hanging undercarriages and tailskids. These were somewhat alleviated in the de Havilland Dragon Rapide by the high-aspect-ratio wing, faired undercarriage and enclosed cockpit. An attraction of biplanes was that they were trustworthy; monoplanes of the time were not.

power) or (Unavoidable drag/Total drag), of only 50 per cent. Moreover, the worst aircraft (such as the Armstrong Whitworth Argosy and Handley Page Hercules) would have needed only a third of the power with which they were provided *if* they conformed to his ideal aeroplane. Put another way, if streamlined, they could fly 60mph (95km/h) faster on the same power.

However, manufacturers and customers knew that power cost money, and many of them, particularly in the UK, interpreted this to mean that speed cost money. This created a circular argument. If airliners were economically condemned to cruise at no more than 100mph (160km/h), streamlining became a secondary consideration. However, if aircraft were cleaned up and flew faster, profile drag became more important. This emphasized the importance of reduced wing area via the use of flaps, improved streamlining to limit flow

separations, and a retractable undercarriage. What many British designers failed to appreciate was that, if all the improvements were made simultaneously, power requirements could be reduced to a fraction of what was actually being used. The consequence was that both the USA and Germany had streamlined aircraft in series production long before the UK. Although the ideal seemed unattainable, it was approached within a few years, so that by the late 1930s the best airliners had efficiencies of around 65 per cent.

Engine cooling drag

In the earliest days of flying, engine cooling was achieved without much thought of the resulting drag. Two almost simultaneous attempts were made to deal with the air-cooled radial engine. In the 1920s it had been demonstrated that the

Reduction in zero lift drag with time. In terms of Melville Jones' 'Ideal Streamline Aeroplane' the Lockheed L.049 Constellation reached about 80 per cent of the 'streamline speed', giving an indication of the progress made in aerodynamic cleanliness over 20 years. The major influences in drag reduction are shown as the move from biplanes to monoplanes, followed by the introduction of retractable undercarriages, close and efficient cowling of engines and the increasing use of flush riveting.

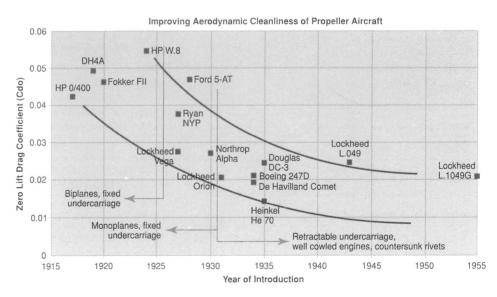

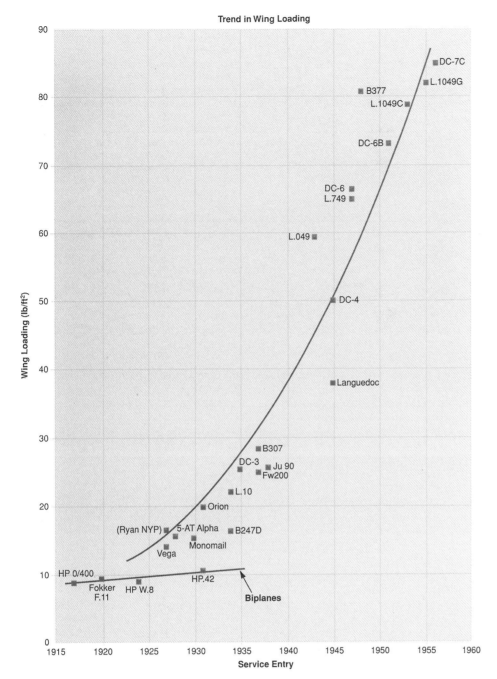

Trend in Wing Loading

Wing Loading (lb/ft²) vs Service Entry

DC-7C
L.1049G
B377
L.1049C
DC-6B
DC-6
L.749
L.049
DC-4
Languedoc
B307
DC-3
Ju 90
Fw200
L.10
Orion
(Ryan NYP)
5-AT Alpha
B247D
Monomail
Vega
HP 0/400
HP.42
Fokker F.11
HP W.8
Biplanes

Wing loading with time (propeller transports). This figure shows that, while the British inclined to stay with biplanes, with their low wing loadings, well into the 1930s, Germany and especially the USA rapidly exploited the virtue of lower drag, albeit at the expense of needing high-lift devices to retain adequate airfield performance. For example, while the first of the 'modern' airliners, the monoplane Boeing 247, appeared without flaps, the DC-1's use of them gave a 35 per cent increase in lift coefficient on take-off and brought even greater gains in lowering the landing speed. By the end of the Second World War cruising speeds were so high, at over 300mph (480km/h), that the aim was to keep drag/wing area down rather than keep the drag down by keeping the wing area down.

	Fairey Fox (biplane, 1930)	de Havilland D.H.88 (monoplane, 1934)	Heinkel He 70 (monoplane, 1935)
Maximum speed (kt) [km/h]	152 [212]	235 [328]	235 [328]
Power loading (kg/kW) [lb/hp]	5.22 [8.6]	7.17 [11.8]	6.8 [11.2]
Profile drag coefficient (wing area)	0.044	0.0197	0.0144
Profile drag coefficient (wetted area)	0.0145	0.0051	0.0046
Percentage of streamline speed	25	74	60

Improved aerodynamics in the 1930s. Advances in propulsion provided the greatest benefits to the performance of early aircraft. Nevertheless, the major improvement (shown by the two later monoplane aircraft) during the 1930s (over the highly regarded Fairey Fox biplane light bomber) came from better aerodynamic design. Indeed, the profile drag of the He 70, aerodynamically the cleanest aircraft then built, shows a gain of three to one over the Fox and, if given the then contemporary fighter power loading of 3.6kg/kW (6lb/hp), was reckoned to be capable of nearly 300mph (480km/h). The D.H.88 was able to achieve 74 per cent of its theoretically possible maximum speed, taking account of its lower wing loading compared with that of the He 70.

Rivets near leading edges were the greatest cause of profile drag. To minimize this element of drag the Vickers Viscount had flush rivets for the first third of the fuselage length (just aft of the propellers) and dome-head rivets for the rest.
(Key – Gordon Swanborough Collection)

cylinders of a radial engine projecting from the nose of a streamlined body increased drag four- to five-fold. In the UK, Townend of the National Physical Laboratory (NPL) made a simple test to see if a ring located around the nose of a body influenced the body drag. He found that in some positions the body had negative drag; it tried to move upstream into the ring. This observation led to putting the ring around the heads of the engine cylinders, giving a considerable reduction in drag. Whether an aircraft with a ring around its air-cooled engine was really as efficient as an aircraft with a watercooled engine was a good question. Perhaps it was simply that biplanes with air-cooled engines were so inefficient that it was quite hard to make them worse.

Almost simultaneously the NACA cowling was developed in the USA by Wieck, using NACA's new 20ft (6.1m)-diameter propeller-testing wind tunnel to test cowlings systematically on a full-scale fuselage. The best cowling reduced the drag by two-thirds and improved cooling, despite the engine being almost completely shrouded. After flight tests in 1928 this development was revealed in a coast-to-coast record flight of 18.22hr by a Lockheed Air Express (a Vega derivative), for which the new cowl increased the top speed from 157mph (253km/h) to 177mph (285km/h), equivalent to a power increase of over 40 per cent.

Flush riveting

In the early 1930s most metal aircraft were held together by rivets with protruding dome-shaped heads. A decade later almost all such aircraft had rivets flush with the surface. To observers outside the aircraft industry this change, if noticed at all, must have seemed straightforward and even trivial. There had always been controversy over the drag reduction achievable from the use of flush rivets. In many cases the gains were disappointingly small, due to the boundary layer becoming turbulent for reasons other than the disturbances

set up by the rivets (for example, wing-leading-edge de-icing systems). Thus flush riveting in the first half of the 1930s was of peripheral importance and lagged behind the major innovations. This lag did not depend on problems in riveting itself, so required no major breakthrough, though it had rarely been used for sheets as thin as those on aircraft. Only when the performance improvements caused by retractable undercarriages, flaps and the like had been realized did it become generally attractive to pursue the lesser gains offered by recessed rivet heads. While the extra cost of flush riveting remained constant, so the smaller gain from flush riveting became more inviting. In some instances manufacturers made limited use of flush riveting by employing it only on the upper surface of the wing near the leading edge, where protrusions are particularly harmful. By the mid-1930s the time was ripe for flush riveting throughout the industry.

The effects of surface finish were also investigated because of concern over the quality of paint application and its deterioration in service. In extreme cases military Service aircraft were found on return to the factory to have 27 per cent more drag than when they had the factory as new, owing to lack of attention to surface finish.

Wing/fuselage aerodynamic interference

Innumerable experimental studies were made of wing position in the early 1930s, regarding the aerodynamic interference generated at the wing/fuselage junction. In particular, the low-wing configuration was found to be by far the worst arrangement from the point of view of drag. Putting a circular fuselage on top of the wing has the effect of producing a pair of rapidly diverging surfaces (formed by the fuselage curvature and the reducing thickness of the wing towards its trailing edge). This steepens an already adverse pressure gradient and almost guarantees flow separation ('burbling', at as it was commonly called in the USA),

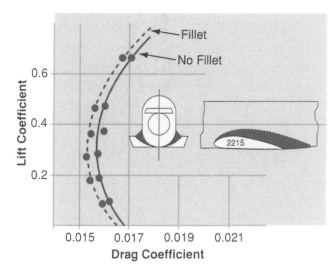

Effect of wing fillets on wing/fuselage interference. Windtunnel testing of the first 1/11th-scale model of the DC-1 revealed some bad characteristics. One of these was that, at the highest speeds, it was subject to buffeting around the wing/body junction. CalTech proposed the use of wing fillets or fairings (the effect of which is to increase the radius of the junction towards the rear of the wing) to smooth out the adverse pressure gradient existing where the wing thickness decreased and met the lower surface of the fuselage. In the low-lift, low-drag condition the addition of the fillet on the DC-1 (with a flat-sided fuselage having its wing mounted below the cabin floor) reduced the minimum drag of the windtunnel model by about 2 per cent and raised the maximum lift coefficient from 1.27 to 1.34. This change alone produced a gain of 17mph (27km/h) in the DC-1's top speed.

resulting in more drag and less lift. The discovery of the beneficial aerodynamic effects of a fillet or wing/body fairing was found during work started in 1931 at the NPL in the UK and at CalTech in the USA (*see* adjacent figure). This largely overcame the problem to such an extent that the disadvantages of the low-wing monoplane could be almost completely eliminated by proper design of the wing–fuselage intersection. What little inferiority remained for the low wing configuration was more than compensated for by its benefits. These included provision for a short and easily retractable undercarriage, the cushioning ground effect on landing of a wing close to the ground, and energy absorption in the event of a wheels-up landing.

Laminar flow

Prandtl had proposed the concept of the boundary layer in 1904, though in UK literature the term does not appear until 1925. The existence of a laminar boundary layer (which gives minimum skin friction drag) was unsuspected in the UK until 1924, when experimental results demonstrated its reality. By 1928 Melville Jones emphasized its importance in an analysis of international wind tunnel tests on airship models. At the time, aircraft wing surfaces were often rough or inaccurate in shape, with heavily ribbed or stretched fabric, corrugated light alloy, wrinkled plywood, or a mass of dome-head rivets along lapped joints (*see* adjacent figure).

With the eventual overthrow of the biplane in favour of the monoplane with retractable undercarriage, drag reduction of the basic configuration concentrated on detail design. During the late 1930s much attention was paid to this. Tests at the NPL showed that excrescences, corresponding to the roughness of fabric-covered wings of the time, resulted in a drag increase over a smooth aerofoil of about 70 per cent. These results ultimately led to more care over aircraft

construction. In addition to retaining a smooth leading edge, where flush riveting had to be employed, advantage could be gained by retaining a smooth surface back to the trailing edge. The rear half of the wing was found to produce about a third of the drag.

Once the dependence of the skin-friction drag on the location of the transition from laminar to turbulent flow was recognized, and wing surfaces were smooth enough for some laminar flow to exist (20 per cent in the case of the He 70's wing), great efforts were made to exploit the possibility of reduced skin-friction drag. This was brought about by ensuring better standards of surface finish and by changes in the section shape, and thus the pressure distribution. It had been predicted in 1936 that, with full laminar flow, skin-friction drag might be reduced to about 10 per cent of then current values. Even though wind tunnel results showed little chance of much laminar flow on aircraft wings, Melville Jones carried out flight tests with a Hawker Hart in 1937 and showed its existence. Paradoxically, no improvement was found during high-Reynolds-number wind tunnel testing.

These results undoubtedly inspired US researchers such as E.N. Jacobs and his colleagues at NACA. It was realized that the flow in contemporary wind tunnels was much more turbulent than experienced in flight, and induced premature transition. Accordingly they developed a wind tunnel with very low turbulence, but not until it was available in 1938 could the striking reduction in drag be clearly demonstrated.

Then followed the breakthrough by Jacobs, who realized that the maintenance of laminar flow depended on a prescription of the pressure distribution (rather than the shape of the aerofoil), from which the aerofoil profile could then be defined. The basic principle was to delay transition by ensuring that the flow continued to accelerate for as great a distance as possible before encountering the region of rising pressure near the trailing edge. In other words, keep the minimum pressure point far back by having the maximum wing thickness at around 40–45 per cent chord. By the time UK experimenters heard rumours in 1938–39

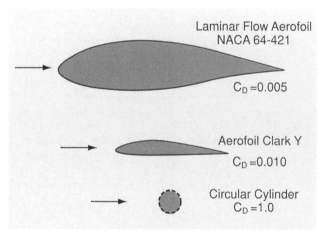

Comparison of drag of a laminar-flow aerofoil with a conventional one (Clark Y). Although it is a much bigger and thicker (21 per cent) aerofoil, the one designed for laminar flow has a drag coefficient half that of the conventional one. The benefit of basic streamlining can be judged by the drag coefficient of the small circular cylinder at the centre of the circle (representative of the wires used on biplanes). The Clark Y was empirically derived by Virginus Clark in 1922, simply by flattening the bottom of one of the best Göttingen aerofoils. It proved to have good lift and, for its time, reasonable drag, the flat bottom easing construction. It was one of the most successful sections of the 1920s, and Lindbergh's NYP *Spirit of St Louis* was one of many types that used it. In addition, its virtues made it attractive for propellers, for which it was used extensively up to the mid-1940s.

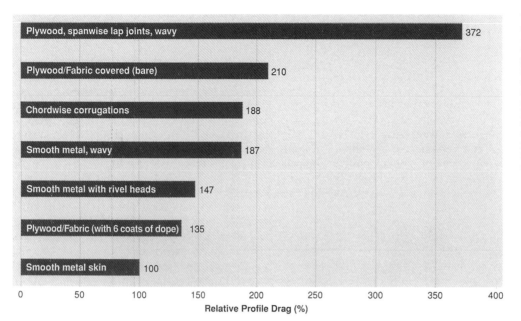

Plywood, spanwise lap joints, wavy	372
Plywood/Fabric covered (bare)	210
Chordwise corrugations	188
Smooth metal, wavy	187
Smooth metal with rivel heads	147
Plywood/Fabric (with 6 coats of dope)	135
Smooth metal skin	100

Relative Profile Drag (%)

The effect of surface condition on profile drag. Results of flight tests in Germany in 1928 showed that smooth, well-doped plywood had 25 per cent less drag than a wavy metal skin and was nearly 10 per cent better than smooth metal with dome-headed rivets. These results were unknown outside Germany, and had to be rediscovered later. Rivets near leading edges were the worst offenders.

Simplified view of the effect of increasing Reynolds number. (A) At low Reynolds numbers there will be a large extent of the boundary layer which is laminar, and transition to turbulence may occur only in the wake, where the boundary layer has separated from the wing surface. A laminar boundary layer, though giving low skin friction, separates easier than a turbulent one and gives rise to extra pressure drag. (B) At increased Reynolds number the transition to turbulence will occur nearer to the leading edge, giving rise to increased skin friction but resistance to separation. (C) Further increase in Reynolds number will move the transition region nearer to the leading edge, leaving very little of the wing covered by a laminar boundary layer.
Note: Reynolds number can be increased by a rise in speed, a larger-chord wing, or flying at low altitude. In addition, premature transition to turbulence will arise due to roughness of the wing surface near the leading edge.

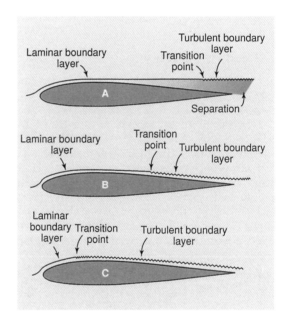

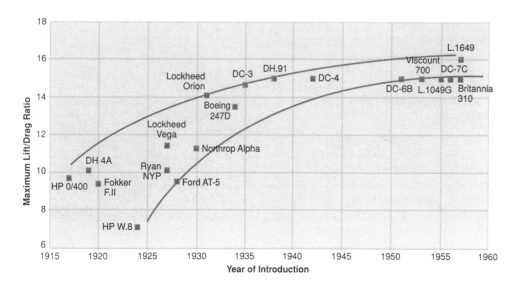

Maximum Lift/Drag Ratio

Year of Introduction

Improving lift/drag ratio. Since aircraft range is a function of speed multiplied by L/D ratio, the efforts made to reduce drag by improved cleanliness and limited span loading (by increased aspect ratio) paid dividends.

of curiously shaped aerofoils with cusped trailing edges, NACA had developed its six-series laminar-flow aerofoils. It was further found during tests in 1939 in the compressed air tunnel at NPL that the aerofoil section should be thin, since this has the added benefit of minimizing pressure drag. This led to the RAE series of aerofoils.

Although these laminar-flow sections have been widely used, their expected benefit was never fully achieved. This was because laminar flow requires a wing surface to be manufactured and maintained in a very smooth condition, lacking in waviness. For waves no more than 6in (15cm) in length the permissible height of a wave had to be less than 1/1,000th of its length. This required an accuracy of construction far higher than that achieved. Moreover, the required smoothness could easily be contaminated by a build-up of insects (a common occurrence), or dirt deposited on the leading edge during take-off. This prompted impractical schemes for coating the wing lower surfaces with paper, later to be jettisoned. However, although the new aerofoils were unable to fulfil their promise, they did accelerate the air more gradually over the upper surface. This yielded a higher critical Mach number (delaying the onset of the drag rise by perhaps 50mph (80km/h)), wherein lay their greatest practical benefit (*see* Compressibility).

The devil is in the detail

Although remarkable improvements to aerodynamics were made in the 1930s, this was primarily because the state of streamlining had previously been so abysmal. The grudging realization that there was a vast margin between the drag standards actually achieved and those theoretically attainable provided a great stimulus to R&D. Clean-up operations were mounted: undercarriages were made retractable, wings were made thinner and their surfaces made smoother by flush riveting, wing–body junctions were filleted, flaps became common, and wing loadings were increased. However, the benefits could be easily undone by lack of attention to detail. Following the Second World War the advent of the jet engine

held the promise of even higher speeds that would require the ushering in of new branches of aerodynamics.

Compressibility

In the context of aerodynamics, the period between the two world wars has been classified as a period of exploitation of rational theories of an incompressible fluid. The speeds of chief interest were considerably below that of sound, though, towards the end of the period, designers began to use propellers having tips that travelled at high subsonic speeds. By the early 1940s fighters in high-speed dives began encountering difficulties produced by air compressibility as the speed approached the speed of sound. Their wings had been designed so that, in level flight, there would be a reasonable speed margin before compressibility struck. This had been done with the experimental data then available; mostly aerofoil tests combined with a limited theoretical understanding of the flow phenomena. However, this work had concentrated on estimating how aerofoil drag would vary with Mach number. What consequences would be encountered as aircraft exceeded the estimated critical Mach number of 0.65–0.7 was unknown. Wind tunnels operating near the speed of sound were of little help in understanding the flow phenomena because of choking and shock-wave reflections. The implications of shock wave/boundary layer interaction were yet to be studied, tested and understood. However, this had little relevance as far as propeller-driven transports were concerned, since the highest cruise speed attained by the mid-1950s was no more than half that of sound.

Drag rise

This is the name given to the behaviour of drag exhibited by high-speed aircraft when they first encounter compressibility effects, and led to the so-called 'sound barrier', a rise in drag so large that many thought it was impenetrable. The development of compressibility drag can be separated into three components. Firstly there is the very gradual drag

Minimum-unstick-speed trials, one of the many tests that a new airliner must undergo as part of its certification process, were successfully completed by the Airbus A330 in June 1993. The minimum unstick speed is a function of the lifting capability of the wing; one of the disadvantages of swept wings is their low lift curve slope.
(Airbus Industrie)

increase that can occur before any supersonic velocities arise. Next there is a somewhat more rapid drag rise as shock waves form and start to spread out. Finally there is the very steep drag rise that usually starts when the Mach number just ahead of the shock wave on the upper surface of the wing exceeds approximately 1.2.

At Mach numbers below those at which shock waves exist, an aircraft's profile drag is composed mostly of skin-friction drag and pressure drag, both of which vary with Mach number. The skin-friction drag coefficient decreases with Mach number because of the thickening of the boundary layer owing to boundary layer heating. On the other hand, the pressure drag increases with Mach number. Consequently, whether or not there is any drag rise in the absence of supersonic flow, and if so how great, depends on the balance between these two components. However, for most aircraft there is a gradual rise.

When localized supersonic flow, terminated by a weak shock wave, first appears on a wing, the dominating parameter is the adverse pressure gradient resulting from the abrupt rise in static pressure across the shock. This will cause at least a thickening of the boundary layer, if not flow separation. Just above the critical Mach number the shock wave is not strong enough to cause separation, and the effects on drag are barely perceptible. However, further increase in speed causes the supersonic region to enlarge and the strength of the shock wave to grow. The interaction between the shock wave and boundary layer will eventually cause boundary layer separation. This prevents the static pressure at the wing's trailing edge from recovering to the freestream value, leaving the aftmost, rearward-facing surface of the wing at a lower-than-expected pressure. This increases the pressure drag, and is one of the main contributors to wave drag. Thicker aerofoils were found to aggravate this undesirable behaviour, and caused it to occur at lower speeds. It was conclusively established in the late 1940s that thinner sections could greatly alleviate these effects and postpone the drag rise to higher Mach numbers.

Thus, despite the great strides made during the 1930–40s regarding drag, it might have appeared that all that was required was careful attention to detail design. However, with the advent of the jet engine and its possible application to commercial transports, the top speed of an aircraft in level flight could no longer be related so directly to its subsonic drag, but was determined by the drag divergence Mach number (Mdiv), beyond which the rapid increase in drag occurred. Research concentrated on means to increase Mdiv rather than to reduce the level of the drag in this condition. A major development was the introduction of wing sweepback.

Sweepback

By 1939 Albert Betz, a Swiss aerodynamicist, had shown that sweepback could be used to delay the onset of compressibility problems arising from local regions of supersonic flow terminating in shock waves in the *transonic* flight regime. German aircraft had appeared in the early 1940s with sweepback, though more for reasons of balance (as on the DC-3 airliner) than for aerodynamic benefits, because leading-edge sweepback was limited to about 20 degrees, a modest level of sweep that had little effect on drag. Nevertheless, Germany's appreciation of the value of sweepback at high speed advanced quickly, and by the end of the war in Europe it led the world in this respect, incorporating sweep into many of its future designs.

In 1945 George Schairer, Boeing's engineering vice-president, was in the Allied teams sent to collect data from the recently-discovered German aeronautical research laboratories. Since Boeing was competing for a United States Army Air Force contract for a new jet bomber at the time, there data were potentially of great value.

Boeing was then researching a way to install jet engines in its bomber. From four different arrangements, one had been selected with straight wings, with four jet engines grouped in the centre fuselage and the jetpipes exhausting over the rear fuselage. This design was scrapped on Schairer's return from

Swept wings and underslung podded engines adopted for the Boeing B-47 Stratojet led to the airliner configuration accepted as the norm today. By contrast, the reluctance of UK authorities to adopt the swept wing in 1945–46 lost Britain a great opportunity that subsequent British transports failed to recover until the early 1960s. (Key Archive)

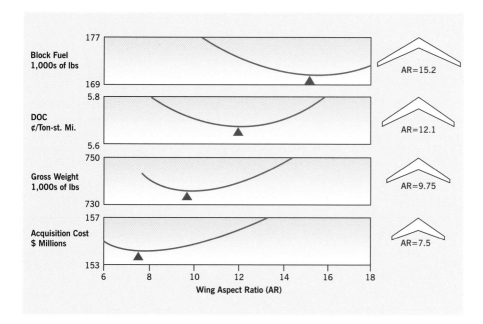

Effect of wing aspect ratio for a transport carrying a 250,000lb (113,250kg) payload at Mach 0.85. This figure shows the effect of aspect ratio on four factors that are important to airline economics. Drag in subsonic flight is partly due to wetted (surface) area and partly to span loading squared $(W/b)^2$. Little can be done to reduce the surface area of the fuselage without reducing its carrying capacity, so the emphasis has to be on wing design. The most efficient subsonic wing from an aerodynamic viewpoint has the highest practical aspect ratio (span²/area) shown by the fuel-burn graph. One limit to aspect ratio is weight, since beyond a certain point the wing weight to resist the bending loads outweighs the aerodynamic benefit.

Europe and, on the basis of the 'acquired' German data, a fresh start with swept-back wings was made, but with the engines still in the fuselage. One month later, using the advantages of long span, the engines were relocated to separated external pods slung on pylons ahead of and below the wing leading edge. Being remote from the wing, the pods overcame Boeing's harsh wartime experience with engine fires on its B-29 Superfortress bomber. Furthermore, being placed well outboard, the engine masses provided favourable aeroelastic effects on the very slender and flexible swept wing. Thus, in the form of the new Boeing B-47 Stratojet, first flown in 1947, the classic layout for long-range aircraft was born and led to the airliner configuration accepted as the norm today. By contrast, the reluctance of UK authorities to adopt the swept wing in 1945–46 lost Britain a great opportunity that subsequent British transports failed to recover until the early 1960s.

Development efforts toward high-speed jet transports began in the USA in the late 1940s. Basic aerodynamic lift, drag and pitching moment data for the initial studies were obtained primarily from NACA tests of swept-wing models. Two-dimensional sweep theory was studied, and generally formed the analytical framework that supported the test results to arrive at useful analytic prediction methods. For example, Boeing had tested a wing for an aircraft about the same size as its eventual 707, but this was swept at only 25 degrees. It was expedient to take the wing and simply rotate it another 10 degrees. Although this was cruder than desired, there was little time for anything more elaborate. In this manner, early swept-wing-transport designers made remarkably successful use of inadequate theory and empirical data.

The benefits of sweepback

Delay and reduction of subsonic drag rise
The most immediate benefit of sweep is its ability not only to delay the subsonic drag rise to a higher speed, but also to reduce the drag coefficients. As shown in an adjacent figure, the effect of sweep is to reduce the velocity component normal to the wing isobars (lines of constant pressure) that, for the time being, are assumed to be parallel to the leading

edge. Sweeping the wing by an angle Λ theoretically allows an increase in the flight speed before sonic flow first appears by $1/\cos\Lambda$. The above reasoning is a simplification, since the flow over a typical swept wing is a complex three-dimensional one, especially at the root and tip. Consequently the simple $\cos\Lambda$ relationship applies only to a yawed wing of infinite span, and the delay in reaching Mcrit is much less than predicted. Although, in practice, sweepback increases Mcrit by only about half the expected amount, the benefits are still well worth having. It could be argued that increasing aspect ratio would increase the wing area free from root and tip effects, but the phenomenon of pitch-up (*see* Stability and Control chapter) places an upper limit on the aspect ratio that can be used with a given sweep angle. The early swept wings had little twist or camber; their basic geometry was generally designed to give good performance at one particular operating condition.

The penalties of sweepback

Despite the benefits of sweep, when it was first introduced much effort had to be devoted to dealing with some serious inherent problems. These included reduced lift at a given AoA and the reduced effectiveness of trailing-edge flaps, both of which resulted in increased take-off and landing speeds. Because, simultaneously, wing loading was rapidly increasing, the problem was compounded, though some relief was obtained by the reintroduction of the leading-edge high-lift devices. Other repercussions of sweep are: increased rolling due to sideslip, tip stalling and pitch-up, and structural and aeroelastic problems.

Reduction of lift-curve slope
Increasing sweep always reduces the lift-curve slope of a wing and increases the AoA for maximum lift. Reduced lift for a given AoA means nose-high attitudes (especially on landing), which restrict pilot view, though this is offset by trailing-edge flaps. The reduced lift slope also limits usable lift for take-off. The AoA for maximum lift cannot be attained because the aft fuselage will strike the ground if the aircraft is rotated more than, say, 15 degrees about the main wheels (*see* adjacent figure). This could be overcome by

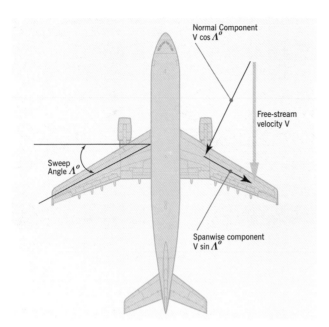

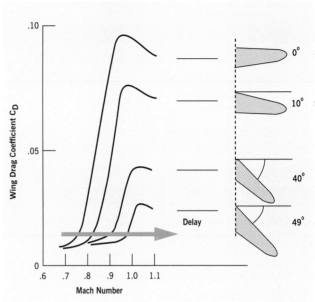

Delay and reduction of subsonic drag rise. The most immediate benefit of sweep is its ability to delay to a higher speed the subsonic drag rise (right figure). As shown (left figure), the effect of sweep is to reduce the velocity component normal to the wing leading edge. Sweeping the wing by an angle Λ allows an increase in the flight speed before sonic flow first appears by $1/\cos\Lambda$ (theoretically for an infinitely long wing).
(Key – Pete West)

increasing the length of the undercarriage legs, but that would lead to problems of stowage, structural efficiency of the wing, and weight. The high sweepback on the Boeing 707 (35 degrees) presented a severe limit to increasing the basic design's passenger carrying potential, as a stretched fuselage would have restricted the take-off angle without a longer undercarriage. Douglas's DC-8 used only 30 degrees and, with its adequate-length undercarriage, had far more stretch potential.

Higher drag-due-to-lift
Lift-dependent drag is primarily a function of span loading squared $(W/b)^2$; that is, it depends on both aspect ratio (b^2/S) and wing loading (W/S). That said, aspect ratio, as such, does not have a direct effect on either drag or performance. It does, of course, play a major part in determining the induced drag coefficient, but a coefficient should not be confused with the physical force it represents. It is drag, not drag coefficient, that must be overcome, so it is span loading (W/b) and not aspect ratio that determines how efficiently a wing performs

its lifting function. The problem for the designer, who must juggle a large number of aerodynamic parameters, is to trade wing area and span so as to arrive at a safe and economical aircraft. In practice it generally turns out that, when sufficient wing area has been provided to give desired stalling speed and cruise altitude, the aspect ratio falls out as an incidental consequence of the other two. Although the induced drag coefficient is seldom out of the aerodynamicist's mind, the main parameters for manipulation are span loading and wing loading. Inevitably, from Boeing's experience on the B-47 (aspect ratio = 9.43 and W/b = 1,750lb/ft (2,600kg/m)), a swept wing applied to transports needed a high aspect ratio to get a low span loading.

Reduction of maximum lift
Sweepback reduces maximum lift at both ends of the speed spectrum. On relatively thick wings of high aspect ratio it reduces the maximum lift with $\cos\Lambda$. In the late 1940s, wind tunnel model tests showed that, at the high-subsonic Mach numbers made possible by sweep, the maximum lift

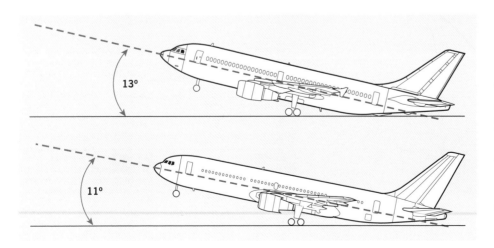

The adverse effect of sweep in reducing the lift curve slope of the wing. This may limit usable lift on take-off because of the risk of the aft fuselage striking the ground, and can restrict the stretch potential of an aircraft. This has to be compensated for by the high-lift system to ensure growth possibility and satisfactory field performance. Shown here are the maximum rotation angles for the Airbus A310 (13 degrees) with a quarter-chord sweep of 28 degrees, and the Boeing 767-200 (11 degrees) with its sweep of 31.5 degrees.

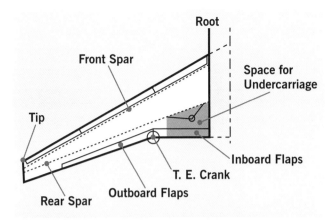

Trailing-edge crank to increase space for undercarriage. Not only is the crank used to house the undercarriage aft of the rear spar, but the extended chord length of the aerofoil section means that high thickness at the wing root (good for low weight) can be used while maintaining a relatively low thickness/chord ratio. Additionally, the crank effectively reduces the sweep of the hinge line of the inboard flaps, so increasing their effectiveness. (Key – Pete West)

Wing disassembly. The wing of a Virgin Atlantic Boeing 747-400 with trailing-edge triple-slotted Fowler flaps in landing configuration. (Key – Malcolm English)

coefficient had fallen to such an extent that it would be impossible to fly straight and level at high altitude without stalling. The B-47 was a notable early example of this effect; at certain easily attainable combinations of aircraft weight and altitude, the low- and high-speed stalling speeds coincided, this region being known as 'coffin corner'.

Reduces effectiveness of high-lift devices

Although moderate sweep of up to 25 degrees can result in an increase in maximum lift, higher sweep reduces the lift generated by thick wings. At low sweep, acceptable lift increments can be achieved by using flaps, so that an increase in wing area is not needed to obtain a specified field performance. At higher sweepback, however, the lift yield from flaps reduces markedly. This loss of effectiveness is due to the outflow along the wing. The sweep at the leading edge of the flap becomes a dominant parameter, and the trailing-edge sweep of wings is generally kept low to maximize the benefit from trailing-edge devices. The resulting kinked planform (which coincidentally provides room for the undercarriage) also minimizes root thickness/chord ratio and increases the depth, and hence strength, of the rear spar and central torsion box (*see* adjacent figure).

The need for the complicated high-lift systems (such as triple-slotted trailing-edge flaps with leading-edge flaps) used in the 1960s and 1970s meant that the weight of high-lift

devices became a significant part of the cost of providing acceptable airfield performance. Today's high-lift systems are simpler. The estimated total weight penalty for a present-day high-lift system for a 6,000ft (1,800m) field length is about 4 per cent AUW, but this is quite modest considering that it effectively doubles the usable lifting capacity of the wing (typically increasing maximum lift coefficient from 1.4 to 2.8).

Aerofoils

German research during the 1940s showed a clear appreciation of the value of reduced thickness for high-speed flight. The thinner sections not only had lower drag coefficients, but also delayed the onset of drag rise due to shock-wave formation. The former was the main argument in favour of thin sections, which, together with sweepback, has been successfully employed on all subsequent high-speed aircraft. However, for transport aircraft a high aspect ratio (and low span loading) was necessary to minimize the lift-dependent drag, but too thin a wing cannot be tolerated because of the structural weight penalty. Moreover, a wing of conventional thickness, permitted by the use of sweepback, maintained reasonably high maximum lift and provided room for both leading- and trailing-edge lift devices, together with useful fuel volume and stowage for the undercarriage. Thicker sections are impractical because the excessive airflow acceleration over the surface produces

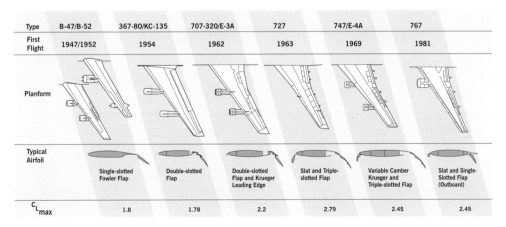

Type	B-47/B-52	367-80/KC-135	707-320/E-3A	727	747/E-4A	767
First Flight	1947/1952	1954	1962	1963	1969	1981
Planform						
Typical Airfoil	Single-slotted Fowler Flap	Double-slotted Flap	Double-slotted Flap and Krueger Leading Edge	Slat and Triple-slotted Flap	Variable Camber Krueger and Triple-slotted Flap	Slat and Single-Slotted Flap (Outboard)
$c_{L_{max}}$	1.8	1.78	2.2	2.79	2.45	2.45

Trends in high-lift devices. The reduction in maximum lift with sweep (Λ) depends on the quality of the lifting device. The rise in aircraft wing loading and the nature of the swept wing's characteristic to reduce not only its own lifting ability but also the effectiveness of high-lift devices led, during the 1950s and 1960s, to increased complexity of lift-enhancing systems. Plain wings approach a $\cos\Lambda$ law, plain flaps are very bad ($\cos^3\Lambda$ or worse), but highly developed systems with slotted leading- and trailing-edge devices follow approximately a $\cos\Lambda$ law. (Key – Pete West)

velocities that exceed the local sonic velocity and lead to premature shock-wave formation. This can be delayed by more sweepback, since 30 degrees sweep plus 12 per cent thickness is roughly equivalent at subsonic speeds to 40 degrees sweep plus 14 per cent thickness. But this degree of sweep, though approached in the late 1960s by the Boeing 747, is difficult to combine with high aspect ratio because of pitch-up.

Early jet transport aerofoils

For the new swept-wing transports that appeared in the late 1950s, both Boeing and Douglas began empirical studies on Mdiv and section maximum lift coefficient of every aerofoil family for which data could be obtained (mostly NACA wind tunnel tests). A Douglas study showed that NACA-modified four-digit aerofoils had a significantly higher Mdiv than the generally accepted NACA six-series laminar-flow aerofoils. Because it was sceptical NACA ran further tests, and these verified the superiority of the four-digit series. The reason behind the better behaviour of the older aerofoils was that they had a 'peaky' pressure distribution and carried a lot of lift on the forward portion. For a given total lift this permitted the local velocity at the aerofoil 'crest' to be lower. The crest is the point on the upper surface to which the freestream is tangent.

Important aerodynamic design goals for the basic aerofoil

High maximum lift coefficient and buffet onset limits for whole flight regime
Delayed drag rise without pronounced drag creep at the lowest possible drag level
Smallest possible zero-lift pitching moment
Good off-design characteristics

In the early 1950s there were no methods for calculating 3-D compressible pressure distribution for swept wings. Empirical relationships were developed from NACA wind tunnel data on swept wings to relate the pressure distribution for a 3-D swept wing at high speed to that of the corresponding 2-D aerofoil in incompressible (low-speed) flow. The procedure accounted for the effects of Mach number, root and tip interference, and sweep.

Jet transport layout

When, towards the end of the 1940s, the jet engine became a promising prime mover for bombers and possibly acceptable for transport aircraft, the traditional piston-engine layout was overthrown. Two entirely different lines of thought emerged. The protagonists of engines in short pods attached to the wings by means of pylons were in the USA, whereas those who favoured engines buried in the wing root were in the UK

In addition to arguments put forward in the text for the buried-engine arrangement, the designers of the Comet also claimed that the height of the engine intakes reduced the risk of FOD; control runs and cabin and de-icing system ducting from the engine compressors were simpler; the mounting structure, in which the engines are hung between wing ribs, is reduced to its simplest form; unlike the podded design, the spacing of ancillary equipment was less closely packed; the close proximity of the engines allowed maximum advantage to be taken of the available fire extinguisher fluid; and, in the event of a wheels-up landing, whereas pods bore the full impact with the ground, the wing installation provided a degree of protection for the engines and fuel tanks. This is a Comet 4C operated by Middle East Airlines.
(Key Archive)

Podded engines	Buried engines
Engine well spaced for safety in the event of fire	Less drag due to lower wetted area and the elimination of wing/pylon/nacelle interference
Short intake and exhaust ducts are good for engine performance	Lower wing loading and cruise lift coefficient gives bigger buffet margin
Mass of engines and pylons give structural inertia relief to wing allowing large wing weight saving	Greatly reduced asymmetric-thrust yawing moment following engine failure
Engine mass ahead of wings gives mass balance against flutter	Lower aspect ratio makes for stiffer wing less prone to aeroelastic problems
Engines much more accessible at low weight because pods are not stressed structures	Low wing loading gives better low speed performance. A higher maximum lift coefficient is available from a clean wing and from a flap uninterrupted by a gap for engine exhaust
Engine pylons have favourable effect on wing airflow by acting like the wing fences needed on so-called 'clean' wings	Low-aspect-ratio wings less prone to pitch-up. Gives reduced induced drag at high lift due to vortex from wing/pylon/nacelle junction

Pros and cons of podded versus buried engines. The arguments above are only valid to a degree, and the subsequent development of large-diameter high-bypass-ratio engines, along with more efficient high-lift systems, settled the argument in favour of high wing loadings, high aspect ratio and podded engines.

Although the high-lift system of the Boeing 767 is less complex than on previous Boeing designs, its performance is highly regarded. This view of a China Southern 767 on approach to land clearly illustrates the leading-edge slats and trailing-edge flaps (outboard single-slotted and inboard double-slotted). (Key – Malcolm English)

and Soviet Union. They used the arguments to support their views as shown in the table opposite.

Overall wing design

The key to the success of any commercial transport aircraft is its ability to carry the design payload over the required range with maximum efficiency and safety at a competitive speed. A major contribution comes from the excellence of the wing design. In 1973 fuel at around 15 cents/US gallon accounted for 20–25 per cent of direct operating costs (DOC) for a long-haul airliner. A 10 per cent improvement in cruise L/D before 1973, achieved using a slightly heavier but more efficient

wing, would have *increased* DOC by 1 per cent. In 1983, with fuel costing well over $1/US gallon, its contribution to DOC was 50–55 per cent, and the same L/D improvement would have *reduced* DOC by 1 per cent. The need for advanced wing design is clear.

It is important to realize that the commercial transport is *not* a point design configuration. Due to the assignment of cruise altitudes and the limited number of step altitude changes allowed by air traffic control during a given flight, and the reduction in aircraft weight due to fuel burn, the cruise lift coefficient throughout a given flight typically varies by as much as ±0.1. Admittedly this is a much smaller variation than a combat aircraft, but nevertheless it cannot be ignored.

The aerodynamic design of a wing is concerned with its planform geometry (area, sweep, span and taper) and its aerofoil cross section distribution (profile, camber and twist) to meet high-speed requirements, together with high-lift device geometry to satisfy the low-speed characteristics for the operations of which the aircraft must be capable.

Once the general planform, aerofoil types, approximate average thickness, design lift coefficient and desired cruise

Flows on a typical high-subsonic transport's wing 'off design'. Even though no airliners regularly fly faster than about Mach 0.87, regions of supersonic flow terminated by shock waves will occur on their wings. Under the right lighting conditions these can be seen with the naked eye. At the design condition the flow should be as shockless as possible. The figure is for a typical wing operating away from its design point, indicating that it is in the outboard region where the two main shocks coalesce to form a relatively strong shock, downstream of which flow separation is most likely to occur. (Key – Pete West)

First-stage parameters	Second-stage parameters
Area	Aerofoil section
Planform	Thickness distribution
Aspect ratio	Twist distribution
Sweep angle	Wing setting angle
Taper ratio	Dihedral versus span
Thickness	Space for fuel, undercarriage & systems
Design Mach number	Load distribution versus span
Design lift coefficient	L/D & buffet boundary
Weight & aeroelasticity	Pitching moment
Low-speed performance	Stalling characteristics
Produceability	Aileron effectiveness

Steps in aerodynamic design of wings (the quality of the design method contributes to a large extent to the wing's aerodynamic efficiency).

General design criteria to be fulfilled in a transonic wing design

Good drag characteristics (profile, induced, compressibility) over a range of lift coefficient (± 0.1) at cruise Mach number

High (ML/D)max with good ML/D characteristics for entire design range (Mach number 0.75–0.85, lift coefficient 0.4–0.6)

No excessive penalties for installation of engine nacelle pylons

Buffet boundary high enough (1.3g margin required) to permit cruising at high design lift coefficients (high-altitude flight)

No pitch-up tendencies near stall and buffet onset

Control surface effectiveness must be maintained

No unsatisfactory off-design performance

Sufficient space (wing thickness to house undercarriage, required fuel volume for design range and high-lift devices)

Must be structurally efficient (to minimize weight)

Must be consistent with aircraft design for relaxed static stability

Must be producible at reasonable cost

Sufficient thickness in areas such as: fuselage/wing junction, planform crank, outboard aileron, to keep structural weight low, increase flutter speed and maintain control effectiveness

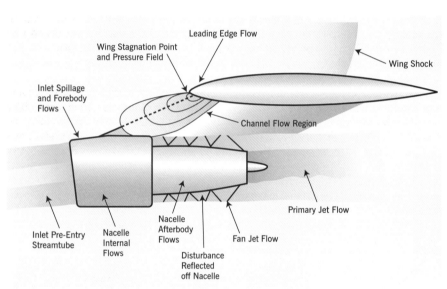

Airframe/engine integration. Very careful studies have to be made to find an installation that avoids any serious adverse interference. As always, the situation is one of compromise between the aerodynamics and a practical engineering installation. This figure gives an idea of the complex flows around a podded installation. The most obvious source of interference is the flow through the channel formed by the lower wing surface, the pylon and the nacelle or nacelle efflux.
(Key – Pete West)

In an attempt to increase aerodynamic efficiency, trials were carried out with a Cathay Pacific Airbus A340 having a third of its surface covered by 'riblets', a plastic film with microscopic grooves. The riblets, which reduce fuel burn by more than 1 per cent, were applied to the upper surfaces of the wing and fuselage and to both sides of the fin and tailplane.
(Airbus Industrie)

Mach number are established, the aerodynamic designer's job starts in earnest. The goal is to design a minimum-weight wing consistent with achieving as much of the aerofoil's 2-D potential as possible, minimizing any profile- or induced-drag penalties and satisfying all of the other design criteria as on the table on page 57.

To obtain as much of the 2-D aerofoil potential as possible typically requires maintaining straight isobars (lines of constant pressure) parallel to the wing leading edge (to keep the shock waves swept), and avoiding any premature flow separation or excessive boundary layer thickening. Many iterations are required involving tailoring of the wing planform, chordwise and spanwise aerofoil thickness, camber and twist. This in the past entailed much trial-and-error wind tunnel testing, with often less-than-superior final designs. This procedure has been revolutionized by the transonic computational methods now always used.

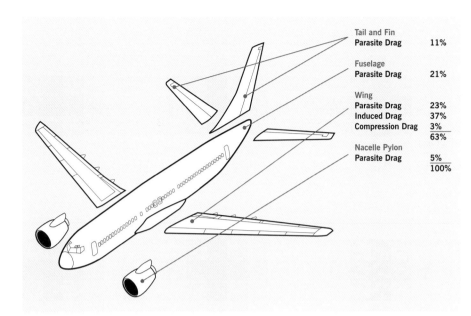

Tail and Fin	
Parasite Drag	11%
Fuselage	
Parasite Drag	21%
Wing	
Parasite Drag	23%
Induced Drag	37%
Compression Drag	3%
	63%
Nacelle Pylon	
Parasite Drag	5%
	100%

Drag breakdown of a typical airliner in cruise. Parasite or profile drag includes not only the friction and pressure drag of the various aircraft components (treated as though they were each isolated), but also the following as a minimum:
Interference drag – addition (or offsetting) of supervelocities of various components
Intersection drag – boundary layer interaction in junctures
Protuberance drag – canopy, antennae, vents, lights, etc.
Excrescence drag – gaps, steps, protruding rivets, base areas, unfaired control surfaces
Ventilation drag – air conditioning and cooling flows
Fuselage upsweep drag
(Key – Pete West)

Drag other than of wings

Since the goal for a well-designed commercial transport is to design and arrange the components other than the wing to have a drag divergent Mach number higher than that of the wing, the dominant factor in achieving acceptable aircraft compressibility drag is the wing. This assumes that interference drag effects will be largely eliminated in the development process (not always a valid assumption). Although there are transonic flow situations at design conditions outside the airline cruising regime where wing-tail interactions are very important, most of the transonic flow design problems faced by the commercial transport designer can be reasonably segregated and attacked individually. Apart from the wing these include: wing/pylon/nacelle interference, wing/fuselage interference, fuselage aftbody/tail surface interaction, and fuselage nose design. No predominant interaction exists, though some have caused more problems than others.

Wing/pylon/nacelle interference

Although wave drag is most often associated with shock-wave formation on the wings of an aircraft, there are often regions where supersonic flow, terminating in shock waves, occurs at speeds well below Mdiv, causing drag to start rising prematurely, or what is known as 'drag-creep'. This was a common problem in the wing/pylon/nacelle region.

The shape of streamlines on a swept wing is such that an effective convergent-divergent channel is formed under the wing just aft of the wing leading edge on the inboard side of the nacelle/pylon installation. This channel provides the potential for large interference penalties due to the supersonic flow and resulting shock waves and separation unless the pylon and nacelle are placed properly. One of the worst examples occurred at a long duct nacelle installation for the DC-8 during prototype flight investigations. Results obtained for a configuration with the nacelle aft-body well back under the wing clearly showed much greater interference drag (twice as much) than had been indicated in the wind tunnel. A similar situation, but of lesser severity, was encountered on early versions of the DC-10. Moreover, engine pods need special treatment quite apart from drag at

high Mach number, since external flow on the pod of a dead engine can affect the permitted take-off weight (TOW) by perhaps 4 or 15 per cent of payload in critical cases.

Fuselage

The fuselage shapes of prewar (unpressurized) airliners were mainly, for reasons of low drag, all of streamline form with a maximum diameter ahead of mid-length. In contrast, all pressurized airliners have almost constant near-circular cross sections for most of the fuselage length for the sake of efficient

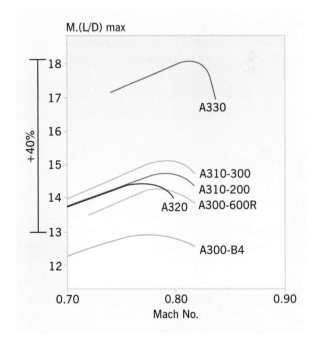

Improvements in cruise efficiency of Airbus aircraft. The general improvement in the parameter that measures maximum 'air miles per pound of fuel' also indicates the Mach number for maximum efficiency, which is highly influenced by wing sweep. The 40 per cent improvement achieved from the A300-B4 to the A330 was won through a mixture of project configuration choices (wing sweep, area, etc.) and technology standards (overall attention to detail in cleanliness, and reduction of interference drag of all the surfaces making up the complete aircraft configuration).
(Key – Ray Whitford)

Lift/drag (L/D)	Drag-rise Mach number (Mdiv)	Rating
±3 per cent	±0.25 per cent	Amazing
±5 per cent	±0.5 per cent	Very good
±7 per cent	±0.75 per cent	Average
±10 per cent	±1.25 per cent	Below average

Accuracy with which the drag at full-scale conditions can be predicted (*c.* mid-1970s). Very little recently published information allows a comparison between predictions and flight-test results because gathering the data is expensive and they are highly proprietary, since they contribute significantly to a manufacturer's expertise.

(low-weight) structural load bearing due to the pressurization loads they bear. The fuselage then terminates in a tapered section, for low drag, with upsweep for ground clearance on rotation at take-off. The latter characteristic is certainly not one to give low drag, and may explain why the drag of many airliners of the 1950s and 1960s compared poorly with the best of the 1930s, such as the Heinkel He 70 and de Havilland D.H.88 Comet and D.H.91 Albatross, but it is a price to be paid for cabin pressurization. It could also have been an indication that, in some respects, design standards had slipped.

In addition, pressurization leads to bulges forming between the fuselage structural frames and stringers. Boeing carried out work on its Model 720 and found that pressurization increased fuselage drag by about 5 per cent. The bulging effect was reckoned to increase the boundary layer thickness, but the major contributors to the extra drag were thought to be pressure leaks and exhaust air associated with the pressurization system. Almost all of an aircraft's external surfaces have to be designed with aerodynamic considerations in mind. Even a substantially cylindrical fuselage needs careful design of its front and rear ends. Not only is drag an issue, but the flight-deck region needs special care to avoid excessive noise.

Aerodynamic tools of the trade

Although the 1950s saw the advent of the jet transport configuration that we know today, much remained to be done to improve the state of transonic aerodynamics to enable the potential of the jet transport to be fully exploited. Up to the design of the Douglas DC-10, Boeing 747 and Lockheed L.1011, wing design procedure was almost totally based on relatively simple methods. This was carried out in conjunction with a somewhat cut-and-try experimental programme to refine the wing configuration once the planform, type of 'conventional' aerofoil, average thickness and design lift coefficient had been determined by an optimization study. Unfortunately for the manufacturer and airline customer, less-than-optimum designs were the result of this approach. In the late 1950s methods started to become available whereby, within a practical time, pressure distributions could be calculated for wings of arbitrary shapes. Instead of picking an aerofoil section out of a catalogue of, say, NACA profiles, wings became individually tailored to give desired distributions. The first application was for the Vickers VC10.

Computers have made an enormous impact on aerodynamics. Calculations that, at the time of the design of the de Havilland D.H.106 Comet 1 (1947) were regarded as

only just feasible, taking two weeks, with the rest of the office staff forbidden to speak to the person doing them, would now take perhaps five minutes on a programmable pocket calculator, and about five seconds on a home PC. On supercomputers that are now the norm, the time taken to carry out the calculations is not an issue, but much more complicated and accurate sums are done. The cry of 'Parkinson' could come from the cynic, but the improvement in the usefulness of the results makes it worthwhile. The computing bill can easily exceed over $1m in a year, and a wing is not put to bed in a year.

Theoretical designs are still backed up by wind tunnel testing, despite predictions that computing would make such testing unnecessary. Indeed, expenditure on tunnel tests exceeds that of computational fluid dynamics (CFD) several fold. A figure of $10 million at 1986 values was quoted for a collaborative project. Over the years the realism of such testing has improved greatly, with better tunnels giving higher Reynolds numbers.

The two most obvious advantages of CFD are the ability to get closer to the optimum design before committing to costly and time-consuming wind tunnel testing, and the ability to produce a design that operates well in more than one flight condition. The older approach to aerodynamic development involved a series of modifications to the design on a high-speed model in a transonic wind tunnel. The end result would then have to be checked on another and larger model in a low-speed tunnel. With CFD, however, the design can be developed for both conditions simultaneously, hopefully with only confirmatory wind tunnel testing.

Supercritical aerofoil sections

Early British sections

By the beginning of the 1960s there were demands to increase the efficiency of subsonic commercial aircraft by postponing the drag-rise Mach number. While much effort had moved to supersonics to support the various SST programmes, attention began to refocus on transonic characteristics, specifically on improved aerofoil sections. Much of the early work to improve Mach number and buffet limits at high subsonic speed was done by Pearcey at the NPL. The basic approach was to contour the leading edge in order to expand the flow rapidly from the stagnation point and generate supersonic flow over the nose region. The expansion Mach waves so created would then reflect as a series of compression waves from the sonic line. These compression waves would then gradually reduce the local Mach number so that the final shock wave was thereby

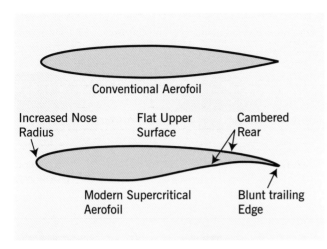

Comparison between conventional and supercritical aerofoils. The conventional aerofoil (NACA 6-series, as used on first-generation jet transports) shows an early drag rise Mach number. Early supercritical aerofoils, although an improvement, suffered because supersonic flow, terminating in shock waves, occurred at speeds well below Mdiv, causing drag to rise prematurely (drag creep). With time the new type of aerofoil has been refined to have a blunt nose, a flat upper surface (to reduce disturbances to its more sensitive boundary layer), and a highly cambered aft section (to give rear loading for increased lift). A blunt trailing edge (first applied on the Airbus A310) has been used to alleviate the steep adverse pressure gradient on both the upper and lower aft surfaces (thereby lessening the likelihood of boundary layer separation), plus the structural and flap/aileron packaging problems associated with the relative thinness at the rear of the profile.
(Ray Whitford)

weakened, causing less severe flow separation aft of the shock and so reducing drag. It was believed that the flow could be decelerated with minimal loss from maximum local Mach numbers as high as 1.4 without the intense shock that would normally terminate such a supersonic flow. Such an ideal situation would admittedly occur for a given aerofoil at only one isolated design point (combination of Mach number and lift coefficient), but it was found that the rate of growth of shock waves away from the design condition was usually slow, making a practical design possible.

The resulting pressure distribution has a marked suction peak near the leading edge; consequently this type of aerofoil was described as 'peaky'. It also featured increased rear loading, achieved by means of a reflex, cusped trailing edge generating large positive pressures on the lower surface. The 'new-technology' aerofoil differed only in that it could carry the supersonic flow further back on the chord, thereby increasing its lift. The extra lift provided helped compensate for the reduced lift from the much flatter upper surface (*see* adjacent figure), itself designed to reduced disturbances to the more sensitive boundary layer on the upper surface. The use of a blunt trailing edge was intended to reduce upper-surface slope, lessening the likelihood of boundary-layer separation. It also helps isolate the upper- and lower-surface trailing-edge pressures. However, peaky sections which deliberately generate high suctions at the leading edge can suffer at high AoA, such as in high-altitude cruise, as a result of excessive shock strength below the design Mach number, causing a loss of lift.

The carrying of appreciable amounts of load near the trailing edge of an aerofoil is not new. Even the old NACA four-digit series carried appreciable loads at the rear, and the six-digit series aerofoils more so. However, the changes in aerofoil design from 'low Mach number design for laminar flow' to 'sonic roof-top pressure distribution' changed the meaning of 'design lift coefficient'.

Both the de Havilland Trident and Hawker Siddeley HS.125 had sections that carried modest amounts of rear loading. In the 1960s de Havilland, along with NPL, carried out many investigations into varying degrees of rear loading as a means of increasing the sonic roof-top design lift coefficient that could be achieved for a given thickness ratio and Mach number. It was clear that any such improvement could, if desired, be used as a means of increasing cruise Mach number rather than lift coefficient, except perhaps at very low lift coefficient. This 'staggered roof-top' feature formed the second component of the rear-loading concept as applied to the Airbus A300B. The research enabled the increase in drag associated with Mach number to be delayed so that either maximum cruise Mach number could be increased from 0.84 to 0.86 or, as in the case of the A300B, a thicker wing could be used for a given Mach number with the resultant 4 per cent saving in wing structure weight of approximately 2,500lb (1,130kg), improved low speed characteristics and a side benefit of increased fuel volume.

American 'supercritical' sections

Further development of Pearcey's pioneering work was continued, much interest being created by Whitcomb's research at NASA Langley, where the description 'supercritical' was coined. This is a misnomer in that all, even early, subsonic transports operating at their most efficient conditions in terms of speed, and L/D, have sizeable local areas of supercritical (supersonic) flow. The Whitcomb sections and subsequent developments have a camber distribution designed to reduce further the adverse pressure gradients by means of an even flatter upper surface. A larger leading-edge radius is used to reduce velocities over both upper and lower surfaces, but especially to attenuate the leading-edge suction peak. More lower-surface camber at the rear was introduced to increase aft loading, but without reducing Mdiv. A reduction in lower-surface velocity is needed to avoid the formation there of a shock wave, the pressure rise through which, superimposed on the pronounced pressure increase of the rear camber, would risk flow separation.

Using supercritical aerofoils

The benefits offered by the advanced sections may be used:

1. To increase Mdiv by about 0.05 for a given thickness ratio and sweep. This increased speed without structural weight penalty improves DOC, which varies almost inversely with block speed. Furthermore, the fuel burn is nearly the same.
2. To allow the use of a thicker wing (though at the expense of increased profile drag) for a given Mdiv and sweep, to improve available wing volume and either significantly reduce the wing structure weight or allow an increase in aspect ratio, or a combination of both.
3. To reduce wing sweep for a given Mdiv and thickness ratio, so improving maximum lift and L/D for take-off and landing, increasing the design cruise lift coefficient and, for a given aspect ratio, decreasing wing weight.

The choice of benefits from these improvements includes a decrease in wing area, giving a reduction in wing drag, particularly if applied as a reduction in wing chord at constant span; an increase in cruise altitude to save fuel on long-haul flights by reducing equivalent airspeed at a

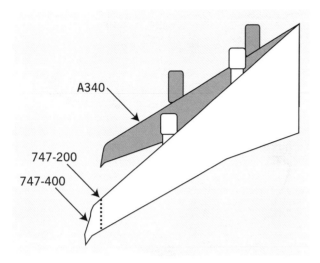

Comparison of second- and third-generation jet transport wing planforms. The Airbus A340 has 80 per cent of the capacity of early Boeing 747s but much greater range. Although improvements in propulsion and structure weight efficiencies also play a part, a substantial contribution to overall aircraft performance comes from the wing, which has about 65 per cent of the 747's wing area but virtually the same span. That is, it is a high-aspect-ratio design using its large span to reduce vortex drag arising from lifting the aircraft's weight in both take-off and cruise.
(Key – Pete West)

constant Mach number; or simply a reduction in Mach number to save fuel for short/medium-haul aircraft.

A combination of any of these attributes could be used, depending on the aircraft's intended role. Because of the emphasis for commercial aircraft on fuel efficiency, the tendency has been to use supercritical aerofoils to reduce sweep and increase thickness, both of which reduce weight, to lower span loading and hence, induced drag. The weight reduction and improved structural efficiency is then used to increase aspect ratio. The higher-aspect-ratio wing makes use of (indeed requires) the increased lifting capability of the supercritical aerofoil, since the desired (most efficient) cruise lift coefficient increases directly with aspect ratio. Significant benefits can be obtained if the design cruise speed is high enough. A typical current short-haul aircraft cruising at Mach 0.82 could benefit its DOC by about 3 per cent and fuel consumption by 5 per cent. In addition, the increase in wing thickness and reduction in wing weight permit the use of higher aspect ratios with less weight penalty than previously. The higher aspect ratio raises the L/D and further reduces fuel consumption by perhaps 8 per cent.

Disadvantages of supercritical aerofoils

Weighed against the supercritical aerofoil, with its extensive aft camber, is its very high nose-down pitching moment. This requires an increased tail download for trim (*see* next section), which increases the required wing lift and, since Mdiv characteristically decreases as lift increases, part of the Mdiv gain is lost. To avoid excessive trim drag, less-than-maximum aft camber may be selected. This also serves to reduce the Mdiv gain. The supercritical aerofoil Mdiv potential gain is shown in an adjacent figure to be about 0.05, though, in practice, the trim requirement may lower this to a gain of about 0.03. Further disadvantages are concerns over the steep adverse pressure gradient on both the upper and lower aft surfaces, plus the structural and high-lift-device packaging problems associated with the relative thinness at the rear of the wing.

Trim drag

Trim drag is caused by the need for the tail to trim the aircraft. It is the difference between the drag of the aircraft balanced in pitch and the drag of the aircraft in the untrimmed condition, for which there is no balancing moment provided by the tail. The lift is required to be the same for both cases. Trim drag consists of the sum of the change in the aircraft tail-off lift-induced drag due to the lift on the tail (usually downwards), the tailplane's induced drag *and* the component of the tailplane's lift in the direction of the downwash at the tail surface.

Trim drag is most strongly influenced by the aircraft (wing–body) pitching moment characteristics and the tail arm. For transports with conventional aerofoils the trim drag at efficient cruising conditions has to be made relatively small, typically being 1 per cent of total drag or less, the lowest values being for aircraft with long tail arms. However, as noted above, trim drag is more important for aircraft with supercritical (aft-loaded) aerofoils. Calculations for one of the experimental wing designs for the A300B showed that, to trim the aircraft, the tail download in the clean configuration was greater than that of the flaps-down case. A considerable saving in tail weight of 265lb (120kg) and fuel to overcome trim drag was achieved by making the two cases of equal severity and increasing wing washout (nose-down twist) and slightly relaxing the section's rear loading. This was done at the expense of a slight reduction to the lift coefficient for buffet onset. Reducing trim drag and recouping the loss in L/D may be achieved by centre of gravity (CG) control, that is by using the tailplane as a fuel tank to maintain the CG in a more rearward position than normal during cruise.

Buffet boundary

The other dominating aerodynamic performance parameter next to ML/D is the buffet boundary, which is more or less completely associated with the wing design. Buffet appears as the structural response to flow separations on the wing. The buffet boundary parameter ($M^2 C_L$) is the square of the Mach number multiplied by its maximum lift coefficient, beyond which the airflow starts to break down causing unacceptable airframe buffeting. This will commonly be caused by turbulent flow in the wing wake impinging on the tailplane. The buffet boundary limits the maximum cruise lift coefficient. The normal encounter with buffeting at transonic cruise conditions occurs when an aircraft hits a strong gust. This will increase the AoA to the point where upper-surface flow separation occurs, typically along the wing trailing edge.

The buffet boundary is usually defined as the first appearance of a 'significant' area of separated flow. This boundary can at times be nearly as important a performance parameter as drag, since the maximum cruising lift coefficient is limited by the requirement to maintain a 1.3g manoeuvre margin to buffet onset. This is required to enable the pilot fly a 35-degree bank angle and have sufficient margin against flow separation occurring in a heavy gust. The peak value of $M^2 C_L$ determines the maximum altitude at which the aircraft can fly for a given wing loading (W/S). Too low a limitation of the desired cruise lift coefficient forces the aircraft to operate at a lower altitude, leading to reduced fuel efficiency, because the specific fuel consumption of jet engines increases lower down. Moreover, the performance loss due to an inadequate buffet margin can be disproportionately higher than just the buffet boundary deficit. This is because of the relatively large increments in assigned cruise altitudes for a given flight direction (east–west) and the difficulties sometimes encountered in receiving clearance from air traffic control to change altitudes.

Furthermore, if the buffet boundary for a particular design is not high enough to maintain the 1.3g margin over the desired range of lift coefficients, then the full potential of the wing aspect ratio cannot be exploited. This is because the desired lift coefficient for maximum efficiency increases with increasing aspect ratio. Little further gain appears possible in this area for a fixed-geometry aerofoil, though variable-camber technology could offer additional improvements.

Wing-root treatment

The aerodynamic performance of the root section of the wing has a dominant effect on the inner wing flow and wing/fuselage interference. One critical part of the wing-root section design is the shape of the nose, which can have a large influence on drag creep (premature drag rise). The designer seeks a type of pressure distribution with low drag in the neighbourhood of the design point and high buffet boundaries, rather than designing for a specific leading-edge radius that then conditions the rest of the profile's surface. Modifications to aerofoil section shape or fuselage waisting, or possibly both, are necessary on swept wings to avoid premature formation of shock waves of low sweep at the wing root. However, it is desirable for an airliner to avoid fuselage waisting and to confine the 'root treatment' to the wing, and a combination of the following actions may be taken:

1. Increase section thickness
2. Move section maximum thickness forward
3. Increase section camber
4. Move maximum camber point forward
5. Introduce some negative camber

Thinning the rear of the aerofoil is not very practical, as the undercarriage has to be accommodated there. Additionally, wing bending stresses tend to concentrate near the rear spar at the root of swept wings, and the rear of the section is already rather thin.

Wing/fuselage fillet

The traditional region for a fillet is at the rear of the wing, where, without a suitable one at the wing/fuselage junction, an area of separated flow would probably result. The designer of any modern transport aircraft with a rather thick root section of 15–18 per cent has to prevent flow separation at the rear by a more or less large fillet (just as in the transports of the 1930s). Besides that, the camber affects the load on the aft section, and the downwash behind the trailing edge can have a large influence on drag as well as lift. The very large increase in wing thickness, up from 14 per cent at the root on the A300 to 20 per cent allowed on the Airbus A310 by use of its advanced supercritical section, made it much more difficult to maintain or improve upon the A300. A predicted worsening of the separation problem, relative to the A300, required the A310's wing trailing-edge fillet to be

Typical drag-reducing fairings are those for the flap tracks and at the wing/body junction, which also serve to house the undercarriage on the Airbus A340. (Ray Whitford)

increased in size and extent, giving a 0.67 per cent drag saving.

There is also a problem at the wing leading edge. Too blunt a nose results in a drag increase due to boundary layer separation in the wing/fuselage corner. A large wing-root fillet is often needed to prevent the separation and reduce the root section velocities to decrease drag. This drag reduction may be 1–2 per cent of the aircraft total drag, and hence it is very important with respect to aircraft performance. The higher the velocity over the root section upper surface and the suction peak at the leading edge, the larger the fillet needed for drag reduction. Without special filleting, the fuselage boundary layer approaching the wing cannot traverse the adverse pressure gradient close to the leading-edge stagnation region. It separates from the fuselage side, rolling up into a 'necklace vortex' that is shed above and below the wing/fuselage junction. The energy going into the wake, and hence drag, depends on the thickness of the boundary layer approaching the wing and the width of flow affected, which is greater the deeper the wing root. With the increased emphasis on fuel economy at the time of the A310 design, it was decided to incorporate a larger leading-edge fillet to suppress the vortex fully, and design the high-lift device around it. This resulted in a 1.3 per cent drag saving compared with the A300.

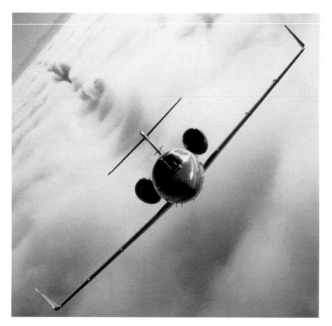

Winglets are not only the prerogative of airliners, they are fitted to a number of business aircraft, including the Learjet 31 seen here. Note the vortices in the clouds created by airflow spilling over the wingtips. Without the winglets there would be even more disturbance and hence drag.
(Learjet)

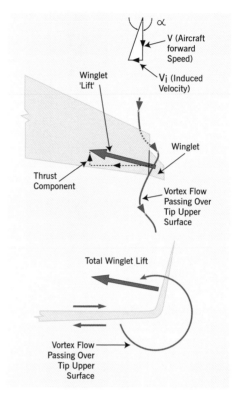

Drag reduction by winglets. For a lifting wing, lower-surface air flows outboard towards the tip, while air on the upper surface flows inboard. The winglet is a small wing mounted in the swirling flow at the wingtip. The crossflow induced by the wing rotates the vector of force on the winglet forward, thus reducing the net drag increment. In this way a well-designed winglet will be significantly more successful than the endplate effect alone.
(Key – Pete West)

Other fairings and fillets

It should be noted that fairings and fillets are often used not merely to eliminate adverse interference, but also to give favourable interference. The flow field around them can serve to induce extra lift on a wing in regions where, otherwise, the local velocities are low. As a result, a critical section of a wing can be unloaded for a given lift coefficient, and drag-rise buffet boundaries improved. Flap-track fairings are a good example. On both the A300 and A310 it was possible to design flap-track fairings that were successful in delaying Mdiv to the extent that, within the cruise flight envelopes, addition of the flap-track fairings actually reduced the total aircraft drag. In both cases the successful fairings increased lift coefficient at a given AoA. It was concluded that this favourable effect was critically dependent on the size and shape of the fairings near the wing trailing edge. It is intriguing that the optimized configuration is not necessarily the one that succeeds in hiding its flap supports within the wing.

Winglets

Lift-dependent drag is derived from the production of lifting forces. Any surfaces with positive lift (including bodies) have lower pressures on their upper surface than on their lower surface. As a result, lower-surface flows move outboard towards the surface tip, while upper-surface flows move inboard towards the centreline (*see* adjacent figure). This flow mechanism is the simple result of flow migrating from a higher-pressure to a lower-pressure region. At the end of the surface these crossflow velocities from the upper and lower surfaces combine with the freestream flow to form a vortical flow that is particularly strong near the surface tips (e.g. wing or flap). When they are fully integrated a net downwash exists that combines with the freestream velocity. The resultant flow that the surface sees is rotated, and the lift

Quite the largest winglet (proportionally) to appear on any Boeing aircraft, those on the Boeing Business Jet are claimed to include fuel-burn savings of 3.8 per cent when fitted to a 737-800 on a 2,750nm flight.
(Key – Malcolm English)

vector rotates with it. The component of the lift vector facing aft forms the lift-induced drag.

While various studies over many years suggested that reductions in lift-dependent drag could be obtained by mounting small vertical surfaces or endplates at the wingtips, the overall benefits were generally small, as the reduction in the trailing vortex drag was only marginally larger than the wetted-area surface friction drag added by the endplates. This differentiates winglets from simple endplates. It was only during the 1970s that that the real potential of tip devices was fully realized. To be effective the vertical surface had to be designed to produce a significant side force. Flow surveys showed that the basic physical effect of a winglet could be interpreted in a variety of ways:

1. As a vertical diffusion of the tip vortex flow immediately downstream of the wingtip, this being the source of the reduced vortex-induced drag.
2. The inward side force on the winglet normal to the local flow direction (inflow above the wingtip), when resolved in the freestream direction, yields a significant thrust component (*see* adjacent figure).
3. End-plate effects of inhibiting flow around the wingtip thus increasing the lift carried by the wing near the tip.

The winglet derives some of its benefit from the loading it induces on the extreme outer wing. This extra lift will serve to reduce the maximum local lift on the wing for a given overall lift, and thus there is the possibility that, at high Mach numbers, there will be a reduction of wing wave drag as well as lift-dependent drag (another example of favourable interference).

It was thought that winglets should be more effective when fitted to wing designs that are relatively highly loaded on the outer wing sections. Some aerodynamicists therefore argued that they would probably only be effective when fitted retrospectively on early wing designs, such as that of the Boeing 707/KC-135 (the subject of the first flight tests). However, the initial test data showed that on both first- and second-generation jet transports an effective winglet gave a larger drag reduction for a given wing-root bending moment than the corresponding span extension. Thus it was argued that, for future jet transports, the wing-winglet should be designed with the wing geometry deliberately chosen to suit the addition of the winglet (just as, on combat aircraft, it had become standard practice to carry weapons at the wingtip to obtain similar benefits).

With a winglet, a higher effective span is obtained with little increase in physical span. The resulting wing-root bending moment is less than that derived from a simple wingtip extension, so structural penalties are minimized. However, on the basis of purely aerodynamic considerations, an increase in span will probably be always superior, though wing bending moments may be greater for a given performance improvement. Thus the application of winglets to existing aircraft as product improvement items has been

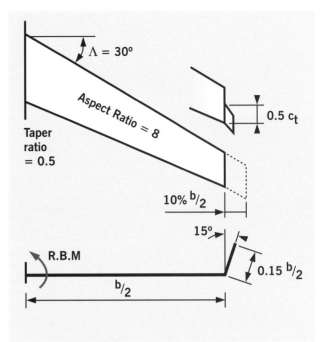

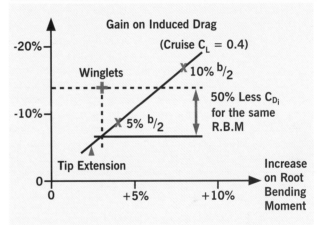

With a winglet a higher effective span is obtained with little increase in physical span. The resulting wing-root bending moment (RBM) is less than that derived from a simple wingtip extension, so structural penalties are minimized. However, on the basis of purely aerodynamic considerations (reduction in induced drag: C_{D_i}), an increase in span will probably always be superior, though wing bending moments may be greater for a given performance improvement. (*AIR International* – Ray Whitford)

Empirical guidelines for winglet design
Avoid rake that would reduce wingtip-region loading
Winglet span (height) should be comparable to wingtip chord length
Winglet toe-out angle is comparable with wingtip twist angle to produce an inward sideforce in the cruise that, when expressed as a coefficient based on winglet area, is comparable to the wing lift coefficient.
Avoid merging of wing and winglet supersonic regions
Winglet cant angle should be selected (typically 20 degrees) for optimum combination of induced drag and wing-root bending moments.
Winglet junction should be treated like a wing-root junction to avoid trailing-edge load build-up
Mounting an additional winglet below the forward lower surface controls the angle of flow ahead of the leading edge of the upper winglet at high AoA (an example of favourable interference)

The essential art of designing an effective winglet lies in the blending of the junction between wing and winglet to avoid adverse interference.

Boeing adopted a swept wingtip extension for the 767-400 in preference to the canted winglet originally proposed. The highly-swept extension saved over 2,000lb (900kg) in wing weight and was considered easier to maintain.
(Key – Duncan Cubitt)

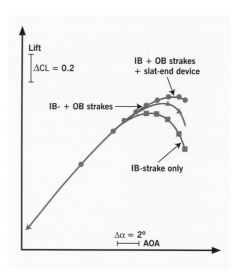

The strength of this vortex shed (from right to left) from the engine nacelle stake on the Boeing 767-300 is far more significant in recovering lift at the wing leading edge slat cut-out for the wing pylon junction than the small core of condensation suggests.
(Ray Whitford)

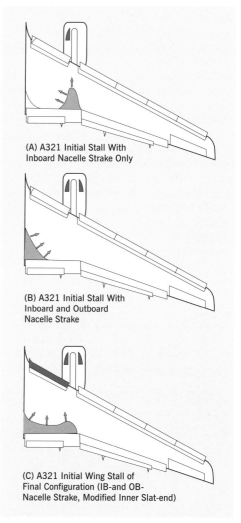

(A) A321 Initial Stall With Inboard Nacelle Strake Only

(B) A321 Initial Stall With Inboard and Outboard Nacelle Strake

(C) A321 Initial Wing Stall of Final Configuration (IB-and OB- Nacelle Strake, Modified Inner Slat-end)

Use of nacelle strakes on Airbus A321. When the A321 entered flight test in 1993 the leading-edge devices were kept similar to those on the A320 for commonality, only inboard nacelle strakes being fitted. Not unexpectedly, windtunnel tests revealed small differences in stall characteristics compared with the A320 due to the new double-slotted-flap system. With the initial A321 configuration the stall started downstream of the slat cut-out (A), so a second nacelle strake was fitted to suppress it. The initial stall then moved to the wing root, and maximum lift was significantly increased (B). The 'slat horn', a small wing/fuselage fairing, was increased in size to control the flow separation at the wing root, showing the effect in (C). The net result of the final configuration was improved handling qualities at the stall, together with higher lift.
(Key – Pete West)

subject to very close scrutiny, as the tolerable increases in wing bending moments are strictly limited. Careful design may therefore maximize the performance benefits available within a given wing strength (*see* adjacent figure).

Controlling flows with vortex strakes

During wind tunnel tests on the Douglas DC-10 a significant loss was found in maximum lift coefficient in the flap-deflected configurations, with leading-edge slat extended, compared with predictions. This resulted in a highly undesirable increase in stalling speed of about 5kt (5.7mph/9.3km/h) in the approach configuration. Initial wing stall occurred behind the engine nacelles and forward of the inboard ailerons. The problem was traced to the effect of the nacelle wake at high AoA, and the absence of the slat in the vicinity of the nacelle pylons. The solution was a pair of strakes (large vortex generators), mounted forward on each side of the nacelles in planes about 45 degrees above the horizontal. The vortices mix nacelle boundary layer air with the freestream and disperse the momentum loss in the wake, then pass just over the upper surface of the wing, continuing this mixing process. The counter-rotating vortices also create downwash over the wing region unprotected by the slat, further delaying premature stall. The effect of the strakes was to reduce the DC-10's required take-off and landing field lengths by about 6 per cent, a very large effect. Nacelle strakes have proved a popular device for other transports (McDonnell Douglas MD-11, Airbus A320/321, Boeing 767) and the vortices they form can be clearly seen under humid air conditions.

Aerodynamic cleanliness

It is apparent that, despite some levelling-off in improvement potential in some fields of aerodynamics, there are still exciting new technologies for future benefit, though the need for attention to detail remains. Despite efforts to minimize drag during the design and production phases, there will be an inevitable drag increase in service due to deterioration of airframe condition. Over a period of time this can include incomplete retraction of moving surfaces, damaged seals on control surfaces, skin roughness and deformation owing to hail or damage caused by ground vehicles, chipped paint, mismatched doors and excessive gaps. All of these are potential money wasters, since the increased drag causes higher fuel consumption.

The fuel-burn penalty depends largely on the location and extent of the problem. Different areas of the airframe are more or less sensitive to alterations in their aerodynamic cleanliness, as shown in the adjacent figure for the A310. Zone 1 surfaces require high smoothness because they are subject to very high local velocities and very thin boundary layers, sensitive to small local disturbances. The zone 3 areas are much less sensitive because of lower velocities and thicker (and turbulent) boundary layers. Seals on moveable surfaces are important. For example, spanwise slat seals are mandatory for the optimization of supercritical

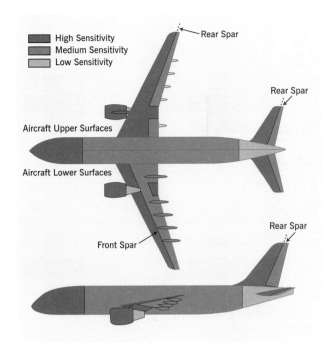

Aerodynamic deterioration. Fuel-burn penalties that arise due to deterioration of aerodynamic surfaces depends largely on the location and the extent of the problem. Different areas of the airframe are more or less sensitive, as shown for the A300/A310. The darker surfaces require high smoothness because they are subject to very high local velocities and very thin boundary layers, sensitive to small local disturbances. The lighter-coloured surfaces are much less sensitive because of lower velocities and thicker (and turbulent) boundary layers. (Key – Pete West)

aerofoils, and one metre of missing seal incurs a penalty of $2,300 per aircraft per year for typical A310 utilization for fuel costing 60¢/USgal. A missing fairing seal at the fin/fuselage junction would cost $3,500 per aircraft per year.

Control surface	Penalty (USgal/year)	Penalty ($/year)	Cost of repair ($)
Spoiler	3,060	1,840	100
Aileron	810	490	150
Rudder	1,350	810	200
Flap-track fairing	680	410	250

Cost of mis-rigged (by only 5mm) control surfaces (Airbus A300/A310; typical utilization; fuel at 60¢/USgal)

Chapter 4

Stability and Control

There was very little change in the stability and control of aircraft in the post-First World War period. This is simply because the desirable design characteristics were attained by about 1918. Since then, the main problems have been to preserve them in spite of the profound changes in the shape of aircraft, and to enable the pilots to control much larger and faster aircraft. The layout of today's jet transports with their swept, high-aspect-ratio wings owes much of its success to the lessons learned from the Boeing B-47 bomber. It was this aircraft that forced the problems of Dutch roll, pitch-up and aileron reversal to be adequately addressed. The digital computer has brought the configuration to full maturity.

Glossary

Static stability: An aircraft whose initial tendency is to return to its equilibrium position after being disturbed (say by a gust) is said to have positive static stability. One whose initial tendency is to diverge from its equilibrium position has negative static stability. One which is neutrally stable merely assumes its new attitude after being disturbed, with no tendency to converge nor diverge. About the pitch axis a commonly used measure of stability is the static margin. In simple terms, this is a CG margin, being the distance along the chord of the wing between the actual CG position and the position where the CG would be for the aircraft to be neutrally stable (the neutral point). If the CG is ahead of the neutral point, the aircraft has a positive static margin and is stable.

Dynamic stability: This refers to the time history of an aircraft's response to a disturbance. An aircraft has positive dynamic stability if, over a period of time, it tends to return to its undisturbed state. An aircraft that, over a period of time, tends to diverge from its undisturbed state is dynamically unstable. An aircraft has neutral dynamic stability if it has no tendency to either move towards nor away from its undisturbed state, though it may oscillate through it.

Stalling: This is, in simple terms, the condition where maximum lift has been achieved. It is the result of flow separation on an aircraft's wings. For simple aircraft (such as those of the pre-swept-wing era) the stalling angle of attack (AoA) is in the region of 15 degrees.

Spinning: Theodore Von Karman, the eminent German aerodynamicist, was asked by Amy Johnson: 'Can you tell me in a few words what causes a spin?' He replied: 'Young lady, a spin is like a love affair; you don't notice how you get into it, and it is very hard to get out of.' A spin is the autorotation of a stalled wing. In a roll, at AoA below stalling, the down-going wing meets the air at an increased AoA and develops more lift, while the up-going wing's lift is reduced. Both effects tend to resist and damp the rolling motion. At AoA beyond the stall however, an increased AoA on the down-going wing produces less lift, whereas on the up-going wing, whose AoA may now

be less than that of the stalling angle, the lift is increased. The combined effect of the two wings is now not to dampen the rolling motion; on the contrary, a propelling moment is applied. Rotation of the fuselage and fin about the flight path at high AoA gives rise to opposing (damping) moments, and a steady rotation rate is reached when the two effects are equal and opposite. Rotation causes a nose-up moment due the centrifugal forces on the nose and tail of the aircraft. This tends to fling them away from the spin axis, the nose-up moment depending on the mass distribution of the aircraft, the rotation rate and the AoA.

Theory versus practice

The foundations of stability and control theory were laid, and well laid, long ago. British mathematician G.H. Bryan placed the whole problem of aircraft dynamics on a rigorous basis in 1911. He introduced the concept of stability derivatives, broke the total aircraft motion down into symmetrical and rotative components, and uncovered the nature of aircraft natural frequencies. Up to that time the mathematical approach had received very little attention owing to the complexity of the mathematics, and also because aircraft of the day could be flown without such knowledge. Bryan's equations of motion showed that there are independent longitudinal and lateral solutions:

Longitudinal: For statically stable aircraft there are two modes of motion: a short-period mode (which for the low wing loading and altitudes of the day were always heavily damped and so ignored) and a weakly-damped long-period mode (named the 'phugoid' by Lanchester). It was found quite simple to obtain longitudinal stability, and no attempt was made to analyse the motions for statically unstable aircraft, or for aircraft of neutral stability, though these were the conditions under which most aircraft of the time were flying.

Lateral: The now well-known oscillatory ('Dutch roll') mode, the rolling mode and the spiral mode. Stability of the spiral mode required reductions in directional stability and an increase in dihedral effect. However, this weakened the damping of the oscillatory mode, and researchers were unsure what to recommend to the designer.

Configurations

By 1910–12 a large number of designers were evolving various configurations and aviators were learning to fly them, many being killed in the process. By 1909 Blériot had created the configuration that became representative of most subsequent aircraft (a tractor aircraft with the propeller directly attached to the engine), with controls in a stick and rudder-pedal arrangement, which was eventually universally adopted. With the rapid development of aircraft during the First World War, designers, through trial and error, developed layouts that had acceptable flying qualities.

Following a series of trials by RAE Farnborough and NACA in the 1940s, United States Army Air Corps/US Navy specifications for stability and control were drawn up and used for many years to guide designers. One of the major conclusions was that, to avoid heavy controls and pilot fatigue, stick force per g during manoeuvring of transports should be less than 50lb. To generate the large forces occasionally demanded, some of the early airliners, such as the Ju 52/3m, were equipped with substantial control wheels. In comparison, most current airliners have computerized flying-control systems, which require relatively light force inputs from the pilot. The Airbus A340 illustrated here, for example, has single-handed sidestick controllers.
(Airbus Industrie; Key – Malcolm English)

One of the great difficulties was to define the necessary or desirable stability margins and associated control characteristics. Designers needed the requirements expressed in terms that could be reflected in their layouts, both as a whole and in detail. They had to be able to judge fairly accurately how the changes, inevitable as a design develops, would affect stability and control.

Wind tunnel testing

Researchers at the time were concerned that design guidance for stability was inadequate, and proper levels of stability were not understood. Two groups set about correcting this via a series of wind tunnel tests (flight testing being regarded as too dangerous and expensive), hoping that they could obtain values for the stability derivatives for use in the newly-stated equations of motion.

The first group was at the NPL, where Bairstow and Melville Jones carried out tests on a model of the Blériot monoplane. However, having obtained the data, the NPL

team seemed hard pressed to know exactly what to do with them, and what they meant to real aircraft. The principal concerns were damping of the long-period oscillation and obtaining a spiral convergence in the lateral case. In retrospect, the tests would have been more meaningful had it been realized that pilots really did not care whether the phugoid damped or not, and preferred high directional stability to a spiral convergence. They were greatly concerned over the motion of aircraft in gusty conditions, feeling that stable aircraft under repeated disturbances might develop dangerous oscillations, though there was no evidence of this having occurred. They concluded that the aircraft should have a little stability, but not too much. Although they stated that the levels of stability required could not be decided upon until there had been correlation with pilot experience, this was not accomplished in a rigorous way until many years later.

During 1915–16 the other group (which included Donald Douglas), under Hunsaker at the Massachusetts Institute of Technology (MIT), conducted wind tunnel tests on the Curtiss JN-2 because it was known to have powerful controls but did not possess any particular degree of stability, especially directional stability (as can be guessed from its small vertical fin, as seen in the accompanying figure). The MIT group realized the need for a control limitation due to forward CG position because, with a large (5 degree) nose-down setting of the tailplane, so much of the available elevator power would be used in trimming at high lift coefficients that nothing would be left for control in gusty conditions. They resisted relating static longitudinal stability directly to CG position.

Both teams concluded that the data they generated would not have real meaning until better information was obtained on what was good and what was bad. This would only come from flight experience and pilots' opinions. One of the first flight tests for stability and control was performed in 1919 at NACA Langley. The results of flight tests on a Curtiss JN-4H 'Jenny' and a de Havilland DH-4 showed that, whereas the Jenny was longitudinally unstable at airspeeds above 60mph (95km/h), it was very stable down to the stall (*see* adjacent figure of elevator angle versus airspeed). This may explain the Jenny's weird reputation. The DH-4, however, with its adjustable tailplane, had stick-fixed stability throughout its speed range and excellent longitudinal stability characteristics.

The flights were significant in showing that finding the elevator and stick force variations with air speed were the fundamental tests, and these trim curves were related to 'stick-fixed' and 'stick-free' static longitudinal stability (described later). The puzzling fact for both teams was that aircraft encountering the instabilities directly forecast by the mathematicians got along quite well and flew anyway. Eventually, when the human being as a control element was brought into the equations, this was understood.

Stability criteria

Much of the knowledge of flying qualities came as a result of aircraft accidents, or incidents of loss of control. Designers' experience was that it was usually sufficiently safe to assume that, when wind tunnel tests gave a pitching moment versus AoA curve having a negative slope of the 'proper magnitude', an aircraft had sufficient pitching stability. What was missing in 1918 was a stability criterion in terms of

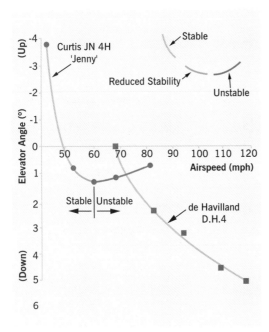

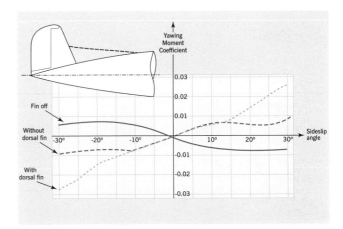

Curves of elevator angle versus airspeed. These are for the Curtiss JN-4H 'Jenny' and de Havilland D.H.4, as measured in 1919 at NACA Langley. An aircraft is described as stable if it requires the stick to be moved forward (elevator down) to decrease AoA and trim at a higher airspeed. It can be seen that the Jenny was unstable (at the one CG position used) at speeds above 60mph (96.5km/h) (the stick needing to be moved aft, giving up elevator, above that speed). The D.H.4 shows stick-fixed stability throughout its speed range. (Key)

The Boeing 307 Stratoliner experienced rudder lock with its original vertical tail. After a fatal accident to the prototype, windtunnel tests, seen here, showed that a long dorsal fin extension would have prevented the rudder locking. Two things must happen before an aircraft is a candidate for rudder lock. Directional stability (yawing moment versus sideslip angle) must be low at large sideslip angles, and rudder control power must be high. Adding a dorsal fin extension has very little effect on the directional stability at low angles of sideslip; by far the greater effect is to delay the fin and rudder stall, thus providing directional stability at large angles of sideslip, as shown.
(Key – Pete West, Dave Unwin)

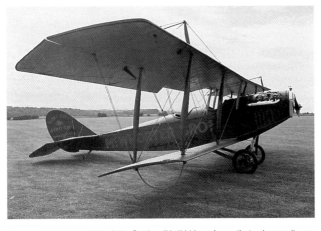

An unusual characteristic of the Curtiss JN-4H 'Jenny' was that, whereas it was longitudinally unstable at airspeeds above 52kt (60mph, 96.3km/h), it was very stable down to the stall.

control forces and movement felt by the pilot and measurable in flight. Doubts still lingered, though, as to whether inherent stability was desirable for certain classes of aircraft. Indeed, some successful aircraft were quite unstable. The design problem was perplexing, and the process by which it became well defined lasted a quarter of a century. The first stage, from 1918 to 1936, was to establish a basic analytical understanding and the practical capability needed for the job of specifying flying qualities. The results of flight-testing were compared with those obtained by wind tunnel testing. The flight tests included measurement of elevator angle and stick force for straight steady flight throughout the speed range.

It was established that there were two conditions of stability: stability with the stick fixed and hence elevator fixed (stick fixed stability), and stability with the control stick released and the elevator left free to float up or down in the airstream (stick free stability). An aircraft has stick fixed stability at a given speed if the pilot has to move the stick back and raise the elevator to maintain trim at reduced speed, and move it forward and lower the elevator at increased speed. It has stick free stability at that speed if the pilot must pull on the stick at reduced speed and push on it at increased speed. For instability the reverse is true in each case. Thus the change of the elevator angle and stick force with speed provided criteria of stability and a measure of controllability, the latter by indicating the amount of control action required to change the steady flight speed. This was a major advance, as it was far better than the customary method of relying on pilot's qualitative comments.

So far as flying qualities were concerned, the leading questions about stability and control appeared to have been answered, at least to the satisfaction of the research community. Even so, the elevator angle and stick force criteria were probably little used by designers, who did not have the luxury of putting their pressing practical problems aside. They preferred to use the pitching moment curve slope. That said, any doubts that inherent longitudinal

During windtunnel tests for the Lockheed Electra in 1934 a model was first tested with a conventional single vertical fin and horizontal tail. With the CG at 33 per cent chord the model showed longitudinal stability at cruise conditions, but at high AoA it was apparent that the horizontal tail was being blanketed by the engine nacelles, causing unacceptably low stability, as shown. It occurred to Clarence 'Kelly' Johnson, in charge of the tests, that the use of endplates on the tailplane would improve matters by increasing the effective aspect ratio of the surface. As finally developed, the endplates were made to serve as fins and rudders, the original vertical fin being eliminated.
(Key – David Stephens Collection)

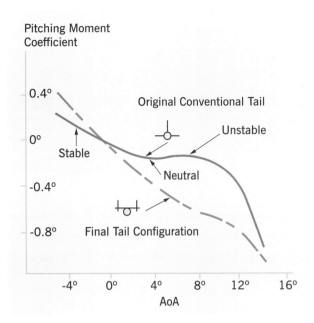

stability was desirable largely disappeared in the 1920s. A contemporary comment was: 'It is true that an unstable machine will not fly very long with hands off, but even in stable machines the pilots do not leave their controls for long, simply because the stick is the best place to keep their hands'. Thus what in 1910 had been controversial, and in 1920 was at least arguable, had by 1935 become obvious.

Flying qualities

By around 1935 a whole variety of aircraft had been successfully developed without any formal handling qualities requirements. Some research organizations were beginning to notice discrepancies between the predictions of theory and the characteristics of real aeroplanes. It was simple to stipulate that an aircraft should be stable both laterally and longitudinally, but what was meant by this

precisely? For example, in the USA a Civil Aeronautics Authority (CAA) bulletin described the test for lateral stability thus: 'With the rudder held in neutral, the aircraft is rolled about its longitudinal axis to a fairly pronounced angle and the control stick immediately released. A sideslip will result, and if the aircraft recovers from the tilted position to a wings-level attitude, it is laterally stable.' When this was written, pilots were going to be very disappointed if they expected to find many aircraft among those certificated by the CAA that were laterally stable according to this definition.

Throughout the period the increasing range and duration of flights extended pilots' exposure to fatigue when they were required to manipulate the controls continually. Higher landing speeds, especially with the introduction of more streamlined aircraft in the 1930s, added to the danger from that source. Moreover, during this period, improvements in cockpit instrumentation made blind flying more commonplace, and the elements of 'instrument flying' needed explaining to 'seat-of-the-pants' pilots. Success was marginal, to say the least, but it was the beginning of a process that was essential if airlines were ever to operate in adverse weather with safety. At the same time, pilots were

In 1942 a series of tests was run by United Airlines to develop a manual outlining simplified procedures for making consistent stabilized approaches and landings with DC-3s, with power being the only variable. It was found that if, in the event of poor visibility, the DC-3 was flown on to the runway at a 3-degree approach angle at the stabilized approach speed and flap configuration, the undercarriage could absorb the shock without any undue hazard. This appears to be the primary basis for the long-accepted 3-degree glideslope. Tailwheel aircraft are traditionally landed on all three wheels at once, using the 'three-point' technique. However, the DC-3's stalling characteristics were such that it had to be 'wheeled on', touching down on its main wheels first.

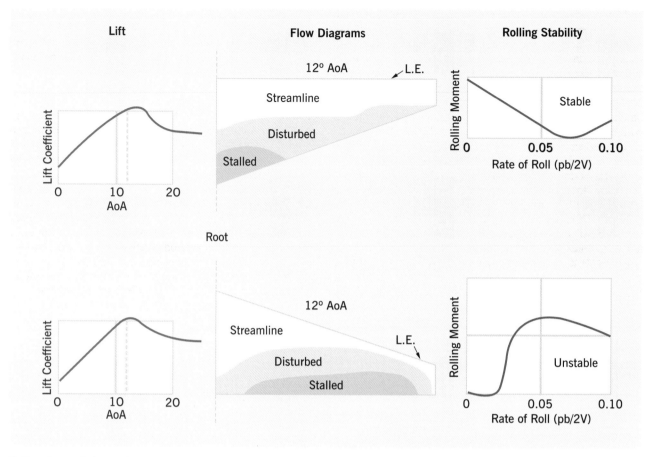

Lift

Flow Diagrams

Rolling Stability

Root

Stalling of tapered wings and rolling behaviour. A good deal of work was carried out on the characteristics of tapered wings during the 1930s. This figure (modified from a 1936 NPL report) shows two wings of 0.25 taper ratio, one forward-swept and the other swept back, along with their lift curves (left). Also shown is the variation of rolling moment versus (relatively low) rates of roll. Where the rolling moment is negative there is stability in roll, and vice versa. In terms of flow separation at 12 degrees AoA, the forward-swept wing stalls at the wing root first, with the separated region spreading forwards and outwards. In contrast, the aft-swept wing stalls at about two-thirds span, with separation spreading forwards, outwards and inwards. It might thus appear that the forward-swept wing is to be preferred. However, at only slightly higher AoA the forward-swept wing becomes unstable in roll. Thus hasty decisions as to the lateral stability of the two wings could be premature.
(Key)

having to give increased attention to peripheral duties, such as radio operation. Thus, from a variety of causes, the art of flying had become more complex. The concentration on static stability was accompanied by lessened concern for dynamic stability. Aircraft that had been made statically stable were almost always dynamically stable. In those cases where the long-period mode was unstable, the instability was mild and readily controllable by the pilot.

Shortly after its introduction the DC-3 suffered accidents, and pilots complained that its stalling characteristics were critical, the aircraft being considered a 'hot ship'. Stalling tests conducted by United Airlines, assisted by NACA, at Langley Field in 1937, were very revealing, and demonstrated how the aircraft should be flown to increase the margin of safety. It was found that the DC-3 had to be taken off and landed in a manner different from the traditional 'three-point' technique. This was accomplished at speeds safely above the stall, which minimized the chance of nosing over on a muddy airfield, or by sudden application of the wheel brakes, thanks to improved brakes and longer runways.

Flying qualities specifications

With enhanced aircraft performance (improved payload, speed, rate of climb, range, ceiling or carrying capacity), the

control of an aircraft was regarded as secondary, provided, of course, that it could be flown safely. Design for stability had to be better related to control, and ultimately to the pilot who flew the aircraft. Only when the performance gains had in part been realized did concentration on problems of stability and control become clearly beneficial. A view of military thinking of the time was: 'At present we simply specify that the aircraft shall be perfect in all respects and leave it up to the contractor to guess what we really want in terms of factors such as: stability, controllability, manoeuvrability and control forces. He does what he can and then starts refining the design; for example, by building new tails, ailerons and rudders until we say we are satisfied.' Unsatisfactory aircraft characteristics were doubtless due in part to the inability of designers to design for what was required, but what was wanted was far from clear. There were good and bad aeroplanes, and pilot opinion could make or break an aircraft without the designer understanding why.

Probably the first attempt to specify flying qualities was made in 1935 by E.P. Warner of MIT, acting as a consultant to Douglas for the first DC-4 airliner (later called the DC-4E (E for 'experimental') to distinguish it from the later and successful DC-4) then under development. The specifications were, for the time, highly detailed. They addressed both longitudinal and lateral characteristics for the full range of flight speeds with flaps and undercarriage retracted and extended. They called for qualitative static stability both stick-fixed and stick-free (as indicated by the elevator angle and stick force gradients respectively). They stipulated that the degree of stability should be 'small'. In keeping with contemporary beliefs, quantitative requirements were placed on damping and time of the long-period oscillation, though with no mention of the short-period oscillation. Concerning elevator effectiveness, it was required that the aircraft should be able to be pitched either up or down by 5 degrees in 1.5sec at the lower end of the speed range, and that the stick force needed to do this or to turn the aircraft with 45 degrees' bank at 140mph (225km/h) in a horizontal circle should not exceed 75lb (34kg). Although the specifications went into more detail than warranted by existing knowledge, they helped to focus attention on flying qualities.

By 1940, RAE Farnborough and NACA had started an exhaustive series of tests (which accelerated during the Second World War) to accumulate data to correlate stability and control characteristics with pilot opinion on aircraft 'flying qualities'. The result was the USAAC-USN specifications on aircraft stability and control that were used for many years to guide designers. Some of the major conclusions were:

Longitudinal:
1. The damping of the long-period oscillation had no correlation with pilot opinion. Otto Koppen, a recognized authority from MIT, said in 1940: 'A lack of damping in the long-period oscillation is usually unnoticed by the pilot who can satisfactorily fly anything that looks like an airplane'.
2. The short-period oscillation with elevator free should be sufficiently damped to have vanished after one cycle. Unsatisfactory damping of this mode was sometimes found, involving coupling between elevator deflection and aircraft motion. Thus the short-period oscillation replaced the long-period one as the focus of concern for designers.
3. Static longitudinal stability stick-fixed and -free was required within certain speed and configuration regimes.

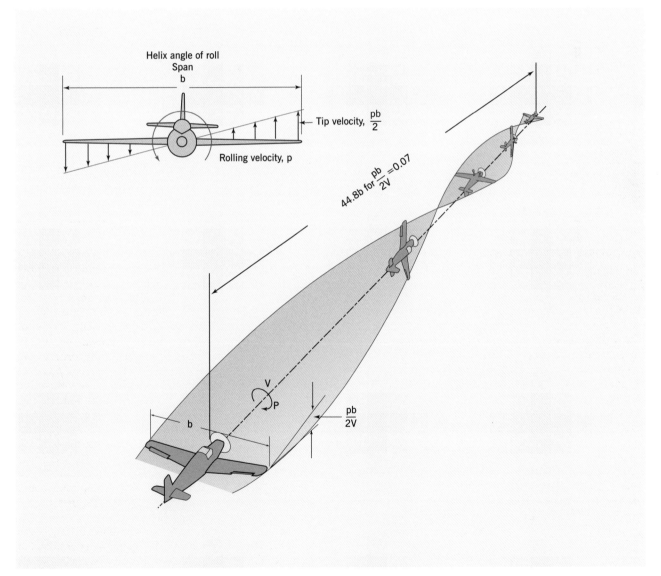

Illustration of the NACA aileron roll rate criterion (pb/2V). At the minimum allowable pb/2V value of 0.07 radians (4 degrees) for transports and bombers, the roll helix angle creates a complete roll in a forward distance travelled of 44.8 wingspans, regardless of airspeed.
(Key – Pete West)

4. Manoeuvring criteria, particularly stick force per g, was important. This criterion seems to have been arrived at independently by Gates at the RAE and Gilruth at NACA, and quickly proved to be the most meaningful to pilots. To avoid heavy controls and pilot fatigue, stick force per g during manoeuvring flight of transports should be less than 50lb (222N), and less than 6lb (27N) for fighters.

Lateral:

1. The damping of Dutch roll was important, while controlling the spiral divergence was not.

2. Rolling performance was measured by the helix angle (pb/2V) described by a wingtip during full aileron roll (where p = rate of roll, b = wingspan and V = airspeed). This aileron roll rate criterion was a particularly troublesome characteristic, and NACA tested 28 aircraft to arrive at it. It was presented in classified form in 1941 and fixed at 0.07 radians for transports and bombers to give a remarkably simple preliminary design criterion (*see* adjacent figure). The ailerons had to be powerful enough to provide the required pb/2V.

3. Directional control was related to yawing disturbances introduced by the lateral control, asymmetric power on multi-engined aircraft and crosswind take-off and landings.

The requirements were stated to be the minimum for satisfactory flying qualities, felt to be obtainable without

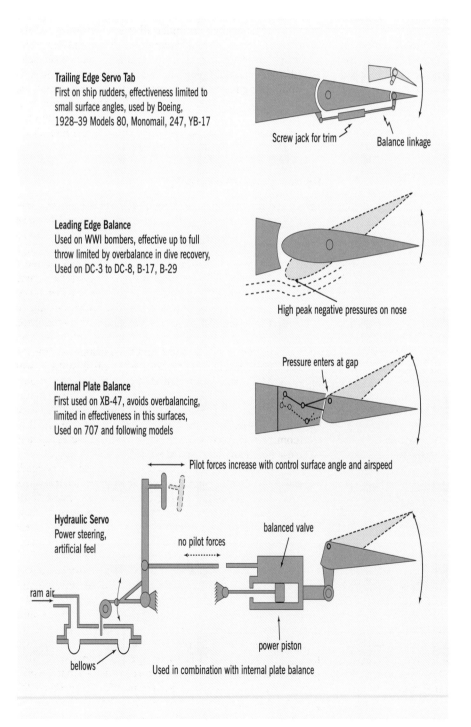

Trailing Edge Servo Tab
First on ship rudders, effectiveness limited to small surface angles, used by Boeing, 1928–39 Models 80, Monomail, 247, YB-17

Screw jack for trim

Balance linkage

Leading Edge Balance
Used on WWI bombers, effective up to full throw limited by overbalance in dive recovery, Used on DC-3 to DC-8, B-17, B-29

High peak negative pressures on nose

Pressure enters at gap

Internal Plate Balance
First used on XB-47, avoids overbalancing, limited in effectiveness in this surfaces, Used on 707 and following models

Pilot forces increase with control surface angle and airspeed

Hydraulic Servo
Power steering, artificial feel

balanced valve

no pilot forces

ram air

bellows

power piston

Used in combination with internal plate balance

Some examples of control surface balancing and power assistance with q-feel. In the days of manual control systems the control forces were almost entirely determined by the aerodynamic hinge moments of the control surfaces. As a result, a great deal of work was done on the means of aerodynamically balancing the controls to reduce the force required from the pilot. With the growth in size and speed of aircraft, a gradual increase in force to full deflection was needed, with satisfactory centring and no dead spots.
(Key – Pete West)

compromising the performance of an aircraft, while the provision of even better qualities was encouraged. New information was gained from almost every new aircraft (60 by 1948) that appeared. In addition, the rapidly expanding performance capabilities of aircraft during this period introduced many new problems, as well as new methods of analysis and new control system design features.

Aeronautical engineers today express amazement that any manoeuvrability criteria besides stick force per g ever existed, and that the idea took so long to develop. That said, it took five years for the aeronautical community to grapple with the problem and come up with the answer. Moreover, government agencies regulating civil aircraft were less influenced by this new work than the military ones. Civil regulations were limited to the minima necessary for safety, the finer points of flying being left to the judgement of designers and operators. The airworthiness requirements of the US Civil Aeronautics Board (CAB) in 1946, for example, while putting considerable emphasis on longitudinal control near stalling speed and with flaps and undercarriage extended, made no mention of stick force per g. Although designers now had a greatly improved understanding of what was wanted with regard to flying qualities, knowledge of how to design for them still left much to be desired.

Flying controls

As with many other mechanical advances, flying controls tended to become increasingly complex. The aircraft of the first 30 years of powered flight operated within a 100kt (185km/h) speed envelope, and control problems were relatively simple. Early aircraft used a direct mechanical linkage between the control surface and the pilot's control column and rudder pedals, normally consisting of an arrangement of multi-stranded wires and pulleys. For these aircraft, which flew slowly, it was possible to hinge a control surface at its leading edge and expect the pilot to be strong enough to deflect the surface against the air loads. For larger and faster aircraft, however, it was found that the forces required to move such a control surface were beyond the strength of a pilot. The control force required rises with increased control angle at constant speed, with a given control angle with the speed squared, and with the area of the surface. The control forces had to be made smaller. This was done by aerodynamically and/or mass-balancing the control surface. Considerable ingenuity went into devising means of reducing the loads in a variety of ways: set-back hinges, horn balances and trailing-edge balance tabs (*see* figure). In this way the pilot supplied some of the force required and the balance provided the rest. The servo tab came into use early on in aviation, and was a feature of most large aircraft, some of which had as many as three rudders to overcome the resistance to turning a forest of struts, wires and nacelles.

The effect of speed on the control surface is particularly severe on the elevator. This is the surface that can cause a pilot the most trouble, either through a lack of elevator control or as a means, inadvertently, to overload the airframe. The predominant effect is due to the dynamic pressure: $\frac{1}{2}\rho V^2$. Designers had evolved a system that operated successfully throughout the limited speed range. The result was that aircraft of 1920 with direct manual control could have their control characteristics decided by the rigger by a rule-of-thumb procedures.

In the field of control balance, big advances were made in the face of difficulty. The Vickers Vimy Commercial airliner of 1919, for example, operated at speeds of 80 to 100mph (130 to 160km/h), at which the pilot could provide the forces necessary for control with little or no aerodynamic balance. In the case of its ailerons, on which the aerodynamic balance comprised 50 per cent of the aileron area, the maximum hinge moment required was probably equivalent to a force in the pilot's hands of around 50lb (222N). For the Avro Lancastrian of 1945 the same movement of surfaces of about the same size was required at 300mph (480km/h), needing nine times the force. The pilot was no stronger, so the aerodynamic balance had to reduce the hinge moment to, say, 1/18th of that of unbalanced ailerons. This was a difficult requirement, but it was met.

On larger, faster-flying aircraft the controls were required to handle reasonably well under all flight conditions. If the designer had arranged the characteristic of the control system to suit the mid-range of speeds, those at the extremes of speed would suffer. At low speed, when effective control is essential during the landing approach, the controls would be sloppy, and at high speed they would be rigid. Moreover, if the control was underbalanced it would be too heavy; if overbalanced it would be too light and, in extreme cases, would lock at the full extent of its travel.

Power-assisted controls

The introduction of the autopilot and an increase in the size of transports in the late 1930s resulted in control balance causing a great deal of difficulty in spite of the most sophisticated aerodynamic devices. In some instances refuge was taken in power boosting; reducing the balance to avoid overbalance problems and replenishing the operating force with power assistance. The control loads were proportioned between the pilot's direct linkage and the power circuit, so that only a fraction (25 per cent) was fed back to the pilot. The power-boosted system was accepted by pilots without adverse comment because the direct mechanical linkage between the control column and the control surface was retained. Moreover, it was felt that excessive development time and money would be required to develop manual control systems for high speeds. Thus power-boosted systems became, for a short while, an accepted method of overcoming increased loads as size and speed increased, and were used on many high-speed aircraft.

There seemed no good reason why they could not be made reliable. All large aircraft had hydraulic systems for undercarriage actuation, and hydraulically operated flight controls were an extension of that already proven system. However, early hydraulically boosted controls were notoriously unreliable, being prone to leakage and outright failures. Among other innovative systems, the Douglas DC-4E prototype had hydraulic power boost, but experience with it was so bad that Douglas reverted to pure aerodynamic balance and used tabs for the production version, the DC-4.

In relation to reliability, a major problem arose concerning manual reversion. It occurred when power failed and the pilot was left with a simple direct-linkage system. He was then confronted by loads much greater than usual. Most power-boosted systems had the loads divided so that the pilot needed to give 1lb (4.4N) of push or pull for every 3lb (6.2N) provided by the booster. The designer had to balance the system to allow for an acceptable degree of abnormal control forces for emergency use. This 3:1 ratio did enable the pilot to control the aircraft manually under most situations; it took effort, but could be done.

Artificial feel

Designers did not take kindly to having to provide a manual reversionary system, as it was then necessary to take steps to ensure that the control surface would not be subject to flutter in the manual mode. In any control system in which all or some of the control loads can be fed back to the pilot's control column, accurate balancing is required if flutter is to be avoided. Commercial aircraft are generally designed to have a 20 per cent flutter margin over the design flight boundary, with a resulting weight penalty to allow for contingencies.

From the pilot's viewpoint, the suitability of a control system is assessed not only by its reliability but also by its ability to feed back to the pilot an accurate representation of the loads on the control surface, such that the pilot will not overstress the airframe. This could be provided by a feel device more or less independently of the hinge moments on the control surfaces. Many new problems were involved with these devices, however, both because of certain undesirable or non-linear force characteristics introduced by the hydraulic control systems and because of the unusual characteristics of some feel devices.

In spite of great efforts by designers, such simple artificial-feel systems (commonly incorporating a spring that increased resistance to control column movement with increasing control-surface displacement) seldom satisfied pilots. At best they were poor substitutes for the real thing. The question of feel now became all-important for safety, as well as convenience. Accordingly, the designer had to provide a load to the pilot's control that would vary as the square of the aircraft's indicated airspeed and the deflection of the control. This resulted in the q-feel device (q being the symbol for dynamic pressure: V^2 as measured by the pitot-static head).

Fully-powered controls

By incorporation of q-feel and other devices that made corrections for angular displacement of the control surfaces and for other variations in the flight conditions, designers were able to develop fully-powered systems that otherwise would have made it too easy for the pilot to overstress the aircraft. Thus the mechanical linkage between the pilot and the control surfaces was eliminated. In place of the wheels, pulleys, brackets, springs and wires, a few obedient hydraulic or electric motors mounted close to the control surfaces were deemed sufficient. However, in the minds of some pilots, leaking or burst pipes or fuzed or failed electrics were a poor substitute for the sturdy length of tubing or tough wire cable that they had learned to trust over almost half a century.

Pilots and operators were not satisfied that it was prudent to send an expensive aircraft into the air entirely dependent on hydraulics or electro-hydraulics, so the manual system was added once again. Naturally, such systems could only be designed to control the aircraft at the lower end of the speed range, as the fully-powered system had eliminated the necessity for mass and aerodynamic balances. The manual system was either very sloppy or required excessive physical effort. A further point that had to be considered was whether the manual system compromised the safe working of the powered system.

Pilots were not willing to relinquish existing tried and tested manual control systems unless the powered systems were shown to be as safe and reliable as the direct rod or wire-cable arrangements. One way to prevent the disaster of losing elevator control, for example, was to duplicate the power control system and actuators and provide alternative power sources. That was a relatively simple solution, except that if an actuator failed or locked solid it might prevent the operation of the standby actuator, so that the duplication might not mean redundancy.

The safer arrangement was to divide each control surface into two sections, each of which had its own actuator with an independent control circuit, and its own source of power and fluid. With effort, the chances of a complete loss of control would then be so remote that there would be little reason to demand that a manual reversion circuit be fitted.

Compressibility

Before the advent of the jet age the influence of high speed on aircraft flying characteristics was restricted to high dynamic-pressure effects that involved problems of distortion and aeroelasticity. These caused difficulties with fabric-covered control surfaces and loss of rolling performance (of fighters) because of wing torsion (twisting) in response to aileron deflection. At the start of the Second World War the knowledge of compressibility was limited, and corrections were applied only to propeller efficiency, airframe drag being considered to increase with speed squared only. The way in which this led to large errors has been addressed in Chapter 3 (Aerodynamics).

Stability problems at high speed were encountered by fighter pilots in dives, when, despite their efforts, the aircraft failed to pull out. This led to the phenomenon being known as 'frozen stick'. There was heated debate among aeronautical engineers of the day as to the probable cause, and the results of their deliberations can be summarised as:

1. Past the critical Mach number, the reduction in slope of the lift curve (increase in lift with AoA), reduction in the rate of change of downwash, and the aft movement of the wing's centre of lift tends to induce a 'tuck under'.
2. A rapid deterioration of elevator effectiveness occurs to a point where all-moving tails may be required.
3. General aircraft buffeting and other phenomena are brought about by the influence of the shock waves lying across the wings.

To exploit the potential of jet propulsion, these effects were delayed and reduced in magnitude by using thinner aerofoils, removing most of the camber, sweeping the wings and using all-moving trimming tails. Mach trim compensators as separate systems continued to be features of transonic aircraft for many years. For example, the Boeing 707 and Convair CV880 had automatic Mach trimmers that put in small amounts of stabilizer trailing-edge-up trim starting at Mach 0.8.

Wing/fuselage interference

Stability and control designers had known for some time that whether an aircraft has a low or high wing influences its static directional and lateral characteristics. It had been established by 1941 that a low-wing aircraft's static lateral (rolling) stability was reduced by about 5 degrees of equivalent wing dihedral compared with a mid-wing type, whereas its static directional stability was increased. For high-wing aircraft the reverse is true. Thus the post-war generation of low-wing airliners had tended towards 5 degrees of wing dihedral.

Sweep intensifies roll-due-to-sideslip

When a swept wing is placed in a sideslip, the into-wind wing experiences an increase in lift because its effective sweep is less. Similarly, the out-of-wind wing has increased effective sweep and generates less lift. The result is a rolling moment that tends to lift the one wing and drop the other, and so right the aircraft. This is known as dihedral effect (*see* figure). A swept wing operating at high lift coefficients in, say, the landing case, can experience such an excess of this contribution to lateral stability that handling may be a problem in a crosswind.

Although Dutch roll may affect any aircraft configuration, the use of sweep tends to aggravate it, as an excess of dihedral effect causes oscillatory instability. Too small a level of directional stability (insufficient fin area) combined with too much lateral stability (an excess of dihedral effect) reduces oscillatory stability. For example, if the correct level of dihedral effect is achieved for high-speed, low-lift coefficient cruise, the relationship between lateral and directional stability may prove to be unbalanced at low speed and high lift coefficient, or even at high speed and high altitude. Fortunately, a low wing has less dihedral effect, but sufficient dihedral is needed to provide clearance for the pylon-mounted engines with a reasonable length undercarriage, but a large fin is required.

Sweep intensifies roll due to sideslip. When a swept wing is placed in a sideslip (to the left for this Boeing 727), the into-wind wing experiences an increase in lift, since its effective sweep is less. Similarly, the out-of-wind wing has increased effective sweep and generates less lift. The result is a rolling moment that tends to lift the one wing and drop the other, and so right the aircraft. This is known as dihedral effect. A swept wing operating at high lift coefficients in, say, the landing case, can experience such an excess of this lateral stability contribution that handling may be a problem in a crosswind. (Key)

Dutch roll

The Boeing XB-47 strikingly revealed that Dutch roll was, in a way not seen before, endemic to the swept wing. The tendency had been detected during wind tunnel testing. Following its first flight in 1947, the XB-47 was not far into its flight-test programme when, at high altitude but at a speed well below its maximum, the aircraft started snaking. This became incrementally more pronounced, with the wings starting to roll, and the aircraft then made a series of S turns with a period of about six seconds. When a description of the motion was relayed to the ground, engineers confirmed that it was Dutch roll.

This put the B-47 Stratojet programme in jeopardy. A Boeing expert in electromechanical devices was asked to build a device that could be interposed between the pedals in the cockpit and the rudder that, without the pilot's intervention, would sense the presence of Dutch roll and damp it out. Within three weeks the XB-47 was fitted with a yaw damper known, for no apparent reason, as 'Little Herbie'. It overcame the problem and was an important step in redeeming the large, swept wing. Every aircraft of similar configuration is now fitted with a yaw damper.

At the time (1949), stability augmentation as a routine design feature had not been established, and it irritated some purists. Indeed, arguing that vices should be designed out of an aircraft, not circumvented by artificial means, Prof Jerome Hunsaker (mentioned previously) commented: 'If the B-47 had been designed properly, it would not have needed

stability augmentation'. Dutch roll had not been eliminated, it had been merely suppressed; in that respect the configuration was inherently unstable. Despite that, yaw damping is required for high-altitude aircraft because of inescapable physical facts. With Dutch roll damping being proportional to air density, no airliner having satisfactory natural yaw damping at low altitude can be expected to have acceptable damping at altitudes above 35,000ft (10,700m). This is true to a lesser extent for high-altitude pitch damping.

Yaw and roll dampers

When an aircraft has a significant Dutch roll that is anything less stable than a reasonably quickly damped motion, some assistance is necessary to avoid a tedious and demanding task for the pilot. Because too large a fin is detrimental to spiral stability qualities, the effective fin area must be increased in some other way. On some early jet transports with manually operated rudders (Boeing 707, Convair CV880) the rudder tended to trail downwind in a sideslip, at least over small angles. This decreased the effect of the fin and made the oscillatory stability worse. Boosting the rudder resulted in it remaining centred, thus restoring effective fin size.

On airliners with power-operated rudders (most of them now), the logical step was to prevent the sideslip starting or building up. This is what a yaw damper does, as it is a gyro system sensitive to changes in yaw that feeds a signal into the

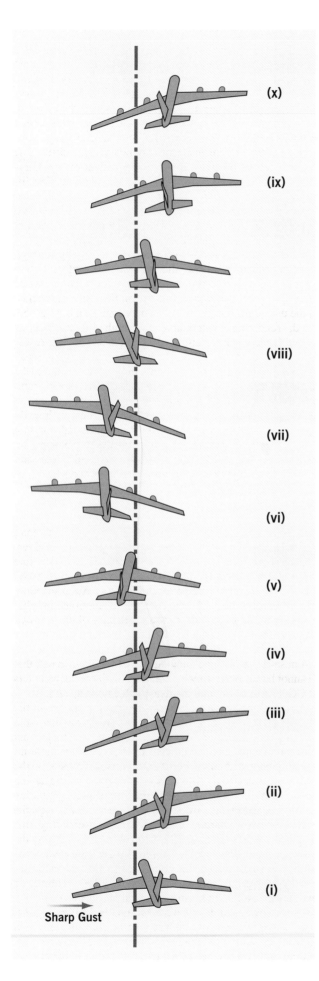

(x)

(ix)

(viii)

(vii)

(vi)

(v)

(iv)

(iii)

(ii)

(i)

Sharp Gust

rudder power unit that opposes the yaw. Some aircraft also have a roll damper, which does substantially the same as a yaw damper but works the ailerons instead. These are not necessarily fitted for Dutch roll damping, but can be purely for roll damping in turbulence on a type in which the rolling inertias are such that this sort of damping is needed (those without wing-mounted engines).

At least one accident occurred to the Boeing 707 due to Dutch roll when, in an extreme case during a training flight, an engine became detached. That said, much of the drama surrounding Dutch roll in the 1960s was not really justified. It was engendered, perhaps, by a lack of knowledge of the subject and possibly by over-exuberance on the part of pilots. It is now reasonable to say that there are no civil jet transports flying which need be the slightest bit demanding in terms of oscillatory stability and control. Most have a 'raw' Dutch roll that is only slowly unstable, when there is any instability, and the others are adequately protected by yaw and roll dampers.

Sweep contributes to tip-stall tendencies

The successful and routine use of wings swept back 30–40 degrees was a source of wonder to stability and control engineers who were active in the 1940s. Such a wing that was tapered by sweeping back the leading edge while keeping a straight trailing edge, giving no more than about 5 degrees of sweepback (DC-3), was deplored at the time. One could expect early tip stall with increasing AoA, wing drop and roll-damping reversal.

Sweepback alters the lift distribution in much the same way as decreasing taper ratio. All outboard sections of the wing are affected by the upwash produced by preceding inboard sections. Thus sweepback, as well as taper, with which it is always combined, leads to higher local lift coefficients towards the wingtips. The highly loaded tips, with their elevated outboard suctions, tend to draw the sluggish, slow-moving boundary layer in a spanwise direction (as shown in the adjacent figure). Such is the effect of boundary layer 'drifting', which tends to clean up the flow at the root, that it tends to accumulate a lot of 'tired' air in the boundary layer at the tip, where there is an adverse spanwise pressure gradient. Drifting of the boundary layer is often blamed as a cause of tip stalling, though an alternative view is that drifting is more a mild encouragement to tip stall than a prime cause. There are certainly enough other reasons, without recourse to this boundary-layer effect. Growth in boundary-layer thickness is aggravated by an increase in either sweep or AoA, because of the increased tip loading which results.

The use of wing sweep intensified Dutch-roll tendencies. The Boeing 387-60, which followed the B-47 in formula but not detail, and the 707, had similarly swept wings, podded engines and a single vertical fin. One 707 suffered fatal loss of control when divergence Dutch roll had the chance to develop. The solution adopted for the 707 was the fitting of a yaw damper, and a ventral fin under the aft fuselage for those 707s certificated for operations on the UK register. The latter increased directional stability, while the rolling moment due to sideslip either remained the same or was very slightly decreased. Dutch roll, resulting from a lateral gust, is shown. (i) Sharp gust from left: translation to right and yaw to left. (ii) Right wing moving forward develops extra lift and induced drag: roll to left and yaw to right. (iii) Inclined lift starts translation to left. (iv) Left wing moving forward: roll to right and yaw to left. (v) Weathercock reaction of fin to translation assists drag in yaw to left. (vi) Inclined lift: translation to right. (vii) Right wing forward: roll to left and yaw to right. (viii) Fin reaction: yaw to right. (ix) Inclined lift: translation to left. (x) Etc. (Key)

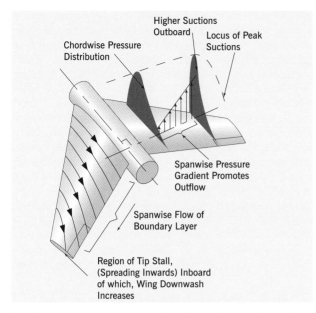

How wing sweep promotes spanwise flow. The suction peak is moved forward on the outer part of the wing and backwards near the root. This is not all, however. Perhaps the most difficult feature is associated with the boundary layer flow, which has a strong tendency to flow spanwise as well as in the freestream direction. This is governed by the lateral pressure gradients. These are larger on swept wings, and the boundary layer flows 'down' the pressure gradient towards the tip. Thus the spanwise flow on the wing upper surface will be drawn towards the most highly loaded part of the span, where the suctions are most pronounced, and then, being retarded (between this region and the tip), it will cause a thickening of the local boundary layer. Such is the effect of boundary layer 'drifting', which tends to clean up the flow at the root but tends to accumulate a lot of 'tired' air in the boundary layer where the load is reduced over the tip, in fact where there is an adverse spanwise pressure gradient. This can then lead to tip stalling. Because downwash from the wing is a inversely proportional to the span squared, the reduced effective span (due to loss of lift at the tips) causes increased downwash at the tailplane, so reducing its stabilizing effect. This further aggravates pitch-up.
(Key)

Ultimately the flow starts to separate in the highly loaded tip region, progressive increase in AoA causing the separated flow region to spread inwards and forwards (*see* the figure on page 72). This is the phenomenon of tip stalling, caused not only by taper but, in this case, also by sweepback. The greater the sweepback, the more critical the effects of tip stalling. This is partly because the lift loss is greater, and partly because the tip region's loss of lift causes a forward movement of the wing's centre of lift, giving an imbalance about the aircraft's CG and exaggerated pitch-up tendencies. Furthermore, the concentration of the lift over the inboard part of the wing will decrease the tailplane's AoA and effectiveness, because the wing's downwash rapidly increases as *effective* wingspan is reduced. Moreover, the part-span vortex shed from the wing may interact with the tip of the tailplane. The resultant loss of lift at the tail is a common cause of pitch-up.

Ideally, an aircraft should stall first at the wing root. This reduces the rolling moment produced by asymmetric stalling, since the stalled area has a smaller moment arm and maintains good flow over the ailerons on the outer wing, thereby maintaining good lateral control to minimize any rolling motion. Furthermore, with the loss of lift occurring inboard first, the downwash over the horizontal tail is reduced, resulting in a reduced tail download and a nose-down pitching moment that tends to push the aircraft out of the high-AoA stalled condition.

The combined effects of sweep and aspect ratio

The degree to which tip stalling can limit the performance of a wing depends largely on the planform, being most accentuated by high aspect ratio and sweep. For a given sweep, the higher the aspect ratio the worse the boundary-layer drift effect, since the length along which the drift can occur is increased. At the same time the chord length shortens so that the ratio of boundary layer thickness to wing chord increases, thereby intensifying boundary-layer drift. The inboard parts of the wing enjoy the equivalent of boundary-layer suction, with a consequent raising of the stalling lift coefficient. Near the tips the reverse occurs, and the local maximum lift coefficient is reduced. This led to the adjacent figure (produced by NACA in 1957) showing the limits (not immutable) of the combination of aspect ratio and sweep.

When large amounts of sweep became necessary for high subsonic Mach numbers, the wings also had to retain acceptable low-speed stalling characteristics. The onset of pitch-up places an upper restriction on the AoA, and hence on the usable lift coefficient. This may impose a limit at low speed, rendering unattainable the high lift coefficients needed for low stalling and landing approach speeds. It was soon discovered that leading-edge devices such as slots, slats, flaps, camber and a blunt nose radius could make the combination of sweep with moderate aspect ratio practicable. Leading-edge slats had been used before the advent of sweepback to correct wingtip stall on heavily tapered straight wings. In addition, crosswind landing problems arose as a result of rolling induced by sideslip. The solution was bigger ailerons, which led to smaller flaps and sometimes a bigger wing to restore airfield performance.

The stalling problem

Airline experience of the 1950s and 1960s showed that, despite many precautions, transports were being inadvertently stalled in the order of 1 in 100,000 flights. This rate was such that the stall had to be made as benign as possible. Airworthiness requirements attempted this by demanding that 'there shall be no large-scale rolling motions and that the aircraft shall pitch nose-down'. Ideally, there are two requirements:

1. A nose-down pitching moment with sufficient strength that it cannot be overridden by a pilot, even with the aircraft at its aft CG limit and with maximum available nose-up control.
2. A sufficiently large and speedy dynamic response in the nose-down sense to give the pilot an immediate and unmistakable indication that he has stalled, and to prevent that attainment of excessive AoA at any stage of the motion.
It is frequently difficult to satisfy the first requirement on the aft CG without undesirably compromising the normal flying characteristics. This requirement may be relaxed, providing that the second one is sufficiently met, because although the system is not foolproof, there is a high probability that the pilot will take the correct recovery action by pushing the control column forward. The difficult case arises when the stall onset is not recognized owing to a mild, natural nose-down pitching motion coupled with the pilot's inability to distinguish AoA from attitude changes. He may then inadvertently penetrate much too far into the stalling regime, with severe danger of spinning or superstall (*see* next section), depending on the aircraft configuration. The post-stall motion is made up of two parts: that due to lift change

and that due to pitching moment change. The dangerous AoA increase is dependent on the magnitude of the post-stall lift loss, while the offsetting pitching effect depends on changes in stall pitching moment and on the aircraft size.

There can be very large differences in angular acceleration in pitch at the stall onset, depending on the aircraft size, layout and maximum lift coefficient. This leads to a significant delay in AoA reduction on modern large aircraft. Large aircraft tend to have a much more sluggish nose-drop than smaller ones. It might be supposed that a safer situation would arise by having a very gradual stall with a small lift loss. While this might make the attainment of excessive AoA less likely, a consensus of pilot opinion is that it is not acceptable because the aircraft has not 'stopped flying'. The lift remains nearly equal to the weight, and subconsciously the pilot may continue to attempt normal flight. There could, however, be a degradation of control and an increase in drag that could lead to the unnoticed development of very high sink rates, resulting in a height loss greater than that involved in a sharp but short-lived stall that was noticed and corrected.

By suitable spanwise grading of the leading-edge devices it is relatively easy to avoid tip stalling with mechanical flaps. Even so, experience indicates that this solved only about one-third of the problem. On the inner wing, which is allowed to stall first, a very exacting sequence of events must be achieved, for not only must the stall occur in the right places, but it must also spread at an optimum rate. If it spreads too quickly, wing dropping and over-sensitivity are likely to occur. If it spreads too slowly the stall will be indefinite. Varying the local geometry of the leading-edge devices is the most effective method of promoting the stall in the desired locations. In terms of design geometry, a useful general rule is that leading-edge devices across the inner part of the wing should, as far as possible, avoid discontinuities, since they tend to inhibit the rapid spread of the stall over the inner wing, leading to poor stall recognition.

Superstall/deep stall

During the 1960s the aft-fuselage location of engines became fashionable, having been pioneered on the Sud Caravelle with its mid-fin-mounted tailplane. Types such as the BAC One-Eleven, Douglas DC-9, de Havilland Trident and Vickers VC10 all featured 'T-tails'. Latent in this configuration was the previously unknown and serious 'deep stall' or 'superstall' threat. To have a deep stall potential an aircraft will either be unstable at the initial AoA of about 16–21 degrees, or will become unstable at an angle well above the initial stall. If the unstable aircraft pitches up to an AoA above the normal stall angle, it may then become stable and trimmed in a fully stalled condition at 35–45 degrees AoA (*see* adjacent figure), the so-called 'locked-in stall'. At such high angles, aerodynamic control surfaces such as elevators

and ailerons are sufficiently stalled to have severely reduced effectiveness, and a highly-swept rudder may have no effect at all because its effective sweep angle is approaching 90 degrees. The controls then lack the capability to pitch the aircraft nose down to escape from this stable, very-high-drag, high-sink-rate condition.

The instability is caused by a combination of fuselage vortices creating an enormous downwash over the inner part of the horizontal T-tail surface, where the local velocity is close to the freestream value, and a helpful upwash over the outer part of the tail, where the local velocity is greatly reduced by the wing wake and, if the engines are aft-mounted, by the nacelle wakes at higher AoA. The stability that reappears at very high AoA results from the tail surfaces moving through the wakes and emerging into the freestream below the wakes.

The locked-in stall is very dangerous. A fatal crash occurred during the testing of a BAC One-Eleven in 1965

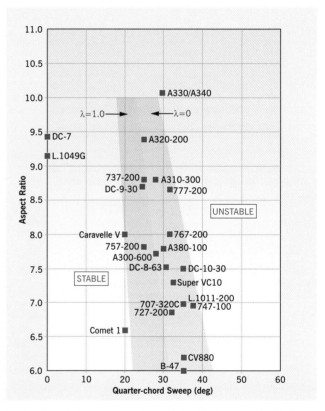

Pitch-up boundaries. These were formulated by Furlong and McHugh of NACA in 1957 (for taper ratios λ=1 and λ=0). With an aspect ratio of 6.0, quarter-chord sweep of 35 degrees and a taper ratio of 0.23, the B-47 wing fell close to the boundary, which applies at low speeds with the tail off. Although not an immutable law it served as a good preliminary design rule, though, with time, experience showed how to combine increasingly higher aspect ratios with moderate wing sweep.
(Key – Ray Whitford – Pete West)

Aircraft type	Stall quality
Piston-engine transports	Good, with natural warning produced by buffet and straight nose drop
Turboprop transports	Degraded with a tendency to roll; stick shakers needed for warning
First-generation jet transports	Good, with natural warning and straight nose drop
Second-generation jet transports	Not good (some very bad); devices needed for warning and qualities

T-tails became popular in the 1960s with the emergence of aircraft with aft-mounted engines such as the BAC One-Eleven, VC10, de Havilland Trident, Tu-134, Boeing 727 and this MD-80 (DC-9 derivative) of SAS, seen on approach to London Heathrow in May 2000.
(Key – Steve Fletcher)

owing to a stable stall that developed during intentional stalling tests at 17,000ft (5,100m). During the 90sec that followed before the aircraft hit the ground it proved impossible to effect a recovery. Subsequent to this accident, all aircraft suspected of being prone to superstall were protected against the stall by a stick-shaker, a visual and aural stall warning, and a standby elevator power system or stick-pusher.

Aeroelastic effects on control

The earliest analytical studies of aircraft stability and control were made on the assumption that they were rigid bodies. This is satisfactory for most low-speed aircraft, despite the fact that many early ones were far from rigid (for example, wing warping was used by the Wright brothers for roll control). However, their speeds were so low that elastic problems were 'lost in the noise' of other difficulties. Next to the problem of flutter, the most important problem concerned the influence of wing elasticity on the rate of roll in response to aileron deflection. Wing twisting in response to control deflection decreased the available rolling moment as a function of dynamic pressure, resulting in an 'aileron reversal speed' above which roll response to lateral control would reverse.

The aircraft that really brought industry's attention to this aeroelastic problem was the Boeing XB-47. Designed in 1945, it featured thin, high-aspect-ratio swept wings at a time when little was known about building such structures. That said, it was anticipated that the wing would be very flexible (it had a wingtip deflection of 10.7m (35ft) between maximum positive and negative loads), and that this would have a very serious effect on stability and control. This is an understatement.

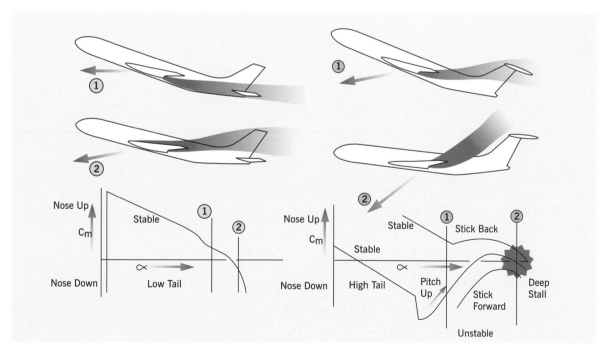

Superstall. Aircraft with high-set tails may be prone to superstall owing to the loss of stability and tailplane effectiveness at high AoA, resulting from the tail remaining in the low dynamic pressure wakes from the wings and aft engine nacelles. This can result in the AoA increasing (due to the rotation and rate of sink following the stall) until the aircraft stabilizes at a high AoA (becomes locked in a deep stall) when the tail emerges from the wake. The designer must provide a means of warning the pilot (typically using a stick shaker) and obtaining sufficient nose-down pitch to prevent the aircraft entering a deep stall (typically using a stick pusher).
(Key – Pete West)

Extreme requirements demand extreme design modifications. Because of the greatly enlarged unpressurized upper fuselage on the Airbus A300-608ST, the dorsal fin was raised and extended, and tailplane-tip endplates were added to restore directional stability to an acceptable level. Similar modifications were required for the Space Shuttle-carrying Boeing 747.
(Airbus Industrie)

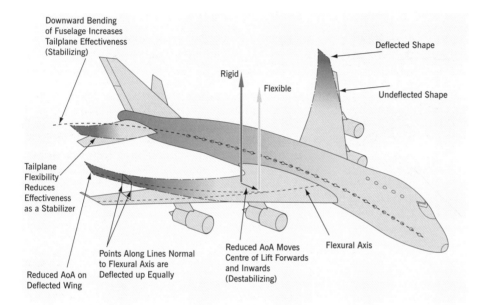

Floppy structures. Aircraft structures are flexible, not rigid, and deflections have significant effects on stability. This figure shows, in exaggerated form, how structural flexibility following an up-gust affects pitch stability. Note that, with an aft-swept flexural axis, points along streamwise lines on the wing are deflected up more at the trailing edge than at the leading edge, producing nose-down twist.
(Key – Ray Whitford – Pete West)

The problem confronting the structural designer was that the torsional stiffness requirements needed to be established so that construction of the aircraft could begin. However, there was no previous experience from which to extrapolate. Wind tunnel techniques had yet to be evolved to handle the elastic problem, and a complete theoretical solution had yet to be developed. Without a computer there was no hope that solutions to the complicated equations could be solved in a reasonable time. Faced with this dilemma, the project engineer calculated the wing torsion in response to aileron deflection and made an estimate of the torsional rigidity required to keep the aileron-reversal speed above the design limit speed. Unfortunately the solution did not account for the fact that, when the ailerons deflected, the wings bent. When they do this, swept wings twist. As a result, the stiffness needed was underestimated, and the B-47's actual aileron-reversal speed was too low.

Spoilers

To overcome the aileron reversal problem on the B-47 a spoiler was tested, but it was not until the Boeing B-52 Stratofortress that the device came into wide usage on large aircraft. The

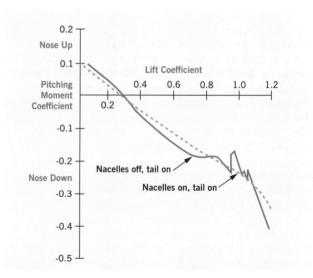

Effect of engine pods on pitch-up. During windtunnel development of the Boeing B-47 it was found that the shape and location of the jet-engine pods had a major influence on low Mach number pitch-up. Originally it had been planned to put the outboard engine pod on the wingtip, but it was found that a location further inboard minimized the probability of pitch-up.
(Key)

Spoilers may be used on swept-wing aircraft for roll control (without the attendant adverse yaw that ailerons tend to produce) and as lift 'dumpers'. These two photographs show Boeing 747-400 spoilers deployed in flight (left) to aid descent, and to assist braking after touchdown (right) by dumping lift to put more weight on the wheels.
(Key – Malcolm English)

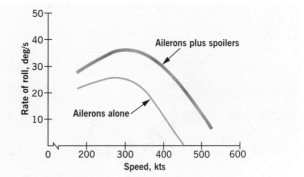

dumping lift to put more weight on the wheels.

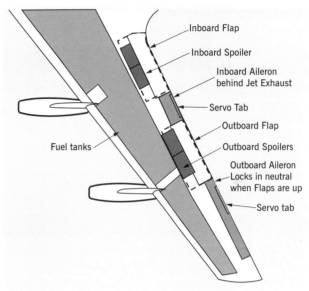

Benefit of spoilers. Aeroelastic deflections of the Boeing B-47 wing gave much-reduced roll rates at high indicated airspeeds and lateral control reversal above 450kt (520mph, 830km/h) IAS (top) using ailerons alone. Flight tests of spoiler-type controls were conducted on an experimental B-47, and demonstrated good responsive lateral control at all speeds. This, and Boeing's experience with spoilers on its B-52, led to the manufacturer using spoilers (in addition to ailerons) for roll control on its Model 387-60 (707 'prototype') as shown (bottom).
(Key – Pete West)

advantage of spoilers is that they provide roll control without the same aeroelastic side-effects as ailerons. Spoilers have lower section pitching moments for a given change of lift than flap-type ailerons, which means they create less wing torsion. Thus the wing structure may be made lighter.

Early flight tests with the Northrop P-61 Black Widow during the 1940s showed an important property of spoilers regarding their chordwise location on the wing. When located at around mid-chord there was a lag in their effect, in the sense that there was no immediate lift or rolling moment change. This was probably because of the time required for the flow disturbance to affect the trailing-edge condition. Spoilers at aft locations, however, were found to have no lag problems. When installed just ahead of slotted wing flaps, spoilers become slot width control devices when the flaps are down, providing an additional bonus of powerful low-speed roll control.

A spoiler acts by dumping lift, pushing a wing down. While this avoids adverse yaw (away from the intended direction of roll and turn, by increasing the drag of the downgoing wing), there is a loss of authority as airspeed is reduced. Therefore, upper surface spoilers tend to be augmented by ailerons for low-speed control, and are a standard feature of modern jet transports. Spoilers are also used symmetrically to reduce lift and increase drag to make fast descents and to assist braking after touchdown by

Command control systems

As soon as autopilots were installed in aircraft in the 1930s it was realized that control of the aircraft could be accomplished merely by changing the setting of the autopilot (or 'George', as it was affectionately known). This method was used during the Second World War to reduce the workload of flying bombers in formation by use of the so-called 'formation stick'. Most autopilots, however, were severely limited in control authority for safety reasons. Control through the autopilot, therefore, could be accomplished only in gentle manoeuvres. It was not until the development of highly reliable triple- or quadruple-redundant automatic control systems that control of the aircraft through an automatic system became practicable.

Active Control Technology (ACT)

On a modern aircraft there are many advantages in the use of command control systems. The weight and complication of the control system can be reduced and, with digital systems, the designer has the freedom to vary control laws after the

Mode	Action	Benefit
Manoeuvre load alleviation	Symmetric negative outboard aileron deflection to move wing loads inboard	Reduce wing bending moments and weight (Lockheed L.1011-500, Douglas DC-10-50, Airbus A330/340)
Gust load alleviation	Negative outboard and inboard spoiler deflection to dump lift, and elevator deflection to pitch aircraft	To reduce gust loads to extend fatigue life or reduce structural weight (A320)
Relaxed static stability	More aft CG to give less inherently stable aircraft with artificial stability provided by active controls	Reduce tail surface areas, drag, weight and fuel burn (A330/340, Tu-204)

Aspects of Active Control Technology

hardware is installed. As shown in the accompanying table, the use of such systems enabled the exploitation of capabilities such as manoeuvre load alleviation, gust load alleviation and relaxed static stability. The use of digital computers provides greater freedom in choice of control laws as well as greater reliability. Quadruplex redundancy is acceptable for military operations, where the accident rate from all causes is in the region of 1 in 10,000 flying hours. This is insufficient for commercial fleets, where 200 airliners may accumulate about one million flying hours in a year. Many modern airliners embrace ACT, with some form of back-up, to provide a measure of artificial stability.

Fly-by-wire (FBW)

The previous technology of control systems transmit pilot commands through steel cables linking cockpit controls to hydraulic jacks. In turn, these jacks or power units move the ailerons, spoilers and elevators. Thus mechanical controls make up a complex cascade of interdependent moving parts. FBW replaces these mechanical links with electrical ones. The pilot sends electrical signals to hydraulic power units that directly drive the surfaces, so reducing the number of moving parts. This simplifies maintenance and helps minimize potential for error. Because electrical signalling requires minimal rigging compared with mechanically-

signalled actuators, it provides quicker, simpler and more accurate repairs.

The FBW approach has its roots in the 1960s, when, for Concorde, available analogue computer technology offered a solution to the special challenges of supersonic flight. The 1970s witnessed the widespread introduction of digital computers, whose rapidly growing power and affordability encouraged manufacturers to make wider use of them.

The major advantage of FBW is the ease with which 'limiting' can be incorporated. With manual control systems the pilot always has the capability to stall the aircraft or exceed its structural limits. Therefore, many of the requirements for aircraft of this type have to do with providing adequate warning to the pilot so that he will avoid these difficulties. With command control systems it is simply necessary to limit the magnitude of the command to values that ensure that dangerous situations are not encountered. This capability is particularly desirable for transports that are not intended for flight beyond normal limits.

FBW controls keep pilots within the speed and manoeuvre limitations of the aircraft's flight envelope. They also allow the aircraft to reach these limits rapidly and continue to fly there without running the risk of exceeding them, something a conventional aircraft cannot do. The benefit comes in unusual situations, when a pilot is forced to make an abrupt manoeuvre (to avoid a collision, for example). It had been

Fly-by-wire systems have their roots in the 1960s, when analogue computer technology matured sufficiently to offer a solution to the special challenges of supersonic flight facing Concorde. The 1970s witnessed the widespread introduction of digital computers, whose rapidly growing power, reliability and affordability encouraged manufacturers to make wider use of them. (NewsCast)

Although some 'purist' pilots might disagree, one of the great advantages of digital flight control systems (FCS) is the ease with which limits can be placed on an aircraft's speed and manoeuvre flight envelope. This can give the pilot what is known as 'carefree handling'; irrespective of the control input, the FCS ensures that none of the aircraft's design limitations are exceeded. An A340-600, seen here at the 2001 Paris Air Show, demonstrates its high AoA capability; the digital FCS keeping the angle just on the limits allowed.
(Key – Malcolm English)

With the exception of the rudder, all of the A320's flight control surfaces are electrically signalled, rather than mechanically as in most commercial aircraft. Removal of extensive mechanical linkages saves weight and reduces the amount of maintenance required. Most importantly, fly-by-wire improves the handling characteristics and reduces pilot workload.
(Airbus Industrie)

shown that pilots have a strong tendency to feed input to the controls progressively, stopping input before getting the maximum out of the aircraft. This is understandable in part, because pilots have no instrument to measure g and must be careful to avoid losing control. In the case of the Airbus A320 (the first civil transport with digital FBW primary control, in pitch and roll), the pilot can achieve more rapid response (2.5g for a pull-up manoeuvre) without fear of breaking the aircraft.

The decision of Airbus to offer the A320 as an FBW aircraft was taken against a background of some 20 years' experience among its partners of applying electrical signalling in military and civil aircraft, including Concorde. However, the old arguments, reminiscent of those used against fully-powered

flying controls, were used against electronic flight control systems, it being claimed that the pilot would not be in total control of the aircraft. Some said it was a mistake that the controls operated by the pilot were not coupled as they were in conventional aircraft. Another argument was whether it was sensible to sell such sophisticated aircraft to countries culturally and economically ill-equipped to operate them safely.

The adoption of widespread digital processing and FBW primary flight control in the A320 focused a review, by certification authorities worldwide, of the requirements for systems and software integrity to meet the necessary standards of aircraft safety. The arguments used by Airbus for FBW included:

- Built-in redundancy, over-capacity and internal monitor. For example, the A320 uses five FBW computers; any one of them alone has sufficient processing power for pilots to fly the aircraft. All five computers work simultaneously; if one fails, another automatically takes over.
- Continual self-monitoring: each computer is actually two computers in one; one continuously monitors the other.
- Concurrent computer design and software-writing: one manufacturer (Thomson-CSF) designs and builds three of the A320 computers; another (SFENA) makes the other two according to a separate design, with different micro-processors (from Intel and Motorola). Independent teams, using different software, program the two types separately (using four different languages), which overcomes the possibility for the same fault to affect all computers at once.

- If failure does occur, pilots can use mechanical back-up controls (tailplane trim and rudder) providing left/right and up/down control to fly the aircraft.
- FBW aircraft remain flyable in the very unlikely event of complete electrical failure. The A320 has six different power sources; a generator on each engine, a hydraulically driven generator, and auxiliary power unit, a ram-air turbine and batteries.

Although often described as a design revolution, FBW is a logical step in experience-based aircraft design. While flight envelope protection and other safeguards promote safer flight, they are no substitutes for airmanship and vigilance, and no technical solution can ever offer infallible protection against every risk.

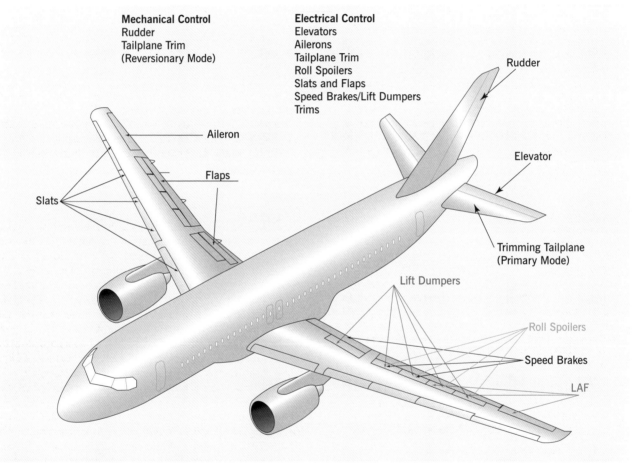

Mechanical Control
Rudder
Tailplane Trim
(Reversionary Mode)

Electrical Control
Elevators
Ailerons
Tailplane Trim
Roll Spoilers
Slats and Flaps
Speed Brakes/Lift Dumpers
Trims

Rudder

Aileron

Flaps

Slats

Elevator

Trimming Tailplane
(Primary Mode)

Lift Dumpers

Roll Spoilers

Speed Brakes

LAF

A320 flight control system. The Airbus A320 was designed from the outset to have an electrical flight control system (EFCS) so that the aircraft would be fully FBW in pitch and roll. Pitch control is by four elevators, each of which is independently powered by a dedicated hydraulic actuator, electrically signalled. The entire tailplane is powered by two or more actuators to trim the aircraft in pitch. Roll control is provided by ailerons located on the outboard third of each wing. At low airspeeds the ailerons are augmented by differential use of the wing spoilers mounted on the upper surface of the wing. The spoilers operate symmetrically as speed brakes (for descending flight) and lift dumpers on the ground (to place more weight on the wheels to improve braking performance). Yaw control is via three independent rudder sections, the control system for which incorporates yaw dampers. Rudder and pitch trim are mechanical to ensure short-period survivability in the event of a total electrical failure. The load alleviation function (LAF) was incorporated in the EFCS to ameliorate the wing loads resulting from sharp vertical gusts.

Chapter 5

Propulsion

Measured by any plausible parameter, such as gross power output, power per weight or per displacement, specific fuel consumption, altitude or speed attained, or total numbers in service, the evolution of the air-cooled piston engine (the type most used for transports) achieved stunning success between 1920 and 1950. Its development comprised not only the vast improvement in basic engine components (cylinders, pistons, internally cooled valves), but also the adoption of innovative subsystems (variable-pitch propellers and superchargers) and progress in other fields, notably fuels.

By the mid-1950s the high-power piston engine had become a hideously complicated device depending on intricate cooling systems and electrical equipment. Intractable problems of cylinder cooling had imposed a practical limit on maximum size of piston engines, and the 3,500hp of the early 1950s was close to the top of their power range. Anyway, adding power would merely accelerate the drop in propulsive efficiency. The introduction of the gas turbine was a major opportunity to reverse the trend towards complexity and weight, opening the door to a vast expansion of air transport partly by raising speed, but mostly by a great surge in usable power.

Wartime turbojets all used compressors that, in general, were not very efficient and were greedy with fuel. Furthermore, they were driven by turbines that ran at such high temperatures, given the available materials, that their lives were relatively short. Nevertheless, these powerplants of low overall efficiency formed the basis for greatly improved types that, after ten years of military experience, became acceptable for commercial service. By the 1960s the technology of the jet engine was poised for a giant new leap. Developments in blade aerodynamics, combustor design, materials and cooling led to the multi-shaft high-bypass-ratio turbofans that were the fore-runners of today's engines. These have now become much more fuel efficient, less polluting and so reliable that they enable virtually unlimited global operations.

Glossary

Bypass ratio (BPR): The ratio of external mass flow of the cold jet from the fan to the mass flow passing through the engine core.

Power loading: Total aircraft weight/total installed power.

Pressure ratio: The ratio of the pressure of the air leaving the last stage of the compressor to the pressure of the air entering the first stage.

Propeller efficiency: Power delivered to the air by the propeller/power delivered to the propeller by the engine.

Propulsive efficiency: Useful propulsive power/engine power $= \dfrac{2}{1 + U/V}$ (where V is aircraft velocity and U is the engine's jet velocity).

Solidity: Ratio of total area of propeller to disc area.

Specific fuel consumption (sfc): The rate at which fuel is burned for a given power or thrust output. For gas turbines a rough rule of thumb, which no one endorses but which seems to work, is: $sfc \propto \sqrt{\dfrac{1}{1 + \text{BPR}}}$

Specific thrust: Engine thrust/air mass flow through the engine.

Specific weight: Engine weight/power output (lb/hp).

Thermal efficiency: Power output/rate of fuel energy consumed. In its simplest form this is expressed as the Carnot (ideal cycle) efficiency $= 1 - \dfrac{T_1}{T_2}$ where T_1 is the lowest temperature in the cycle (typically at inlet) and T_2 is the maximum turbine entry temperature (TET).

Turbine entry temperature (TET): Temperature of the gas leaving the combustor and entering the turbine.

T/W (thrust/weight ratio): The engine thrust divided by engine weight.

UK engine development

The end of the First World War brought a widespread feeling that the aeroplane had already caused enough trouble and was not something to be encouraged by a world at peace. Consequently there was a rapid fall in the rate of progress and a great change in the orientation of industry in all countries. The unfavourable commercial outlook led the majority of companies that had embarked on wartime aero-engine production to revert to their pre-war activities and abandon aero engine work. Even the few survivors had a hard struggle to keep going in the immediate post-war years because of large war-surplus stocks of engines that took years to liquidate.

By the end of the war the high-power watercooled engine had been well developed, as represented by the French 220hp (164kW) Hispano-Suiza, the British 360hp (268kW) Rolls-Royce Eagle VIII and the standardized American engine, the 400hp (298kW) Liberty. While most engines used by Britain during the First World War were of French origin, from about 1913 to 1916 a large part of UK engine development had been carried out by the Royal Aircraft Factory (RAF) at Farnborough. It was there, in 1915–16, that Gibson and Heron carried out the first systematic research on the design of air-cooled cylinders. Ultimately accepted as the basic principles, their findings were:

1. Adequate valve cooling could be obtained only if the valves were inclined to each other at a broad angle, so that sufficient cooling air could flow between them.
2. Contrary to common belief, two valves were superior to a greater number, at least up to the size and power contemplated at the time.
3. Cylinder barrels should be open at the end, the entire head being of aluminium, since less weight of this metal was required to conduct away heat.

4. The head should be of one piece (since metal-to-metal joints were difficult to maintain in good thermal contact), designed to give the shortest possible heat escape route, with the largest cross-section, for the heat generated.
5. The barrel was better cooled by integral fins than by having the head cover it like a muff.
6. The head should be attached to the steel barrel by screwing and shrinking it on.

Very little effort was made in France and Germany during the war to develop air-cooled engines of much over 150hp (112kW), though in 1917 the British government began to support a number of projects. A competition was held for an air-cooled radial engine of 300hp (225kW), not more than 42in (1.06m) in diameter and weighing not more than 600lb (270kg). This was inspired by the desire to avoid the unreliability of watercooled systems, with their leakage problems. It was reckoned that 25 per cent of failures in service were due to the cooling system (another 20 per cent being due to oil systems).

Armstrong Siddeley Jaguar

Probably the most outstanding work done by Farnborough was the design of what became the classic head of the new type, forming the basis of the RAF8, a 14-cylinder two-row radial engine of 1,374in³ (22.5-litre) displacement. The radial form was chosen in preference to the in-line vee because, for a given number of cylinders of given size, it had a much smaller crankcase and was therefore much lighter. A fixed radial was chosen in preference to the popular rotary primarily because it was believed that it would give much more power, even before deducting from the gross power the 25 per cent or so that was lost in the windage (air drag) of the rotating cylinders.

However, in 1916, following accusations that the RAF was intruding upon the industry's domain, Farnborough was stripped of the right to design complete aircraft or engines. Consequently the new engine went to Siddeley-Deasy, accompanied by some of the Farnborough personnel, and eventually became known as the Armstrong Siddeley Jaguar. By the middle of 1920 a redesigned Jaguar with increased displacement of 1,512in³ (24.8 litres) was producing 300hp (225kW). By 1923 it was rated at 360hp (268kW), and a year later it passed its 100hr Type Test at 425hp (317kW).

Bristol Jupiter

Also in 1917, the Ministry of Munitions had given the Brazil-Straker company a production order for 200 Mercury engines. This 14-cylinder, two-row 1,223in³ (20-litre) engine, designed by Roy (later Sir Roy) Fedden, was independent of Farnborough's work. The follow-on in 1918 was the Jupiter, a nine-cylinder single-row radial of greater size: 1,753in³ (28.2-litre) displacement and 52.5in (1.33m) diameter. At the low aircraft speeds of the time the increased diameter was not thought to be a serious disadvantage. Brazil-Straker, having been renamed Cosmos, concentrated almost entirely on the development of the Jupiter. The company's principal reason for undertaking the new engine was simply the complete faith shown by the British government in the single-row configuration because of its ease of production. For a given power, single-row engines could be built with considerably less (20–25 per cent) labour than a two-row of the same

displacement, though equal displacement would normally give somewhat more power in a two-row engine.

At this time the consensus was that anything more powerful than the 450hp (336kW) watercooled Napier Lion was unnecessary, and that higher power would be impractical without water cooling. Fedden's target was 500hp (373kW), air-cooled. The cost of Jupiter development was far higher than anticipated, and in 1920 Cosmos folded. Eager to have the Jupiter continue, the UK government prevailed upon the Bristol Aeroplane Company to take over Cosmos. Fedden, as chief engineer of the newly-created Bristol Aero Engine Department, estimated that within two years he could produce a Jupiter weighing no more than 650lb (295kg). It was the first engine to pass the Air Ministry's new 100hr Type Test (which had replaced the 50hr test originally introduced in 1919), at a normal rating of 385hp (287kW) at 1,575rpm. The engine was shown at the 1921 Paris Salon Aéronautique, where it was acclaimed and rewarded by a government order for forty-two engines.

Jaguar versus Jupiter

Throughout the period from 1922 to 1926 Armstrong Siddeley was the dominant British manufacturer of air-cooled engines. The company's position was inherently strong because it had an airframe manufacturing arm, Armstrong Whitworth Aircraft, and consequently could be sure of having airframes designed around its engines. In 1926 it introduced its Argosy, an eighteen-seat transport powered by three Jaguars, which entered service with Imperial Airways on the London-to-Paris route. This was the first British transport with air-cooled engines to go into regular service, and the first British one to make commercial aviation a paying proposition. Once established, no more airliners were built around the standard civil watercooled Rolls-Royce Eagle and Napier Lion.

Although its output was greater, the Jupiter II was far from being the equal of the contemporary Jaguar. Nevertheless, in 1923 the Jupiter IV was type tested and, besides having a maximum rating 36hp (27kW) higher than the Jupiter II, it was more reliable. Development of the engine continued at a rapid pace, and within three years important improvements were made. One was the replacement of the cast aluminium crankcase by a forged one. An engine with this modification passed its type test in 1925 and, though there was no noticeable increase in power, the Jupiter VI was 7 per cent

Replacing the earlier Jupiters' cast aluminium crankcase with a forged one reduced the weight of the Jupiter VI by 7 per cent. It was used on the D.H.66 Hercules, with which Imperial Airways started its UK–India service, later extended to Australia.
(Key – Gordon Swanborough Collection)

lighter. Besides being used in several military aircraft, it was adopted for the new de Havilland three-engine D.H.66 Hercules introduced in 1926, with which Imperial Airways started its UK–India service, later extended to Australia.

Jaguar outclassed by Jupiter

By 1926 the Jaguar and Jupiter were on about equal footing. There were two features of the Jaguar however, that were superior: its Farnborough-designed geared centrifugal supercharger, the first of its kind (*see* later), and its aluminium cylinder head. The advantage of the Jupiter lay in its higher output, partly offset by its 60 per cent greater frontal area. The Jaguar had a longer time between overhaul (TBO) in commercial service, but the Jupiter's general standard of workmanship was better. During the period from 1926 to 1929 Bristol succeeded in surpassing Armstrong Siddeley's achievements in both features that constituted the Jaguar's advantages. This was primarily due to the efforts made to produce a special Mercury engine for the 1927 Schneider Trophy contest. The second major improvement in the Jupiter after 1926 was the development of a geared version (*see* later). This was not only a reliable means of reducing propeller rpm, but it also helped solve the vibration problems when running at high speeds. Production of the Jupiter VIII and IX started in 1928, both having a maximum speed of 2,200rpm that increased maximum output to 525hp (391kW) for the IX. However, throughout the evolution of the Jupiter up to 1928, its fundamental weakness was its poultice cylinder head.

About 1926–27 two new factors entered the picture. Firstly, the output of the Jupiter was obviously pushing the cooling capacity of its cylinder head to its limit. Secondly, in 1926 US air-cooled radial engines appeared with cylinders that, although they were descended from the original Farnborough work, were much improved and far superior to their UK contemporaries. The first step taken by Bristol was to adapt the Jupiter to have the cast all-aluminium head used on the racing Mercury. Although it was successful in operation, production was excessively costly owing to the high rate of scrap. The US cylinder heads were cast, but British foundry techniques were inferior, and Bristol decided to use a forged head with machined fins.

In 1929, with the market for Jaguars rapidly shrinking, Bristol began production of the new F (Forged) series of Jupiters. The Handley Page H.P.42 Hannibal, ordered in 1928 by Imperial Airways for its India route, was originally designed for either four Jaguars or Jupiters, but soon standardized on the Jupiter XIF. The basic reason for the eclipse of the Jaguar was simply its lower power and insufficient development, which was also true of its supercharging. While it is true that the Jupiter had 16 per cent more displacement, the smaller cylinders of the Jaguar should have been capable of more power per unit volume. Furthermore, the problem of torsional vibration, which was perhaps the most serious obstacle to radial engines in 1920, was gradually solved for single-row engines during the 1920s. It was not truly solved for double-row engines until the 1930s.

Origin of US air-cooled engines

As in Europe, the US market for aero engines was depressed by the glut of war-surplus units, many of them unused, which were offered for sale at a small fraction of cost. It was impossible to sell even a much superior new engine for civilian use until the mid-1920s. For about ten years after the end of the First World War, vee-type liquid-cooled engines led by the Liberty dominated the engine field in the USA. Consequently there was no reason whatever for private capital to risk any appreciable funds in the development of new aero engines. Until 1925–26 the only adequate financing for R&D was provided by the US Government.

The history of high-power air-cooled engines in the USA began with a design competition announced in 1919 by the US Army, which, aware of the progress being made in Britain, issued a specification calling for an engine to develop 350hp (260kW). Although it was not the winning design, Wright's nine-cylinder R-1 of 1,454in^3 (23.8 litres) did develop the power, but it had many faults, the worst of which concerned its cylinders. After testing in 1920, Wright rebuilt it with new cylinders developed by Heron with the US Army at McCook Field. He had moved to the USA, and introduced a great aid to cylinder performance and extended valve life; the sodium-cooled exhaust valve. In 1923 a specification was issued for a new engine, the R-1454 (R: radial; 1,454in^3 (23.8 litres)), incorporating fundamentally changed design features.

The entire industry was invited to submit bids, the lowest bidder being Curtiss. The engine was to deliver at least 390hp (290kW) at 1,700rpm, and to have provision to use a new cylinder with automatically lubricated valve gear then being designed by Heron. This became standard on US air-cooled radial engines, and it proved to be a feature of great utility. The first R-1454 was delivered nine months after the signing of the contract. On test it delivered up to 405hp (302kW) at 1,650rpm, and before the end of 1925 the 830lb (376kg) engine had passed a 50hr Type Test consisting of 45hr at 90 per cent of its normal 390hp (290kW) and 5hr at fully rated power. However, by 1926, when flight tests with the R-1454 began, a much better engine had appeared.

Formation of Pratt & Whitney

In 1925 a number of Wright's most highly experienced personnel broke away to found the Pratt & Whitney Aircraft Company, where they designed and built, in five months, the famous R-1340 Wasp. It not only delivered slightly more power, but, of 1,344in^3 (22-litre) displacement, it weighed only 650lb (295kg) and was a good deal cleaner and more reliable. The US Navy agreed to buy it in quantity if Pratt & Whitney could produce an engine meeting certain specifications. The R-1340 demonstrated such decisive superiority over the Curtiss R-1454 in comparative flight tests that all future development of the latter engine was stopped.

Instead of having a cast crankcase, as used on all previous US radials, the Wasp differed in having a cleverly designed forged crankcase. It was much lighter and saved even more weight proportionally than the Bristol Jupiter, as its design was better suited for forging to minimum weight without excessive scrap. It was astonishingly successful for a new engine, being type tested at a normal rating of 400hp (298kW) at 1,900rpm at sea level. The US Navy ordered 200, and commercial sales of twenty-eight engines for use on the Boeing Model 40 mailplane followed even before the first US Navy order had been filled. These engines were delivered before the end of 1927, the receipts completely amortizing the cost of development with a satisfactory profit.

In 1927 the R-1340 Wasp was probably the best unsupercharged, direct-drive, air-cooled engine in production anywhere, with a specific weight (weight/power) equal to that of the Jupiter VI. The poultice head of the Jupiter was distinctly inferior, however, and had to be re-bedded at intervals of 300hr at most, and the valve gear was open and allowed water and dirt to enter it and oil to be spattered over the engine. Its inadequate cylinder cooling meant that its output was near its limit, whereas the output of the Wasp was rapidly increasing. It was not until Bristol put its F-series Jupiter into production in 1929 that the British engine was again on equal footing with the Wasp. It was still some time, however, before a US engine equalled either of the two British engines, Jupiter and Jaguar, in two respects: geared drive and supercharging.

Geared propellers

During the First World War British designers had shown that aircraft performance was improved by the use of gearing between the propeller and the engine, 'to provide the aeroplane with a gearbox'. The gearing gave the propeller a lower rpm than the engine to improve propeller efficiency. (The Wright brothers knew this in 1903, and geared down their twin pusher propellers through shafts and chains.) If an engine equipped with a fixed-pitch propeller is operated in level flight at all altitudes with sea-level air (via supercharging) in the induction system, the rate of revolution will steadily increase with altitude. The power output will increase in proportion to the increase in rpm. If the propeller is designed for maximum permissible rpm at the maximum altitude at which it is desired to operate, the available engine power is considerably reduced at any lower altitude. Take-off could become impossible. Conversely, if the propeller is designed to allow maximum rpm at sea level, engine power in level flight has to be reduced as altitude is increased.

Although Britain was stopping almost all production of direct-drive high-power engines by 1928, there was no demand for geared engines in the USA. However, in 1927 it had been shown that, with unsuitable propeller blade angles holding down engine speed, only half of an engine's power was being converted into useful work on take-off. By using variable-pitch blades a rate of climb of 500ft/min (150m/min) could be almost doubled. What was needed was a propeller that would enable the engine to maintain constant speed at all altitudes.

Variable-pitch propellers

By 1916 the knowledge required for propeller design was reasonably well in hand, but systematic propeller data for the aircraft designer were almost non-existent. In the USA, apart from the excellent beginnings by the Wright brothers in 1902 and 1903, little of note had been accomplished. In Europe, Stefan Drzewiecki, beginning in Russia in 1885 and continuing in France, had developed a theory for the calculation of propeller performance with the aid of measured aerofoil data. Experimental work on propellers began in earnest in the UK, France and Germany around 1910, and by 1913 comparison between theoretical and experimental data in the UK showed that the theory, though quantitatively unreliable, provided a useful guide to the design of efficient propellers. Practical but individual designs were giving efficiencies of 70–80 per cent (propeller efficiency is defined as propulsive power delivered by the propeller to the air compared with shaft power absorbed by

the propeller from the engine). Systematic performance data, however, were limited to the small amount obtained by French structural engineer Gustav Eiffel at his private laboratory in Paris. How widely the European knowledge was disseminated in the USA by 1916 is unclear, but certainly most of it was known. W.F. Durand of the newly formed NACA, established to enable the USA to catch up with Europe in the development of aeronautics, proposed an experimental study of model propellers using methodology similar to that used for marine propellers. By the autumn of 1917 a report of the testing of forty-eight different propellers had been published.

The earliest commercial propellers were of the fixed-pitch two-bladed wooden type, shortly paralleled in use by fixed-pitch metal propellers of the Reed twisted-blade type. Work done in Britain on early experimental variable-pitch propellers, installed in biplanes with fixed undercarriage, was technically successful, but the very modest overall gain in performance did not justify the added weight, complexity and cost. However, a very important step in aviation came in 1928, when the aviation community was introduced to the Hele Shaw-Beacham variable-pitch propeller. At the time, though, few could foresee the use of such a device. Britain's aversion to it was partly due to the fact that the UK had developed propeller reduction gear to a high state of efficiency and reliability. This, together with the typical low wing loading of around 10lb/ft² (49kg/m²), made the heavier and more complex device appear unattractive. A major step was the development of the adjustable-blade propeller,

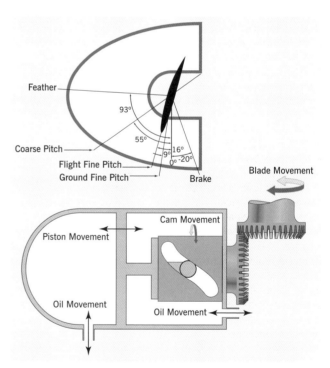

The pitch range of a propeller blade and a simplified pitch-change mechanism. The modern propeller, as well as performing its primary task of converting shaft power to thrust efficiently, carries big responsibilities for the engine and airframe. Reversing is only one example of the way in which the propeller is enlisted to improve aircraft performance. Auto-pitch coarsening is another. At take-off the ability to maintain performance after engine failure often depended upon the propeller's ability to coarsen pitch automatically, so that sudden uncontrollable windmilling drag is immediately relieved. Moreover, the other refinement, called synchro-phasing, reduced vibration and 'beat' by ensuring that the blades of each propeller moved in a fixed angular relationship to each other. The effect of synchro-phasing is to make all the propellers turn at the same speed and angular position.

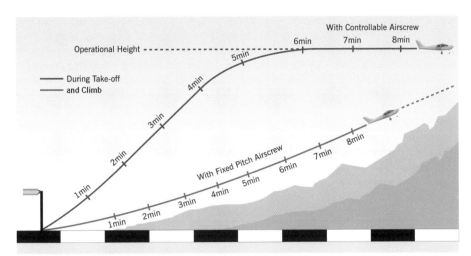

Variable-pitch propellers. A contemporary (1930s) illustration of the benefits of variable-pitch propellers, showing the much-improved climb performance with the blades working at their best angle as speed changes. It was left to Hamilton Standard, owned by Pratt & Whitney, to develop a truly practical hydraulic variable-pitch propeller, used commercially for the first time in 1933 on the Douglas DC-1. After 1933 variable-pitch propellers, both hydraulic and electric, were increasingly widely used. This made it possible for monoplanes with their higher wing loadings to take off within reasonable distances, and to land slowly while still maintaining high efficiencies at high speeds and altitudes.

which, by *ground* adjustment of pitch, permitted the adoption of a setting reasonably suited to the particular requirements of the aircraft–engine combination using it. None of this type, however, developed the real potential of the powerplants.

It was left to Hamilton Standard in the USA (owned by Pratt & Whitney) to pioneer and develop the first practical two-position, variable-pitch propeller. This could be adjusted from the cockpit to a low pitch position reasonably consistent with the low airspeeds of take-off and initial climb, during which the engine could be speeded up to develop its rated power more fully. Thereafter it could be set to a high-pitch position for reasonable efficiency in cruise at reduced rpm and higher airspeed. Even in the USA, though, it would have been dropped had it depended solely on military support. It was not until the advent of the all-metal, well-streamlined monoplane with retractable undercarriage that it was worth the trouble. Indeed, without the variable-pitch propeller the opportunity to exploit increased engine power could not have been taken.

Notably, the variable-pitch propeller was used commercially for the first time in 1933 on the Douglas DC-1, whereupon both hydraulically- and electrically-controlled types were widely used. They made it possible for monoplanes with high wing loadings to take off within reasonable distances and land slowly, but still to maintain high efficiencies at high speeds and altitudes. Indeed, it was found that only with a variable-pitch propeller could the Boeing 247D of 1934 take off with a reasonable payload from high-altitude airfields in the Rockies. The resulting orders allowed further development of the device, leading to the constant-speed controllable-pitch propeller, which by governor control would maintain a desirable take-off rpm for maximum power, permitting a continuous advance of propeller pitch with increased speed.

US air transport in the 1920s

The Wright J-5 Whirlwind, the first US air-cooled engine to have a fuel consumption as low as that of contemporary watercooled engines, was extensively flown on Fokker F.VIIB/3ms from 1925 and Ford 5-ATs from 1928. Although this was a limited expansion, the situation was as different economically from what it had been only a few years before as it was technically. The first factor in this growth was a considerable increase in the use of high-power engines.

When it was first introduced, in 1933, the revolutionary Boeing 247, seen here, came without variable-pitch propellers. Shortly afterwards, as the single Douglas DC-1 was taking shape, it became clear to Douglas that it would be substantially heavier than originally estimated. It would thus not be able to meet single-engine take-off requirements unless variable-pitch propellers were installed.
(Key Archive)

From 1927 the Pratt & Whitney Wasp showed a compelling economic advantage: its lower weight for equal power permitted an increase in payload. It was largely for this reason that the cost of carrying airmail was now half of that incurred using de Havilland D.H.4s with Liberty engines. It was cheaper to buy a modern engine with a TBO of 300hr than to recondition a Liberty requiring major overhaul every 75hr to maintain the same service. This presaged a great expansion in civil operations, and launched a long series of genuine commercial airliners designed around air-cooled engines. In 1928 and 1929 the Wasp became the alternative choice for the Whirlwind on the Ford and Fokker trimotors.

Supercharging

'Supercharging' refers to the pre-compression of air ingested by a piston engine, usually by means of a centrifugal compressor. It was used:

1. At sea level, to supply the engine with air more dense than atmospheric in order to increase power.
2. At altitude, despite the decreasing density, to supply air at least as dense as the engine could use, thus preventing any decline in power.

That said, supercharging would have been largely lacking in

commercial value without the development of the variable-pitch propeller.

Supercharging at sea level creates serious difficulties with detonation, as described later. In the case of air-cooled engines, their inability to use high levels of supercharging was probably their greatest weakness at the time. Although US air-cooled engines actually had more 'built-in' supercharging than the production version of the premier US liquid-cooled engine, the Curtiss Conqueror, there was enough evidence to prove that the liquid-cooled engine could handle more supercharging (when superchargers were available to deliver it, that is). This was partly because the air-cooled engines were deficient in cooling at altitude: indeed, they were barely adequate near sea level. Difficulties arose because the air density decreases proportionally more than the temperature difference between the ambient and the cylinder cooling fins increases.

The other part of the problem for air-cooled engines was detonation at altitude. Despite the air being colder, compressing it to sea-level density results in the cylinder delivery temperatures being substantially above those at sea level. The mixture of fuel and air could be compressed to a much higher temperature without causing detonation in a liquid-cooled engine than in an air-cooled one. This was particularly true with the inefficient 1930s' superchargers that could attain maximum pressure ratios of 1.85:1 with efficiencies of 65–70 per cent. Nevertheless, in the USA at least, the comparison was more potential than actual, since the only superchargers capable of maintaining full engine power to altitude were turbosuperchargers. These were highly experimental, with so many difficulties that they were a decade away from service. Contemporary turbochargers normally had compressor efficiencies of 70 per cent at most, and turbine efficiencies of roughly 60 per cent, giving an overall efficiency of only 40 per cent.

Furthermore, though the liquid-cooled engine's potentially higher performance at altitudes of 15,000–20,000ft (4,580–6,100m) was argued, at no time in the 1930s did this possibility offer much assurance of a market. One of the most critical problems had always been take-off, and since the liquid-cooled engine was likely to produce less power for a given weight, the potentially better performance at altitude was of little use. Another reason why high-altitude performance had little attraction in the 1930s was the discomfort of flying at high altitude without a pressure cabin, something that did not arrive until late in the decade.

The decline of the liquid-cooled engine, 1928 to 1932

When the first successful high-power air-cooled engine appeared in the USA in 1926, its much lower specific weight led to its rapid adoption for a wide variety of applications. Simultaneously, British air-cooled engines were also driving watercooled types from the commercial market. The same low weight that made the air-cooled engine commercially desirable quickly led to its general acceptance for military payload-carrying aircraft. Moreover, by the end of the decade many (but by no means all) responsible people in the industry were convinced that the day was close when civil transport would create a market exceeding that of the military services.

In 1927 there were four US manufacturers able to spend appreciable sums of their own money on development: Pratt

& Whitney, Wright, Curtiss and Packard. Of these, the first two were exclusively producers of air-cooled engines, but Curtiss and Packard had so far been successful only with liquid-cooled types. Belief in the superiority of the air-cooled engine for most uses, and in the growing importance of the civil market, was so strong that Packard quit the liquid-cooled engine field. Furthermore, within four years all development of the Curtiss Conqueror stopped.

Moreover, Lindbergh's transatlantic flight in 1927 in the Ryan NYP, powered by a 220hp (164kW) Wright J-5 nine-cylinder air-cooled radial, focused attention on the engine type. This was undoubtedly a great stimulus to the industry, making it much easier to obtain capital from ordinary investors. In 1925 and 1926 the Pratt & Whitney Wasp had for the first time been developed and marketed at private risk. Virtually all new private financing of aero engine development was devoted to the air-cooled type. Development of liquid-cooled types throughout most of the 1930s continued to be done only for the US Government, just as in the 1920s.

Maintainability and reliability

Once the air-cooled engine had been adopted for commercial operations, a wealth of experience rapidly accumulated to improve their reliability markedly. Military Services continued to use liquid-cooled engines, but never did the sort of routine flying that contributes most to establishing reliability. The simplicity of the air-cooled engine gave it a certain and undisputed advantage: it had no parts that were not in the liquid-cooled engine, whereas the latter had all the parts of the former, plus a liquid system with coolant, pump, piping and radiator. The absence of these components made for less maintenance and, what was equally important, the maintenance that had to be done was much easier on the exposed cylinders of the radial than on the liquid-cooled in-line engines of the 1920s, where a whole bank had to be dismantled in order to reach individual cylinders.

Number of engines

Early US transports were single-engined or tri-motored. With no clear definition of engine-out requirements in the 1920s, and given the prevailing spirit of adventure, there was general industry, if not public, acceptance of single-engine aircraft. There was a broad assumption of the three-engine principle, in which engine-out performance gave an adequate ceiling. In spite of the disadvantages of fire risk, noise, dirt and vibration, there was no serious industry objection to an engine in the nose. The trimotors might be ponderous, but they were perceived as less risky than twin-engine aircraft. The third engine gave a better margin of safety. A comprehensive engineering study issued in 1931 seemed to prove that an economically sound transport could not be built with just two of the available engines. One engine appeared acceptable, three and four were eminently satisfactory, but two were shown to be quite unsound. This finding was quickly proved erroneous by subsequent developments. With its Model 247 Boeing set an almost unattainable goal; a twin-engine aircraft so aerodynamically clean that it would be able to climb with a full load on the power of one engine.

In 1932 Wright introduced its first really successful high-power air-cooled engine, the F3 model of the R-1820 Cyclone, that marked not only an increase from 575hp to

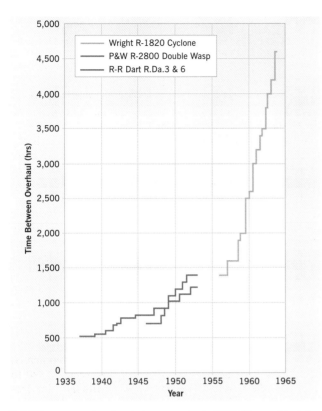

Reliability expressed as time between overhauls (TBO). Whereas it took the Wright R-1820 Cyclone twelve years to double its TBO, the much more complex Pratt & Whitney R-2800 Double Wasp achieved this in commercial service on the Douglas DC-6 in a little over half the time. The inherently simpler Rolls-Royce Dart gas turbine started where the R-2800 left off, and rapidly achieved TBOs inconceivable with piston engines.
(AIR International – Ray Whitford)

700hp (429kW to 522kW), but a great increase in reliability. It was chosen by Douglas for use in its new airliner, the DC-2. This reinforced the belief that by far the largest part of the market for large engines would go to the air-cooled type. Wright was further convinced of this by recent experience. In 1929 Transcontinental Air Transport had tried some Curtiss Condor transports with Conqueror engines, but had soon switched to Ford 5-ATs with air-cooled Wasps.

Greater power from a single engine

The acceptance of the nine-cylinder single-row radial layout as a sound type is well illustrated by the Bristol Jupiter, which was built under licence in fourteen countries. The notable exception was the Armstrong Siddeley Jaguar, with fourteen cylinders staggered in two rows, which had been in production since 1921. However, the conclusions to be drawn from the history of this engine by 1930 were uncertain. Although from about 1923 to 1926 it had been used in the most successful British fighters, for transports it had never been equal to the big single-row Bristol Jupiter, whose power increased more rapidly. The Jaguar was not evidence that a two-row radial could be built with a great deal more power than a single-row engine.

Cylinder dimensions are restricted by the square-cube law, by which increasing the volume increases the heat, while the area of the cylinder walls through which cooling is possible rises in lower proportion. Thus a size was reached where cooling became an almost insurmountable problem. Opinions differed as to the practicality of two-row radials. In this early stage of the art of air cooling there were always serious difficulties with the cooling of single-row engines, let alone those with two rows. At Bristol, Fedden, who had already established a reputation in the USA as the 'dean of the air-cooled engine', initially resisted this complication. While US manufacturers were more concerned with civil engines and Bristol with military, it was not uncommon for transatlantic calls to be made to discuss the technical problems the companies encountered. On one occasion Luke Hobbs of Pratt & Whitney was asked why his company had not built a two-row engine. He replied: 'Because Fedden hasn't'.

Multi-row engines

By 1930 it was generally agreed that a single-row radial, or one row of a multi-row, had reached its limit of displacement at about 1,800in³ (29.4 litres). The 1,860in³ (30.5-litre) single-row 'B-series' Hornet of 1930 had nine cylinders of 207in³ (3.4 litres) each. No successful radial ever had more than nine cylinders in a single row, and no successful one ever had cylinders of greater individual displacement than the Hornet. Multiple double-banked cylinders in radial

Douglas chose the F3 model of the Wright R-1820 Cyclone for use on its new airliner, the DC-2. The Cyclone was Wright's first really successful air-cooled high-power engine, and its reliability gave passengers confidence in the twin-engine (rather than tri-motor) configuration.
(Key – Duncan Cubitt)

No successful radial ever had more than nine cylinders in a single row, and no successful one ever had cylinders of greater displacement than the Pratt & Whitney Hornet, seen here powering a Boeing Model 40B-4.
(Key Archive)

formation demanded much experimentation in the shaping and placing of the baffles to give uniform cooling without hot spots. There was a limit to power, and the only solution that could provide a considerable increase at the beginning of the 1930s was the two-row radial or a four-bank of X or H form. So, as the need for greater power became evident, a gradual change-over to double-row engines took place.

There was direct competition between the two US builders in a class where the real profits lay, that of highest power. Wright could depend on a certain backlog of almost uncompetitive business in the Whirlwind class, and Pratt & Whitney could do the same with the Wasp. There was no hesitation on the part of either to risk a good share of its gross revenue in development in order to secure future profits. After beginning experiments with two-row engines in 1929, Pratt & Whitney had decided to develop an engine of 1,830in³ (30-litre) displacement as its first of this type. For any smaller displacement, single-row engines were preferable because they were lighter and simpler. Even the R-1830 Twin Wasp was intended to produce only 15–20 per cent more power than the single-rows. For four years after 1930 the R-1830 was the largest engine under development. It passed its Type Test in 1933 but did not reach a 1,000hp (746kW) rating until 1936.

In the radial form, the one best suited to air cooling, more than eighteen cylinders was out of the question in a two-row engine, and the use of more than two rows presented complex new problems, not only in cooling but in mechanical design. By 1939 the Wright and Pratt & Whitney radials had established themselves as supreme in the commercial transport and heavy military aircraft fields, largely as a result of their impressive record of reliable performance, low fuel consumption and ease of maintenance. By 1937 two air-cooled engines were under development in the USA, the Wright R-2600 (42.6 litres) and Pratt & Whitney's R-2800 Double Wasp of 45.9 litres. By enlarging the R-1830 Twin Wasp's cylinders and increasing their number to eighteen, power was increased to 2,000hp (1,490kW). By the end of the Second World War the outstanding R-2800 was producing 2,800hp (2,092kW) on 115/125-grade fuel. Although it was started in 1940, the even bigger four-row 28-cylinder R-4360 Wasp Major (71.4 litres) missed World War Two, first qualifying in 1942 at 3,000hp (2,237kW), and by 1945 it was producing 3,500hp (2,610kW).

Wright fought back mainly with its fourteen-cylinder R-2600 of 1,700hp (1,268kW) and the eighteen-cylinder 54-litre R-3350 Duplex Cyclone of 2,200hp (1,640kW) with two General Electric turbosuperchargers, used initially on the Boeing B-29 Superfortresses. The Wright Turbo-Compound was an R-3350 with three General Electric

An engineer working on one of the Pratt & Whitney Double Wasp engines of Air Atlantique's DC-6.
(Key – Duncan Cubitt

turbochargers to put power into the crankshaft. By this means the power rose eventually to 3,700hp (2,760kW) and made possible the Lockheed Super Constellation and DC-7C, the last engine being delivered in 1957.

Detonation and fuel anti-knock quality

Detonation is over-rapid burning of the fuel/air mixture, and occurs when the fuel's temperature and pressure become excessive. The First World War brought the initial awareness of detonation problems (knocking) and pre-ignition in aero engines. As a result, from 1916, the Royal Dutch Shell Oil Company supported research by Harry Ricardo into the performance of fuels, which showed that, with an increase in compression ratio, certain fuels developed a tendency to

No fewer than three General Electric turbochargers were used to boost the power of the Wright Turbo-Compound to 3,700hp (2,760kW), thus making possible the Lockheed Super Constellation.
(Key Archive)

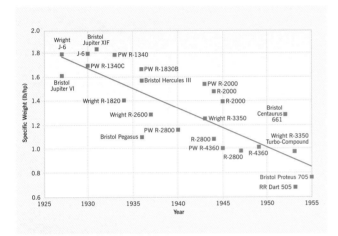

Specific weight reduction (that is, more power per weight) with time. The first successful high-power air-cooled engines showed an even more compelling economic advantage: their lower weight for equal power permitted an increase in payload. This was largely responsible for the fact that the cost of carrying airmail was cut in half when the Pratt & Whitney R-1340 Wasp-powered Boeing 40 appeared in 1927. During the twenty years between 1930 and 1950 specific weight reduced by over 40 per cent, while engine power increased by a factor of six. Note the weight reduction possible by the introduction in the 1950s of turboprops (Dart and Proteus). The degree of scatter is due more to the imprecise data on engine weight than anything else. (1lb/hp = 0.61kg/kW)
(*AIR International* – Ray Whitford)

detonate in the cylinder. The contemporary 80/20 fuel (80 per cent petrol, 20 per cent benzole) of just over 70 octane led to detonation and pre-ignition, when a cylinder would blow its top, with flames shooting from the head joint. At this time the right chemical combination had been found by trial and error on the part of the engine makers to give satisfactory results. It was not until 1925 that Edgar in the USA formulated the system of octane ratings, which allowed various fuels to be compared accurately.

From the work of Ricardo and later researchers the effects of various compounds in fuel were gradually understood. In 1921 Midgeley and Boyd, sponsored by General Motors, discovered the detonation-preventing properties of tetra-ethyl lead (TEL), which been studied during hostilities for possible use in chemical warfare. While TEL was more readily accepted in the USA, gaining approval of it in the UK and Europe was an uphill battle. Indeed, it was well-nigh impossible to persuade car manufacturers to become interested in lead; TEL was expensive and there were questions over its toxicity. Nevertheless, of the increase of some 30–40 per cent specific power (power/displacement) realized during the 1930s, 15–20 per cent was directly attributable to the improvement in the anti-knock quality of fuel.

By the late 1950s the high-power air-cooled piston engine, sophisticated and efficient though it was, was ending its long

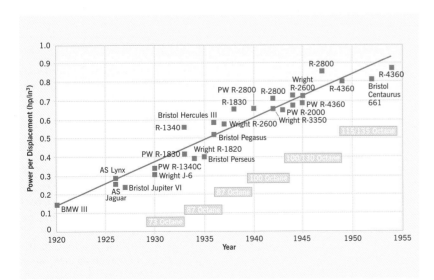

Improving specific power (power per piston displacement). Progressive developments in fuel, with a view to reducing the tendency to detonate, did more than anything else to render possible the high performance of later engines, contributing 30–40 per cent of the improvement. Since the realization during the First World War that the incidence of detonation set a limit – and, in those days, an early limit – to power output, extensive research into fuels was carried out. Engineers took full advantage of it, at first to raise the compression ratio and thereby gain thermal efficiency. When that had reached the practicable limit, further increases in mean cylinder pressure were achieved by supercharging. The increase from 73 to 100 in octane number permitted an almost threefold increase in mean cylinder pressure, but at the cost of almost doubling both the maximum gas pressures and the intensity of the heat flow. Throughout the years 1925 to 1945 it was a neck-and-neck race between the chemist and the engineer. At times the chemist was ahead and the engineer at frantic pains to stiffen the structure and working parts and to improve the cooling of the engine in order to take advantage of the improved fuel, while at other times the engineer took the lead. (1hp/in³=45.5W/cm³).

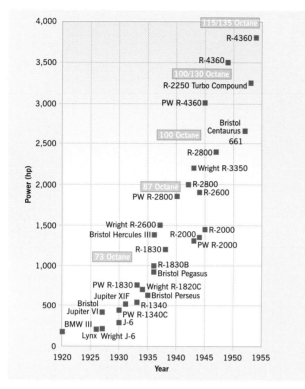

Power increase over the years, contributed in part by increasingly higher-octane gasoline. In the decade before the Second World War Britain had only one producer of high-power air-cooled engines, Bristol. However, total sales for civil transports of all British engines averaged only thirty per year in the late 1920s to early 1930s. The outstanding high-power US wartime engine was the eighteen-cylinder 2,000hp Pratt & Whitney R-2800 Double Wasp. This was a progressively developed and reliable type that built up a superb reputation. (1hp=745W).
(Key – Ray Whitford)

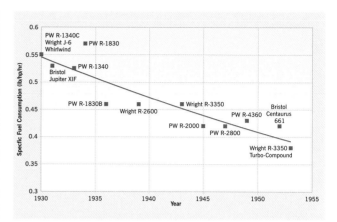

Gradual reduction in specific fuel consumption (sfc). Even the earliest civil piston engines were quite efficient, as heat engines go, although by modern standards they were heavy and unreliable. During the 1930s US air-cooled engines, the only ones specifically developed for commercial service, had lower fuel consumption than the best European liquid-cooled engines, which were designed primarily as fighter engines at a time when combat range was considered relatively unimportant. In 1937 PanAm regularly achieved an sfc of 0.45lb/hp/hr from its Wright R-2600 Double Cyclones in Boeing 314s on transpacific service, while on the test stand (where fuel cooling was less necessary) various US air-cooled engines were repeatedly tested at under 0.4. That said, the introduction of turbo-compounding was the only very significant improvement but this was at the end of large-piston-engine development. (1lb/hp/hr = 0.61kg/kW/hr).
(Key – Ray Whitford)

and distinguished life in aviation as the gas turbine began to make its appearance for commercial use. The last and most advanced example was the Wright Turbo-Compound. Thus, from the 13hp (9.7kW) Wright brothers' home-built four-cylinder watercooled engine of 1903, the power of the piston engine had steadily increased by a factor of over 280 and its weight/power had been reduced by more than 10.

Turboprops

Gas turbines had emerged independently from the work of four individuals: Whittle in the UK and von Ohain, Wagner and Schelp in Germany. Only Whittle and von Ohain directed their efforts towards a turbojet from the beginning. Before the gas turbine revolution the holistic airframe/piston-engine/propeller system produced such astounding increases in total system performance that many in the aeronautical community, especially in the USA, rejected all alternative systems. They were nearly blinded to the promise and to the necessity of the gas turbine for civil use.

While it was clear to some in the UK (though by no means all) that the gas turbine was the prime mover of the future and the days of the reciprocating engine were numbered, engine designers were reluctant to abandon the propeller. This still had large potential for efficiently converting energy into thrust, so controversy raged as to whether the new breed of turbine aircraft would be powered by turboprops or turbojets. A strong school of thought, with sound technical arguments, held that, in spite of the promise

of the turbojet-powered de Havilland Comet, the next step should be towards turboprops. The turboprop offered a smooth, relatively simple powerplant with potentially high reliability and power. As a result, a number of successful turboprops were produced in which the high energy of the residual gas stream was converted into shaft power. This was achieved either by adding additional turbine stages to the basic core, or by using a separate free turbine driving a co-axial shaft into a propeller reduction gearbox.

The fuel consumption of the turboprop was, with development, as good as that of an economical piston engine, at the former's proper operating altitude. Comparing the Rolls-Royce Tyne in the Vickers Vanguard with the Wright Turbo Cyclone in the Douglas DC-7C, the cruising specific fuel consumption (sfc) of each was about the same at 0.4lb/hp/hr (0.24kg/kW/hr), as shown in the adjacent figure. Moreover, it had taken twenty years or more to get the piston engine to 1,000hr of operation between overhaul in airline service, and about another five years to reach 1,500hr. The turboprop reached 1,500hr in two to three years' operation, the Rolls-Royce Dart running at 3,000hr by 1960. Bristol Aero Engines, with economical operation in mind, designed and developed its 4,000hp (3,000kW) Proteus. This was troublesome in its early stages, but settled down after intensive development and was operated successfully in the Bristol Britannia with an overhaul life of 7,500hr.

The Vickers Viscount was the first turbine-powered civil aircraft to enter widespread service (1953), and was very successful in that it attracted traffic from piston-engine rivals and had no turboprop competitor. The Viscount was followed by the Vanguard, Lockheed Electra and Britannia, with larger and more powerful engines. Although the Britannia, delayed three years by certification difficulties, had long range, it was accepted that the turboprop was most suitable for short/medium ranges, and the main debate concerned long-haul operations. The high-speed jet transport was thought by

Two of the first turbine-powered civil aircraft to enter widespread service were the Vickers Viscount and Vanguard (foreground), seen here at London's Heathrow Airport about 1964.
(Gordon Swanborough Collection)

many to be unsuitable. This was because of the apparently insuperable difficulty of building such aircraft with adequate range and payload at what was then considered to be an acceptable TOW, and able to use existing runways.

Propeller efficiency

By proper design a propeller can be produced to satisfy speed and load conditions efficiently, provided the combination of aircraft speed and propeller speed are low enough to avoid propeller-tip compressibility. In the neighbourhood of 500mph (800km/h) tip compressibility decreases propeller efficiency sharply. Similarly, the altitude at which propellers would function efficiently is limited. Thus it would have posed insurmountable problems to propel a transport aircraft with turboprops at the speed (500mph+) of the forthcoming jet transports. The development of an 8,000–10,000hp (6,000–7,500kW) turboprop (allowing for propeller efficiency) would have been a lengthy process in itself, certainly exceeding the time taken in getting a comparable turbojet into the air. On this basis Rolls-Royce made the fundamental decision not to develop a turboprop after the Tyne, a decision comparable with the one it had made ten years earlier regarding piston engines.

Aircraft range performance

Great emphasis is laid on the Breguet range equation:

$$\text{Range} = \frac{1}{c}\left(\frac{VL}{D}\right)\log\frac{W_{start}}{W_{end}}$$

With proper allowances for fuel reserves and other flight margins (about 8 per cent for long-haul flights), this formula works well in describing the payload/range performance of jet aircraft. The VL/D portion can be described as the aerodynamic efficiency (as seen in Aerodynamics chapter as M×L/D), c is the specific fuel consumption (sfc: fuel flow rate/thrust) of the engines, and the weight ratio $\frac{W_{start}}{W_{end}}$ represents a measure of structural efficiency (structure weight forms a large part of W_{end}).

Turbojet efficiency

The turbojet demonstrates obverse characteristics. Firstly, because the exhaust velocity of a conventional turbojet

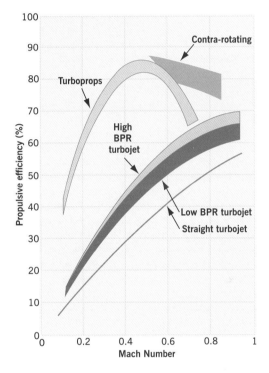

Comparative propulsive efficiencies versus Mach number. At Mach numbers below about 0.6 the turbojet is less efficient than a propeller-type engine because its propulsive efficiency depends largely on its forward speed. The turbojet is most suitable for high speed, whereas a propeller's efficiency drops off due to the compressibility effects at its tips. However, though the turbojet was initially used for jet transports it was rapidly superseded by turbofans of increasing bypass ratio. These gave not only improved fuel efficiency, but also reduced noise levels. The fuel crisis of the early 1970s led to a resurgence in the propeller in the form of single and contra-rotating, very thin, highly-swept multi-bladed propellers in the form of the unducted fan, which could operate at very high efficiency at cruise speeds up to Mach 0.8. General Electric and Pratt & Whitney both flew them in the 1980s, but interest waned with the subsequent falling-off in fuel prices and perceived passenger resistance to a return to the propeller.
(Ray Whitford)

cannot be reduced much below 1,000mph (1,610km/h) (1,200mph (1,930km/h) is more common), it suffers large propulsive efficiency losses at low flying speeds. The aircraft speed at which a turbojet starts to be acceptably efficient is above 400mph (645km/h), and even then the turbojet wastes 60 per cent of the fuel's energy. Secondly, because the less-dense air at high altitude, which at 33,000ft (10,050m) is about one-third that at sea level, produces less drag on the aircraft, and because the lower ambient temperatures at high altitude (23 per cent lower at 33,000ft) improve engine thermal efficiency, turbojets are increasingly efficient above 20,000ft (6,100m). Furthermore, the speed for maximum range, where VL/D is greatest, increases with altitude.

In its early days the turbojet was considered to be greedy with fuel. This is not strictly true as, according to pressure ratio and component efficiency, it did as well as the piston engine when relating fuel consumption to equivalent power. It was the propulsive efficiency that was low at contemporary flying speeds, and this showed up in high fuel consumption. The nearer the speed of the aircraft is to that of the jet velocity, the higher the propulsive efficiency and the better the fuel consumption, all other things being equal. So when an aircraft is flying at around Mach 0.8 the turbojet's propulsive efficiency is higher than that of a conventional propeller.

Fuel consumption

In the early 1950s it was realized that it would be some time before the turbojet's sfc would be less than twice the equivalent of improved turboprops or the latest compound piston engines. The figures are not directly comparable, but they pointed to the serious turbojet range and economy problem. However, if the ratio was compared at cruise altitude and speed, the fuel consumption of a turbojet was only around 1.4–1.5 times that of the most advanced turboprop then proposed, and only 1.25 times that of the best piston engine. When the advantages in terms of reduced weight and drag that accrue from the use of turbojet were factored into the equation, these ratios of fuel consumption began to look less daunting.

Gas turbines could operate adequately on a wide variety of fuels, and since fuel costs were going to be a large percentage of direct operating cost as the range of turbine transports grew, this factor could not be neglected. An important consideration in realistic studies of commercial operations was the validity of assumptions of fuel reserves. A tentative

	Comet 2	Britannia 100
First-class seating	44	63
Block speed (mph)	412	323
Still-air range at maximum payload (statute miles)	2,240	3,020
Fuel consumption (seat-mile/gal)	20	33

Turboprop versus turbojet. In summary, the Comet (turbojet) was very fast (in 1952) and reasonably economical, whereas the Britannia (turboprop) was reasonably fast and very economical.

suggestion was to assume a 45min weather hold at 20,000ft (6,100m) at destination, followed by a descent to attempted landing, then a climb-out to 20,000ft and a diversion of 300 miles (480km), followed by an additional hold of 45min and final descent. This appears to be a fairly drastic reserve requirement, but it was not incompatible with contemporary operational requirements under adverse weather conditions. There had been a tendency for design engineers to minimize the importance of operational fuel reserve requirements (the difference between zero-fuel and landing weights). These had, on many occasions, severely penalized payload in inclement weather operations.

Much additional information had to be obtained to establish the most efficient turbojet operating altitudes. It seemed a realistic conclusion, based on reasonable relations of wing loadings, speeds and powerplant characteristics, that an altitude range for efficient jet transport operations would lie between 30,000–35,000ft (9,100–10,600m). Much thought was given to commercial jet operations to 40,000ft (12,200m), but by 1953 this was reckoned to be a somewhat undesirable altitude, at the base of the stratosphere, with prevalent turbulence and high wind (jet stream) conditions. There was also the serious problem of the relatively high idling fuel consumption. Taxi strips and holding areas would need to be provided to permit high

Although the Bristol Aero Engines Proteus turboprop was troublesome in its early stages, it settled down after extensive development and operated successfully in the Bristol Britannia with an overhaul life of 7,500hr.
(Key Archive)

taxying speeds to conserve fuel and minimize taxying distances.

Doubts over jet transports

Following the Second World War it was apparent that a passenger could be carried across the Atlantic for a smaller expenditure of fuel by air than by ocean liner (though not in such comfort). The fuel was important, not only for its own cost, but for the other costs depending upon it: maintenance and engine power.

By the early 1950s the USA was lagging behind in the use of gas turbines for commercial aircraft, while Britain had the Viscount, Comet and Britannia, and Canada had the Avro Jetliner. These were still of little interest to US airlines or manufacturers, which dominated the international long-range transport arena with piston-engine DC-6s, Constellations, Stratocruisers and DC-7s. They were, for the most part, making a profit. Worldwide travel had become a reality, and engine and aircraft reliability had attained new heights. Passengers were happy with the comfort of flying at the higher altitudes delivered by the pressure cabin. Why gamble with something as new and untried as the turbojet-powered airliner, whose fuel consumption was so high that its range was shorter than that of the large piston-engine airliner?

It appeared that the low fuel efficiency and thrust/weight ratios would not permit ranges greater than New York–Chicago. Operating costs were going to be well above those of the piston engine aircraft of the time. The USA's manufacturers looked at the jet decision in two ways. Either in one leap they would leave the opposition looking archaic, or they would end up with a speculative aircraft that no airline had asked for, and which would entail changing every detail of operations from maintenance to airport handling, and would need safety certification according to rules that did not even exist.

That said, the new gas-turbine aircraft that had been designed in the UK and the engines that powered them were much nearer commercial service than any parallel projects in the USA. In the spring of 1950, after a trip to the UK to see the British aircraft, John Herlihy of United Airlines commented:

> The inescapable conclusion is that medium and large transport aircraft of the near future will be powered by gas turbines. The principal controversy is whether the propeller turbine or jet turbine is the more suitable and it is seen as a difficult question to resolve. All gas turbines bring to transport aircraft the advantages of low weight and drag, negligible oil consumption, higher operating speeds, and quiet vibrationless flight. I do not consider that our company can safely undertake the financial risk of buying any new additional types of conventional piston engine aircraft, inasmuch as they are already rendered technologically obsolescent by these turbine powered transports.

An airline's view

It was self-evident that the public would appreciate the much greater speeds and smoothness of operation. The prospect of changing from gasoline to a cheaper and less-volatile fuel, kerosene, was also enticing. Nevertheless, when United Airlines made a careful analysis of the possible use of the Avro Jetliner on its route structure it became apparent that, with a range less than that of the DC-6, the speed advantage

was not great enough to compensate for the number of refuelling stops it would have to make on a transcontinental trip. The DC-6 could make the trip in shorter elapsed time and with much less fuel. This conclusively demonstrated that practical and economically viable turbine-powered aircraft required as good or better range capabilities than current piston-engine types.

A successful jet airliner for United Airlines needed transcontinental non-stop capabilities with a reasonable payload. Using state-of-the-art aerodynamics, propulsion and structural design criteria, its Technical Development Group established specifications for a hypothetical aircraft. It was to have seating for seventy-five to eighty passengers, with a maximum payload of 22,000lb (9,900kg) and a maximum TOW of 200,000lb (90,800kg). This hypothetical aircraft was run over six simulated daily flights for a period of fifteen months. Dispatch procedures were as though the aircraft and flights were real. Cruise altitudes were 35,000–40,000ft (10,600m–12,160m) and speeds were 520–560mph (840–900km/h), depending on weight, altitude and temperature. The results of the first year's simulations were very encouraging regarding the practicality and reliability of jet transport operations. They demonstrated that the much higher speed of the aircraft made scheduling easier and more accurate. Additionally, it was shown that combinations of adverse circumstances that were not planned for (such as weather changes and traffic problems) were very rare. Again, the much shorter flight times were a distinct advantage in this regard. During the whole fifteen months there were only eight diversions. However, United's' economists and passenger service agents concluded that the airline did not need nor want aircraft larger than the DC-6 with a capacity of about fifty to fifty-five. It was essential to maintain frequency of service, and a larger aircraft would not be able to maintain profitable load factors.

US jet transports

Douglas was showing no signs of giving up on the propeller. Its latest design, the DC-7 (1953), was being sold convincingly as a state-of-the-art airliner to extend the company's hold on the airlines beyond the 700-plus DC-6s it would sell. The DC-7 had long range, was economical to operate, and Douglas was trusted. It might have propellers, but it represented the thing the airlines liked about Douglas: nothing fancy, everything well proven.

On the other hand, Boeing, with its Model 367-80, seemed to many to be 'pushing the future too hard'. Moreover, it had a serious disadvantage in trying to sell it to the airlines: the secret classification attached to its engine, the Pratt & Whitney J57. This was destined for the B-52, so little could be revealed of its performance. Furthermore, its overhaul and maintenance costs could not honestly be stated to be reasonable, any more than its reliability would be equal to that of piston engines. This was not helped by military turbojet experience, which was averaging only 500hr between engine removals. Engine reliability decreases with TET and speed but with some benefit to sfc, but military engines derated for commercial operations implied reduced thrust/weight. In addition there was the endemic problem of foreign object damage (FOD).

Inevitably, as for the previous generation of piston engines, there was the vexed question of reconciling the installed versus uninstalled engine performance (that achieved on the manufacturer's test-bed). However, the J57 was the only engine that had gained enough usage (in the military) to justify application to civil operations, and the engine manufacturer was confident that airline experience would be much better. Indeed, Pratt & Whitney agreed to guarantee that hourly overhaul and maintenance costs would not exceed a stipulated amount.

Boeing in 1954, and Douglas in 1955 (despite much initial reluctance), each offered a long-range jet transport, though both aircraft (the 707 and DC-8) turned out to have marginal range performance and economics, being originally powered by a civil version of the J57, the Pratt & Whitney JT3C. However, at the time these aircraft were able to offer competitive operating cost and range, firstly because they were much larger than existing piston-engine airliners, and secondly because the wing design and engine sizing were not compromised to allow operations from existing runways. The proclaimed advantages of these aircraft to operator and

passenger were such that airlines realized that they could not afford not to have them. In 1955 PanAm started the bonanza by placing launch orders for both types, and was followed by a stampede of the other leading operators. In the event United Airlines placed an order with Douglas for thirty DC-8s with a passenger capacity of 125. Pressure was then applied on major airport authorities throughout the world to begin programmes of runway extension and strengthening unforeseen a few years earlier.

Installation benefits of pods

Wherever possible it is desirable to use an identical engine installation across the board, and to have as much as possible of the engine assembly associated with the aircraft, rather than with the engine. A uniform engine build-up meant that engine changing could be accomplished in a minimum of time. With podded jet engines it was not necessary to change

Early jet airliners, such as the Boeing 707, were able to offer competitive operating costs and range, firstly because they were much larger than existing piston engine airliners and, secondly, because the wing design and engine sizing were not compromised to allow operations from existing runways. (Lufthansa)

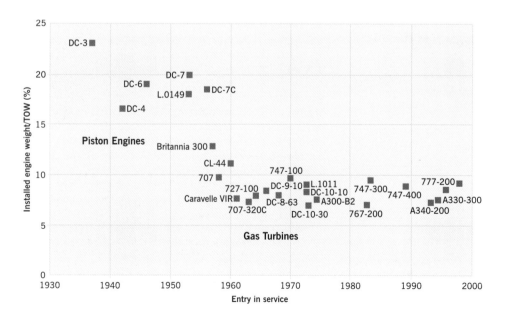

Propulsion weight as a fraction of take-off weight. One of the great virtues of the gas turbine is its high power or thrust/weight ratio. This figure, showing the ratio of installed engine weight (engine, fuel system, exhaust and thrust reversers) to the aircraft's maximum TOW, demonstrates the impact that the gas turbine's introduction had by cutting the ratio in half. (Ray Whitford)

a lot of aircraft parts, as was common with piston engines. The engine mounting had to be arranged in such a way that the engine could be hoisted into position and the attachments to the aircraft quickly made. It was equally desirable that systems associated with the engine, which might require switching as a result of an engine change, be readily accessible and easily replaced. A good example is the oil system, which, if it becomes contaminated, needs to be either cleaned or replaced at the time of an engine change. On some jet engines it was possible to mount the oil system entirely upon the engine. Although desirable from many maintenance standpoints, this was not always a good safety feature, as an appreciable quantity of oil could remain in the nacelle and present a fire hazard.

Podded engines offered the ultimate in accessory maintenance and change capabilities. It was not difficult to arrange the accessories in such a way that they did not seriously influence the drag of the pod, yet were easily accessible. This was valuable since, in most cases, the accessory choice and installation could be very versatile and changed during design without conflict with primary structure. Ease of access was achieved because of the lack of structure around the engine, which is secured at a minimum number of points, with the pylon reaching back to the wing spars.

Engine position

Finding the best place for engines involves virtually all the disciplines of aeronautical engineering. Airliners with piston engine/propellers were restricted to wing-mounted powerplants. With the advent of the turbojet the old problem of where and how to mount engines reappeared. Turbojet experience was beginning to show that there was less likelihood of catastrophic types of failures than with current

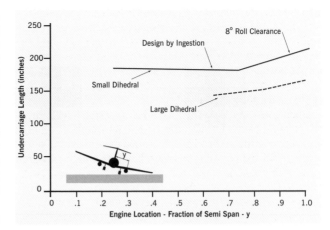

Variation of undercarriage length with spanwise engine location. Another adverse effect of an outboard engine location is the need for a longer undercarriage when the engine is located too far outboard, as illustrated. The length of the undercarriage has to increase to allow for minimum engine clearance at extreme aircraft attitudes at touchdown. This constraint becomes increasingly severe with increasing relative engine size, though it can be relieved by greater wing dihedral (as in the Boeing 777).
(Key – Pete West)

reciprocating engine/propeller combinations (piston or propeller breakaway). The problem of turbine disc failure was severe in the early days of jets. The tremendous amount of kinetic energy involved releases highly destructive forces. Even today there is no design requirement to contain a disintegrating disc fully. Boeing had consistently used podded engine arrangements for its jet bombers (B-47 Stratojet and B-52 Stratofortress) because they effectively insulated the aircraft from the most serious effects of engine break-up.

The turbojet offered several different mounting arrangements: submerged wing mounting, pod-mounted along the wing and aft-fuselage. Even in Britain in 1954 there was an awareness that engine diameter was going to grow and that podding was a more flexible means of accommodating that growth. The engine location influences

Over thirty years separate the design of the Douglas DC-8 and Airbus A340, but similarities endure. This figure, scaled for equal wingspans, shows some differences. For example, the A340 has lower wing sweep and its engine locations are different. Of course, the A340 shares a broadly common wing with the A330 twin, which, for reasons of engine-out minimum control speed, requires its two engines to be located more inboard that optimum for a four-engine design. In compensation, to gain structural inertia relief, the A340's outboard engines are about as far outboard as possible, consistent with flutter requirements, and required an increase in vertical fin area.
(Key – Pete West)

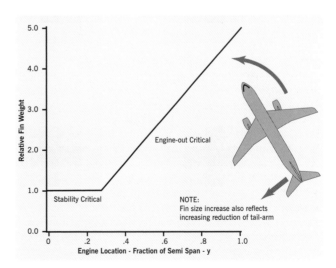

Effect of engine spanwise location on vertical fin weight. A factor that favours engine location outboard on the span of the wing is relief of wing bending moments, but this comes at a price. In particular, the size (and hence drag and weight) of the fin increases in magnitude steadily for spanwise positions greater than about 30 per cent, as shown. This is due to the unfavourable yawing moment that results from an outboard engine failure.
(Key – Pete West)

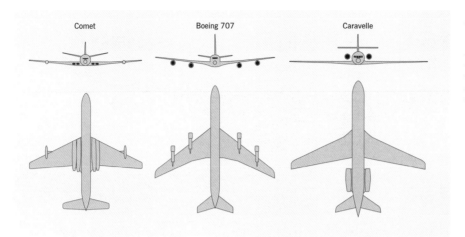

Comet   Boeing 707   Caravelle

Different concepts of engine location. By the mid-1950s three different jet-engine layouts had flown, of which only two are now in current production. Sud Aviation set the trend in rear-engine design (and spawned a whole variety of rear-engine airliners) with the world's first short-haul jet, the Caravelle, which entered service with Air France in May 1959. (Key – Pete West)

The advantages of wing-mounted engines, such as those of the DC-8, include high intake efficiency with least adverse effect at high AoA, fuel lines to engines do not pass through the fuselage, and more freedom for engine location (being less constrained by CG position than rear-engine layouts).
(Key – Alan Warnes)

the cruise drag decisively, exacting high performance and speed penalties from an installation that is less than very good. The structural weight of the aircraft is also affected in many ways by engine location. Putting the engines on the wing will reduce the weight of the wing, and the relief of airloads, flutter, and the effect upon stalling speed are all factors to be considered in the design of the installation. The placement of the engines also influences the location and size of the empennage and control surfaces. Large yawing moments can be produced in engine-out cases, affecting directional control requirements. Furthermore, the weight of the propulsion system is an important factor in locating the CG of the aircraft, which affects longitudinal stability and control requirements. Attention has to be given to jet-flow effects on flap and control surfaces to prevent unfavourable interactions. Airfield performance is particularly sensitive to engine location and size, because it influences the maximum lift coefficient of an aircraft as well as its L/D in the high-lift mode. Engine location also affects the engine noise heard on the ground, because it may be shielded by the airframe.

Aft-fuselage mounting

Both wing-mounted and fuselage-mounted engines have their good points as well as their problems. Careful analyses

are necessary to determine which of the two is better for a given operation, aircraft type and engine. At the time of the Vickers VC10's design evolution in the late-1950s, the current fashion in engine positioning was in pods beneath and forward of the wing (Boeing 707, Douglas DC-8 and Convair 880). However, the Sud-Aviation Caravelle was highly innovative, with engine pods attached to the rear fuselage, and had flown in 1955. It was with these configurations that the VC10's layout had to be compared.

Vickers was unhampered by any previous existing data or 'logical development of a current military type' constraint. The company's jet experience (specifically with its Valiant bomber) embraced 'clean wing' design without podded engines. The influence of the British short runway requirements, compared with the US military 'miles of concrete' designs, laid down certain guidelines. In the case of the rear-engine VC10 it was realized that its fundamental drawback was its wing's lack of inertia relief, which produced an inherently higher empty weight. This was a penalty that its high-lift aerodynamics and predicted field performance promised to overcome. In design for high Mach numbers there was little doubt that aerodynamicists would prefer to start with a clean pair of wings than a podded set, and would have greater confidence in the accuracy of their predictions. As far as Vickers was concerned, it was difficult

Although engines mounted on the wing will undoubtedly save wing weight because of the inertia relief they give, there is potential for a loss of lift. In designing its VC10 Vickers-Armstrongs was concerned with airfield performance, and the aircraft's clean, fully-flapped wing was reckoned to be a better route. This is the VC10's first flight, from the Vickers-Armstrongs airfield at Weybridge on 29 June 1962, after a take-off run of 2,150ft (655m).
(BAE Systems)

to find any aerodynamic aspect of a rear-engine layout that was more difficult than with wing-mounted engines.

At the time of committing to the VC10 there was considerable heart-searching to ensure that the right road was being taken, in view of the heavy outlay to which the airlines were already committing themselves for the first generation of large jet transports. Some of the arguments used for the different engine mountings are indicated in the table below. To Boeing, though, the Russians (Ilyushin Il-62) and British (VC10) were penalizing their aircraft designs by hanging the engines on the rear fuselage. In the case of the Russians it was thought they just did not have the wind tunnel data and the engineering sophistication to hang them from the wings. In the case of the British there was less excuse. In the event, the benefit of the VC10's improved take-off performance had largely been rendered redundant by the time the aircraft was ready for service: major airports had extended their runways to accommodate the big US jet transports.

The use of aft-mounted high-thrust engines implies that the aircraft will get heavier not only because the engines get

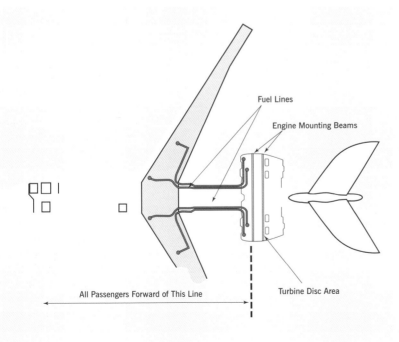

Layout of fuel system, engine mountings, turbine discs and passenger area for a rear-engine aircraft (Vickers VC10). Everyday perception of the rear-engine layout appeared to harbour major doubts over the supposed risk of interrelated mechanical engine damage. In the event of a turbine disc failure there appeared to be only a small chance of a fuel line being severed, or a passenger being struck. That said, other aircraft with detail differences have suffered such occurrences, together with hydraulic system failures.
(Key – Pete West)

Fuel Lines

Engine Mounting Beams

All Passengers Forward of This Line

Turbine Disc Area

Wing-mounted-engines	Aft-fuselage-mounted engines
Less acoustic damage to fuselage but more to wing	Reduced cabin noise and extent of fuselage exposure
Avoids the need for T-tail and potential superstall problems. No restriction on tail position, but fin needs to be large.	Much better asymmetric-thrust handling qualities yields a smaller fin. The necessary T-tail increases fin effective aspect ratio and tail arm length.
Separated engines less subject to sympathetic failure.	Less likelihood of engine damage in taxying accidents or wheels-up landings.
Avoids aft fuselage added structure and weight; allows for greater underfloor cargo hold behind the wing.	Uninhibited choice of wing dihedral and engine intake height could give shorter and lighter undercarriage.
More passengers for a given fuselage length	Little trim change due to thrust variation.
High intake efficiency with least adverse effect at high AoA.	Reduced risk of FOD, especially from reverse thrust.
Fuel lines to engines do not pass through fuselage.	Remoteness of engines from fuel tanks.
More freedom for engine position: good balance qualities and easier loadability arising from smaller CG travel.	Odd number of engines can be accommodated, but centreline engine intake and rudder size compromises necessary.

Wing- versus aft-fuselage engine position. In the late 1950s the argument with regard to engine placement was between wing and aft-fuselage mounting. However, the net effect of all the factors above cannot be determined without a detailed analysis of a particular configuration. Though it appears that the wing-mounting protagonists have won, and all large airliners have now adopted this configuration, production of designs with aft-mounted engines continues, especially for business-jet applications. This table should be read in conjunction with the Aerodynamics chapter.

heavier, but also because more area is needed at the back of the aircraft to provide additional stabilizing surfaces for the aft-moving CG and lengthening forebody. The forebody must be lengthened relative to the aft-body to balance the added weight at the back of the aircraft. As a consequence, the spread between the CG position of the full aircraft and empty aircraft increases. When the weight of the engines

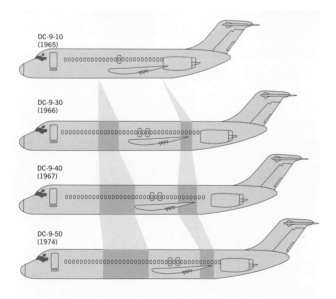

Stretching rear-engine aircraft. As engines get bulkier and heavier, configuration problems become more difficult. This is particularly true when the engines are located long distances from the aircraft's CG. The forebody must be lengthened relative to the aftbody to balance the added weight at the back, and, as a consequence, the spread between the CG at full payload and the CG of the empty aircraft increases rapidly. Nevertheless, Douglas found with its DC-9, even in its earliest days, that it could be stretched by 28 per cent (DC-9-10 to DC-9-50) to carry 54 per cent more passengers over increased range.
(Key – Pete West)

Noise considerations. In promoting its VC10's rear-engine configuration, Vickers-Armstrongs used the argument that not only was the aircraft's tailplane well clear of wing downwash (at low AoA), but that the noise damage to it was reduced compared with wing-mounted engines. That was until 'screech' (a noise component at 90 degrees to an exhaust jet full of shock waves) was discovered. That said, the proportion of airframe surface subject to engine noise, in particular the passenger cabin, is greatly reduced. Moreover, the forward-projected noise, directed towards the ground, from rear-mounted engines can be blanked by the wing.
(Key – Pete West)

becomes increasingly large, the efficacy of the aircraft with aft-mounted engines diminishes rapidly.

Noise considerations

In the immediate postwar years the public remained sympathetic to aviation. The industry had helped win the war, and there was still an element of prewar pioneering about its products. Up to that time, the noise limitation of engines was never taken into consideration during the design phase. Airliners flew in to and out of airports at whatever height the airlines and the airworthiness and airport authorities decided, with no thought for the population living beneath the flight paths. Then concern began to grow over airport noise levels. It had become evident that the problem was not strictly of noise, but had subjective elements: interruption of sleep, fear of crashes, annoying vibrations, radio and TV interference. These were tentatively addressed via operational constraints on direction and altitude during climb-out and approach. However, in the view of many in the industry certain factors worked on the manufacturers' behalf. Once people became accustomed to them, the high noise levels of jet engines would be of comparatively brief duration and only associated with take-off. Moreover, gas turbines needed less ground running.

But others thought that there could be no avoidance of industry's basic obligation to substantially reduce the annoyance of aircraft operations in the vicinity of airports. Without basic corrections, an increased frequency and intensity of noise had to be expected as movements multiplied and engines increased in size and thrust. In the early 1950s large piston engines were producing sound levels of 100 to 105dB and, with conventional propellers, of 115 to 120dB; with the introduction of the turbojet, levels of up to 125dB were anticipated.

When the pure-jet transport entered service in the late 1950s there was an almost immediate outcry from communities around affected airports against the new, and higher, noise levels. These were recognized to be quite unacceptable, and beyond what could be reduced simply by operational restrictions. In consequence, limits on take-off noise based on the then average levels from existing propeller aircraft were imposed at a number of major airports. Air movements, previously numbered in hundreds, began to reach thousands per year.

In 1963 a UK government committee under Sir Alan Wilson stated that, to maintain the current level of noise exposure, a fall in noise level of 10dB from individual aircraft was necessary as air movements increased. This implied that airport limits should be reduced accordingly. The industry had completely misjudged the strength of the tide of protest, amid a prevailing pessimism among scientists and engineers about providing a solution, something which required a re-examination of the basic principles of sound generation. The work of Lighthill, Lilley and Ffowcs-Williams in the UK, and others elsewhere, did much to

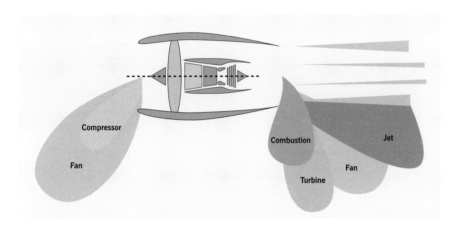

Sources of engine noise, showing their directivity and relative amplitudes. The main sources are the propulsive jet, the compressor, turbine and combustion. Because of shockwaves forming at the fan blades' leading edges at supersonic tip speeds (occurring mainly on take-off), the fan is a dominant noise source in high-BPR engines.
(Key – Pete West/Ray Whitford)

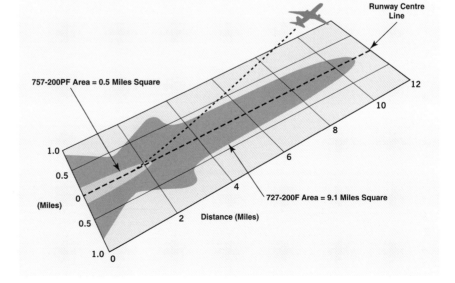

Noise footprints. Concern over airport noise is especially important for cargo airlines, which would ideally like to operate around the clock. This figure shows the comparative 90dB take-off noise footprints of the Boeing 727-200F (Freighter) and 757-200PF (Package Freighter) operated by United Parcel Service (UPS) at its Louisville, Kentucky, hub. The much quieter 757-200PF was a major factor in the UPS decision to be the first operator to order the aircraft.
(Key – Pete West/Ray Whitford)

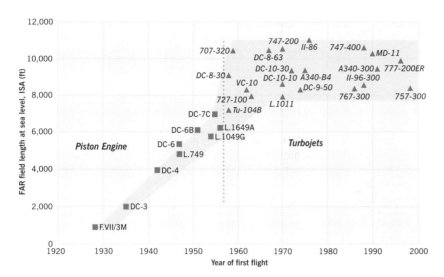

Take-off distance trend. This shows the increased take-off length required as piston engine aircraft grew in weight. By the mid-1950s required field lengths had grown to 7,000ft (2,100m). For the late-1950s introduction of the early big jets, such as the Boeing 707 and Douglas DC-8, runways were extended to around 12,000ft (3,650m), to cope with wing loadings increased by 20 per cent, combined with the poorly lifting swept wing. Note that current airliners have to operate from runway lengths built for the early jets.
(Ray Whitford)

The results of a 1993 NASA study showed that thrust reversers are not cost-effective, in that they do not offset brake-wear cost (thrust reversers cost around $150,000/aircraft and are complicated and heavy). That said, pilots like the additional security, especially for wet/icy runways, and operators also appreciate the flexibility due to shorter taxi times. Here an Airbus A340 has its four blocker-door-type thrust reversers in operation with the nosewheel off the ground. On this aircraft a thrust reverser failure is automatically countered by cancelling the symmetrically opposite reverser.
(Key – Duncan Cubitt)

explain the origin of jet noise, its propagation and control. Studies showed that the sound pressure level generated by a jet is proportional to a high power of the jet velocity V (V^4 and V^8, depending on the jet's Mach number). The first mechanical means of reducing noise was by the use of silencers that simply entrained more air into the exhaust to lower the jet velocity. By the 1970s, environmental considerations had become a fundamental part of the equation, whether in regard to a new aircraft or airport.

Thrust reversers

The arrival of the jet transport resulted in a mix of jet- and propeller-driven aircraft using the same airport. The maximum traffic frequency was dependent upon the aircraft having the highest required approach speed and the one having the lowest climb-out speed. Since the jet transport would presumably satisfy climb performance, it was therefore necessary to ensure it had a satisfactorily low approach speed. It was predicted that, by 1960, the required take-off distance would be nudging 8,500ft (2,600m), a maximum of 7,000ft (2,130m) for domestic operators and not more than 10,000ft (3,050m) for any long-range aircraft, bearing in mind that the cost of airport real estate was becoming prohibitive. Practical limitations on runway length were also an effective means of impressing on the aircraft designer the necessity of limiting approach and landing speeds.

For a low-drag jet airliner without thrust reversal, safe operations depended on an efficient landing technique, good runway characteristics and aircraft braking. Spoiler effectiveness decreases rapidly with loss of speed, and could not be regarded in any sense as the equivalent of reverse thrust for landing safely under all conditions. This had been seen from operations with the Boeing B-47, which required a drag 'chute. Reversible-pitch propellers had been introduced in the USA in 1951, shortly before Boeing began serious studies of jet transports. They offered greater deceleration than brakes alone (without an anti-skid device), especially on icy runways. This was not possible with a turbojet; indeed it was only with difficulty that were they applied to turboprops.

The mandatory factors affecting the design of thrust reversers are conflicting: the elimination of difficulties that had been met with reversible-pitch propellers (inadvertent thrust reversal following electrical failure or pilot error), design for maximum reliability, the incorporation of fail-safe characteristics, and the fact that no reduction in engine life nor adverse engine behaviour could be tolerated. Some weight penalty had to be accepted.

Compressor types

Centrifugal compressor

All but one of the British Second World War turbojets used the centrifugal compressor. This was the type that both

Although centrifugal compressors, such as the one illustrated here, were simpler and stronger than axial types, they had limited growth potential; hence the universal use of axial-flow engines on airliners today. (Rolls-Royce)

Whittle and von Ohain had chosen for its simplicity and ease of development, aided by previous supercharger experience. It was not very efficient, but was rugged and much less expensive than the axial-flow type, and the simple turbojets' performance was little affected by the type of compressor used, anyway. De Havilland stuck to the centrifugal type after the war, developing the Ghost of 5,000lb (22kN) thrust from their wartime design, the Goblin, and using it in their own fighters. As the de Havilland Comet 1 went into service in 1952 with Ghost engines of 4,450lb (20kN), so battle was joined on the relative merits of the centrifugal versus the axial compressor.

Axial compressor

Most German engines had used the axial-flow compressor that subsequently became standard for turbojets. This consists of spool assemblies carrying aerofoil blade sections mounted in a casing carrying stator vanes. The compressor is a multi-stage unit and, to begin with, the amount of work (temperature rise) per stage was small, about 10°C (18°F) with a pressure ratio of approximately 0.2:1 per stage. A stage is one row of rotating blades followed by stator blades. An additional row of fixed inlet vanes was provided to guide the air into the first row of rotating blades. There is a gradual reduction of the annulus area between the rotor shaft and the stator casing; this is to maintain a constant axial velocity of the air as its density is increased throughout the length of the compressor. The pressure rise results from the diffusion process in the rotor and stator blade passages.

Rolls-Royce continued to develop turbojets with the centrifugal compressor until the end of the war, when it was ready to produce the Nene of 5,000lb (22kN) thrust. The influence of A.A. Griffith, who had joined the company from RAE Farnborough in 1939 to work on a turboprop with an axial-flow compressor, was not manifest until Rolls-Royce started to design its AJ.65 (axial jet 6,500lb thrust) in 1944. Compared with the centrifugal compressor, the axial type bristled with difficulties, and there were many aerodynamic and mechanical problems to be solved before the axial compressor could be regarded as a sound substitute for the well-proven and rugged centrifugal type. The axial's blades

were fragile and vulnerable to FOD. The problem was compounded by the proponents of the axial claiming not only 8–10 per cent higher efficiency over a wider pressure range, but also a higher pressure ratio. The centrifugal compressor suffered high losses associated with the tortuous flow path and higher tip speeds. However, the axial was smaller in diameter and could have its capacity more easily increased by adding more compressor stages, whereas the centrifugal needed its diameter increased.

Whittle's centrifugal engine had been designed for a pressure ratio of about 4:1 at about 80 per cent efficiency. For the AJ.65 (later named the Avon), Griffith was postulating (on paper) a pressure ratio of more than 7:1, requiring twelve compressor stages (with 20°C/stage) driven by a single-stage turbine. The advantages of the higher pressure ratio and the axial's higher (85 per cent) efficiency made the goal worth achieving, especially in terms of fuel consumption. However, as Sir Stanley Hooker put it: 'We leaped into the deep end and landed in such trouble that it took about seven years before the AJ.65 got a clean bill of health'. It had taken only seven months in the case of the centrifugal Nene.

When taking over Power Jets' gas turbines in 1943, Lord Hives of Rolls-Royce said to Whittle: 'Just leave it to us, we will soon design the simplicity out of it'. That said, compared with Whittle's baseline sfc of 1.05lb/hr/lb, the AJ.65 reached 0.84lb/hr/lb. It was reckoned that increasing the pressure ratio to 12:1 should give a 12 per cent reduction in sfc. At the time this was thought to require seventeen stages of compression, though it became apparent from work at Britain's National Gas Turbine Establishment (NGTE) that a temperature rise per stage of 30°C (54°F) was possible. This could reduce the number of stages by a third, meaning that the AJ.65 would need only eight stages (driven by a two-stage turbine) for a pressure ratio of 6.5:1, or twelve stages for a pressure ratio of 12:1. This opened up new possibilities for increased thrust/weight. The Avon with 6,500lb thrust was introduced in 1949 and was eventually developed to its 532 version to produce 12,600lb (56kN) for the Sud-Aviation Caravelle VI-R of 1960.

Off-design operations

Consequently, the transition to the axial compressor was inevitable. Unfortunately, one of its characteristics is a sharply-tuned surge line, which made it extremely difficult to operate at part loads and low speeds while maintaining high efficiency at the design point. In the aerodynamic design of an axial compressor, the fundamental dimensions are fixed by the pressure ratio, with each stage designed to do an equal amount of work on the air in compressing it. As the air passes from one stage to the next, the height of each blade row is made smaller than the preceding one, in order that the velocity along the compressor remains constant. This meant (for the Avon) that the outlet area was only about 25 per cent of the inlet area, an arrangement that was satisfactory when the engine was running at full speed at its design pressure ratio. However, at lower speeds, during starting and acceleration, the pressure ratio was very small and the inlet and outlet areas were totally mismatched. For example, when starting, with the pressure ratio only about 2:1, the outlet area should have been 80 per cent that of inlet area (because of the reduced air density), so the flow was extremely restricted and could not easily leave the compressor exit. This caused the blades at the front to stall, vibrate and, not infrequently, snap off. At low engine speeds, conditions could exist where, even if combustion could be initiated, there was insufficient power in the turbine to accelerate the engine. It was vital to have rapid and dependable acceleration in case of a required go-around on landing. This had to be assured without invoking surge, and without having to maintain too high a percentage of rpm and thrust on approach with its aggravation of the landing deceleration problem.

Multi-shaft engines

Thus the axial compressor was found to require airflow control. Many solutions were considered, but only three were really practical. They were as follows:

1. The first used variable inlet guide vanes and stators (first patented by Rolls-Royce in 1949), up to seven stages in some instances, to permit stall-free starting and acceleration. The vanes/stators then automatically swivelled to their design position as the engine speed rose.
2. The second solution used interstage bleeding from the compressor, again permitting the front stages to become

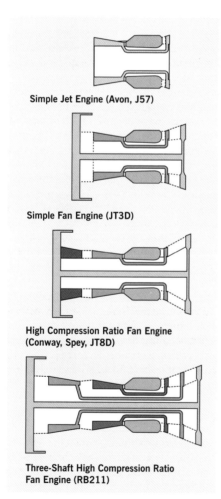

Simple Jet Engine (Avon, J57)

Simple Fan Engine (JT3D)

High Compression Ratio Fan Engine (Conway, Spey, JT8D)

Three-Shaft High Compression Ratio Fan Engine (RB211)

Overall layout of jet engines. Broadly speaking, the four original types of civil jet engine were designed to have pressure ratios in the region of 6:1, 14:1, 20:1 and 27:1 respectively, with corresponding bypass ratios of 0, 1.5, 3 and 5. The last type, initially represented by the Rolls-Royce RB.211, differs from US engines of similar performance (Pratt & Whitney JT9D and General Electric CF6) in that they retained the two shafts with some compressor stages on the LP shaft behind the fan. The advantages of separate IP and HP shafts, as used by Rolls-Royce, appear mainly during off-design operation, including starting.
(Key – Pete West)

unstalled. As the engine accelerated, so the bleed valves closed.
3. A better method, though mechanically more difficult, was to divide the compressor into low-pressure (LP) and high-pressure (HP) sections, each driven by its own turbine via concentric shafts. Having two shafts allows the speed of each to vary to meet the needs of its compressor, thereby reducing the mismatch of the front stages of each. This gave two moderately loaded compressors, which it was possible to handle and, given proper design, a very flexible arrangement was achieved. Twin-shaft compressors combined with variable stators entered service in the mid-1950s (Bristol Olympus and Pratt & Whitney J57 and J75).

The use of multiple shafts has an additional benefit for design point operation. The LP compressor must not operate with a blade speed that is too high in relation to the local speed of sound, lest the efficiency falls sharply due to shock-wave formation. The temperature rises (causing the local speed of sound to rise also) so that the blade speed of the HP compressor can be significantly higher without large losses. With a compressor on a single shaft there is a severe limit to how much the blade speed can be increased, because this can only be done by increasing the mean radius. By splitting the compressor into two it is possible to allow the HP compressor to rotate much faster.

Combustion chambers

The gas turbine is an enormous swallower of air. A turbojet of about 20,000lb (90kN) thrust takes in over 8 tons of air per minute, which is equivalent to a 60ft (18m) cube of air at sea level. It takes a given air molecule about 0.02sec to pass completely through an engine. Combustors are required to burn large quantities of fuel with the huge volumes of air supplied by the compressor, then release the heat so that the air is expanded and accelerated. A relatively small proportion of air is used for burning (to heat up the rest), the total then being ejected at high velocity (via the turbines) to give jet propulsion. Combustion has to be maintained in a stream of air moving with as low a velocity as possible, around 15ft/sec (4.6m/sec), so that the flame will remain alight throughout all engine operations. Burning has to be accomplished with minimum pressure loss and maximum heat release in the limited space available. Furthermore, the fuel and the air have to be intimately mixed, since fuel droplets burn from the surface. Both time and oxygen are required to consume them. While the stoichiometric (chemically correct) mixture strength in the primary combustion zone of a gas turbine is about the same as that of a piston engine (fifteen parts by weight of air to one of fuel), the overall air/fuel ratio going through the engine is somewhere between 150–200:1. If the turbine blades are not to suffer local overheating, a stream of heated gas of known temperature distribution is needed.

In early combustion chambers fuel was fed under high pressure to atomizing jets which sprayed a cloud of fine droplets into the burning region. For many years, palliatives were sought for its most severe disadvantage: it was not possible to maintain the high pressure needed for proper atomization, except at maximum fuel flow. Thus at take-off, where the fuel flow is 100 per cent, the fuel pressure may be 1,000lb/in^2 (6.9MN/m^2), giving good atomization; but at idling the fuel flow may be only 10 per cent and the pressure only 10psi. This low pressure results in the burner emitting a

Powered by General Electric CJ-805 turbojets, a Convair CV880-22 of Seagreen Jet Transport makes a smoky take-off from Antigua in October 1982. Excess carbon in the exhaust gases was a by-product of increasing the pressure ratio of early turbojets.

spluttering jet containing small, medium and large droplets, each of which need different periods of time to burn. This can wreck the desired fuel distribution and fuel/air ratio, lay down carbon deposits causing turbine blade erosion and a smoky jet, and promote flameout when the pilot opens or closes the throttle.

Engine pressure ratios were quite low (about 8:1) at the time that most developments for good combustor design were taking place, but as they increased and the pressure in the combustor rose, trouble began to be experienced with carbon in the exhaust gases. From a performance point of view this had little significance, and probably explains why smoky exhausts were tolerated for some time, though environmental concerns were beginning to grow. As the numbers and utilization of jet aircraft increased, so the time at idling speed rose and unburned fuel and toxic gas emissions, particularly in the environs of big airports, became a growing nuisance. Idling combustion efficiency was never very good, and in the early days of gas turbines figures as low as 80 per cent were not unknown. Up to pressure ratios of 10–12 the vaporizer combustion system was much less prone to smoke than atomizer configurations, and in some cases it was thought that this was an inherent characteristic of vaporizers. The smoke problem was mitigated, if not eliminated, by careful adjustment of local air/fuel ratios in the primary and immediate secondary zones and attention to mixing and combustion processes.

Combustion chamber types

Historically, the combustor has always been one of the hardest components to get right, and problems with combustion held up the Whittle engine for many months. Von Ohain avoided this in his engine tests (flown in 1939) by burning hydrogen instead of kerosene. The original multi-chamber Whittle design had reverse flow to slow the flow leaving the compressor, to ensure flame stabilization, but it suffered a large pressure drop, one of the most difficult problems with early engines. Later a 'cannular' system was evolved, though current engines all use completely annular combustors that make the most of a very restricted space, give better mixing and are more reliable. From the beginning, techniques of wall cooling progressed in parallel with increases in TET, with the two main objectives of improving the uniformity of cooling and using less air. Air was becoming a valuable and diminishing commodity, being increasingly required for combustion, flame-tube and turbine cooling, and for dilution of the gas that was too hot, at a flame temperature of 2,000°C (3,630°F), to enter the turbine.

Fuel

One of the advantages that Whittle foresaw for the gas turbine was the ability to use heavier, less-volatile and therefore safer fuels than gasoline. That said, it was recognized that design of the combustion chamber had far greater influence on performance than relatively minor variations in the fuel used. The first specification for aviation turbine fuel was issued in 1950, based largely on maximum availability with satisfactory characteristics, that might or might not produce a satisfactory fuel at minimum cost. It called for good-quality kerosene already in production, with a freezing point of −40°C (−40°F). This freezing point was accepted with some reservations, but it was regarded as the best compromise between aircraft requirements and availability. However, military aircraft flying at 40,000ft (12,200m) were not infrequently encountering temperatures of −60°C (−76°F), so a freezing point of −40°C for the fuel was considered marginal. For military aviation it was recognized that a wartime demand for turbine fuel would exceed the availability of suitable kerosene, so a 'wide-cut distillate' type of fuel was selected. Such a fuel could be readily made from practically any feed stock at almost any refinery in the world. The American JP-4 fuel (cheaper than kerosene) was typical of the specification laid down in 1954, but its use by some airlines in the 1960s provoked vociferous arguments over safety.

Turbines

Turbines are used to drive the compressor and accessories. The power is extracted from the hot gas released from the combustor as it expands to a lower pressure and temperature through the turbine. The design of the nozzle guide vanes and turbine-blade passages are broadly based on aerodynamic considerations. The aerofoil shapes used are such that the turbine functions partly under impulse and partly under reaction conditions. The blades experience an impulse force due to the initial impact of the gas on the blades, and a reaction force resulting from the expansion and acceleration of the gas through the blade passages. To produce the required torque, a turbine may consist of several stages, each stage being one row of turbine blades and a row of stationary nozzle guide vanes. The number of stages depends on the number of shafts and the relationship between power required from the gas, the rotational speed at which it must be produced and the diameter of the turbine permitted. For a given shaft output the mean blade speed has a considerable effect on the maximum efficiency, since relative velocities are important for moving blades, frictional losses being proportional to velocity squared.

The case for high TET

Low sfc requires high thermal and propulsive efficiencies. Thermal efficiency is largely independent of engine low-pressure performance, but is very dependent on the difference between the maximum (TET) and minimum (intake) temperatures. Although the higher the TET the better, at a constant pressure ratio increasing the TET increases thrust, but at the expense of sfc, due to reduced propulsive efficiency arising from the higher jet velocities. Fuel consumption can be reduced by an increase in pressure ratio, but this means an increase in compressor length. Since the compressor is driven by the turbine, this also involves an increased expansion ratio and hence more turbine length, both of which increase engine weight. The initial tendency was for low stage loading by increasing the number of stages. The use of multiple stages of turbine expansion to obtain additional power or improve efficiency went hand-in-hand with increase in pressure ratio. Consequently, there was a significant fall in fuel consumption up to high pressure ratios (particularly at higher TETs), though beyond a certain value this was offset by a decrease in thrust/weight. There will be an optimum value of pressure ratio, depending on aircraft range. For short-haul operations the two parameters are of roughly equal importance; for long-haul, sfc is about four times more important than thrust/weight.

Turbines operate in an extremely hostile environment, with high temperatures and tip speeds (up to 1,300ft/sec (400m/s)) that give very high stresses. The first Whittle engine ran at a maximum TET of about 750°C (1,380°F). Today's maximum (take-off) TETs are around 1,450°C (2,640°F) with a flow velocity of 2,000ft/sec (600m/s). There was always a case for operating at increased TET, but it has to be consistent with the life of the engine. The higher the TET, the more often parts need replacing. This conflicts with the needs of operators, who require reliability and long times between overhaul. This could only be obtained by significant developments in the field of metallurgy to produce the best possible heat-resisting materials and the maximum economic degree of turbine blade cooling.

Engine materials

While all turbine components have to operate at elevated temperatures, bearings and discs are simpler to cool, are amenable to accurate stressing and do not cause an undue amount of trouble, though failures have occurred. The real problem lies with the blading, both fixed and rotating. Blades are subjected to gas flows where neither velocity nor temperature is uniform. This can cause buckling, cracking and burning of nozzles, and, on occasion, creep failures of rotating blades. They are also subject to fatigue from a multiplicity of exciting sources that can cause resonance, sometimes blade-only or occasionally, if one is unlucky, a coupled resonance between blade and disc.

In Britain the original specification for a turbine blade material called for an alloy that would have not more than 0.1 per cent extension in 300hr under a stress of 3tons/in² (46MN/m²) at a temperature of 750°C (1,380°F). This is the thermal creep property of a material, similar to the everyday (without the temperature effect) nature of washing lines that stretch with time, and the reason why violin strings should not be left taut. This characteristic had to be combined with the highest possible resistance to oxidation and other corrosive attack, while simultaneously being sufficiently workable to enable forgings to be produced without excessive difficulty. Two materials met this specification, Rex 78, a nickel-chrome-molybdenum alloy produced by Firth Vickers (used for nozzle blades) and Nimonic 80, a nickel-chrome alloy made by Mond Nickel (used for turbine blades). Although nozzles are not subject to centrifugal loading, they operate at very high temperatures and, because their configuration is simple, are fabricated as hollow blades, either sheet metal or cast, and air-cooled.

Over the years the properties of turbine blade alloys were improved. With this, however, came manufacturing problems, as materials that will not deform or break at high temperatures will be correspondingly difficult to forge, as they were in the mid-1950s. To forge a blade it was squeezed, while almost white hot, between two dies having the correct shape to form the blade with a head (for the tip shroud) and root. The blade was then machined to a smooth finish all over, to precisely the correct size and profile.

Up to around 1960, uncooled turbine blades forged from Nimonic materials coped with temperatures of around 1,000°C (1,830°F). The manufacture of blades from castings (having better creep properties) was realized to be inevitable, at least by Bristol Aero Engines. Although difficulties arose owing to lack of stability in the cores and erratic grain size, these problems were overcome. The Bristol company abandoned forged blades soon after 1960, casting its blades instead by the 500-year-old lost-wax process. Casting

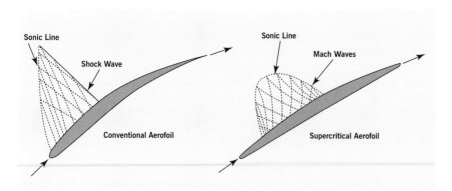

Fan blade evolution. A fan blade of conventional aerofoil shape with flow acceleration to supersonic speeds and a consequent shock wave is shown on the left. A big advance occurred in fan design with the incorporation of supercritical aerofoil technology (to achieve shock-free flow), which gave lower losses over a wider range of blade AoA at all subsonic Mach numbers. This, together with blade sweep, has enhanced fan performance.
(Key – Pete West)

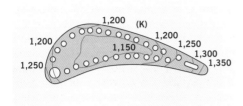

Typical temperature contours for a cast air-cooled turbine blade of the late 1960s. Of note are the high temperatures at both the leading edge *and* trailing edge, which has to be thicker and blunter than aerodynamically desirable. Up to 1960, uncooled turbine blades forged in Nimonic alloys were adequate to cope with temperatures up to 1,250K. Thereafter, air-cooled blades were necessary, demonstrating in this case that the core of the blade could be kept to 1,150K. (Note: 1,250K is 977°C)
(Key – Pete West)

Pressure and temperature are increased steadily as air passes through the compressor stages with a reduction in annulus area. This is an eight-stage intermediate pressure (IP) compressor for a three-shaft Rolls-Royce Trent. (Rolls-Royce)

enabled the use of materials that were intrinsically stronger than Nimonic alloys but too hard to be forged or machined. The blades were cast to the final dimensions, with a mirror finish, with no machining apart from precision grinding at the root. Cast blades proved to be much stronger and, despite their brittleness and susceptibility to thermal stresses, they were much better.

Consequently, cast blades were used for many (but not Rolls-Royce) high-temperature (HP) stages, with complex cooling configurations (*see* next section), with the cooler LP turbine stages remaining as forgings. Cast materials of an alloy such as PK24 had the advantage of being able to withstand about 35°C (60°F) more than forged Nimonic material for the same thermal creep life. The disadvantage was that due to its crystalline structure, the cast material had only about 60 per cent of the fatigue strength of the forged. Both creep and fatigue strengths are vital properties for turbine blade materials. It was subsequently found that a better cast blade could be made by arranging for the crystals to form in the direction of their length: directionally-solidified blades. A still better blade was obtained by growing each blade as a single crystal, which is the norm for today's HP blades.

During development of the Rolls-Royce Trent 800 three-spool engine it became clear that the intermediate-pressure (IP) turbine blade material CMSX-4, used in the lower-rated Trent 700, would have inadequate creep life at the elevated temperature needed for increased thrust. The alternatives were either to introduce cooling (*see* next section), as for the HP turbine blades, with the consequent loss of performance and increased complexity, or to develop a more advanced alloy. The latter route was chosen and a new single-crystal alloy, RR 3000, was developed from CMSX-4 (to run about 35°C hotter than its predecessor) in half the time of previous alloy development. This may seem a small increase in temperature, but it allowed the new blades to remain uncooled, offering significant benefits in terms of mechanical design, engine performance and cost. This enabled the Trent 800 to be certificated at 90,000lb (400kN) thrust instead of the planned 84,000lb (373kN).

It has been estimated that a further 200°C (360°F) increase in TET will be required over the next twenty years to satisfy airlines' demand for improved performance. Although a fourth-generation single-crystal alloy may be possible, the nickel-based alloys are close to their temperature limits. Much of the future increase is likely to come from thermal

barrier coatings (TBC), ceramic coatings with low thermal conductivity that effectively insulate the metal from the hot gas stream. A critical issue for these coatings, however, is the problem of loss of coating through spalling, because of the difference in thermal expansion coefficients. This requires strain-tolerant TBCs, to accommodate the size mismatch between the metal and coating during thermal cycling, using fibrous grain structures. Further increases in temperature are likely to require the use of ceramic matrix composites (CMC), which offer significant weight savings due to their lower density.

Cooling

Early in the 1950s the NGTE initiated a programme to examine the feasibility of cooling turbine blades and to find the maximum continuous operating temperatures that might be used with existing materials. It was concluded that the optimum cooling configuration used a multiplicity of small holes within the blades. Turbine blades and discs are cooled by 'cold' air at around 530°C (985°F) from the compressor being blown along the holes. In 1955 the introduction of air-cooled blades allowed a jump in TET of 100°C (180°F). Rolls-Royce was one of the pioneers of air-cooled turbine blades, and in 1958 some Avon engines were operating at TETs of around 1,030°C (1,890°F), almost 250°C (450°F) hotter than the Avons that first went into service. All Rolls-Royce blades were forged in a Nimonic high-nickel alloy, able to retain adequate strength at about 900°C (1,650°F). In the company's Conway bypass engine, designed in the mid-1950s, the peak gas temperature was about 1,100°C (2,010°F), so the cooling had to keep the blades 200°C (360°F) cooler than the surrounding gas.

A major problem was to obtain a hole pattern through the blade contour and extending into the root, where it could pick up cooling air, and which would be consistent in form and reliable in manufacture. Techniques such as spark erosion and electrochemical machining did not exist. Manufacture therefore followed two lines:

1. Forging the blades and then drilling holes radially down them. Just where these had to be was found by trial and error,

so that after the rough blank was forged the holes were in the correct position. This process, however, was a nightmare, because microscopic variations between cooling holes in successive blades meant that the cooling would be uneven. An alternative was to forge the blades in two halves and then braze the halves together after machining the air passages.

2. Casting the blades with integral cooling passages by the lost-wax process. An additional benefit of the move to casting was that the process enabled more complex cooling passages (with roughness elements to encourage heat transfer to the cooling air) to be incorporated.

A further development was to use small holes or slits in the blade surface to provide film cooling. This was used initially for the lower surface of the blade, then later for the upper surface. To achieve greater cooling and avoid corrosion requires a continuous film over the whole surface: transpiration cooling. Instead of producing a film through rows of holes or slits, cooling air was led to the upper surface through a porous matrix.

The choice of TET is a balance between engine performance and turbine life. There is also a balance between TET and cooling-air requirements, since extraction of cooling air from the compressor reduces the efficiency and thrust of an engine. Engine component efficiencies constitute a major problem, with blade-tip leakage and cooling losses reducing individual stage efficiencies. Even using high contemporary (1960) efficiencies (compressor 90 per cent, combustor 90 per cent and 90 per cent for the turbine), the overall losses amounted to a 32 per cent reduction of thrust and a 21 per cent increase in specific fuel consumption. A 2 per cent increase in the efficiency of all components was equivalent to an increase in TET of 250°C (450°F). The problem was how to achieve the maximum cooling effect, to make use of the increase in power, without incurring too high a penalty through an uneconomic quantity of cooling air.

Turbine cooling is an expensive technology to develop. Because raising the allowable temperature can have such a big effect on engine performance (analogous to the sodium-cooled valves of the 1920s piston engines), cooling technology is one of the areas where competition is most intense. The HP turbine blades in the Bristol Olympus 593 for Concorde operated at 1,250°C (2,280°F), much hotter than contemporary Rolls-Royce production engines. Rolls-Royce was aware of the Bristol experience, and planned to

switch eventually, but designed its RB.211 (for the Lockheed L.1011) to use forged and machined Nimonic HP turbine blades to withstand 1,250°C, roughly 150°C (270°F) above what was then current state-of-the-art. For blades limited by creep, their life (at a given level of cooling and material) is halved for every 10–20°C (18–36°F) rise in temperature of the metal, so the RB.211 blades were prone to early failure. This was also a severe problem for early Pratt & Whitney JT9Ds. It was predicted (correctly) in 1970 that by 1980 TETs would have reached 1,350°C (2,460°F), and by 1990 they had reached 1,450°C (2,640°F).

Gas turbine configuration

Single-shaft turbojet
The single-shaft jet engine, although simple, light and cheap, is limited in pressure ratio and hence thermal efficiency. It has low propulsive efficiency because of its high jet velocity. For the same reason it is noisy.

Two-shaft turbojet
A variation of the simple turbojet is the higher-pressure-ratio two-shaft turbojet, in which the compressor is split into two separate parts, each driven by its own turbine. The first of the two-shaft turbojets were the 10,000lb (44.5kN) thrust Bristol Olympus (Avro Vulcan), Pratt & Whitney J57 (Boeing B-52) and 13,000lb (57.8kN) civil JT3C (Boeing 707 and Douglas DC-8).

Low-BPR turbofan
This is a two-shaft engine with the LP compressor driven by the LP turbine and the core (HP) compressor driven by the HP turbine. The flow through a turbofan is divided into a bypass stream and a core stream. BPR is the ratio of bypass mass flow of the cold jet from the LP compressor (or fan) to the mass flow passing through the core. In low- and medium-BPR turbofans (Rolls-Royce Conway and Spey, Pratt & Whitney JT3D and JT8D), all the air entering the inlet passes through the LP compressor. A selected percentage of that air then flows through the core (HP compressor, the combustor and the turbines). In so doing, some of the intake air supercharges the HP compressor and hence the core. The higher the pressure ratio and TET, the greater the thermal efficiency, provided the efficiency of each compressor and turbine can be maintained. On the other hand, the higher the thermal efficiency, the

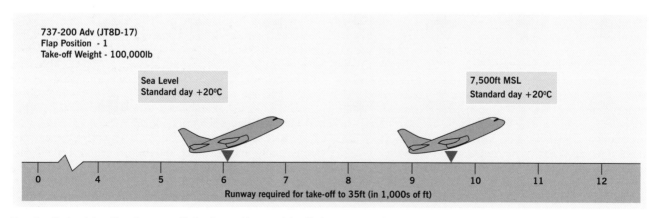

Density effect on take-off performance. All aircraft are subject to weight-altitude-temperature (WAT) limitations, and suffer take-off performance loss when operating at altitudes other than sea level. This figure illustrates the effect of altitude on combined aerodynamic and engine attainment for a Boeing 737-200Adv, where the field length is increased by 60 per cent when operating from an airfield at 7,500ft (2,300m) above mean sea level. (Key – Pete West)

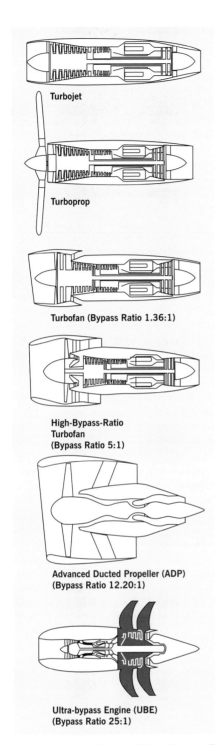

Turbojet

Turboprop

Turbofan (Bypass Ratio 1.36:1)

High-Bypass-Ratio
Turbofan
(Bypass Ratio 5:1)

Advanced Ducted Propeller (ADP)
(Bypass Ratio 12.20:1)

Ultra-bypass Engine (UBE)
(Bypass Ratio 25:1)

The broad range of aero engines developed for airliner use. The so-called ultra-bypass engine (UBE) was more commonly known as the unducted fan (UDF), developed and test flown in the 1980s as a highly fuel-efficient powerplant to counter the rise in fuel costs in the 1970s. (Key – Pete West)

The first bypass engine to enter service was the Rolls-Royce Conway (1960). Initially it was rated at 17,000lb (75.6kN) thrust with a core mass flow of 280lb/sec (127kg/sec) and a BPR of 0.3. The BPR being less than unity consequently meant the Conway still had a high jet velocity and was noisy. As for US manufacturers, General Electric had experimented with a front fan on a single-shaft engine in 1952 but, unsurprisingly, found it difficult to start and run.

Chronologically, Metropolitan Vickers was the first to produce a bypass engine, and adapted its F.2 model to an aft-fan configuration in 1943. Although the engine was built and run it never entered production, possibly due to mechanical difficulties in making and sealing the combined fan/turbine assembly. It weighed more, but the thrust/weight ratio was increased and, more significantly, its sfc (static) was reduced by 35 per cent. The aft-fan, however, did fly as the General Electric CJ805-23B (*see* adjacent figure) on the Convair CV990 of 1960 as the first US turbofan. Having faced the impracticality of putting a fan on the front of a single-shaft engine, General Electric was led to the aft-fan. Its CJ805 single-shaft turbojet with variable stator vanes was derived from the military J79 designed in 1953. There was no need to make great changes in the turbojet itself but, unlike the front-fan, the aft-fan did not supercharge the airflow through the engine core. Moreover, the aft-fan was not as easy to install on a single-shaft engine as a front-fan was on a two-shaft one. However, as the fuel consumption advantages of the fan engine became clear (a 28 per cent reduction in cruise sfc was claimed for the CJ805-23B), all makers adopted the turbofan for civil use.

Pratt & Whitney realized the turbofan concept by simply attaching a fan to the front of its existing JT3C turbojet, which then became the JT3D turbofan (1962). Its conversion entailed removal of the first three stages of the LP compressor and their replacement by two fan stages, the fan extending well outside the compressor casing, plus adding a stage to its turbine. Initially the engine developed 17,000lb (75.6kN) with a core flow of 180lb/sec (82kg/sec), and total mass flow of 450lb/sec (200kg/sec) with a BPR of 1.5 and an overall pressure ratio of 13. Both the Conway and JT3D were installed on variants of the Douglas DC-8 and Boeing 707, but the JT3D was a vastly more successful engine in terms of numbers built. Pratt & Whitney developed its J52 turbojet in similar fashion to produce the remarkably successful JT8D turbofan (over 14,000 built over twenty years) for the Boeing 727, 737, Douglas DC-9 and Sud-Aviation Caravelle 10–12s.

In this simplified treatment it is assumed that all of the power from the HP turbine is used to drive the HP compressor. In reality a relatively small proportion is taken to drive fuel pumps, generate electricity and provide hydraulic power for the aircraft. Similarly, it is assumed that all of the air compressed in the core passes through the combustor and turbines, though some is bled off to pressurize the cabin and de-ice some surfaces of the wing and engine nacelles. Most of the power from the multi-stage LP turbine is used to compress the bypass flow (whence most of the thrust), only a small proportion being used to raise the pressure of the core.

High-BPR turbofan
A further significant development in compressor design was needed before the full advantages of bypass airflow could be exploited properly. This was the development of fan blade aerofoil sections that enabled supersonic tip speeds to be

greater the jet velocity, the kinetic energy of which is wasted on being released to the atmosphere. The propulsive efficiency would therefore fall. However, the remaining (bypass) air, directed around the core, provides a propulsive jet of 'cool' air at the expense of the velocity and power of the hot core jet. The turbofan then has a higher thermal efficiency owing to its higher pressure ratio, and a better propulsive efficiency owing to its lower overall jet velocity. This gives a reduced sfc without serious penalty in engine weight.

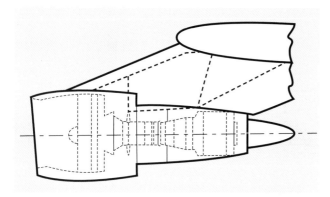

Typical wing/pylon/nacelle/engine mounting for a high-BPR turbofan. This engine is hung from a main mounting between the high- and low-pressure turbines and a forward one at the high-pressure compressor inlet flange. A thrust pin is provided at the rear mount, and links stabilize the engine at both front and rear.
(Key – Pete West)

and achieved a pressure ratio of 1.68, with an efficiency of 82 per cent at the design point, but up to 90 per cent at 96 per cent speed. The titanium-alloy blades had sharp leading edges with blade thickness/chord reduced to around 5 per cent to run at tip speeds up to Mach 1.5.

Turbofan development advanced to much higher BPRs, with the blades of the first stage of the axial compressor extending way beyond the intake lip to act as a large fan propelling five to eight times as much air as went through the engine core (BPR = 5–8). Some (Pratt & Whitney and General Electric) have 'booster' or IP stages just behind the fan on the LP shaft to compress the core stream before it enters the core proper. At cruise the fan and booster might have a pressure ratio of about 2 and the HP compressor a pressure ratio of about 16, to give an overall pressure ratio of 32. However, the disadvantage of these two-shaft high-BPR turbofans now becomes clear. The LP fan and IP compressor being in one unit, if the tip speed of the fan is Mach 1.5, then the tip speed of the IP compressor is very much lower, owing to its smaller diameter. As a consequence, the work capacity of the IP blades is now low, and more stages must be used for a given duty. Nor can the full pressure ratio of the combination be exploited, owing to the difficulty of matching the fan and IP compressor when driven by one shaft.

Hence the three-shaft high-pressure-ratio turbofan was born. In this, the LP fan, the IP compressor and the HP

used without loss of efficiency due to shock-wave formation. Many research teams around the world tried to develop a fully supersonic fan in the 1950s, but without success. At the NGTE a major effort was mounted between 1945–55, but it was concluded that a transonic fan, in which only the outer part of the blading operated at supersonic speed, had far better prospects. The NGTE's first transonic fan ran in 1956

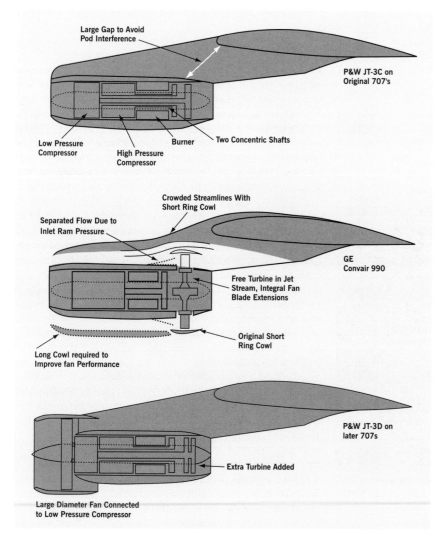

Large Gap to Avoid Pod Interference

P&W JT-3C on Original 707's

Low Pressure Compressor

High Pressure Compressor

Burner

Two Concentric Shafts

Crowded Streamlines With Short Ring Cowl

Separated Flow Due to Inlet Ram Pressure

GE Convair 990

Free Turbine in Jet Stream, Integral Fan Blade Extensions

Original Short Ring Cowl

Long Cowl required to Improve fan Performance

P&W JT-3D on later 707s

Extra Turbine Added

Large Diameter Fan Connected to Low Pressure Compressor

Turbofan evolution in the USA. Despite its success in the military field, it took General Electric more than twenty years to establish itself in the first rank of manufacturers of commercial engines, beginning with the less-than-successful single-shaft CJ805-23B turbojet. The CJ805-23B's aft fan was not easy to install as a front fan, and did not supercharge the airflow through the engine core. Moreover, it weighed more for a given thrust, but, as the fuel consumption advantages of the CJ805-23B became clear, Pratt & Whitney added a fan to the front of its JT3. The choice of two shafts by Pratt & Whitney over General Electric's single shaft with variable stator vanes was crucial. It was relatively simple to add a fan to the front of the JT3, coupling it mechanically to the LP compressor, which the fan supercharged. Although the CJ805 programme was not a commercial success, without it General Electric would not be in the airline engine business today.
(Key – Pete West)

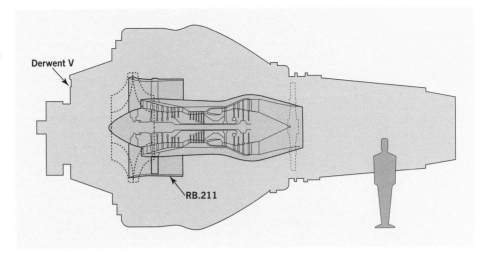

Size comparison. The Rolls-Royce Derwent V first ran in 1945, giving 2,600lb (11.5kN) thrust, but was quickly developed to 3,500lb (15.5kN). Here it is shown scaled-up for comparison with the RB.211 (first run in 1968 at 38,000lb (169kN) thrust, both giving 50,000lb (222kN) thrust.
(Key – Pete West)

Derwent V

RB.211

compressor are independently driven, and each can be designed for its optimum pressure ratio and efficiency at its required duty. This arrangement, though mechanically complicated, dispensed with the need for blow-off valves or variable stators, and allowed each of the three components to rotate at its optimum speed, thereby improving the overall aerodynamic efficiency and flexibility. This was exemplified by the Rolls-Royce RB.211 of 1970, in which the desirable speed relation between the spools were: fan 3,600rpm, IP 6,800rpm, HP 10,000rpm, so that, with its fan design pressure ratio of about 1.5, and a core pressure ratio of 16:1, the overall pressure ratio became 24:1, giving a high thermal efficiency.

One aspect of the RB.211 that proved disastrous was the use of lightweight carbonfibre material for its wide-chord fan blade, developed for the engine in 1968. This had been encouraged by the performance of these materials in the RB.162 lightweight lift engines for vertical/short-take-off-and-landing aircraft. While aerodynamically sound, the carbonfibre 'Hyfil' blades failed to withstand the impact of foreign objects, notably birds, and the programme was stopped in 1970. With retained confidence in the concept of

the wide-chord fan blade, however, Rolls-Royce started a ten-year research programme into honeycomb-reinforced hollow titanium wide-chord fan blades, which were first introduced in the RB.211-535E4 engine. By 1996 Rolls-Royce had nearly 20 million hours of experience with this design, and all of its civil engines above 25,000lb (110kN) have these types of fan blades, giving a considerable advantage in terms of weight, aerodynamics and bird-ingestion capabilities. Further development led to the introduction of the super-plastically formed/diffusion bonded (SPF/DB) wide-chord fan, with higher strength, lower weight and lower unit cost.

The future

Multi-stage three-dimensional steady viscous calculations now permit the design of complete compressors, and this computational technique has allowed secondary losses (such as flow separations) to be reduced. Other benefits are the ability to increase blade loading without increasing loss, and better axial matching of multi-stage compressors that permit reduced blade numbers and stages. On the fan, this technique has been used to design the swept fan blade, increasing flow capacity (and hence thrust) and efficiency. Developments in unsteady computational fluid dynamics (CFD) will lead to improved understanding of stall and surge phenomena, perhaps reducing the number of variable vanes (conventionally used to control stall) by the use of advanced casing treatments and active control. All of these advances should lead to a more accurate and reliable design process, and would enable the current Rolls-Royce Trent engine, for example, to produce the same work with two fewer IP stages and one less HP stage, with approximately 20 per cent fewer aerofoils in the remaining stages, while increasing efficiency by 1 per cent and providing cost, weight and performance benefits to the customer.

As for turbines, improved analysis techniques will allow significant increase in blade lift coefficients (30–40 per cent) without extra loss. The increased lift coefficients will allow lighter, cheaper machines. Accurate unsteady CFD will allow prediction of supersonic aerofoil interaction effects, which will allow the use of contrarotating statorless turbines, with their high efficiency, low weight and reduced cost. Multi-row CFD for turbines should yield, through better matching and flow control, a progressive increase in stage-specific work. It should be possible to reduce the number of stages required for a given duty, giving both cost and weight reductions.

Although axial compressors are more vulnerable to birdstrikes than centrifugal types, they are nonetheless very resilient. This RB.211 was powering a Boeing 757 when it hit a flock of geese. The engine continued running at full power until the aircraft returned safely to the airport.
(Rolls-Royce)

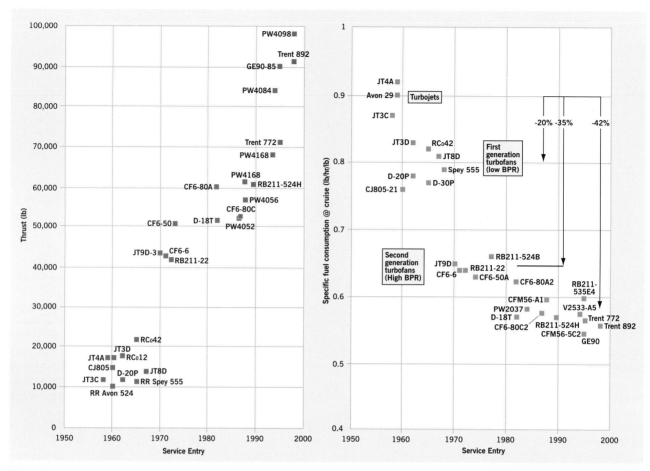

Uninstalled sea-level static thrust growth with time. The big step up arose during the late 1960s for the new widebodies (Boeing 747, Douglas DC-10 and Lockheed L.1011). The overall trend of 20,000lb/decade for the most powerful engines has accelerated since the beginning of the 1980s to accommodate the long-range widebody twins.
(Key – Ray Whitford)

Uninstalled cruise specific fuel consumption with time. The first generation turbofans with an sfc of around 9.8lb/hr/lb converted about 25 per cent of the energy content of the fuel into thrust, the second generation achieved 35 per cent (though maintenance costs were disappointing), whereas the best of the current engines reach around 40 per cent and are achieving this is longer lives and far greater reliability.

As materials become stronger and their tolerance of higher temperature increases, the sfc of commercial engines will decrease. At present, the limit of operation of an engine is as likely to be determined by the compressor delivery temperature as by the TET. Whereas TET is open to increase by increasing the amount of cooling air, the compressor delivery temperature alone defines the conditions that its material must withstand. Today's engines have such high pressure ratios (around 40:1) that the temperature rise in the compressor is so large that, at the exit from the HP compressor, it is difficult to withstand the high stresses in the rotor. Thus it is not only the turbine that has a temperature limit. If the rotor is made of titanium alloy the upper temperature limit is about 600°C (1,110°F), whereas if nickel-based alloys are used it may be 700°C (1,290°F). However, nickel alloys are much heavier, so titanium is preferred whenever practical. There is a balance to be struck between allowable stress, weight and temperature, which depends on the application and the relative desirability of low weight and low fuel consumption. Additionally, the higher temperature of the air entering the combustor before the fuel is burned means that, because the fuel is the only source of power, the temperature rise due to the combustion of fuel must be maintained if the power output of the engine is not to decrease. If overall pressure ratios are to increase there must be major changes

in compressor materials or substantial improvement in compressor efficiency. This implies even higher TETs requiring continued research into high-temperature materials.

Fuel efficiency

The early Pratt & Whitney JT3D turbofan that gave the Boeing 707-320B of 1962 its greatly improved fuel efficiency had a comparatively small fan (BPR = 1.4) that left the engine nacelle only slightly larger in diameter. Larger subsonic aircraft with their economies of scale remained a vague notion without a sufficiently large engine. To get significantly reduced fuel consumption required a much higher BPR turbofan that, although proven in principle, had yet had to show that it could meet the same standards of reliability as the first generation. In seeking what it regarded as stopgap airliner until the supersonic transport arrived, Pan Am was given details of such an engine in 1965. This was the Pratt & Whitney JT9D of 41,000lb (182kN) thrust, almost double that of the JT3D, and with a BPR almost four times greater. Pratt & Whitney had entered this engine in competition with General Electric's TF39 to power the USAF's CX-HLS very large long-range airlifter, which became the Lockheed C-5A Galaxy. However, PanAm did not equate either engine with an airliner designed around it by Boeing or Lockheed. It

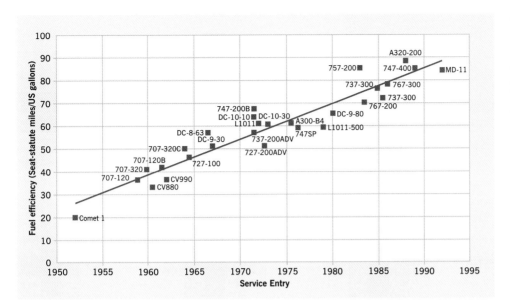

Airliner fuel efficiency. This graph, in terms of seat-mile per US gallon (s-m/gal), shows a consistent performance improvement of around 5 per cent per year since the 1950s. For example, the Airbus A320-200 achieves almost double the s-m/gal of the larger but same-capacity Boeing 727-200Adv. The trend shown has fuelled an enormous expansion in the air transport industry unimagined following the Second World War. A large part of the improvement came from lower engine sfc, improved aerodynamics and increased aircraft seating capacity. (Key – Ray Whitford)

expected to have to wait until a winner emerged for the USAF contract to adapt an airliner from the military design. However, the competition had stimulated a new generation of turbofans in the USA. The TF39, with a BPR of 8, was selected for the C-5A, much of the credit going to Gerhard Neumann, general manager of General Electric's aero-engine division. In Britain, Bristol Siddeley Engines and Rolls-Royce were studying high-BPR engines but lacked funds to build one, apart from the RB.178, which ran in 1966.

Although it is desirable that an engine has a low sfc, the goal for airlines is not the lowest sfc but the engine that will generate greatest profit. There is a tendency for engine weight to increase as attempts are made, via higher BPR, to increase efficiency and lower sfc, so there is a natural trade-off between them. Propulsive efficiency rises and sfc falls with BPR, though the *rate of change* of both declines. Eventually the penalties associated with the engine weight increase, nacelle drag and the difficulties of mounting engines underwing (increased undercarriage length, nacelle/wing interference drag) outweigh the benefit of high BPR. Hence the optimum BPR for generating profits will be lower than that for minimum installed sfc. The economic effect of engine weight and sfc on direct operating cost (DOC) depends on a large number of variables, many specific to a particular airline. Fuel price is also an important part of airline operating expenses. Fuel cost varies with many factors, including the market price (which differs from one carrier to another due to their bargaining power), but is about 40 per cent (at 80¢/US

gallon) of the DOC of a large long-haul (3,500nm (6,500km)) aircraft. A 1 per cent drop in fuel price does not, therefore, make much impression on the total costs, but a 1 per cent reduction in fuel weight which must be carried at take-off can be worth about 5 per cent increase in payload (because payload is only about one-third that of fuel load and about 9–10 per cent of TOW, giving a much greater influence on operating profit. Thus the emphasis in aircraft/engine selection and operations rests heavily on fuel efficiency.

Despite great improvements in fuel efficiency, the modern airliner still consumes fuel liberally. In terms of seat-miles per US gallon (s-m/gal), airline fuel efficiency improved from 20 in 1952 to about 55 within two decades (*see* adjacent figure), which is in the range of the private car with no one but the driver. In terms of national policies to conserve fuel by encouraging people to use mass transit, airlines appear profligate, though, of course, the benefit of air travel is speed. One step the airlines took was to purchase new and larger fuel-efficient aircraft and to retire older ones. Between 1973 and 1983 there was an increase of about 73 per cent in passenger-miles, while total fuel consumption actually dropped, albeit slightly, and fuel efficiency increased to 70s-m/gal. Unfortunately this impressive gain in efficiency was dwarfed by the astonishing rise in fuel prices of that decade. The 1990s trend was to improve engine performance by using higher pressure ratios and lowering sfc, to ease maintenance by dividing the airframe and engine into a small number of replaceable subsystems, and to minimize emissions.

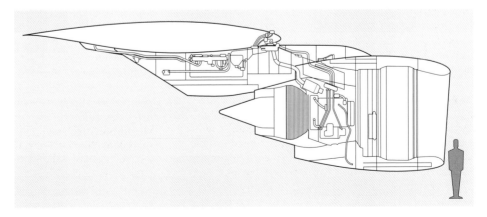

Pratt & Whitney PW4073/PW4084 installation for Boeing 777-200. This figure gives an indication of how the wing leading edge and pylon are tightly packed to accommodate fuel, hydraulic and power lines, pneumatic ducts and control cables. Also noticeable is the small height of the inlet above the ground, the forward cant of the intake face (to accept the flow upsweep ahead of the wing) and the very short length of diffuser ahead of the fan. (Key – Pete West/Ray Whitford)

Due to the larger relative size of the nacelle, considerably more windtunnel testing and analysis had to be carried out for the Boeing 747 than for the 707 (seen here at London Heathrow about 1960) to solve the wing/nacelle integration problem. Of prime concern is the length of the fan-cowl relative to the length of the nacelle. For the 747 it was found desirable to put the exit plane of the fan cowl ahead of the wing leading edge to minimize interference on that part of the wing. A short fan cowl has other losses, however, so this solution is not always the best.
(Key – Steve Fletcher, Ray Whitford)

Engine/airframe integration

Integration of a new engine with a new airframe represents one of the greatest opportunities for success or failure of the combination. A properly integrated engine installation is the best balance between performance, weight, maintainability, life and cost. Overemphasis on any one will produce a non-optimum design that could result in reduced benefits for an airline. The introduction of high-BPR turbofans brought about renewed problems of airframe–engine integration because of their much larger intake diameter (Pratt & Whitney JT3C turbojet 39in (1m); JT9D turbofan 96in (2.44m)). Not only are the direct aerodynamic problems more difficult, but configuration problems resulting from the size of the engine constrain the aerodynamic design more severely than was the case for slim turbojets. For its turbojet-powered 707 Boeing found that, with 'proper' pod design for the JT3s, only the nacelle skin friction drag was of primary interest. The pods increased the aircraft skin friction drag by about 18 per cent, which under cruising conditions

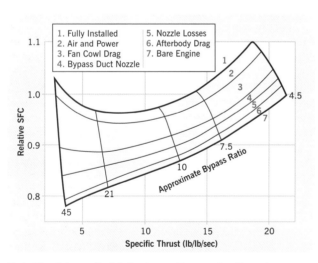

Typical breakdown of installation losses. By convention, the engine manufacturer guarantees 'stream tube' performance and accounts for all losses that occur within the engine. The nacelle losses are accounted for as part of the airframe drag. It is worth noting that what you see in published tables of engine performance cannot be what you get. Engine makers test their products independently of the aircraft to which the powerplant is to be fitted, and the tables make no allowance for installation losses. There is a big difference between bare-engine and installed-engine performance, in this case specific fuel consumption. For a turbofan of BPR 4.5 at Mach 0.8 at 30,000ft (9,000m), the sfc penalty due to installation is around 14 per cent. The penalty incurred from increasing BPR and consequent nacelle wetted area is apparent. (Specific thrust is thrust divided by air flow rate: lb/lb/sec.)
(Key – Ray Whitford)

represented a 9 per cent reduction in aircraft L/D. Because of the larger relative nacelle size, considerably more wind tunnel testing and analysis had to be carried out on the Boeing 747 than on the 707 to solve the wing/nacelle integration problem (*see* adjacent figure).

Designing engine installations for low drag is one of the more challenging problems of aerodynamics, not just because of their nacelles' large bypass duct and external wetted areas. Moreover, it is not sensible to design just for low drag. Analysis of the flow is complex, involving the interactions from the different components. Given the many factors it is difficult to generalize, but, broadly speaking, the drag problem is harder to solve when the nacelle size increases relative to the size of the wing. Moreover, there are many other considerations that make the problem more difficult. The selection of a good nacelle installation is the result of compromise with aerodynamic drag, one of many factors, albeit a dominant one.

With increasing BPR, engines become heavier, which means more lift-dependent drag (proportional to the weight squared). This effectively reduces net thrust (and increases sfc) and payload, so revenue declines. For the early generation of high-BPR (≈ 5) engines (JT9D, RB.211, CF6), the penalty in sfc associated with the nacelles was about 9 per cent, for which the drag breakdown was 1 per cent for the inlet, 2 per cent for the bypass duct and 6 per cent on the outside. Even when designing for a Mach 0.82 cruise there may be regions on the nacelle where low supersonic (Mach 1.2) flow exists. Careful design has to avoid shockwaves (giving abrupt compression) likely to lead to flow separation. Furthermore, if the BPR gets very large the aircraft itself begins to suffer because adequate ground clearance is needed, so a longer and heavier undercarriage is required. Moreover, airflow around the wing is further influenced by the engine. Thus the propulsive efficiency benefits of high-BPR engines cannot wholly be translated into performance benefit.

Even in deciding the pylon geometry there is a possible conflict between what is required to delay shock-wave onset and what is needed to give the optimum effect on other parameters, such as the span loading (W/b) and lift-dependent drag. Interfaces at the wing/pylon/nacelle must minimize weight and drag and are tightly packed to accommodate fuel, hydraulic and power lines, pneumatic ducts and control cables. Traditionally, wings have been designed in the absence of the interference effects of the engine installation, whereupon nacelle position and support-pylon geometry have been designed to minimize any adverse interactions.

Nacelle installations are notoriously fraught with interference problems. Probably the most difficult was the Boeing 737-300/CFM56 combination, where the need to keep modifications of the aircraft to a minimum forced the fan cowl exit very close indeed to the wing leading edge. Some upward tilt and flattening of the lower surface of the pod (to maximize ground clearance of the much-higher-BPR engine) is evident.
(Key – Steve Fletcher)

'On-condition' engine maintenance

In the early 1950s, when the first gas turbines went into commercial operation, 1,500hr TBO was considered a satisfactory target based on piston-engine experience. By the mid-1960s, however, it was becoming easier to keep airliners in the air and turn them around quickly on the ground. The turbojet had reached an astonishingly high level of reliability, with TBOs exceeding 10,000hr, whereas the best piston engine had managed only 2,500hr. Subsequently, TBOs progressed until, in 1965, Air Canada, with the co-operation of a progressive airworthiness authority, adopted 'on-condition' maintenance of the Rolls-Royce Conway engines on its Douglas DC-8s. At the time of the changeover the Conway's TBO stood at 6,700hr. Not all of its operators adopted on-condition maintenance, but they eventually extended their TBOs to 14,000hr with one or more intermediate hangar checks. The objectives of the new philosophy were to: check that the engine was delivering specification performance; detect mechanical deterioration to prevent failure; give accurate location of parts needing attention; and minimize maintenance costs. With the long lives that were being reached the fixed overhaul concept became meaningless, because, even with an acceptable unscheduled removal rate, few engines reached the declared figure without intermediate hangar visits dictated by condition.

On-condition maintenance is more economical because only those parts of the engine that are known to be life-limited are overhauled. This is in contrast to the old system (still used by Russia into the 1990s), in which the complete engine was overhauled, irrespective of condition. The changeover was a gradual process rather than sudden step, but any new engine had to be launched recognizing the evolution that had taken place, and planned to take advantage of its economics. One aspect of on-condition operations was the need for systematic sampling, preferably from natural failures, to gain advance warning of expected changes in parts and hence a possible demand for spares in excess of the provisioning programme, or a sudden increase in unscheduled removals. This constant monitoring, determining the cause of failures, redesigning parts and designing new ones, meant they were retrofittable across entire engine fleets. This not only improved performance but allowed airlines to maintain fleet standardization and lower inventory costs. The sampling also helped indicate the ultimate rework interval for expensive parts to prevent deterioration reaching a point where repairs became very costly or impractical. Another aspect was the progress towards higher TETs and the fact that, as with a turboprop, temperatures in cruise and climb for turbofans dictated life and made close control and monitoring of operations at high TETs essential, if economies in hot section maintenance were to be made. Engines are now operating for times in excess of 30,000hr 'on the wing' between major overhaul/ retirement, or entail 20,000-flight cycles.

Deterioration in service

Deterioration in component efficiency has to be expected during an engine's working lifetime. This is due to dirt, foreign object damage, erosion of compressor blades, wear and increased clearances, sometimes with a contribution due to burning and cracking of turbine nozzle guide vanes. The effect on fuel consumption warrants careful attention. Even with dressing and blending carried out, the performance loss is not fully recovered when the engine is finally overhauled. Although the increase in sfc may be only 1 per cent after five years of operations, the cumulative effect on fuel costs is such that there is a high premium on designing and developing parts more resistant to such deterioration. Consideration had to be given to the relative economics of some parts' replacement against fuel cost. The usual procedure to cope with a fall in component efficiency is to increase the TET to maintain thrust. Indeed, one sign that an engine is due for overhaul is when the TET exceeds a set value for a given thrust or fan pressure ratio. For example, loss of 1 per cent of HP compressor efficiency might be compensated for in terms of thrust by about 20°C (36°F) rise in TET, whereas a 1 per cent loss in HP turbine efficiency could be corrected by a 3°C rise in TET. The sfc would rise by about 0.5 per cent for the loss of efficiency in fan, HP compressor or either of the turbines. If all components lost 1 per cent of their efficiency the cumulative effect could easily require increasing TET by 30°C (65°F), with consequent reduced engine life. However, the increased TET can overcompensate the thrust loss because the higher temperature increases the exhaust jet velocity's contribution to thrust but does not show up on the flight deck as increased shaft speed.

Reliability

Ultimately an airline, much less a passenger, cares not so much about the efficiency of an engine as its safety. An engine simultaneously needs high rotational speeds and temperatures, low weight and extraordinary reliability, each of which pull in different directions, and compromises have to be made. The engine aerodynamicist would like thin blades but, for mechanical reasons, they have to be thicker. Moreover, the mechanical designer has to find a way to hold the bearings and supply and remove the lubricating oil. This tends to mean robust structures that conflict with the aerodynamicist's wishes, but it is a battle the mechanical engineer is likely to win.

The two major elements of DOC, upon which the engine manufacturer can act to achieve an improvement, are fuel and maintenance costs, which (excluding price-related depreciation) jointly account for around 50 per cent of total

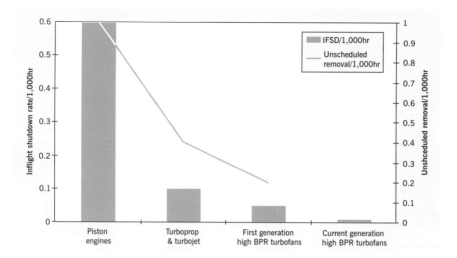

Engine reliability in terms of in-flight shutdown (IFSD) rates and premature removal was vastly improved from the piston-engine era. Although the powerplant is only one of the causes of delay (in the 1970s engines were responsible for about one delay in every 100 departures), it was clear that every effort had to be made to improve reliability. However, compared with the piston engine, by 1970 IFSD rates were 90 per cent lower and unscheduled removal rates were 80 per cent lower. Nowadays, IFSDs are rare, all modern engines having a rate below one per 100,000 flight hours, and most pilots will not experience a compulsory shutdown during their career. (Key – Ray Whitford)

DOC for long-haul aircraft (40 per cent for short-haul). Inevitably, the underlying physics means that trade-offs must be made to achieve the optimum solution. Thus an engine maker can focus design effort to achieve the best reliability and hence lowest maintenance costs, or focus on lowest fuel burn. To get the best possible reliability requires the engine to be designed with a large core. This leads to lower core temperatures, which means the manufacturer can use proven technology evolved over several generations of engine, and can insert new technology only when it benefits the customer. The engine designed for reliability can achieve significant maintenance cost improvements, while remaining competitive in terms of fuel burn. Conversely, an engine manufacturer can adopt a design philosophy of minimizing fuel burn. This will lead to very-high-BPR designs driven by small cores. As a result, the core runs at higher temperatures using high risk, immature, technology. This can lead to lower levels of reliability and consequently higher maintenance costs to achieve any fuel-burn improvements.

For a large twin, 2 per cent saving in fuel translates to a 1 per cent lower DOC, while a 10 per cent maintenance cost saving is required to achieve the same DOC reduction. Thus it would appear logical to invest in efforts to reduce fuel consumption. However, experience has shown otherwise. The biggest advantage in service from an engine optimized for fuel consumption is 4 per cent, but typically the benefit is only 1–2 per cent. The maintenance costs of these same engines, however, would carry a penalty of between 50–100 per cent worse reliability. Thus the engine designed for reliability has an inherent DOC advantage of around 6 per cent.

Moreover, unreliable engines carry a hidden cost burden that has a big impact on airline profitability. This stems from unplanned events such as rejected take-offs (RTO), inflight shutdowns (IFSD), delays and cancellations that disturb airline schedules. Hub-and-spoke systems that are used by all major airlines are particularly vulnerable to such disruption. One IFSD can cost 3 per cent of an annual fuel bill for a single aircraft; fuel must be dumped (to reduce landing weight), the engine may need removal (sometimes away from base), and passengers may need overnight accommodation.

Engine reliability and maintainability recorded steady increases during the 1980s, and new engines entering service in the 1990s showed even greater promise. However, lowering the contribution of propulsion to aircraft DOCs proved to be a double-edged sword for engine manufacturers, who traditionally made the bulk of their money through the sale of spare parts and refurbishment. At the beginning of the 1980s an engine would consume itself in about eight years. In other words, an engine would require spare parts approximately equivalent to its original value by the end of that period. By the 1990s that interval had stretched to 25 years owing to continuous process and component improvements, and on-condition maintenance. Shop-visit rates were cut by a third, despatch reliability increased to 99.9 per cent, and sfc deterioration improved by 4 per cent over the engine's lifetime.

Extended-range operations (EROPS)

Extended range is defined in the context of operational guidelines promulgated by the International Civil Aviation Organization (ICAO) almost 50 years ago. These safety rules focused on the reliability of piston engines used in the early 1950s, when accident rates for twin-engine aircraft were nearly twice that of four-engine types, and when shutting down one of four engines on a transatlantic crossing was a not infrequent occurrence. The regulations required that an aircraft should be able to lose two engines and reach a suitable airport after flying for 90min on the remaining engines. In the USA a more restrictive approach was taken to reduce the risk of catastrophe ensuing from failure of both engines of a twin to acceptable levels. All two- and three-engine aircraft were limited to routes that put them no more than 60min at one-engine-operative cruising speed (about 400 miles (650km)) from an adequate airport. Early twinjets were bound by the same regulation but, as jet engines became more reliable, the FAA granted exemptions for trans-Caribbean twinjet operations, first up to 75min and then 85min. In 1964, after the introduction of the first trijets (de Havilland Trident and Boeing 727), and drawing on the favourable experience of turbine transports, the USA rule exempted three-engine aircraft.

The rules have been evolutionary for good reasons, as confidence gradually grew in the jet engine's reliability. However, development of new guidelines for extended-range twin operations (ETOPS) by airworthiness authorities was not a simple task, and was naturally met with a great deal of scepticism. Commonsense argued that it was safer to fly with more than two engines. Nevertheless, in 1980, aircraft manufacturers began to examine the possibility of EROPS with their twins (Airbus A300 and Boeing 767). As the new generation of twins replaced the old trijets, far from finding

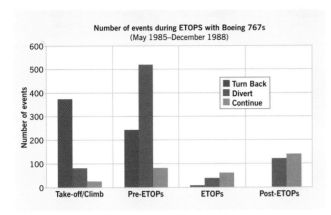

Number of events during ETOPS with Boeing 767s (May 1985–December 1988)

Boeing 767 ETOPS history, May 1985–December 1998. This is a summary of 1,665 reported events out of a total of over one million ETOPS flights, showing that 99.87 per cent of the flights reached their destination airport. (Key – Ray Whitford/Boeing)

themselves with a more flexible fleet and benefiting from new technology, some operators found their options more restricted. Because the jump to the widebody trijets (Lockheed L.1011 and Douglas DC-10) was too big for some airlines, long-range versions of the new twins were the only sensible replacements for the 707s, DC-8s, CV-880s and VC10s that for a generation were the world's means of long-range transoceanic air travel. The Boeing 767ER and A300B 4 had the range of the old four-jet types, and on some routes were the only commercial answers, though initially this inferred a longer route to keep within the 60min limitation. Large high-BPR engines were maturing to a high level of reliability, and gave the new twins sufficient thrust so no more than two engines were required. Furthermore, engines are expensive to buy and maintain, so reducing the number of them offered an immediate advantage. Implicit in this is the trend that the cost/thrust drops as engines get larger. Consideration of redundancy levels indicated that twins designed in the late 1970s would require less maintenance than the four- or three-engine aircraft of late 1960s and early 1970s design.

The regulatory authorities were put under pressure to reassess the whole situation to determine what was prudent for the new twins. The mid-1980s were transition years for ETOPS regulations and standards. The threshold for ETOPS was 60min at one-engine-speed, and in 1985 ICAO provided guidelines for obtaining type design and operational approval for operations of twins beyond 60min. Certification depends on three factors: in-service experience to demonstrate that the aircraft and engine systems are reliable; type design approval to ensure that sufficient redundancy is built into all systems (electrical, cargo fire suppression, auxiliary power unit, cooling for avionics) for reliability en route; and operational approval to cover route planning, crew training and engineering fitness.

By the end of the 1980s it was expected that approvals would be given for operations beyond 120min. Approval went up in a staggered sequence, initially 75 or 90min, then 120min and, until recently, 180min. This meant that twins could be cleared to fly approximately 1,200nm (2,200km) from the nearest suitable airport, greatly increasing the number of alternative airports available to allow virtually unlimited global operations. America took the lead in

ETOPS by simple force of geography. The west coast of both the North and South Americas lies along the emptiest expanse of ocean, the eastern Pacific, and Hawaii (the first group of islands of the north-eastern Pacific) is a US State. Only transatlantic flights between Europe and Brazil, and from northern Africa to Central America, were really affected by the 120min restriction (because of a no-go region between West Africa and the Caribbean).

Initially the ETOPS-configured Boeing 767 was analysed on the basis of an 8hr flight that was up to 120min from an alternative airport using both ETOPS and non-ETOPS service experience. The review showed that the actual performance of the electrical system was eight times better than originally predicted. Subsequently the analysis, redone for a 10hr flight up to 180min from an alternative airport, showed that there was ample margin to meet 180min requirements. Engine temperatures and stresses are far higher during climb than on the long slow drift down that follows an engine shutdown. Additionally, engine manufacturers assume that the remaining engine has only half the reliability normally demonstrated. Over 13,000 Boeing 767 ETOPS flights by twelve operators were made from May 1985 to the end of 1986, with only twenty-five reported events: twenty-one of the flights experienced turnbacks or diversions and four continued to their destination, representing a 99.838 per cent success rate, compared with 99.222 per cent for Boeing 747s. Thus the newer 767 demonstrated a higher arrival assurance than the 747. This is not altogether surprising, given the later technology of the aircraft and its engines.

That said, American Airlines, at the forefront of ETOPS with its 767s, initially experienced too many diversions for its liking. The simple explanation was that toilets were prone to overflow. Engine-related occurrences accounted for only about a quarter of the fifty-six diversions out of 160,000 North Atlantic crossings. The situations in which aircraft turned back included four for medical reasons, four for toilet problems, three for fuel-system faults, two for electrical malfunctions and two for avionics or flight-control snags.

EROPS was the new acronym for what used to be ETOPS. The argument for the renaming was that safety standards should be just as high for airliners flying long transoceanic routes, regardless of the number of engines. The reason why multiple engine failure is not automatically given as a more important safety consideration for twins than for three- or four-engine aircraft is simple. Multiple powerplant failure (for reasons such as fuel starvation and, remarkably in 1982, ingestion of volcanic ash) has always been a 'common cause' failure, and with a common cause it does not matter how many engines an aircraft has. What EROPS requirements attempted to do was to eliminate the 'common causes' experienced of the past.

In-flight shutdown (IFSD) rates

The dramatic improvement in engine reliability was the key factor in allowing twins to fly on extended routes, and is one of the most significant commercial successes of recent times. Compared with IFSD rates of 0.6 per 1,000 engine hours for the best piston engines, and 0.1 for the early turbojets and turbofans, rates for second-generation turbofans dropped below 0.02, with 0.01 for current engines. To be eligible for EROPS, rules in the early 1990s required the worldwide fleet of an aircraft type to have had 250,000 engine hours of

For an aircraft with two engines, loss of one on take-off is very serious, and significantly more powerful engines are required to meet the engine-out case. An Airbus A330-300, for example, at a maximum TOW of 478,000lb (217,000kg), requires a thrust to climb out from the remaining engine of 62,000lb (276kN). To satisfy this requirement, the type is equipped with engines having an uninstalled thrust of between 64,000–67,500lb (285–300kN). (Key – Dave Allport)

experience, with 75,000 of those hours on the specific airframe for which EROPS was sought. In addition, the IFSD rate had to be no higher than 0.05 per 1,000hr for 120min operations, and 0.02/1,000hr for 180min operations. Newer engines have consistently lower IFSD rates, and achieved maturity much faster than the first generation of high-BPR turbofans. The occurrence of engine failure is now very rare; up to 1995 there had been 35 million ETOPS flights and fewer than 100 IFSDs. However, in many more cases one engine had had to be throttled back, but not shut down, and these do not show up in the figures.

Number of engines

Many factors affect the design of an aircraft. For example, the number of passengers to be carried, the distance to be travelled and runway length determine the size of the aircraft. These, in turn, have differing influences on the key characteristics and design of the engine, the fuel consumption of which affects the range and DOC. Take-off thrust is determined by runway length, range and payload and the number of engines, again affecting DOCs. It might be imagined that, if a short-range widebody twin and a long-range four-engine aircraft both require 65,000–75,000lb (290–330kN) static thrust, then the same engine will meet the needs of both. However, the payload and range of twins tend to be dominated at the design limits by engine take-off thrust and engine weight. This arises partly from engine-out requirements, but also from basic aircraft design. Engine sfc and noise play their part in the engine configuration, but are less critical if reasonably competitive. For a four-engine long-range aircraft, low fuel burn and noise are major design factors. Thus the same 70,000lb (310kN) engine is unlikely to give the optimized aircraft design for a twin-engine and a four-engine aircraft. Although there are exceptions, the engine for the twin will ideally have a lower BPR with a smaller diameter fan and bigger core, the latter to keep the engine temperature manageable for reliability at the highest thrusts and to meet top-of-climb thrust conditions. The powerplant for the four-engine aircraft needs a higher BPR to give the best sfc (and so fuel burn) and noise. Thus the fan will be larger and the core smaller, the size of the core being determined by physical

constraints or top-of-climb thrust requirements. Recognizing the need to satisfy a number of planned aircraft designs, a range of thrusts and BPRs will be required.

Loss of thrust on take-off

Regardless of the number of engines, airliners must be able to fly safely even if one engine fails completely; the engine-out condition. The most severe engine failure case is at decision speed (V1) just before take-off rotation. It is mandatory for the remaining engine(s) to produce enough thrust for the aircraft to climb out. For a twin this means that there must be twice as much thrust as that just necessary to get the aircraft into the air. For a four-engine aircraft the same rule requires that there is 4/3 times as much thrust available. The minimum allowable climb gradient is 3 per cent (almost 2 degrees), so that, assuming the take-off L/D is 10, the thrust must be at least (1/10 + 0.03) times the weight. So for a four-engine Airbus A340–300 with a maximum TOW of 606,000lb (274,000kg) the total minimum thrust required is 78,800lb (350kN). If one engine fails, the thrust required from each of the remaining engines is 26,270lb (116.8kN). Engines of uninstalled 31,000–34,000lb (138–151kN) thrust (depending on type) are used for the A340–300, so the thrust from the three remaining engines is sufficient, even allowing for installation losses, power offtakes and momentum drag losses during the take-off run. For the two-engine case, loss of an engine on take-off is much more serious, and significantly more powerful engines are required to meet the engine-out case. In addition, twins typically have smaller wing loadings that allow lower take-off speeds.

The twins' *all-engines-running* greater excess power allows the aircraft to spend less time climbing, and, because of the lower wing loading, to climb to a higher altitude of 39,000–43,000ft (11,900–13,100m) to achieve its maximum ML/D. Thus setting a higher initial cruise altitude for twins allows the same engine to operate nearer its design point at cruise (because the lower-density air reduces net thrust) *and* produce the necessary thrust at take-off to cope with loss of an engine.

In summary, this means that for a four-engine aircraft no major compromise is needed to cope with loss of an engine at take-off, and the total installed thrust can be fixed by the climb requirement (particularly top-of-climb). This can be fairly close to the condition for cruise, at which the lowest fuel consumption is paramount. With the twin, however, some adaptation is needed, resulting in a higher cruise altitude.

Loss of thrust during cruise

Airliners normally cruise at an altitude such that their ML/D is near its maximum. At this condition the engines are sized such that they produce just enough thrust to equal the drag. If thrust is lost from an engine there is not enough additional thrust available, by increasing the fuel flow to raise TET, from the remaining ones to compensate without causing a rapid shortening of engine life.

When a shutdown occurs the crew has several options, depending on the circumstances. It may select various power settings, speed, level-off altitudes and diversion times to a landing site. For example, if the situation is urgent (such as smoke in the cabin), the pilot has the option of flying at a lower altitude at the limit Mach number. When low-altitude weather contains icing or undesirable turbulence (not always known), a higher altitude can be selected. When there is neither a weather problem nor a time emergency, a wise choice is to use no more than maximum cruise thrust. The normal procedure is to descend to a lower altitude, where the higher air density allows the remaining engines to increase their thrust. To retain the maximum ML/D at the lower altitude, the lift coefficient must be maintained close to its value at cruise. With the flight speed inversely proportional to the air density, speed is reduced. Now L/D is increased slightly with reduced Mach number (but the drag is higher because of the 'dead' engine and the use of rudder to counteract the yaw of the asymmetric thrust). If L/D does remain constant, the total thrust required for steady flight from the remaining engines is exactly equal to that at the cruise condition before engine failure, since aircraft weight is initially unchanged.

Engine sizing

Since thrust is roughly proportional to air density, it falls rapidly with altitude. Engines needs sizing so that they operate at an efficient condition while producing the required thrust at the altitude that will put the aircraft at its optimum ML/D. Since most of the flight is spent in the cruise condition, this is the engine operating point most important in determining the total fuel consumption and range. The critical condition for sizing is the top-of-climb, when the aircraft is still climbing as it approaches cruise altitude. Engines used on a four-engine aircraft, which give adequate thrust at top-of-climb, will (as noted above) also give ample thrust on take-off under normal conditions. Commercial engines are allowed to operate for a continuous period of no more than about 5min at maximum take-off power. This represents a very small proportion of the total flight time and, because very little fuel is used in this condition, sfc at take-off (the lowest) is irrelevant (though often the one quoted). At the take-off setting the TET is so high today (1,425°C is 300°C higher than the melting temperature of the materials from which turbine blades are made) that an engine would deteriorate rapidly if allowed to operate for long, whereas at the cruise point the TET is 250°C lower because of lower intake temperature and thrust setting, so the rate of deterioration is low.

The TET is important because increasing its value makes the pressure drop across the core turbine smaller in relation to the pressure rise of the core compressor, and thereby increases the power available from the LP turbine responsible for driving the fan (whence comes most of the thrust in high-BPR engines). Increasing TET also raises the cycle efficiency, provided the pressure ratio increases by an appropriate amount. It is the ratio of (absolute temperature) TET to compressor inlet temperature (T4/T2) that is crucial. Reducing the compressor entry temperature, as occurs at altitude, has a similar effect to increasing TET on the ground. The design point in the sense of lowest fuel consumption *and* longest life should, therefore, correspond to the cruise condition, but the engine must have the capacity to generate some additional thrust to allow the aircraft to climb, so the design condition for limiting the thrust is usually the requirement at top-of-climb, where T4/T2 is the highest.

Considering the need to improve fuel consumption concurrently with the need to reduce cost, very high component loadings will be necessary to enable high pressure ratio, BPR and TET to be used, giving the same or fewer stages of compression and expansion than today's engines. The challenge will be for the aerodynamicist to design for high efficiencies and for materials engineers to produce high-strength, high-temperature capability at low cost.

Conclusion

For commercial aircraft, economy is the overriding consideration and, consequently, high-BPR turbofans dominate the scene. While theoretically there are larger gains to be made from ultra-high-BPR engines, the practicalities of installing these engines tend to negate their theoretical advantage compared with continued development (in Rolls-Royce's view) of the three-shaft engine layout. The three-shaft engine has a real advantage in that it can be developed to an overall pressure ratio of about 60:1 and a BPR of 10 in a direct-drive configuration before the number of LP turbine stages exceeds that used in today's two-shaft engines (six).

When considering a new project, three main objectives must be taken into consideration when evaluating a new technology: safety and reliability; profitability (so its use can reduce costs and maximize revenue); and compatibility with the environment. The future will see greater emphasis placed on the other elements in cost of ownership, namely first cost, reliability and maintainability, and a holistic approach to customer support, all of which will be considered during design in order to reduce the cost of air travel.

Chapter 6

Structures and Materials

In meeting the 1930s demand for increased speed many developments were required, one of the most exciting being stressed-skin structures. From the structural engineer's viewpoint the revolutionary nature of this concept virtually halted the continuation of the two-spar, braced-frame structure and demanded fundamentally new thinking.

According to Samuel Butler, the nineteenth-century philosopher: 'Life is one long process of getting tired'. So it is for aircraft structures. Metal fatigue was brought to the general public's attention by two crashes of de Havilland Comets in 1954. The emergence of fatigue and the design philosophies to deal with it are examined here, along with the introduction of jet transports and the lengths of their working lives.

Glossary

Aeroelasticity: The aerodynamic effects arising from structural flexibility.

Flexural axis: For a wing this is the loci of a series of points on the surface where, if a vertical load is applied, only bending, not twisting, occurs.

Flutter: Violent flapping of a wing or tail in the airstream, rather like a flag. It arises due to the surface's flexibility in both torsion and bending

g: The term g relates to acceleration due to gravity, which for the purposes of atmospheric flight, has the value of 9.81 m/s^2 (32.2 ft/sec^2). When an aircraft is flying with no acceleration in any direction it is referred to as being in 1g flight. During a turn the aircraft experiences an acceleration towards the centre of the turn. The force that pushes the pilot into his seat is equal to his weight times the number of g that the aircraft is pulling.

Limit load: The maximum load that an aircraft is expected to experience in normal operation.

Ultimate load: The limit load multiplied by 1.5. The structure must support the ultimate load before it fails.

Load factor (n): Expressed as a pure number of g: n = lift/weight.

Stress: Load per unit area.

Wing loading (W/S): Aircraft weight/wing area.

Biplanes versus monoplanes

Compared with nineteenth-century engineering, the need for really lightweight structures was a new one. However, the wings of an aircraft are subject to bending forces, very much like a bridge, and since there was a good deal of precedence, bending loads could safely be dealt with. Wing spars, of 'I' or box section, were continuous beams on three or more supports, each bay of a biplane carrying an axial load in addition to the lateral load from the forces of the air.

Early aircraft were built mainly of wood and mild steel tubing, with coverings of fabric that, when doped, shrank to give a taut surface. The biplane's strength resided in the spars and the external bracing. The ribs were necessary to hold the fabric covering to the correct profile, but they did not contribute very much to the strength (and the fabric even less so). Strength calculations were fairly straightforward, for the structure was no more than an ordinary braced girder. Nevertheless, it was some time, and many lives were lost, before the stressing conditions to which an aircraft is subject were more fully understood.

One way to test a wing at less than one-g loading; 69 young people on a wing of a 4–6-seat Dornier Komet operated by Lufthansa, about 1924. (Dornier)

The solid members needed not only to take tension but compression, and since the principal danger here is buckling, such components needed to be as thick as possible for their weight. The importance of weight economy required improvements in structural design, interplane struts providing a good example. Weight and drag could be reduced by tapering a strut towards each end. It was shown that a continuously tapered strut could save 15 per cent in weight. For ease of manufacture a straight-tapered strut, with the central half parallel and the ends half the linear dimensions of the middle in cross-section, lost only 2.5 per cent of the optimum.

Biplanes were dominant because of their lightness and safety, though they incurred high maintenance costs owing to their complexity and had higher drag. However, because of the perceived aerodynamic efficiency of the monoplane, without the interference of two adjacent sets of wings and drag of the large number of struts and bracing wires (though the difference in speed of the two types was marginal), there was a strong inducement to built them. Because the reasons for the many monoplane failures (*see* later) were not understood, though, they were regarded as structurally unreliable.

Resistance to torsion

It was not often realized that the wings of an aircraft are, in addition to bending, subject to large torsional or twisting forces. If no proper provision was made to resist these, the wings could be twisted off. Torsion can be resisted by any kind of box or tube, the sides of which may be continuous or of lattice construction. In either case the walls of the box are subject to shearing stresses. The biplane used lattice girders to provide an efficient torsion box, in an inherently very robust form with little weight. This is a very much more efficient way of resisting torsion than depending on the differential bending of two main spars, as in monoplanes. In the UK it was thought not much could be done about this, and the amount of rigidity that could be obtained in a monoplane, even with wire rigging, was quite limited. This was not the case in Germany, with its experience of thicker and rigid-skinned wings. Consequently, in the UK, monoplanes were thought to be more dangerous, so much so that they were banned by the Royal Flying Corps for a brief period before the First World War. Thus, by 1918, the traditional biplane had become the safest of aircraft structures.

Materials

The materials used were the cheapest and most easily worked: wood, fabric, steel wire and tubing. Aircraft were hand-built with the least expenditure, by local joiners and mechanics. Spruce and birch were the most-widely used timbers, having strength/weight ratios that compared favourably with those of modern heat-treated aluminium alloys. However, wood has disadvantages: pronounced anisotropy (variations of strength in the ratio of 150:1, depending on the direction of loading relative to the grain); changes in shape and dimensions; strength loss due to moisture absorption; inconsistent structural properties common to natural products (no two pieces the same); *and* it burns. Moreover, in the many torrid climates where aircraft were beginning to operate, timber-framed wire-braced structures required frequent re-rigging with changes of

humidity. Moreover, some insects found soft northern timbers more palatable than native hardwoods.

Wood largely persisted throughout the First World War because demand was immediate and there was no time for the theoretical and experimental work that would have been entailed in changing over to metal, even if designers thought it desirable, which few did. Steel tubes did begin to appear for interplane struts, while steel wires, streamlined if external, were used for bracing. Thoughts of changing from wood to metal were current even before the First World War, but at its outbreak they had to be shelved. They were revived, however, as the large amount of wood required for military aircraft construction revealed one of its major limitations; the increasing scarcity of high-grade timber. The most suitable types were imported from overseas, requiring large volumes of shipping that was needed for the transport of troops and food, so poorer-quality timber was substituted.

Wood versus metal

The most obvious and significant change in the interwar period was from wood-and-fabric to metal construction. Provided it maintains weight efficiency, metal has a number of advantages. It is more reliable, with less variation in its properties, less affected by climate and weather, and not subject to microbe attack. Steel was the metal to which designers first turned (the new aluminium alloys suffered from corrosion problems, and Alclad (*see* later) had not yet arrived). However, mild steel, in the acceptably light gauges, offered insufficient structural rigidity and, being fourteen times denser than spruce, it needed to develop a high stress to compete. Although numerous steel-framed (and even steel-skinned) aircraft were built, they were an unhappy compromise at best.

The characteristics of metals demanded new techniques and expertise, both in detail design and in construction. There could be no straight swap of member for member (although this was done), and parts needed forming in thin-walled sections. However, the walls of steel spars usually had to be so thin that solid drawing was out of the question. The answer for wing spars and struts was the use of high-tensile-steel strip, fluted to avoid local buckling. The design of these flutes was more art than science, as was the design of the tools for making them. Empirical rules, quite reliable in the design of biplanes, were found to be inadequate for heavily loaded wing spars for a monoplane.

Aluminium alloys

As early as 1894 the use of aluminium for aircraft had been discussed at the Aeronautical Conference held in Chicago, but its cost would have been prohibitive, even though it had fallen by 95 per cent over the preceding decade. Pure aluminium is unsuitable as a structural material because of its low strength. However, when alloyed with other metals, such as zinc or copper, the strength of the aluminium base is vastly improved. Indeed, in Germany in 1909 Alfred Wilm, seeking a way of producing extruded aluminium cartridge cases, accidentally discovered that aluminium containing 3.5 per cent copper and 0.5 per cent magnesium as unintended impurities spontaneously hardened after quenching, with a large increase in strength.

The principal alloy, under the name Duralumin (commonly known as Dural), was produced in various

Although not the most aerodynamically efficient surface, the corrugated outer skin of the Junkers Ju 52/3m, so stiffened, paid for its weight by the reduction in internal structure, with no ribs except at the ends, while in the fuselage there were no stringers. (Key – Duncan Cubitt)

forms. However, there was resistance to its use, partly because of innate conservatism and partly due to the problem of corrosion, to which the alloys were more prone than pure aluminium. Not until 1927, when Alcoa in Canada introduced cladding of alloys with a very thin aluminium coating ('Alclad') in connection with the US Navy's airship programme, was the corrosion problem largely overcome.

Cantilever monoplanes

The first effective stirrings towards metal construction were begun in Germany before 1914 by Dr Hugo Junkers, who stood out as a pre-eminent contributor to aeronautics. By 1914 Junkers had come to two very-far-reaching conclusions. The first was that, due to its durability and uniformity, metal was preferable to wood as the basic material for aircraft construction. The second was that, because of the need to reduce profile drag to a minimum, the monoplane would replace the biplane. The result was the J1, or 'Tin Donkey', of 1915, a tin-plated-steel, smooth-skinned, all-metal unbraced monoplane. It was heavy and, together with the use by Count von Zeppelin of aluminium alloy for the lattice framework structures for his airships, led Junkers to switch to Duralumin skinning with corrugations running fore and aft. The skin was much stronger than flat sheet, but the corrugations imposed a drag penalty, though this was slight at the cruising speeds of 75mph (120km/h) then current. Thus the advantages of the robust and durable metal structure were to some extent offset by their aerodynamic 'dirtiness'. The stiff skin paid for its weight by reduced internal structure.

When the Junkers F.13 first flew, in 1919, it was a winner. Unlike other civil aircraft it was a low-wing cantilever monoplane that carried four passengers in, for the time, a comfortable cabin, and it was powered by an engine of only 240hp (180kW), roughly half the power of rival aircraft. The Junkers monoplanes were far superior in general serviceability to their wood, wire and fabric competitors. The metal skin contributed to the strength of the structure by helping the internal spars to carry the shear loads, but it was not stressed to the extent of the 'modern-type' stressed-skin airliners of the 1930s. Nevertheless, the F.13 was tough enough to last thirty years in such harsh environments as the Russian Arctic, Amazon jungles and the goldfields of New Guinea. This started an evolutionary process. A number of other designs of all-metal construction were built in quantity by Rohrbach Dornier, Fokker and Ford, some of which also had corrugated skins. These were widely used in many countries, and by the late 1920s such aircraft were becoming common and proving outstandingly successful.

The British view

In Britain, most designers and the Air Ministry did not heed Junkers's pioneering efforts, and it was another decade before the UK accepted the thick-section metal-skinned monoplane. It kept the traditional fabric-covered biplane, merely substituting metal members for wooden ones. It was argued that fabric covering, especially when it could be re-doped, gave long service, and re-covering encouraged overhaul.

The Metal Wing Company tried to provide some advanced thinking in steel-strip construction, and this influenced the designers of Boulton & Paul, Armstrong Whitworth, Gloster and Fairey. Duralumin was being developed to greater strength, workability and corrosion resistance, and its protagonists were competing with the 'steel strip' school of thought. This had been fostered by the Air Ministry in 1924, when it prohibited the use of wood for the main load-carrying parts of the structure of future aircraft, though this did not encourage progress to the extent of the German work on thick-section monoplanes. Even in 1924 the UK *Handbook of Strength Calculations* (Air Publication (AP)970) listed only the properties of steel tubes, and, although Duralumin was mentioned, it was given a yield strength of only 13.5 tons/in^2 (210MN/m^2), and there was no guidance as to its use. Although it was easy to repair, this worried the UK authorities and held up metal construction. When this was coupled with the discovery that Duralumin had no really satisfactory fatigue limit, firms were inclined to back the UK Aeronautical Research Committee's policy of retaining conventional methods of construction.

Light-alloy construction received its first major thrust forward in the UK as a result of the R 100 and R 101 airship programme. Their designers made use of the most up-to-date structural theories and, with many experiments to support them, produced a body of knowledge that spread rapidly in the 1930s as UK aircraft manufacturers began to recognize the advantages of aluminium, which offered approximately 60 per cent weight saving over steel, for a moderate strength reduction. From this point on, aluminium alloys became the principal materials used in British airframes.

Buckling

The transition from the wood, wire and fabric of early aircraft to the modern metal semi-monocoque or framed construction was not dictated by some sudden surge of fashion, but was a strictly logical step in aircraft design once certain loadings and speeds were reached. The general trend of design was towards the hard-skinned monoplane, in which the loads, as far as possible, were taken in the skin. By the late 1920s a smooth surface was essential, and the most obvious way to attain this was to use a metal skin. However, this was heavy, as there was a limit to the thinness of the sheet that could satisfactorily be held to shape with a reasonable number of supporting ribs. The need to save weight meant that every possible piece of material needed to contribute its full quota to strength and stiffness.

There is no difficulty about taking tension in a thin membrane. The problem is how to take compression without the skin buckling. What really happens in failures of this sort is that the structure finds some way of evading an unduly high compressive stress, usually by moving 'out from under' the load; that is to say, by running away in a sideways motion (for example, an end-loaded ruler that buckles). The ability of sheet metal to carry an increasing load after it had begun to buckle, regarded as failure for conventional structures, was crucial to the development of metal aeroplanes.

Stressed-skin construction

Strength calculations became much more complex, for not only did the structure have many redundancies, but failure by elastic instability (buckling) had to be considered in many components, as well as failure by direct tensile stress. Dr Herbert Wagner, who in 1925 was working for Rohrbach in Germany, first theoretically analysed the diagonal tension field of a thin metal sheet rigidly supported along its edges. Although not reported until 1928, nor widely recognized until the early 1930s, this provided the theoretical foundation for future progress in stressed-skin structures. It was the most exciting subject in aircraft design of the period, and formed the basis for the development that resulted in aircraft structures in which the spars, ribs and skin are all integral parts of the stressed system. Although it is now commonplace, the conception of the stressed skin and its rapid development was an engineering triumph.

The most difficult practical problem, however, was that a completely new technology had to be created. Designers in the early 1930s had to switch from familiar diagonally braced structures to tension-field shear walls (Wagner

beams) and shell construction employing stressed skins. The emphasis shifted from determining stresses by conventional classical engineering methods to securing stability against buckling with the minimum expenditure of material and weight. To save weight it was necessary to achieve a deeper section, for example by rolling corrugations into the sheet for the outside skins, as with the Junkers designs. The objections are obvious, and it became the practice to stiffen and strengthen metal skins by riveting stringers to the inside surface to share the load with the spars. Thus the whole formed a shell, stiff in bending and therefore unlikely to buckle. The stressed skin proved sufficiently strong both for fuselages and wings, and offered both cleaner design and lighter weight. Gradually and concurrently, the development of high-strength aluminium alloys and fabrication techniques for working sheet metal provided the means to fashion this new structural form.

In 1928 Jack Northrop in the USA independently and empirically developed structural methods similar to those implied by Wagner, and devised a similar type of

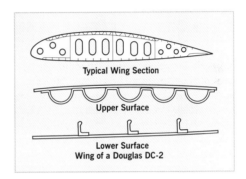

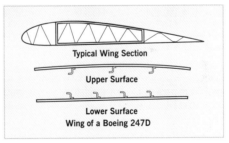

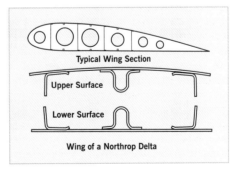

Stressed-skin wing construction of the 1930s. In contrast to earlier designs, in which the skin took predominantly torsion and shear, the stressed skin takes bending loads as well. The upper skin takes compressive end loads, while the lower skin carries tensile loads. The Douglas DC-2 wing had three shear webs, the Boeing 247D was of Warren truss-type with two shear webs, whereas the Northrop Delta had four shear webs. For structural efficiency in terms of weight, designers do not want to provide material that carries little or no stress. This means that, as far as possible, material that lies close to the neutral axis is discarded in favour of material far away from it. Of course some material is needed near the neutral axis to carry the shearing stresses, but thin webs could suffice.

(Key – Pete West/Ray Whitford)

It is apparent that one of the best ways to absorb the energy of impact in a crash landing is to permit destruction of the structure. How much better it is for that structure not to be the fuselage, in which the passengers are housed, but rather the wings and engine installations. An additional benefit of a low wing, such as on the DC-4 seen here, is that, in the event of having to ditch on water it is relatively easier for passengers to evacuate the aircraft. (Key Archive)

construction for a flying-wing he was building. Aluminium sheet was pressed into channel sections, and the channels were then riveted together to make up the wing. The horizontal members formed the skin and the vertical members formed the wing spars, while additional sheets were riveted in to form the ribs. It was a relatively cheap form of construction, which was why Northrop had chosen it. Testing showed it was stronger than expected, and the skin did not collapse after it began to buckle. Even after it developed permanent buckling, and so had failed by normal standards, it was still able to carry around 90 per cent of its 'failing' load. Northrop's designs were heavier and less elegant than Wagner's, but somewhat stronger and, initially, cheaper to build. A modified form of Northrop's structural technique was applied to the Douglas DC-1, -2 and -3, and partly accounts for the longevity of the DC-3's structure.

Flush riveting

Aircraft of the early 1930s were held together by dome-headed rivets. A decade later almost all large aircraft had rivets flush with the surface. To observers outside the industry this change, if noticed at all, must have seemed straightforward and even trivial. It did not require a major breakthrough, but aircraft performance had improved to the point that the aerodynamic drag of protruding rivets was no longer economically acceptable. Besides stressed skins, modern designs incorporated all the major innovations: retractable undercarriage, flaps and variable-pitch propellers. These raised maximum speeds; from the 170mph (274km/h) of the Northrop Alpha of 1930 to the 220mph (354km/h) of the DC-3 of 1935. Even Douglas, however, continued to use protruding rivets, and only when sufficient performance improvements had been realized did it become attractive to pursue the lesser gains offered by recessed rivet heads. Designers of flying-boats, realizing that any protuberances caused a high drag on take-off from water had, since the mid-1920s, used flush riveting on thick-skinned planing surfaces.

By the mid-1930s the time was ripe for flush riveting throughout the industry. But, to incorporate it, changes in production methods were needed. Skins were so thin relative to the size of the rivet that the machined countersink would have to penetrate through one sheet into the next. This was detrimental to the strength and rigidity of the joint, and some other way to form the recess had to be found. Again the solution was easy to perceive in principle. Deform each sheet by pressing a conical dimple around the hole, and accommodate the rivet head in the outermost of the nested dimples. This method had been employed by the Hall-Aluminium Aircraft Corporation in 1929, and experience showed that it worked. With dimpling, all the basic ideas required for flush riveting were in hand.

The task that remained for the industry was to learn how to introduce flush-riveted joints economically and reliably in volume production. With as many as 160,000 rivets in a medium-sized aircraft and 400,000 in a large one, design, fabrication and installation of riveted joints reportedly constituted 40 per cent of the total cost of a typical airframe. Because of this large number, riveting is a mass-production operation, even though aircraft production is not. As with all mass-production operations, small savings mount up.

Flush riveting became widespread, so that by the late 1930s fifteen US manufacturers were using it. Douglas, at the insistence of its aerodynamicists, adopted flush riveting for its DC-4E (1938), which had a maximum speed of 245mph (394km/h). By the late 1940s, although flush riveting had progressed, it left something to be desired regarding tightness of joint and smoothness of surface. If the head did not sit firmly in the recess the joint would yield under load; if the top of the head was too high or too low the surface was not aerodynamically smooth. Eventually it was realized that, by deliberately making the head stand proud, it could be made smooth by carefully milling away the excess after joining. This also had the benefit of giving greater tightness, since the hammer, with its impact concentrated entirely on the top of the rivet head, forced it firmly into the recess. A power-driven, hand-held milling tool that would not mar the surrounding surface was developed.

Aeroelasticity

This term covers phenomena arising from the fact that an aeroplane is not a rigid body, but will deflect under load and can oscillate (a euphemism for shaking itself to bits) in a great many ways. Early analytical studies of aircraft were made on the assumption that they were rigid bodies. This was satisfactory despite the fact that many early aircraft were far from rigid. Indeed, wing warping was used by numerous manufacturers for roll control. However, speeds were so low that aeroelastic problems were 'lost in the noise' of other difficulties. All the same, anyone who has flown in an airliner will probably have noticed that, especially in turbulent air, the wings flap and the engine pods nod.

By the early 1920s a number of limits to safe flight were imposed by structural flexibility. Four different effects were identified in the case of wings: divergence, aileron reversal, wing bending/torsion flutter and control surface flutter. The first two are static in the sense that they depend only on the aerodynamic and elastic forces.

Divergence

Divergence can occur if a lifting surface's aerodynamic centre is ahead of its flexural axis. This will cause twisting, resulting in an increase of AoA towards the tip to the extent that, in a too-flexible structure, the increased aerodynamic loads lead to further distortion and so on, progressing to structural failure. The reason that failure does not occur is that the aerodynamic forces are not sufficient to overpower the restoring elastic ones. All that is likely to happen if the speed is low is an oscillation that damps out with time, as energy is dissipated within the structure. However, aerodynamic forces (and hence the twisting) increase with speed squared, so that there is a balance between the air forces tending to produce the twist and the elastic forces trying to resist it. However, if the speed is high enough or the torsional stiffness low enough, the twist will increase and there is a critical speed (divergence speed) at which the twist becomes infinite. To avoid disaster an aircraft must be restricted to flight speeds less than the divergence speed. The question was, how much less? The *limiting* value was set at 50 per cent.

Aileron reversal

A desirable feature is a wing very stiff in torsion, and this is where stressed-skin construction has an advantage, but often at the cost of more weight than is necessary from the viewpoint of pure strength. There is another consideration that demands more torsional rigidity: the efficiency of the aileron control. If a wing is too weak in torsion, application of aileron twists the wing to such an extent that the rolling moment due to the ailerons is largely offset by a moment of the opposite sign due to the twist of the wing. In an extreme case the rolling moment may be reversed, so that the use of ailerons will roll the aircraft in a direction opposite to that intended. By the early 1930s further increase in speed, without much increase in wing density and torsional stiffness, led to aircraft approaching the boundary where aileron reversal would occur. Again, it is a function of dynamic pressure (predominantly V^2), resulting in an 'aileron reversal speed'. The problem was overcome by increasing the wing's torsional stiffness.

The strength and stiffness in twisting of a box or tube depends upon the square of its cross-sectional area. Thus a torsion box of large cross-section, such as a biplane structure,

required little material and was light. The wing of a monoplane is made by turning the wing itself into a torsion box, with a skin of wood or metal. Even if a much thicker wing is used compared with that of a biplane (18 per cent thickness ratio, versus 8 per cent), the cross-sectional area of the box is very much smaller. So, to get adequate torsional strength and stiffness, designers were forced to use comparatively thick and heavy skins. With today's much thinner (12 per cent) wings, a relatively high proportion of wing weight and expense has to be devoted to resisting torsion.

Flutter

Flutter is a high-frequency flapping in the airstream (like a flag), caused by a struggle between the aerodynamic forces

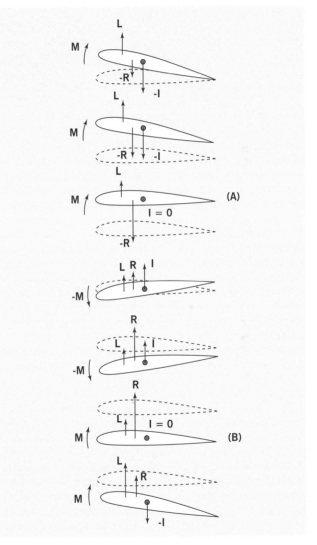

Wing bending/torsion flutter. Three forces act on a wing in flight: L, lift acting through the aerodynamic centre; R, structural stiffness acting at the flexural axis of the wing; and I, the wing's inertia (mass x acceleration) acting through the CG. If the wing is given an upward impulse and the CG is aft of the flexural axis the AoA will increase, increasing the lift. The stiffness R resists this motion, building up in strength to slow the wing's upward speed. At maximum vertical deflection (A) the inertia is zero, R is a maximum and the wing twists nose-down to its original AoA and lift. With R a maximum the wing springs back downwards, with the inertia acting upwards, which twists the wing leading edge down, reducing the AoA and lift, causing the wing to bend downwards. As soon as it passes the neutral position (shown by the dotted outline), the wing's stiffness builds up the other way, slowing the motion until the maximum downward deflection is reached. At this point (B) the lift is at its undisturbed value, inertia is again zero and the wings starts springing upwards. This starts the process all over again. (Key – Pete West/Ray Whitford)

In the final stage of its structural testing programme, a 69ft (21m) A340-500/600 wing test section deflected almost 16ft (4.8m) when applied with one and a half times its 'design limit load'. This confirmed engineers' calculations of its performance, and assured the safety and structural integrity of the new wing design. (Airbus Industrie)

and the stiffness of the surface's structure. Because it involves oscillations, inertial forces also play a part. It can arise when a wing, tailplane or fin is relatively flexible in bending and torsion. This is guarded against by increasing the stiffness of the parts, not by increasing their strength. During the 1920s wing loadings increased from roughly 10lb/ft^2 (48.8kg/ m^2) to 20lb/ft^2 (97.6kg/m^2), which led aircraft into the risk of encountering wing bending/torsional flutter. Again, there is a critical speed below which flutter will die out, and above which it will be maintained. Investigation of flutter in the UK started in 1925 because of accidents that seemed attributable to its cause. The speeds of some aircraft had reached the point where the various modes of wing and control-surface flutter were in danger of losing damping and, consequently, design requirements were established to prevent flutter.

Main-surface flutter

Main-surface flutter arises primarily from a combination of dynamic bending and twisting distortions of the surface (bending/torsion flutter), and the speed at which it occurs (the critical flutter speed) primarily depends on the torsional vibration modes of the surface. Torsional stiffness plays a large part, but it is also heavily dependent on inertia effects, especially those of large concentrated masses, such as engines. Investigations into flutter in the 1920s did much to eliminate its danger as speeds increased and, as a result, flutter accidents became rare. Increasing the torsional stiffness by a larger factor than the bending stiffness is more effective in raising flutter speed than raising both stiffnesses by the same factor. The disproportional increase can be achieved in two ways. Firstly, by increasing the depth of the wing box, though this would lead to a thinner skin to maintain stresses at the same level. Because of skin buckling, however, the stringer area would then have to be increased, leading to higher bending stiffness that would cancel the increased torsion/bending ratio and would not provide the

desired aeroelastic improvement. Secondly, it can be achieved by increasing the skin thickness, which would indeed increase the torsion/bending ratio, but would give a skin thicker than that required by load considerations, thereby producing a weight penalty.

Control-surface flutter

Flight experience had shown that control-surface flutter could cause the control column to be wrenched from the pilot's grasp. Inertia and trail characteristics of control surfaces (aileron or elevator) can modify the overall aerodynamics of the system so that an initial disturbance is amplified, or the tendency to overshoot the original condition is increased. The cure for this was by means other than structural stiffness: mass-balancing the control surface (adding weights to the control ahead of its hinge line). However, each new form of balance on controls (geared tabs, spring tabs and so on) brought its own crop of troubles. The situation was eased by the introduction of power-operated and irreversible controls.

Gust loads

Gusts due to atmospheric turbulence produce changes in wing AoA, thereby subjecting aircraft to sudden changes in lift from which normal accelerations result. For small aircraft at low speeds of under 200mph (320km/h) the accelerations produced by gusts were less than manoeuvring loads. However, as speeds became higher, particularly for the larger aircraft that were not expected to perform severe manoeuvres, normal accelerations decreased, while their higher speeds aggravated gust effects. During the 1930s such effects were covered by designing for artificially high manoeuvring normal accelerations, but later the more logical approach of designing for entry into a given gust was adopted. For simplicity, the aircraft was treated as flying straight and level into a sharp-edged gust of vertical velocity

Early testing of the Boeing Stratoliner revealed elevator flutter at around 240mph (386km/h), only 18mph (29km/h) faster than its recommended cruising speed. The CAA report on the fatal Stratoliner accident of March 1939, which killed many of Boeing's top technical people, including its chief engineer and chief aerodynamicist, concluded that disintegration of the Stratoliner had begun after a stall test with flutter in the elevator. A Douglas C-74 was lost in 1946 when elevator fabric bulging between the ribs increased the trailing-edge angle, causing pitch oscillations that broke off the wingtips; later C-74 elevators were metal covered. A related problem had occurred on the fabric-covered Spitfire ailerons early in the Second World War, as a result of which the type was eventually given metal skins, the top and bottom skins providing a sharp trailing edge.
(Key – Dave Unwin)

V, usually of the order of 25 to 50ft/sec (7.6m/s to 15.2m/s), chosen to give the peak acceleration observed in practice for the class of aircraft concerned. The value of the gust speed specified was at that time determined not by direct measurement of gusts in the atmosphere, but by examination of the strengths of current wings, including some that were thought to have failed because of gusts. By 1940 it was conceded that data on gust loads were reaching statistical dimensions, and from such statistics it was clearly unreasonable to design to withstand all possible gusts. Some reliance had to be placed upon operational factors, such as pilot skill, navigation aids and flying routes.

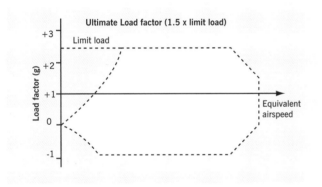

Flight envelope from V-g records. For many years wings were stressed on the basis of the flight envelope, which defines the range of speed (V) and normal acceleration (g) at each speed. The first efforts in the UK to obtain statistical loading data began in the Second World War with the purchase from the USA of the V-g recorder (introduced by NACA in 1937). The boundary of the V-g record was the first real-life version of the flight envelope used for design. With accumulation of V-g records it became possible to calculate the frequency of occurrence of a V-g boundary. This development paved the way for the broad concept that the ideal requirement was one that said 'such and such an event must not occur more often than one in X million flights'. What was not known was whether, under very abnormal conditions, a wing might be subject to higher loads. To deal with this (and possible errors in manufacture and deterioration in service) the maximum design loads are multiplied by a factor of safety (1.5).
(Key – Ray Whitford)

Graded gusts

Airworthiness requirements were modified when it was realized that the gust velocity builds up to a maximum over time, and aerodynamic lift takes several chord lengths of travel to rise to its full extent. The aircraft also starts to rise under the load, and its wings flex upwards during entry into the gust, thereby reducing the change in AoA. The sharp-edged gust assumption had led to overestimation of the normal acceleration. By 1944 the practice grew of calculating the motion of, and loads on, flexible aircraft. Allowance was made for the load relief resulting from vertical flexure of the wings during entry into the gust as they passed into a 'graded' gust on the assumption that the gust velocity increased linearly with time to a maximum over a specified distance. These effects were lumped together into an alleviation factor (<1), by which the change in load was multiplied. The increased altitudes at which aircraft now cruised led to the need to make a guess at the variation of gust velocity with height. Subsequent large-scale collection of gust statistics allowed gust velocities to be calculated on a probability-of-occurrence basis, and these broadly confirmed the inspired guesswork of earlier times.

From gust encounter data assembled from a worldwide fleet of a range of aircraft, it was found that the number of design limit loads (2.8g) would be most likely to occur on the descent, when the aircraft is flying fast down into gustier air at low altitudes, and where the wings have lost most of the benefit of inertia loading from their fuel. Typically, the probability of meeting 'limit load' came at every 32,000 aircraft hours (about once every ten years). Assuming a utilization of 3,000hr per year, the aircraft would be subjected to 44 per cent of ultimate (1.5 times limit load) once a month, 55 per cent per year and 66 per cent once in every ten years. Furthermore, the chance that an aircraft would meet the ultimate load would be extremely remote, even though it would experience 40 per cent of it fairly often. This seemed to fit in with the usually accepted idea that the limit load could be expected to occur once in the lifetime of an aircraft. Then a factor of 1.5 was put on this load to cover uncertainties of load estimation and distribution, detail stressing and structural deterioration.

Accident-rate philosophy

While many early accidents were caused by stalls and spins, structural failures were not uncommon. The idea of discussing the philosophy of the accidental failure of a structure due to loads exceeding its strength sometime in its life arose in the 1930s. This was when military aircraft were being produced in large numbers and 'accidents' to a given class of aircraft became sufficiently numerous to give rise to the discussion of 'accident rates'. Then, as now, most 'accidents' were due to a variety of causes, with pilot error and (then) engine failure being the most common, whereas accidents clearly due to structural failure seldom exceeded

The Vickers Viscount of the 1950s was the last large UK aircraft to allow post-buckling wing surfaces, after which much thicker skins were used. This is a Viscount 810 with a specially strengthened structure permitting it to cruise at 400mph (640km/h) when the more powerful Rolls-Royce Dart 541 turboprops became available in 1961.
(BAE Systems)

1–2 per cent. Experience showed that safety of the structure could be expressed as accident rate per flying hours. The structural accident rate was in the region of one per ten million flying hours. The number of civil aircraft built to a given design might be 100, and the life of each (for a variety of reasons) 20,000hr. Thus, even if one of these aircraft failed due to some structural collapse, the structural accident rate will be five per ten million hours, and therefore likely to be regarded as excessive. In the Second World War the number of aircraft to one design exceeded 1,000 and the life of each (due mainly to military action) only about 1,000hr. Again, if only one of these 1,000 aircraft failed structurally (not through enemy action), the accident rate would appear as one per one million hours and be quite unacceptable even for military pilots, even though the risk of death from other causes was much greater.

Post-war airline experience confirmed this tendency to react against structural failure very strongly, and led to the conviction that structural accident rates should not exceed one per ten million hours. It also made designers realize that, although every effort must be made to preclude structural failure, this ideal cannot be achieved, at least not without so loading the structure with excess material as to reduce the payload to an uneconomic extent.

The life of a structure

The major problem was to achieve lightweight structures that would not collapse. This was not always achieved on either count. During the 1930s considerable advances were made in design techniques, stress levels were not excessive and materials were forgiving. In addition, aircraft were designed to be taken apart, and frequently were, for checks on corrosion and C of A inspections. The accident-rate philosophy started with the assumption that a structure has a finite life. This was all too evident in the case of 1930s aircraft. Utilization rates of aircraft were low. The Handley Page H.P.42, for example, achieved about 1,500hr/year, and many aircraft were retired before they were ten years old. Even long-lived flying-boats never exceeded more than

10,000 flying hours. By the 1950s, however, airliners were being designed for 30,000 flying hours or ten years.

The basic aim of accident rate analysis was to learn how to choose strength factors so that structural accident rates should be as small as possible, consistent with efficient production and operation. Until about 1942 the choice of strength factors had been more influenced by the load aspect than by consideration of the properties of the structure used.

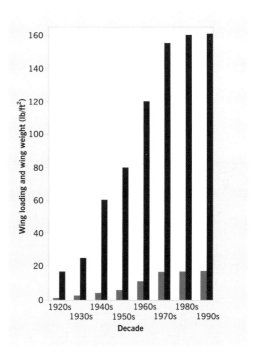

Wing weight. Metal-covered wings on 1930s aircraft were much heavier than the older wood-and-fabric type, though they were not necessarily heavier in relation to the weight of the aircraft. The old type weighed about 1lb/ft² (Wwing/S) and was used on aircraft with a wing loading (W/S) of 6–10lb/ft². The metal wing weighed 2–3lb/ft² or even more, but the wing loading of the 1930s airliner was 20–30lb/ft², so the wing weight to total weight ratio was almost unaltered. Because metal construction was much stiffer than fabric and wooden structures, there was a gain in safety from flutter, but fabric coverings were still used where extreme stiffness was not important.
(Key – Ray Whitford)

Indeed, they had been treated separately, and henceforth efforts had to be made to bring the two together. In so doing, allowances had to be made for the frequency of occurrence of loads of different magnitudes, together with variation in strength among aircraft produced to a given design. It is now common practice to specify life in the context of repairs and replacements.

By the 1950s there were innumerable detail design differences between manufacturers, but the basic principles of design and construction had become relatively uniform, based on sound engineering principles and on knowledge of how to achieve adequate strength and stiffness for minimum weight.

Fatigue

Designers have had to contend with the fatigue of metals for a very long time. It was recognized as a distinct form of failure, where materials break under fluctuating loads at much lower values of stress than their normal static failure stress, about 150 years ago. All parts of an aircraft structure are subjected to alternating loads that occur continuously during its life. As a progressive failure mechanism, material degradation and damage starts with the first loading cycle and progresses until a finite crack appears, which then grows until there is complete failure of the structure. For an aircraft, fatigue is really slow death over millions of cycles, though, unlike fatigue in a human being, rest does not bring recovery and there are no external symptoms until cracks appear. An everyday example is the failure of a paper clip through repeated bending.

The smaller the ratio of working stress to ultimate stress, the greater the number of loading cycles that can be sustained before fatigue cracks develop. The fatigue life of a structure is determined by this interval, together with the interval in which the cracks propagate to the point where the structure becomes unsafe. The latter interval should be such that, on the basis of vigilant inspection and maintenance procedures, cracks can be detected and dealt with before a failure occurs.

Stress concentrations

Small holes and notches are a good way of starting fatigue failures, and serve well to start ordinary static fracture (perforations in postage stamps, for example). However, for cracks the situation is much worse, because while cracks may be short (of the order of centimetres), the radius at the tip of the crack may be less than a millionth of a millimetre, and the stress at the tip of the crack may well be 100 or more times that elsewhere. For example, in cutting glass we do not attempt to cut right through, but instead make a shallow scratch on the surface. The weakening effect of the scratch has little to do with the amount of material removed, but has a lot to do with the sharpness of the scratch. However, even without man-made stress-raising notches, nature provides them liberally, and materials always contain small holes and cracks even before a structure is made from them.

It is well known, however, that the overstressed material at the tip of the crack tends to flow in a 'plastic' sort of way, and so relieves itself of any serious excess of stress. The sharp tip of the crack could be considered to be rounded off, so that the stress concentration is reduced, though this is far from the whole story. Though a crack leads to failure, less severe stress concentrations are also induced by other forms of geometry, such as rapid changes in section, joints and cut-outs. Anything that is elastically 'out of step' with the rest of the structure will cause a stress concentration. In areas such as these, levels of stress much higher than average are encountered.

In 1920 A.A. Griffith of the RAE published a paper on fracture and introduced the concept of 'critical crack length', below which a crack would be safe and stable and not normally extend, but beyond which it would be self-propagating and very dangerous. Such cracks spread faster and faster, and inevitably lead to an 'explosive', noisy and alarming failure and, quite possibly, a funeral. According to the Griffith doctrine, a crack shorter than the critical length should not be able to extend at all, and therefore, since all cracks start life as short ones, nothing should ever break. However, for all sorts of reasons, cracks of less than the critical length do manage to extend themselves. The main point is that they generally do this so slowly that there is time to spot them and deal with them. The most important consequence of all this is that, even if the local stress at the crack tip is very high, even much higher than the material's tensile strength, the structure is still safe and will not break so

Boeing 777 fatigue tests completed the equivalent of 120,000 flights (twice the expected lifetime) in early 1997, two years after starting. Operating around the clock, the tests accomplished the equivalent of 250 90min short-haul flights per day. One hundred computer-controlled hydraulic actuators simultaneously applied loads to simulate taxying, flight manoeuvres, wind gusts and landings. In addition, pressurization cycling was accomplished by repeatedly pumping 46,000ft^2 of air into the fuselage.
(Key Archive)

long as no crack is longer than its critical length. This is why cracks, scratches and holes are not more dangerous than they are.

Early fatigue experience

The absence of relevant fatigue data did not seriously embarrass aircraft designers before the Second World War, as they had been designing short-lived aircraft for wartime purposes, when life was scarcely measured in hours over three figures. It was not until the war that consideration began to be given to fatigue failure in relation to loading history. Previously it had been customary to design the structure with sufficient static strength to withstand the most severe expected gust or manoeuvre load likely to be encountered without making any specific provisions against fatigue. This policy had been largely satisfactory, partly because, until about 1935, the relatively ductile 2000 series (copper-rich) aluminium alloys used (*see* later) had fatigue endurance limits, and partly because flying lives were quite short. When failures did occur they were rarely catastrophic (often being associated with some obvious source of vibration), and were usually attributed to poor detail design and hence were not difficult to cure. This absence of trouble may have lured some designers into a false sense of security.

Towards the end of the Second World War a number of bombers, in spite of an average short life due to military action, did achieve 1,500hr. Some of these had wing spars made of higher-strength, zinc-rich 7000-series aluminium alloys that had recently become available. These allowed structures to be designed to function at higher stresses, and were seized upon as a means of reducing weight while maintaining strength levels. It was not appreciated that they were much more sensitive to fatigue failures and cracking, and had shorter working lives than the apparently 'weaker' ones. During conversion to the new alloys, wing spars of equal static strength suffered a five-fold reduction in fatigue life.

Evidence had begun to accumulate that fatigue failures in aircraft were increasing both in numbers and severity. In the UK little was done until the end of the war, and even then there was a reluctance to take fatigue seriously. Designers, perhaps with some justification, had hitherto accepted the comfortable doctrine that, if they designed for enough strength, fatigue would look after itself. However, in 1945 a US Stinson airliner crashed in Australia with the loss of ten lives. Investigation by the Australian authorities showed that the cause was a fatigue failure in a welded steel tube in the wing. Then a Martin 2-0-2 suffered a similar accident and crashed in 1948.

Emergence of fatigue as a design parameter

In 1947 Dr A.G. (later Sir Alfred) Pugsley of the RAE pointed out that, even on the scanty evidence then available, the actual life of conventional wing and tailplane structures allowed little if any leeway over that commercially needed. He and others drew attention to adverse design trends, warning that, in addition to strength and stiffness, fatigue would become a major factor. Contributing to fatigue was the insatiable demand for minimum-weight structures. This goal had led to the cutting from the structure of much of the excess material once used because of ignorance of the exact amount of applied and allowable stresses. Despite the warnings, expert opinion as to the seriousness of the problem was by no means unanimous, and work on fatigue

did not proceed very quickly until 1951, when two events occurred that swept away the doubts. During an inspection of a suspected fatigue area, one of the lower caps of a Vickers Viking spar was found to be completely severed by fatigue. At about the same time, a de Havilland Dove in Australia suffered a fatal accident due to fatigue failure of the lower cap of one of its spars. A sister aircraft that had flown a similar number of hours was found to be seriously cracked in the same region.

An urgent drive was started to establish the safe lives of the spars of existing aircraft. Despite ignorance of the loads to apply and the small scale of laboratory equipment, experiments showed on a comparative basis what was good and what was bad, such as the avoiding of sharp corners and abrupt changes of cross-section. At first it seemed that tests on the apparently critical portion of the spar would suffice. However, tests by the RAE showed the value of fatigue testing on a *complete* wing, as the principal failure occurred in the spar at a point not previously thought critical. In one case, in which the skin contributed significantly to the strength, the tests induced cracks of a potentially serious kind in the skin.

The causes of this emergence of fatigue as a major factor in design were not hard to find. With the revival of civil aviation after the Second World War, airliners had greater utilization and longer working lives were expected: 30,000hr being considered necessary, whereas 10,000hr would previously have been thought high. Their greater speeds and sizes, calling for higher wing and other loadings, produced more severe bumps in turbulence. Consequently, mean stresses rose. It was probably this trend, rather than the more insidious and far-reaching material effects mentioned above, that focused attention on fatigue. The seriousness of the situation was highlighted in 1954 by catastrophic pressure cabin in-flight failures of two de Havilland Comet 1s.

Loading history

Although the causes of fatigue were fairly clear, its elimination as a threat to aircraft safety was a different matter. Fatigue has two major facets: the prediction of the fatigue strength of a structure, and knowledge of its loading history. Information was lacking on both counts. An obvious first step was to obtain data on the behaviour of structures under fluctuating loads. To measure the load history in service, counting accelerometers were installed in many transport aircraft. From the fairly sparse information gained, deductions were made of the frequency of occurrence of various levels of load. Since failure occurred when the load exceeded the strength, by taking the two variables together it was possible to assess, for an acceptable failure frequency, the required mean strength. It was necessary to lay down some standard for fatigue resistance, and when enough experience had been obtained a provisional criterion was specified. The rule was that a structure should withstand two million cycles of alternating load equal to 7.5 per cent of the static ultimate design strength, superimposed on the load in undisturbed level flight.

Aluminium alloys

The history of aluminium alloys from 1939 onwards is essentially a story of competition between three groups: nickel-free Duralumins, derivatives of aluminium-copper-nickel-magnesium alloys, and aluminium-zinc-magnesium alloys. The substantial weight savings offered by the 7000-

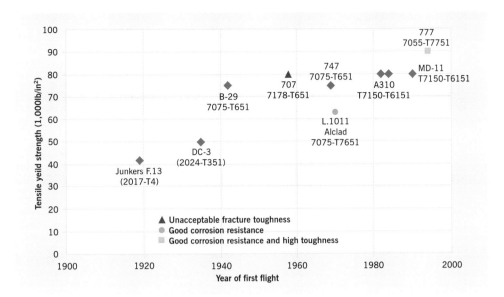

The evolution of 2000- and 7000-series aluminium alloys for wing skins (yield stress corresponds to 0.2 per cent elongation). There has been a steady progression in the development of Al-Zn-Mg-Cu alloys (7000 series) used primarily in compressively loaded structures such as upper wing skins, internal ribs, frames and undercarriages. The new 'clean' 7000 series give zinc strength and copper fracture toughness. On the Boeing 757 and 767, and on sensitive parts of current production 737 and 747 airframes, the manufacturer chose the new higher-strength materials with fatigue-tolerant properties the same as, or better than, the baseline 2024 and 7075. Using the advanced aluminium alloys saved 1,100lb (500kg) of 767 structural weight and 700lb (315kg) on the 757. (Key – Ray Whitford)

series (Al-Zn-Mg) high-strength alloys proved too strong an attraction at the end of a wartime era dominated by short-term considerations. Party to blame for the early wing-spar failures, they gained a tarnished reputation due to their premature introduction. The long-term effects of fatigue and crack propagation, and corrosion, were largely overlooked. Since the new alloys were prone to at least one of these weaknesses, many aircraft suffered frequent minor failures, even if they escaped catastrophe. While it could be said that there was a growing appreciation of the magnitude and frequency of repeated stresses to be expected, there was a dearth of facts on the relative merits, in terms of fatigue strength, of the known light alloys.

Tension leads to fatigue

Aircraft structures are usually designed primarily for static strength and, to achieve a given strength economically, it is necessary to ensure that as much of the structure as possible is in tension and to as high a level of stress as is consistent with safety. This predisposition for tension is partly due to the desire to avoid the inefficiencies introduced by buckling in compression, and partly because metals have higher limiting strengths in tension than in compression. However, this makes such structures particularly prone to fatigue.

Largely owing to their experiences with materials that were introduced in the 1940s and 1950s, engineers tended to adopt a 'once bitten, twice shy' attitude. With increased knowledge of the potential problems, designers of 1960s aircraft were faced with a dilemma. They could either use more of the weaker but well-tried materials to lower the working stress in order to obtain a cheap and reliable structure at the expense of some weight, or use new high-strength materials in order to reduce weight, though at the likely expense of delays in a programme and increases in cost. Eventually, two variants of the aluminium-zinc alloy, specifically and very successfully developed for high stress-corrosion resistance, became available in 1960, the first being the 7075 alloy with the T73 heat treatment.

Well aware that every use of a material involves a compromise, in which the properties of the various available materials vary with application, engineers have to select by balancing one factor against another. Of course, while

materials of high static strength will continue to be much sought after, the environment for an aircraft structure is such that other properties (ductility; ease of manufacture; corrosion-resistance and amenability to protective treatment; fatigue strength; reliability, for instance in freedom from liability to sudden cracking and fracture; and fracture toughness, exemplified by resistance to fast propagation of cracks under load) are of equal, or even greater, concern. The situation facing designers in selecting their alloys means they have to consider for each component whether the critical loading is static tension (or shear), static compression or tensile fatigue. For pressure-cabin and lower wing skins, two areas prone to fatigue due to the long-continued application and relaxation of tensile stresses, the standard material is 2024-T3 (Al-Cu-Mg). Introduced in 1931, this remains the yardstick for good fatigue resistance. For upper wing skins, which have to resist mainly compression as the wing flexes upward in flight (since positive load factors are always higher than negative ones), 7075-T73 is commonly used.

Pressure cabins

The skin of a pressure vessel performs two functions. It has to be gas-tight (fuselages actually operate on a constant leak principle) and to carry the stresses set up by the internal pressure. The effect of cabin pressurization is to create loads to expand the cabin, which puts the skin in tension, acting in both directions parallel to the surface. The stress in the third direction, perpendicular to its surface, is usually negligibly low. For a cylinder the circumferential stress is twice the longitudinal stress. This has probably been noticed by anyone who has fried sausages. When the skin bursts, the slit is almost always longitudinal as a consequence of the circumferential, not the longitudinal, stress. Hence the need for reinforcing frames along the length of the fuselage. There is also a force stretching the fuselage along its length, which is equal to the pressure difference multiplied by the cross-sectional area of the fuselage. This load is taken by the fore and aft bulkheads, windscreen and associated structure.

With the growing use of pressure cabins following the Second World War, the need to make repeated loading tests on their structures became evident. The first tests were on windows and panels, and portions of the cabins. The test

Fatigue Testing. Fatigue tests to two lifetimes (100,000 flights) were completed in eighteen months for the 767 and fourteen months for the 757 (shown below). For both aircraft, more than ten years of repeated load experience was simulated before their first revenue flights. Applied loads included five levels of taxi, manoeuvre load factors, and gust velocities with an application frequency proportioned to their expected service lives. (Key – Ray Whitford, Key Archive)

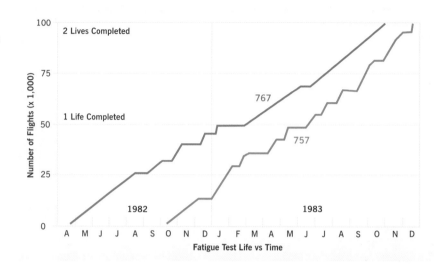

medium was air, and the danger of this procedure soon became apparent. Failures were like explosions, and precautions had to be taken to avoid flying rivets and bolts. Water was soon adopted as the pressurizing medium, since the destructive energy of air is of a higher order of magnitude than that of water. But simply filling a pressure cabin with water under pressure did not suffice, since the weight of water causes a pressure difference between the top and bottom of the cabin. Tanks had to be constructed in which the whole cabin could be immersed, so that the pressure due to the water inside and out was the same. These tanks were equipped for both static and fatigue tests by applying cyclic variations in pressure. Nowadays, pressurization cycling and the risk of explosion are reduced by filling the fuselage with Styrofoam blocks to decrease the explosive energy.

The Comet 1 fatigue failures

It was clear from such testing that the rate of growth of cracks could be anything from very slow inspectable cracks up to explosive tearing. Crucially, though, no specific attempt was made to relate the results to a safe fatigue life of the pressure cabin. At the time, expert opinion was that sufficient fatigue strength could be gained by designing for twice the working pressure differential. This attitude persisted until 1954, when, following the two Comet accidents, the RAE built a tank to accommodate an entire cabin with its wings attached.

This permitted the simultaneous testing of a wing and cabin under repetitive external loads from flight and landing and internal pressure. With the production Comet 1 that was tested (with riveted window reinforcement plates, rather than the de Havilland test sections in which the plates were Reduxed (glued)), a catastrophic failure occurred after the equivalent of only 9,000 flight hours, the origin of which was a tiny fatigue area (a rivet hole an eighth of an inch in diameter) that explosively developed into a crack several feet long. Alarmingly in this case, this test result was not an innocuous matter capable of inspection before reaching dangerous proportions. Pressurization, by the fluctuation of the circumferential tension in the cabin skin with change of altitude, had introduced a severe form of fatigue loading.

In the case of early pressure cabins (such as those of the Boeing Stratoliner and Lockheed Constellation), in which the pressure differential was low at 4psi (0.27bar), the use of minimum practicable skin thickness ensured a low general stress level. However, for a fuselage with a differential pressure of 8psi (0.55bar), a diameter of 10ft (3.05m) and a skin thickness of 0.028in (0.71mm), the hoop stress is 17,000psi (1.17MN/m²). The stress at riveted seams away from a large cut-out might be 23,000psi (1.59MN/²), or 35 per cent of the ultimate static strength, giving a corresponding average life of 30,000 cycles or a safe life of 10,000 pressurizations. This suggests that there is no serious problem. However, there are inevitably cut-outs in the skin to accommodate windows and doors, and these, without reinforcement, can double, treble or quadruple the stresses. For instance, if stresses near a cut-out rise to as little as 50 per cent above the mean level, the mean life falls to about 5,000 cycles, or a safe life of 1,700 pressurizations. In the case of the Comet 1 the stress near the corners of the small radio-aerial windows on the top of the fuselage was reckoned to be over 40,000psi (2.76MN/m^2), significantly higher than had been previously believed.

Safe-life design

The troubles over fatigue led to rival philosophies in structural design. Assuming that failure is in the end inevitable, one school favoured the 'safe life' concept. In this, an attempt is made to guarantee a certain life during which a component or whole airframe is classified as safe. The concept depends on the assessment of the accumulation of damage from the sequence of loadings during its life. This requires a study of the load variations and reversals thought to be likely. By comparison with the stress-versus-number-of-cycles curve for the material, the safe life in flying hours (after which the component is likely to become unsafe, since it has inadequate static strength left when cracked) could be found. The safe life so obtained was presumed to be consistent with odds in the order of 1,000 to 1 against failure occurring, if an aircraft flew up to its safe life. At that time, under the safe-life concept, the part is scrapped, whatever its apparent condition.

Defining safe life is relatively straightforward; ensuring that it remains valid is not. Since it depends on the way the aircraft is operated and maintained, the approach relies heavily on statistical methods and fatigue data. In most cases, accurate specification of the loads and their resulting damage is either difficult or impossible due to experimental scatter. It is also vulnerable to incorrect design assumptions and manufacturing errors. Furthermore, account needed to be taken of the variation of life of nominally identical structures. This was found to have a scatter of around 10:1, which on the basis of stress equated to a scatter of ±30 per cent. The consequences of such scatter are serious.

Safe-life's inadequacies

It became necessary to introduce a 'life factor'. Suppose the average life of a spar was 30,000hr, then, by raising this five-fold (a life factor of 5) to give 150,000hr, even with a generous allowance for scatter there would be little doubt about the safety. To achieve this would mean reducing stresses by about 35 per cent, requiring an increase in the bottom spar size by about 50 per cent. This would not necessarily mean a 50 per cent increase in weight, as not all sections of a spar are critical. If a heavier spar were used, static strength considerations would no longer be important in design, so a material with lower ultimate properties could be used. Thus, perhaps a 25–30 per cent increase in spar weight would put the design beyond fatigue troubles, but this is still a big weight penalty.

Furthermore, the safe-life factor means that, when the safe-life point is reached, many components have not actually experienced the effects provided for, having consumed only a small fraction of their useful life, yet they have to be retired or replaced. This is waste, but it is the price for safety using this method. However, there is one final point

that is the *coup de grâce* for the safe-life concept. That is, even assuming a safe life could be established to guard completely against failure, there are other sources of structural damage, trivial in themselves, that cannot be permitted to destroy an aircraft. Damage can arise due to corrosion, stones flying off runways, and punctures from tools and ground servicing equipment during maintenance and handling. The fuselage must not be destroyed by a turbine disc disintegrating or a thrown propeller blade. A pressure cabin should not blow up because of small-arms fire by a demented passenger. Moreover, there was the difficulty of predicting fatigue damage, both in location and in time of occurrence, after some years of service, when the structure itself would not even be the same as that tested in the design stage because of the repair schemes and modifications incorporated by the operator. The only advantage a safe-life structure offers to operators is that they can plan structural replacements on a scheduled basis.

Summing up, it was concluded that the safe-life concept was impractical as a means of providing safety from catastrophic failure. In one form or another it had been adapted by the designer to provide a structure as free from fatigue cracking as the state-of-the-art, the economics of the aircraft and the manufacturer's reputation for a reliable product would allow. By 1955 many workers in the field felt that the state of affairs that necessitated fixing safe lives was totally unsatisfactory.

Improved detail design could lengthen fatigue life by a factor of 5–10. However, there was the realization that, despite the large life factors applied, it was not uncommon for the most elementary errors to creep in. Production practices had to be improved, as it was not unknown for a spar to fail under test at a fraction of its expected life because of a stress concentration caused by a tool mark at a bolt hole concealed from inspection. In addition, long-term improvements in the fatigue characteristics of materials were needed. They had to be more highly resistant to crack growth, in addition to having a large allowance on critical crack length. Since freedom from cracking cannot be guaranteed it was concluded that the safe-life concept was, for many components, an inadequate and impractical means to provide safety from failure.

Fail-safe design

To quote the US CAB in 1956: 'It shall be shown by analysis and/or test that catastrophic failure is not probable after fatigue failure or obvious partial failure of a single principal structural element'. These words enunciated the fail-safe design philosophy for all subsequent transports. This is based on:

1. The acceptance that failures will occur for one reason or another despite all precautions taken against them, and that airframes had to be designed to cope with them. Thus, should a failure occur in a structural member, the load it normally carries is shed via an alternative path to other members.
2. A system of inspection so that failures may be detected and repaired in good time. Because the strength reserves in the fail-safe mode are usually well below those of the intact structure, a failure must be found and appropriate action taken within a short time compared with the normal life of the structure. Thus, in order to maintain the safety of a fail-safe structure, an inspection programme must form an

Integrally machined Airbus A310 front and rear spars (below left). A truly fail-safe spar design must not fail when a shear beam is damaged for any reason. Here, multiple beam construction has the advantage of supplying alternative load paths for tension in case any single beam web should fail. Assuming that a fatigue crack would start as usual at the wing lower skin, it would probably run upward through the web unless stopped in some manner. This design features a crack stopper, in the form of a continuous stringer about a third of the way up the shear web from the lower skin. The remaining two-thirds of the shear web would be able to sustain considerable load should the lower one-third be broken. This form of construction gives weight saving at reasonable cost compared with a multi-part fabricated spar type (right).
(Key – Ray Whitford/Pete West, Airbus Industrie)

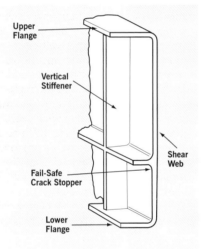

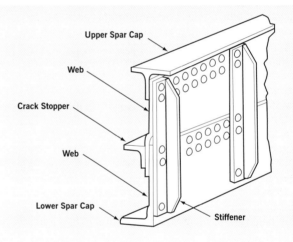

integral part of the total design. This inevitably implied that the amount of structural inspection would need to increase, presenting an added burden on the operator. However, the life of the structure would be considerably extended. Moreover, an aircraft would have higher sale-on value, instead of being virtually worthless, or at least expensive to reconstruct, at the end of its life.

3. An adequate reserve of strength in the damaged structure, so that, during the period between inspections in which the damage lies undetected, ultimate failure is extremely remote. This meant that the crack propagation rate had either to be slow or, if fast, had to be stopped by a barrier of some type. Furthermore, at any time during the period between inspections the remaining structure had to withstand those loads that the aircraft might expect. The residual strength was specified at 80 per cent limit load, based on analyses of two Douglas DC-6s after in-flight partial failures of their wings.

Although it received great publicity, fail-safe design was not new, having been used on biplanes when flying wires were duplicated. Indeed, when examined, the measure of safety achieved was due to a fail-safe approach. Multiple engines, dual controls, emergency systems, alternative airports; are all examples of it. The catastrophic failures that had occurred could, it was argued, be traced to the absence of fail-safe design. The serious failures that did not produce catastrophe were certainly not the result of a safe-life approach, but were due to the fact that those structures did indeed fail safe, whether it was intentional or not. When, in the 1950s, a propeller blade failed and passed through the pressure cabin of a Lockheed Constellation at 20,000ft (6,100m), it was safe failing that made it an incident rather than a catastrophe.

It was argued that the use of the phrase 'fail safe' was just a sales gimmick, and disguised weight penalties. However, it was found that in most cases a design needed only minor modifications to make it fail-safe. The fuselage was usually the first part of the aircraft to be considered when the subject of fail-safe design was raised. This was because of the catastrophic way in which fuselages fail if they do not fail safely. Typical fuselages were shown to have inherently good

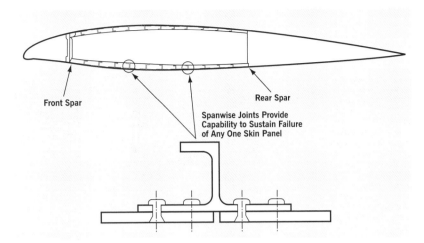

Wing splices. Multiple wing splices and careful selection of materials with slow crack propagation rates are examples of fail-safe design. The Boeing 707 wing was designed so that complete fracture of any one skin panel could be tolerated by making the splice stringer heavy enough to arrest cracks, so limiting their length. These crack stoppers provide a second line of defence against structural damage being missed during inspection. (Key – Pete West)

Front Spar

Rear Spar

Spanwise Joints Provide Capability to Sustain Failure of Any One Skin Panel

fail-safe properties, even though these were not specifically considered at the time of design. Skin panels may be allowed to crack over part of their length; frames and stringers, may crack completely; and, if holes appear, the internal pressure drops, thus relieving the load.

Inspectability

By themselves, fail-safe design features are not enough to safeguard against failure unless the structure is accessible for inspection such that defects can be found in time, before they become too extensive. The degree of cracking that can be tolerated before the structure becomes unsafe is the criterion. A crack that starts after an inspection should not propagate to critical length before the next inspection, at which point it should be detectable.

Apart from the important consideration of the extra protection against accidental damage afforded by the fail-safe structure, the essential difference between safe life and fail-safe is one of degree. A safe-life element cannot be regarded as fail-safe, however slowly it cracks, if there is a risk of accidental damage. Conversely, an element cannot be regarded as fail-safe unless cracks are found reasonably early. If a failed element in a fail-safe structure remains undetected for a long time, then, because adjacent elements are overloaded, the structure will deteriorate eventually to a safe-life condition. Therefore the structure cannot be regarded as fail-safe unless all the elements can be inspected.

Safe-life versus fail-safe design

While use of the terms safe-life and fail-safe may imply that there are two distinct paths for building certifiable structure, the situation is not so clear-cut. Both design concepts are equally necessary to create a structurally safe and operationally satisfactory aircraft. To ensure that an aircraft will perform satisfactorily in service, its structure is designed for four main failure modes: static ultimate strength (1.5 times design limit load); fatigue life (crack initiation); fatigue life of damaged structure (inspection interval); and static residual strength of damaged structure (80 per cent limit load). Thus the designer has really only one overall objective: structures that have a high degree of reliability and safety during their intended lives, so they include both fail-safe and fatigue resistant safe-life concepts.

Since fail-safe versus safe-life is a matter of degree, every item has to be treated on its merits. Pressure cabins (with

The British Aerospace 146 demonstrated best practice in design for ease of inspection. It is extensively bonded, eliminating at least 100,000 fasteners, each a potential crack starter. The aircraft was designed to have a crack-free life of 40,000 flights. Instead of a life factor of two on fail-safe joints, the 146 designers applied a factor of five, and higher in fatigue-critical areas. This cost less than 30lb (13.6kg) on the original aircraft.

crack-stoppers) are always fail-safe, but the slavish following of fail-safe principles on every detail is not necessary. It is technically permissible to continue to fly aircraft containing indisputably safe-life elements by imposing a very frequent inspection schedule on the part in question (and in many instances this is done today). Those which show a short fail-safe life, and where structural redundancy cannot be provided (for instance, under-carriages), are designed as safe-life structures. On the other hand, components that have a finite fail-safe life and contain structural redundancy (such as wing skin-stringer panels) are designated fail-safe structures. Structure in which a load-bearing part is external rather than internal is preferable from an inspection viewpoint. Experience showed that structures with heavy skins and light spars usually gave adequate warning before serious loss of strength, while heavy spars with thin skins did not.

Fail-safe's inadequacies

It must be accepted that the structural design complexity of modern aircraft and the large number of manufacturing processes involved in its production result in a vast scope for undetected shortfalls. When an aircraft enters service it does so with all the problems that were unforeseen by the designers and with latent defects built in during manufacture. Numerous small failures, and the time taken to spot them and carry out repairs, make total reliance on fail-safe philosophy impractical. Fail-safe design is usually based on a life-factor of 3 rather than 5, and within a given fleet of aircraft cracks are bound to occur, however safe they may be, so a good crack-free life is also necessary. The problem lies in cases of accidental damage, careless manufacture, severe deviations from the design flight plan (turbulence, heavy landings) and in-service use for many more years than originally planned. Nowadays, an airliner needs to be flown for over twenty years in order to be economic and is designed to accumulate 60,000 flight hours. It is therefore necessary to ensure that the airframe can reach the required life before the accumulation of damage renders the aircraft unsafe.

Damage-tolerant design

The debate over designing structures for a safe life or safe failing resulted in a compromise: damage tolerance. Originally introduced in the US MIL-STD-83444 *Airplane*

Damage Tolerance Requirements of 1974 and adopted for civil aviation, this was a shift in structural philosophy from the fail-safe stance of the late 1950s. Two events played prominent roles in shaping present damage-tolerance philosophy. The first concerned the General Dynamics F-111. In 1969 an F-111 crashed, as the result of a wing separation, after only 107 flight hours. The cause was a crack, present before the aircraft was delivered, which rapidly grew to critical length. The second event concerned the Lockheed C-5A Galaxy. During the projected four lifetimes of fatigue testing its wing developed multiple site damage well before one lifetime, and so failed to meet USAF requirements.

In practice the fail-safe concept is unduly simplistic, since there are always likely to be some inherent flaws present in the airframe. The damage-tolerance approach recognizes this, and seeks to predict the rate of growth of such damage as well as incorporating design features to delay crack growth. Fracture arrest is provided in stiffened skin structures (wing and fuselage) by careful selection of stringers, frames or straps, their sizes, spacing, materials and fastening. Fuselages can

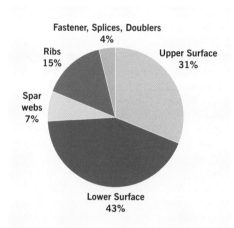

Lockheed L.1011 wing weight breakdown. By the time the Lockheed L.1011 was being designed, two serious problems that had been hampering airlines were fatigue and corrosion. Thus the design requirement at the outset was to strive for freedom from corrosion and a long crack-free life. Here, the distribution by weight of material in the TriStar's wing box shows the large proportion used in the lower wing skins to lower stress levels to resist tensile fatigue. This is balanced by a relatively small percentage allocated to splices and doublers, and is a typical breakdown for a skin/stringer arrangement. Although weight would be saved using integrally machined skins, this method of construction has not been generally favoured by US airliner manufacturers. (Key – Ray Whitford, Key – Mark Nicholls)

One of the events that played a prominent role in shaping present damage-tolerance philosophy concerned the General Dynamics F-111. In 1969 the 94th F-111 crashed while performing a low-level bombing run when it was pulling only about 3.5g, less than half the design limit load factor. The cause of the crash was the separation of the left wing at the pivot fitting after only 107 flight hours, resulting from a crack present before the aircraft was delivered, which grew to the critical length during the 107 flights.
(Key Archive)

sustain a broken frame (or strap) plus a skin crack through two adjacent bays. The permissible crack is of the order of 20–40in (51–102cm), making inspection relatively easy, because inspectors should be looking for cracks a few inches long.

Since it had become possible via the use of fracture mechanics (beyond the scope of this book *and* its author) to calculate crack growth, as an alternative to predicting when cracks will start, each critical location is assumed to have a minute flaw from the day the aircraft is built. The principle differences between the original fail-safe criteria and those of more recent times are that the first required 80 per cent limit load residual strength for a fatigue failure or obvious partial failure of a single principal element, whereas today the criteria require the same strength as before, but also include structural damage at multiple sites and the inclusion of damage growth rate considerations in the inspection programme. In other words: 'Think of cracks and design your aircraft around them'. Psychologically beneficial, damage-tolerant design can often be included with little weight penalty. In practice, the degree of damage that can be tolerated is determined by the rate of crack propagation relative to inspection intervals.

The evaluation of structures under fatigue strength calculation methods is intended to ensure that catastrophic failure is extremely unlikely (safe-life design) and that economic targets, such as low costs of maintenance and repair (damage-tolerant design) are met. Typically, the simulation of at least two lifetimes provides a high safety standard, since scatter in loads and material data is covered sufficiently. New regulations provide guidance for structural reassessments required to ensure safe operations of older aircraft. Proper maintenance and supplemental inspections permit continued safe operation of these aircraft until economics dictate retirement.

Nowadays, designers try to design structures to accommodate cracks of predetermined length. The crack length has to be related to the size of the structure, and also to the probable service and inspection conditions. Where human life is concerned a 'safe' crack should be long enough to be visible to a bored inspector working in bad light on a Friday afternoon. Taking advantage of damage tolerance has a price; higher inspection costs, better inspections and more repairs. All the same, if safety is expensive the alternative is much more so.

Structural implications of sweepback

With the coming of jet airliners in the 1950s, straight wings were replaced by thinner swept-back wings. The latter have a larger structural span than a straight wing of the same area and aspect ratio. Moreover, sweepback introduces additional torsion because the applied loads on the wing act significantly aft relative to the wing root. This requires more structural material, leading to an increase in wing weight. In addition, the wing-root torsion box contained within the fuselage also has to be heavier, since it carries the kink loads imposed when the wing loads are transferred to the fuselage. The torsion loads are reduced by reduced sweep of the rear spar (which, coincidentally, makes room for the undercarriage). It might reasonably be expected that the

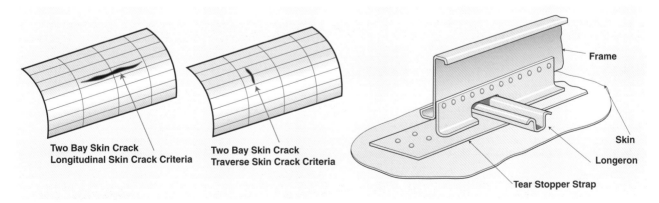

Tear straps. Repeated pressure-induced tension loading is a critical fatigue condition for airliners. Consequently they must have a fail-safe design, and this is achieved by using fail-safe tear straps ('crack stoppers'), designed to contain a failure within controllable limits by stopping a crack when it reaches the strap, whereupon the strap carries the load that the skin has given up. Tests have shown that a 20–40in (50–100cm) crack can be sustained without catastrophic failure.
(Key – Ray Whitford/Pete West)

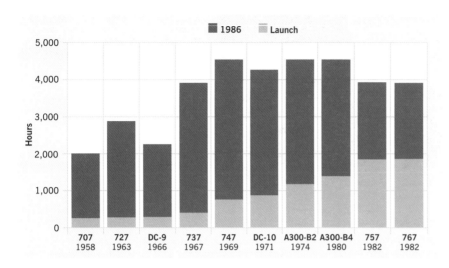

Maintenance intervals. Complete airframe and service 'C-check' maintenance intervals for early jet transports were quite short. As experience with their design and operation grew, both their launch and in-service intervals have been extended remarkably. For example, the Boeing 707 was launched in 1958 with 250hr checks, but by 1986 this had grown to 2,000hr. In contrast, the 747 (below) started at 750hr, which by 1986 had reached 4,500hr. The Heavy C checks on widebodies take around 10,000 man-hours over two weeks and are done every 15–18 months, depending on utilization.
(Key – Ray Whitford, Key – Malcolm English)

weight of wings relative to empty weight would have increased dramatically. However, the increase has been small, partly due to the inventiveness of structural designers and partly to the steady rise in wing loading (W/S).

The effect of wing bending on the actual distortion of the structure is that the swept-back wing, when bent upwards, tends to twist nose down, thereby offloading the tip. From one point of view this is beneficial, as it eliminates the tendency for swept-back wings to diverge under load. However, the nose-down twisting of the tip can have important implications for pitch stability, since the wing's lift centre then tends to move forward and inboard, increasing the pitch-up tendency.

Aeroelasticity

Aileron reversal
Aeroelasticity is concerned with stiffness, not strength, and the interacting effect on aerodynamic loading of aircraft control surfaces, wings and empennage. By the end of the Second World War cantilever ratios (semispan to root thickness) had increased to over 15, and serious consideration had to be given to aeroelastic effects. Wing twisting in response to aileron deflection is a function of dynamic pressure (predominantly speed squared), so that as speed doubled the associated loads quadrupled. This had become a serious design problem for Second World War fighters. The problem was exacerbated with the advent of the jet transports

owing to their higher speed potential and their thin, high-aspect-ratio, swept wings.

Traditional aircraft had used ailerons at the wing trailing edge for roll control, so aileron reversal was not new, and was commonly cured by increasing the wing's torsional stiffness (making it more resistant to twisting). This meant added weight.

Since strength is always a requirement, the designers' task is to provide both the necessary strength and stiffness at the least weight. It is vital to establish that an aircraft's aileron reversal speed is beyond the maximum speed attainable. What was needed was a device that applied rolling moments to the wing without twisting it, or, in other words, a surface (spoiler) that applied an increment of lift nearer the flexural axis instead of near the trailing edge. Only limited experience had been gained with spoilers by the end of the Second World War, though aileron reversal problems with the Boeing XB-47 (see Stability and Control chapter) with its very flexible wings meant that it was the last aircraft Boeing built that used outboard ailerons for high-speed control.

Flutter
Design for flutter prevention is another factor that has to be considered, and the price of freedom from flutter is eternal vigilance. Torsional stiffness plays a large part, but, because flutter is a dynamic phenomenon, it is also heavily dependent on inertia effects, especially those of large concentrated masses (engines). In contrast to divergence, it must be

Aircraft with T-tail configurations, such as the Tupolev Tu-154, tend to have a relatively flexible fin. This calls for extra caution and detailed evaluation to ensure acceptable flutter characteristics.
(Key – Malcolm English)

considered as more probable on a swept-back surface. The aim is ensure that the flutter speed is at least 20 per cent greater than the aircraft's design diving speed, the criterion being based on the ratio of dynamic pressure at flutter speeds to dynamic pressure at Vd/Md (dive speed/dive Mach number) having to be at least 1.5. This is analogous to the 'safety factor' applied to the limit load to obtain the ultimate load.

The wing-flutter characteristics of aircraft with wing-mounted podded engines is complicated by the lift generated by the engine pods themselves, particularly those of high-BPR turbofans. It is not possible to draw generalized conclusions on the effect that pods have on wing flutter because the solution of the problem is subject to many variables in addition to pod position and size. The flutter speed is influenced by the sideways bending motion of the pod and the torsional stiffness of the outer wing. Stiffening the wing region near the pylon can be more effective than stiffening the wing near its root. Other important factors are the stiffness of the pylon holding the engine, and just how far the engine CG is ahead of the wing flexural axis. However, due to lift on the nacelles, moving the engine forward can make an aircraft more flutter prone, contrary to simple ideas about flutter.

Integral construction

Aircraft surface structure must conform to shape and clearance requirements while supporting specified loads. Generally these loads include normal pressure loads; bending (wing and fuselage), which causes axial stresses in surface elements; and torsion, which puts shear in the skin. Stressed-skin construction was developed to meet these requirements with high efficiency in terms of weight. Essentially, such a structure consists of:

1. The external skin.
2. A system of stiffeners (stringers) that rigidize the skin locally and, together with the skin, carry the major surface stresses.
3. A system of regularly spaced internal supports (ribs) that establish the column length or the bending length of the skin/stringer combination to resist buckling and to transfer shear loads.
4. The spars, parallel to the stringers, whose purpose is chiefly to preserve the shape and carry beam shear.

Generally there is taper in size and strength of all elements along the length of the assembly.

During the 1930s era of thick-section wings it was sufficient to use one or two simple spars with heavy booms (spar caps) for bending and to rely on the enclosed leading edge, or perhaps the differential bending action of the two

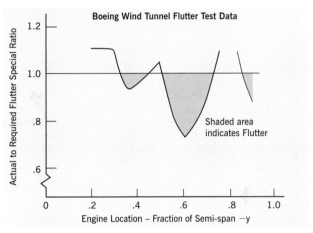

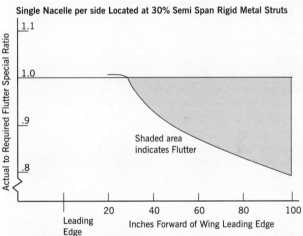

Flutter. Spanwise engine location effects upon flutter speed are shown in the figure (top), where it can be seen that flutter speed is very sensitive to engine position. Evidently some spanwise positions will require an increase in wing torsional stiffness and the attendant increase in weight to provide adequate flutter speed margins. The graph below shows that moving the engine forward makes the aircraft more flutter prone, owing to aerodynamic lift on the nacelle, contrary to simple ideas about flutter.
(Key – Ray Whitford/Boeing)

spars, for torsional stiffness. While the main box covers could be interrupted for access holes and undercarriage, torsional stiffness had to be maintained by local strengthening.

Evolved over many years, stressed-skin construction used flat aluminium alloy sheet as the base material. This would then be cut to shape and then bent, stretch-formed, pressed or rolled before riveting or bolting in appropriate jigs. An aircraft component was therefore produced from a series of low-cost sheet items, but considerable labour was then expended in the jigs, where the items were located, drilled, countersunk, disassembled, deburred and finally sealed,

Advantages	Disadvantages
Inherent stability in compression due to intrinsic solidity of extruded, forged or machined sections.	Large capital outlay on special plant and equipment, hence overall economics need careful scrutiny.
Considerable reduction in number of parts, joints and fasteners, saving cost and time in fabrication, organization and paperwork including stress-approved drawings.	Manufacturing difficulties; huge forgings and extrusion presses needed, also complex skin milling tools.
Good resistance to fatigue due to lack of holes, joints, fasteners etc., and less to inspect.	Expensive close-tolerance machining and quality control.
Reduction in sources of leaks in integral fuel tanks; structural form good for integral fuel tanks.	Double curvatures difficult to produce; even single curvature not easy.
Appreciable weight saving possible (5 per cent of structure weight, 1 per cent of TOW), hence improved performance.	The larger the component the greater the chance of production errors; expensive to scrap large components.
High surface finish, free from manufacturing distortions, gives reduced drag, especially at high speed.	Modifications and repairs difficult to introduce.
Inherently thicker sections match requirements for increased stiffness (skin thickness was more easily tapered to coincide, for example, with the spanwise decrease in bending loads).	Once special plant and equipment installed there is a tendency to justify capital expenditure by using it wherever possible, regardless of merit.

Integral construction

protected and fastened. In the late 1940s the need for reduced production costs led to the investigation and development of large sections of integrally-stiffened structures in place of the usual multi-piece skin/stringer construction. With torsional stiffness being of primary importance, structural efficiency increased as well because, as speed increased and wings became thinner, it was necessary to place as much material as far from the axis of twist as possible, enclosing the biggest area within the wing box. Much thicker skins were needed that were difficult to wrap, high-powered rollers were required for curving the skins, and machining was necessary to attain the required degrees of surface finish.

As the name implies, integral construction means that complicated sections are formed in one piece rather than by assembling separate elements to form a built-up structure (using skins and stringers, for example). There are several methods: machining from plate or billet, forged or rolled as a sheet product, or extruded.

Engine position and inertia relief

With the basic concept of designing large-span wings to lessen lift-induced drag, it is crucially important to keep weight to a minimum. However, the long, slender cantilever beam (the structural wing box) can become excessively heavy as span increases and wing chord, and hence wing depth, is reduced. Attention to the distribution of mass, mainly engines, fuel, and the order in which the tanks are emptied, is an obvious way to keep down the loads in the structure, as this can help relieve the wing bending moments. The extra negative bending moments produced by the engine/fuel masses are easily handled by a structure primarily designed for positive bending.

From its experience with its B-47 Stratojet and B-52 Stratofortress bombers, Boeing concluded that distributing four engines along the span of an aircraft the size of its Model 387-60 (the 707 prototype) was likely to make the aircraft

1,500–3,000lb (680–1,360kg) lighter than one with engines mounted elsewhere. A counter-argument was that the lower-aspect-ratio wing-box structure of the buried-engine layout (de Havilland Comet) was inherently stiffer, and aeroelastic problems were less severe. Boeing acknowledged, even in 1953, that there was no indication that the correct wing-pod mounting of turbojets had any significant effect, favourable or otherwise, upon the ratio of empty weight/TOW of an aircraft (since any benefits were likely to be applied in other areas) as compared with wing-root mounting. However, having gone on to apply its podded layout to the 707 and subsequent models, the company gained increasing experience with a layout that worked, and has stuck with it. Of course, with the introduction of the turbofan engine, especially of the high-BPR type currently in use, there is no feasible way of mounting the engines *within* the wing structure. The benefit of inertia loading has been taken about as far as it can in the long-haul transport, in which 60–65 per cent of the TOW is in the wing. For short-haul aircraft this may be 35–40 per cent.

In all of the types having rear-fuselage-mounted engines the advantage of bending relief was abandoned in pursuit of a cleaner wing and the notional reduction in internal noise, though even the most lavish quantities of soundproofing would not weigh any more than the extra metal required in the wings.

Structural weight fraction

A commonly-used measure of structural efficiency is the structure/weight ratio (Ws/TOW). By the late 1930s it had been noted that structural weight of landplanes varied from 25 to 35 per cent of the total. The slightly downward trend in this measure of efficiency (shown in an adjacent figure) is a tribute to designers, who, in the face of the requirements for increased complexity and more severe operational environment (demanding greater structural strength and stiffness), were able to make such an improvement possible. This was partly

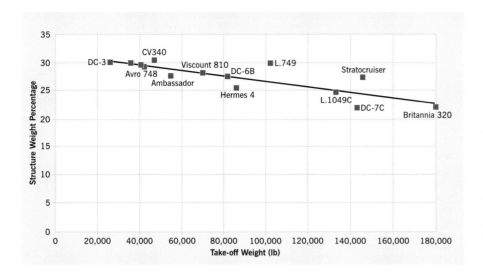

Structural fraction. Achieving a downward trend in the structural fraction (a measure of efficiency) of propeller-driven airliners is a tribute to designers in the face of the requirement for increased complexity and a more severe operational environment. Such an improvement was made possible partly through the use of improved materials, but primarily through new design concepts and by increasing wing loading. This is one of the reasons wing loading grows with aircraft size (allowed by high-lift device advances). (Key – Ray Whitford)

due to the use of improved materials, but primarily to new design concepts. The structural weight ratio has remained roughly constant for all subsequent large airliners.

The greatest gains arise if advances in structural efficiency can be assured in the project stage of design. The change in structural efficiency is here defined as the change in weight of a structure of given external shape designed to withstand a given distribution of load. A 10 per cent gain in structural efficiency would lead to a structure 10 per cent lighter. At the project stage, if payload, performance and strength are held constant, a saving in structure weight is also accompanied by savings in fuel, the use of smaller engines, smaller wings to keep the same wing loading, and so on, so that the saving in the aircraft's TOW to do the same job is much greater than the weight saved in the structure alone. This is the so-called 'growth factor' that may lie in the range 2–5 (i.e. 1lb in weight saved can reduce total weight by 2–5lb and, of course, vice versa).

Design for low weight

The objective is to provide a structure that will permit the aircraft to do its job most effectively, that is with the least total effort, spread over the whole life of the aircraft from initial design until the aircraft is retired. There is, therefore, no all-embracing simple criterion by which the success of the structural design can be judged. It is not sufficient to believe that the percentage structure weight is of itself an adequate measure of effective design, either of the complete vehicle or of the structure itself. Nevertheless, the percentage structure weight is a useful measure, provided its limitations are recognized. The weight breakdowns in terms of structure percentage of subsonic airliners over the years show a remarkable consistency, irrespective of powerplant. Judging by the consistency within the three classes (short-, medium- and long-haul), it appears that, despite changes in the structural art, the undoubted gains in structural efficiency have been absorbed in the optimization process and are not necessarily shown by reduced structural percentages.

The configuration of the various structural components in an aircraft is rather limited, mostly because the structural engineer tends to come off second best when confronting the aerodynamicist. There is, of course, an interaction between all the factors affecting a design, but aerodynamic performance virtually dictates the external shape and configuration, and the structure has to be fitted inside a

prescribed envelope. A good example is the provision of increased aspect ratio, at the expense of structure weight, which may give better fuel economy in the cruise and reduction in total aircraft weight.

The magnitude of the task can be imagined by recalling that the structural weight is between 25 and 30 per cent of the TOW and the payload about 15 to 20 per cent, depending on

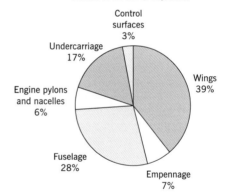

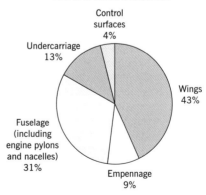

Weight breakdowns. A comparison of structural weight breakdown for the Boeing 707-320 with wing-mounted engines and the Vickers VC10 with rear fuselage-mounted engines. Although the overall structure weights are similar, the figure shows the greater weight put into the VC10's wing because of its lack of inertia relief from engines, whereas it saves on fuselage and engine-pylon weight.
(Key – Ray Whitford)

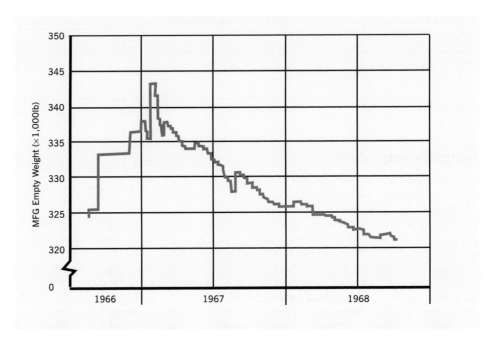

Weight reduction. Early in 1967 Boeing ran into serious weight problems with its 747 design. The figure shows the history of the weight reduction programme, during which more than 20,000lb (9,000kg) was removed by the time of roll-out in 1968. Boeing had calculated that every 1,000lb (450kg) over the contracted weight would cost an airline $5,000 a year in sacrificed payload, passengers and cargo. PanAm insisted that the performance guarantees based on a 655,000lb (297,000kg) aircraft contained in the contract signed in April 1966 should pertain to the actual 710,000lb (322,000kg) 747. (MFG: Manufacturer) (Key – Ray Whitford)

role. Therefore, if the structure weight can be reduced by 15 per cent, a feasible target, the payload can be increased by 30 per cent. This sort of increase will make any design competitive on direct operating cost (DOC) alone, and this benefits through-life cost, which more than offsets the increase in initial cost. A saving of only 880lb (400kg) in a medium-haul aircraft of the A310 type means four extra passengers, a mere 0.5 per cent of the total weight or a cost reduction in fuel of up to $25,000 a year.

Ageing aircraft

Whereas, in the 1950s, airlines kept their aircraft for only six or seven years, today twenty or even twenty-five years is normal. Design goals are initially determined for a life of twenty years and, as of 1990, 32 per cent of the world's fleet was over twenty years old. Twenty years is a rule of thumb for what is called the 'economic design life', the point at which, according to the FAA, 'a substantial increase in maintenance costs is expected to take place in order to assure continued operational safety'. This period was established on both financial and technical bases. In the first case, an airline expects an amortization period of at least twenty years, and, in the second case, it is reasonable to expect that breakthrough technologies generally tend to make the older-technology aircraft less economical to operate. To meet the twenty-year requirement, manufacturers design and build for a minimum average useful life of forty years. This provides the customer with a high probability that the aircraft will be relatively free from fatigue or corrosion problems for twenty years, provided routine maintenance is properly performed.

The longer an aircraft is operated, the more likely it is to develop structural damage, and over half of the Service Difficulty Reports published by the FAA deal with structure. It is in airlines' long-term economic interest to avoid the additional costs that result from unscheduled repairs. This can be done by a systematic approach to the overall inspection requirements of the airframe, engine and other components. This approach has to take into account the

statistics of the occurrence of damage, various non-destructive detection techniques and the probabilities of detection of certain classes of defects, loads and damage deterioration properties, inspection intervals, human factors, costs benefits and repair technology.

Chronological age is only one factor in assessing the safety of an old aircraft. Another is the number of cycles it has gone through, a cycle being one take-off through one landing. At 60,000 cycles a short/medium-haul aircraft has met its economic design life even if it is not twenty years old. Fatigue and corrosion (a function of age and environment, rather than cycles), and to a lesser extent improper maintenance, have been recognized as the main causes of structural failure of ageing aircraft. Although their failure mechanisms are quite different, and require their own specific approaches to prevention and detection, they are particularly harmful when occurring together. This happened to the Aloha Airlines Boeing 737 that lost the top half of its forward fuselage in 1988.

Design for long life

Nominally there are four basic design criteria that must be met: ultimate strength, fatigue resistance, damage-tolerance characteristics and corrosion prevention. These can be quantified by establishing two design goals: overall structural loadings and the design life of the aircraft. These not only specify the extreme structural requirements, but also the length of time (years, flight hours and landings) the aircraft should operate without suffering degradation due to fatigue and corrosion.

The design of load-bearing structures is a balance between:

1. The amount of material required to prevent structural failure from one of the extreme loading conditions (ultimate strength).
2. The amount of material required to sustain structural integrity with certain levels of hidden or undiscovered damage (damage tolerance or fail-safe).
3. The amount of material required to delay the onset of

widespread cracking until the aircraft has reached its useful life (fatigue resistance).

4. Care and protection from the harsh environment in which components may exist (corrosion resistance and inspectability).

This is done through a process of selecting design-limit stress levels, materials and design.

Design for longer life?

For most short/medium-haul aircraft a service life of 60,000 flights without major structural repairs is a typical figure. It would seem that the higher the design fatigue life relative to this service life, the better. Yet, however good the detail design, choice of materials and utilization of fatigue-life-improving processes such as shot peening, it is the stress levels that fix the time when cracks occur. The only sure way to increase the life is to reduce the stress levels, and this means increasing the structure weight and therefore the DOC. The increase in life is close to the fourth power of the reduction in stress in the case of a pressure cabin cycle of zero to maximum pressure once per flight. Thus doubling the life requires about a 17 per cent reduction in stress and a 20 per cent increase in weight, if this is proportional to stress. However, only a part of the structure is designed by fatigue requirements, and thus the total structure weight may be increased by only 6 per cent. Such an increase in structure weight would raise the DOC of a typical 140-seat twin-engine short-haul transport by about 1.5 per cent. It is therefore not necessarily sensible to specify a design life higher than is really necessary.

For the aircraft type considered, the total airframe maintenance costs represent about 6–7 per cent of DOC. These costs include the systems, undercarriage and engine equipment (but not the bare engine) as well as the structure. With the structure accounting for only 10 per cent of the total airframe maintenance cost, and assuming that doubling the design life will halve the cost of maintaining the structure, the resulting reduction in the DOC would be about 0.3 per cent. Thus, taking into account the weight penalties involved, the effect of doubling the design fatigue life is a net adverse effect of over 1 per cent on DOC. On this basis it would not be cost-effective to increase design fatigue life beyond current values. In the absence of detailed cost relationships, manufacturers have found that designing to a mean fatigue life of about twice the expected service life (two times twenty years) seems to give acceptable structural maintenance costs.

Materials

Structure weight, and therefore the use of light materials, has always been important. When a modern fully-loaded subsonic medium-haul airliner takes off, only about 20 per cent of its weight is payload. Of the remaining 80 per cent, roughly half is empty weight and the rest is fuel and consumables. Hence any saving in structure weight can lead to an almost corresponding increase in payload, or improved performance (increased range, higher cruise altitude, improved airfield capability), or a smaller aircraft could perform the mission. It is not, therefore, surprising that manufacturers invest heavily in weight control.

The history of the development of aluminium alloys and steels, which for decades were the dominant metallic materials used in aircraft structures, is a catalogue of

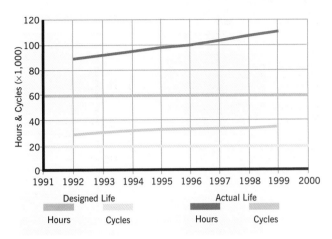

Design lives. The design life of the Boeing 747-100, both in flight cycles and hours, was greatly exceeded by fleet leaders. During 1996 a 747-100 operated by TWA passed the 100,000 flight hours milestone, and by 1999 it had gone on to 111,600hr. The two major structural issues on the type were replacement of the fuselage frames in the Section 41 (flight-deck) zone, and modifications to the engine pylons. In contrast, the fleet leaders of Lockheed L.1011 TriStars, whose original design life was 115,000 cycles, 210,000hr, and which entered service two years later than the 747, had reached only 36,800 cycles and 83,000 flights by the end of 1999.
(Key – Ray Whitford)

improvement of those material properties of first concern to the designer. Several factors influence the choice of the structural material for an aircraft but, of these, strength allied to lightness is the most important. That said, other properties have varying, though sometimes critical, significance: stiffness, toughness, resistance to corrosion, fatigue and the effects of local heating, ease of fabrication, availability and cost. The checking and comparison of all these parameters to make a choice represents an iterative process, which starts from the specification and project requirements, and takes account of the operational environment as well as the properties of the candidate materials. A compromise is always necessary because there are many different and conflicting requirements.

Suffice it to say that alloys of steel and aluminium, which became the mainstay of aircraft structures in the first half-century of flight, have far from run their course, and will continue to find a place for some decades to come. Inevitably, each new success is regarded only as a jumping-off point for the next even-better materials. However, while recognizing a continuing future for the 'conventional' materials, some thought must also be given to the prospect for other materials with a growth potential, such as may conceivably lead to their virtually ousting conventional aluminium alloys. Nevertheless, a word of caution is necessary about the introduction of any new materials: they should never be used in circumstances where inspection is impossible or difficult.

Composite materials

Historically, aluminium alloys have been the primary material for aircraft, but the demand for low structural weight and high stiffness has exceeded the capability of 'conventional' ones. Since the 1980s, non-metallic fibre-reinforced plastics (such as carbonfibre composites) have been increasingly accepted, and airliners have used a growing amount of these new materials, though this has

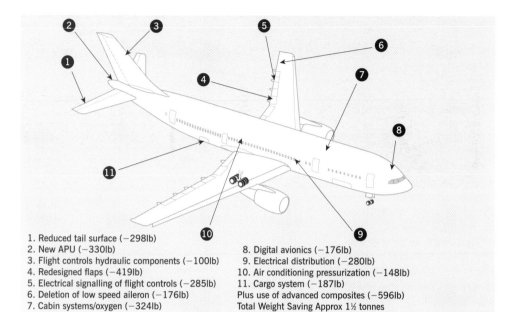

Weight reduction. In stretching the A300B4 by three fuselage frames, Airbus took the opportunity to apply a weight reduction programme in producing the A300-600. The lengthened fuselage (stretched by 63in (1.59m)) allowed the use of the smaller A310 tailplane. Only the major contributors are shown. (Key – Pete West/Airbus Industrie)

1. Reduced tail surface (−298lb)
2. New APU (−330lb)
3. Flight controls hydraulic components (−100lb)
4. Redesigned flaps (−419lb)
5. Electrical signalling of flight controls (−285lb)
6. Deletion of low speed aileron (−176lb)
7. Cabin systems/oxygen (−324lb)
8. Digital avionics (−176lb)
9. Electrical distribution (−280lb)
10. Air conditioning pressurization (−148lb)
11. Cargo system (−187lb)
Plus use of advanced composites (−596lb)
Total Weight Saving Approx 1½ tonnes

lagged behind their use in trend-setting fighters. This is due to cost being a more important consideration, and a general conservatism deriving from greater concern for safety and preparedness to adopt a more wait-and-see policy.

Carbonfibre composites

Carbonfibre composites (CFCs) are the most important material to be introduced into aircraft structures in the last thirty years. They consist of immensely strong, high-modulus (stiffness) small-diameter fibres set in a matrix of epoxy resin that is mechanically and chemically protective. The fibres provide the basic strength, while the matrix stabilizes the tiny fibres and acts to redistribute the load in shear between fibres in the case of fibre failure. At the level of design strains for these materials (0.4 per cent), fatigue is not a problem, and designs are based on their static properties.

Because of the remarkable specific (by weight) properties of CFCs, they offer weight savings of 20 per cent or more, even when allowances are made for hot/wet conditions and

Date	Alloys	Remarks
1903	Aluminium	8 per cent copper engine parts used by Wright brothers
1916	Unknown alloy	First aluminium used in structure (Breguet in the First World War)
1927	2017-T4 (Alclad)	First Alclad aluminium product introduced
1928	2014-T6	2014 introduced and used for forgings (Al-Cu-Mg)
1931	2024-T3 (Dural)	2024 introduced (Cu 4.5 per cent, Mn 1.5 per cent, Mg 0.6 per cent); still very widely used
1943	7075-T6	7075 introduced (Al-Zn-Mg-Cu), high strength but neglected long-term effects
1951	7178-T6	7178 introduced
1954	7079-T6	7079 introduced into USA from Germany
1957	2020-T6	Aluminium-Lithium (Al-Li) alloy introduced
1960	7075-T73	T73 heat treatment overcame stress corrosion problems and had higher strength with cracks present but 10 per cent less static tensile strength. Later used on Boeing 747 upper wings
1971	7050	Improved balance of properties
1974	2020	2020 alloy removed from Alcoa product line
1978	2224, 2324, 7150	Boeing uses new alloys for 757, 767 and 737-300
1980+	2090, 8090	Continuing development of Aluminium-Lithium alloys

Little improvement occurred in 2000- and 7000-series aluminium alloys between 1930 and 1960, but they should not be assumed to be fully developed, since a stream of incremental improvements continue to be achieved. These include improved high strength (Al-Zn), better damage tolerant (Al-Cu) and the more novel Al-Li variants. However, although advances continue in materials, structural design and manufacturing methods, and cost considerations, play an ever-increasing role in ensuring a competitive product.

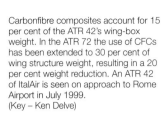

Carbonfibre composites account for 15 per cent of the ATR 42's wing-box weight. In the ATR 72 the use of CFCs has been extended to 30 per cent of wing structure weight, resulting in a 20 per cent weight reduction. An ATR 42 of ItalAir is seen on approach to Rome Airport in July 1999.
(Key – Ken Delve)

notch effects, compared with 2000- and 7000-series aluminium alloys. However, the resulting structures have been much more expensive than their metal counterparts, due in part to the expensive raw material and the fact that the major emphasis is on maximum weight reduction. To accomplish this objective the design approaches have concentrated on structural simplification, reduced part count and the elimination of costly design features. The ability to mould complex shapes reduces waste material and reduces the number of parts by a factor of three, thereby reducing joining costs. For example, a CFC aileron designed for the Lockheed L-1011 TriStar was 26 per cent lighter, had 205 parts instead of 398, and required 2,574 fasteners rather than 5,253.

The general lack of sufficient toughness and damage tolerance is still proving a problem for all composites. The vulnerability of brittle materials to impact and to stress concentration is not a new problem, and it occasionally catches designers unawares, even with metals, most recently Al-Li (*see* next section). Low-velocity impact may be invisible from the outside (it can cause either internal delamination or 'back face' tensile failure). Stress concentrations are also extremely dangerous for materials whose through-thickness strength may be only a fortieth of its in-plane values. However, the properties achieved so far in what is still a relatively young technology (CFCs were announced by RAE Farnborough in 1966) are modest compared with the theoretical, and improvements in matrix materials and in the reinforcing fibres are continuously being made.

Composites versus metals

For composites to become more competitive with traditional aluminium alloys, most operations and maintenance per-

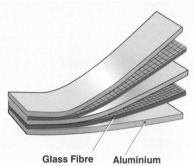

Glass Fibre   Aluminium

GLARE. Glare is a fibre/aluminium alloy laminate that could reduce the weight of fuselage structural components by 15–28 per cent. It uses 0.2–0.3mm fibreglass pre-preg and 0.3–0.5mm aluminium alloy. Its advantages over aluminium alloy are its lower density, greater strength, fatigue and damage tolerance, and corrosion resistance. The most fatigue-critical area of a fuselage is the top skin, because tensile stresses from bending and pressurization are additive. It is in this region that Airbus is using Glare on its A380.
(Key – Ray Whitford/Pete West)

sonnel agree that the costs of using them must drop significantly. Central to cutting those costs will be improvements in maintainability, reliability and repairability. Composites first saw use in cosmetic and non-load-bearing components, but designers today are relying on composites' strength/weight characteristics to use them in primary structure. The performance benefits remain outweighed by the higher cost of their manufacture and maintenance in the field. They have a better initial service record mainly because of their corrosion resistance and fatigue properties, but they are, nevertheless, more prone to impact damage, the economic repair of which has typically been limited to minor damage.

Made in Australia, the 33.8ft (10.3m)-long all-composite rudder on the Boeing 777 weighs 315lb (143kg) and is the largest all-composite primary structure on any Boeing aircraft.
(Key – Tony Dixon)

Characteristic	Composite	Metal
Fatigue	Much better than metals	Problems
Corrosion	Much better than metals	Problems
Load/strain relationship	Linear strain to failure	Yield before failure
Failure mode	Many	Few
Transverse properties	Anisotropic (therefore weak)	Isotropic (same properties in all directions)
Notch sensitivity/static fatigue	More sensitive/less sensitive	Sensitive/very sensitive
Mechanical properties variation	High, mostly in compression and transverse direction	Normal
Sensitivity to hygrothermal environment	Sensitive to hot/wet conditions	Less sensitive
Through-thickness crack growth	Growth/no growth phenomena	Slow growth
Delamination	Problems	No problems
Initial and in-service flaw/damage size	Not well-defined	Defined
Damage inspectability	Problem	Adequate

Current evidence shows that repair costs for composite structures can exceed those for conventional metal by a factor of at least two. Parts with substantial damage must be replaced, with the cost and out-of-service time for such work, combined with the special facilities required, making major repairs impractical. In the event of the need to replace entire items with significant damage, such as a complete fin, the reinvestment required to replace the damaged item is not seen to offset the relatively modest fuel-burn reductions sufficiently. There is also the hazard associated with the dispersal of the fibres in accidents and fires, and in their ultimate disposal. In the striving to obtain the best performance it is relatively easy to leave these issues for someone else to worry about in the future, but they may all rebound eventually.

Most conventional structural materials, such as steel, aluminium alloys and titanium, are roughly equal in terms of specific stiffness. For this reason large expenditure has been put into developing new materials such as CFCs. Depending on their application these may or may not be effective, but what is certain is that they are expensive and their production requires a lot of energy.

Aluminium-Lithium alloys

Prompted by the large increase in oil prices in the mid–late 1970s and the threat of CFCs, the aluminium industry put considerable effort into the further development of Aluminium-Lithium (Al-Li) alloys. The great attraction of these is their reduced density, about 10 per cent less than that of typical 2000-series alloys, whereas they have about the same strength as conventional 7000-series alloys. Moreover, they are about 10 per cent stiffer than conventional alloys and have very good fatigue properties. In many circumstances Al-Li offers comparable benefits to CFCs, especially where the loading is in compression or is strongly two- or three-dimensional. Al-Li alloys are not entirely new and have been around since the 1920s. Were it not for technical and

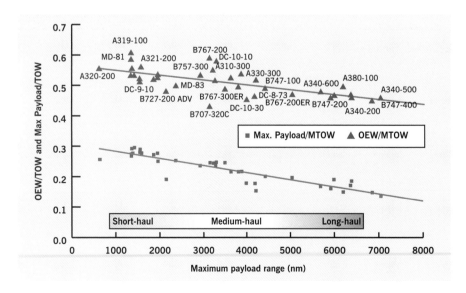

Weight fractions. Variation in maximum payload and operating empty weight (OEW) fractions of maximum take-off weight (MTOW) with maximum (not typical) payload range. Unsurprisingly, payload is traded for range. With structure weight representing about 50 per cent of OEW, lighter structures can benefit payload range.
(Key – Ray Whitford)

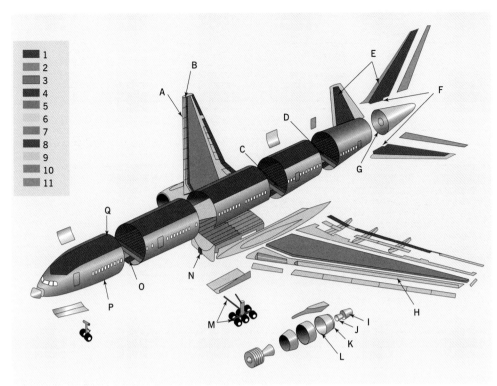

Materials usage on Boeing 777. Of note is the use of aluminium alloy 7150-T77 on the fatigue-critical upper fuselage stringers subject to tension due to fuselage bending and pressurization. (Key – Ray Whitford/Pete West))
Key: Alloys: 1. Ti 10-2-03. 2. 2XXX-T3, -T42, -T36. 3. 7056-T77. 4. 7150-T77. 5. Ti 6-4 b-ELI 6. Ti 15-3-3. 7. Ti b21S
Composites: 8. Toughened CFRP. 9. Pitch core. 10. ATL CFRP tape. 11. AL mesh.
A. Upper spar chord. B. Upper skin & stringers. C. Floor beams. D. Seat tracks. E. Fin & tailplane. F. Tailplane attachment fittings. G. Aft bulkhead. H. ECS ducting. I. Tailcone outer sleeve. J. Tailcone plug. K. Aft core cowl. L. Inner thrust reverser cowl. M. Truck beam & braces. N. Keel beam. O. Belly stringers. P. Fuselage skin. Q. Crown stringers.

production uncertainties, much of today's airframes would already be manufactured from them. Primarily because of the high cost of lithium, safety precautions in casting, the need for scrap segregation and handling, and closer control of processing, product costs are more than three times those of conventional aluminium alloys. However, manufacturers can use existing equipment to machine it, and workers need no special training. Manufacturers in the USA, especially, have been more cautious in their use of Al-Li, regarding the benefits of the material's lower density as being almost entirely offset by its questionable damage-tolerance properties and increased cost, together with the ability of industry to supply the material. Indeed, in 1991 Boeing gave up its plan to use Al-Li extensively on its 777.

Material	Energy to manufacture (Joules × 10⁹ per ton)	Oil equivalent (tons)	Specific stiffness (MNm/kg)
Mild steel	60	1.5	26.9
Titanium	800	20	26.7
Aluminium	250	6	26.0
CFC	4,000	100	100

Approximate energies required to produce various materials

An A340-300 of Olympic Airways. If 1 tonne of structure weight on such an aircraft is saved, this reduces take-off weight by up to 1.5t due to reduced fuel consumption. This allows redesign of the structure saving another 0.2t, which feeds back into the system to give a final reduction in take-off weight of 1.7t. A reduction of 1kg saves about $1,000 over the life of an aircraft, depending on its use and the cost of the part. In addition to being 20 per cent lighter than its aluminium alloy equivalent, the CFC torsion box of the A330/340's fin has less than 100 parts, compared with over 2,000.
(Airbus Industrie)

Wing load alleviation. Wing load alleviation in passive form was pioneered for commercial transports by Vickers for the VC10, using symmetric upward deflection of the ailerons at high operating weights to reduce outboard wing loads, hence reducing wing bending moments. Active manoeuvre load alleviation was introduced by Lockheed in the late 1970s for the L.1011-500, using symmetric aileron deflection in response to pilot commands to modify the spanwise loading and hence wing-bending moments. Active manoeuvre load alleviation was introduced by Airbus on the A330, using fuselage-mounted accelerometer signals to trigger rapid aileron and spoiler deflection in upgusts, thus reducing the applied gust loads.
(Key – Ray Whitford/Pete West)

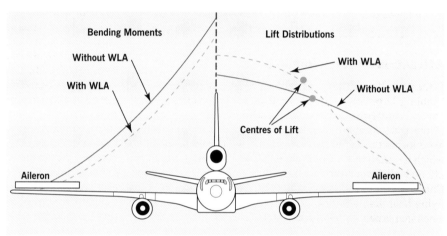

In an attempt to save weight, the A330/340 wing was the first on a civil transport aircraft to incorporate significant amounts of Al-Li alloys in the secondary structure. For some years these promised significant weight savings (7–10 per cent), but have still not been brought to full maturity. Their cost/weight effectiveness remains marginal, but has now reached the stage where sheet and extrusions in the wing leading- and trailing-edge structure became viable. Emirates was the first airline in the Middle East to take delivery of the A330-200.
(Airbus Industrie)

Chapter 7

Flying Boats

During the early 1920s the slow pace of aeronautical development was even more pronounced in flying boats, which did not experience the acceleration of landplane developments at the end of the decade. The biplane configuration dominated flying-boat design, and most efforts were aimed at military uses. However, by the middle of that decade serious consideration was being given to the flying boat for commercial aviation. This chapter deals with the unique design aspects of flying boats, the attempts to achieve transoceanic performance in the 1930s and the flying boat's inevitable demise following the Second World War.

Attraction of the flying boat

In the years before the Second World War, airports capable of handling large long-range aircraft were few in number and non-existent in many parts of the world. However, most areas of the world that were of interest for trade and commerce were located near bodies of water. These natural resources, which required little development, allowed unrestricted take-off and alighting that could be made directly into wind. Consequently, more scope existed for the development of the flying boat than was possible with the landplane, especially when increasing size was taken into account.

The landplane was thought by some to be rapidly approaching a limiting size, whereas the upper limit for the flying boat was thought to be very remote at the beginning of the 1930s. This was because the landplane was limited by the size of airfields, which were generally surrounded by obstructions and therefore required low take-off and landing speeds and a high initial rate of climb. These requirements conflicted with performance judged on a payload/engine-power basis. Moreover, with increasing aircraft size the design of the undercarriage presented difficulties owing to the need to absorb the energy of landing. Another serious problem was the high loading on the wheels when taxying, and the consequent damage to the airfield surface and the attendant maintenance cost.

On long over-water flights the flying boat offered the prospect of a safe descent in the event of an engine failure, a very real possibility with the relatively unreliable engines of the time. The chances of surviving a descent in rough seas were low, so this advantage was more psychological than real, yet a number of cases were reported in which passengers and crew survived a descent on the open ocean. However, flying boats cannot withstand the same rough seas as ships, and scheduled operations were limited to coastal waters and lakes. Moreover, loading/unloading and servicing posed considerable problems. No passenger wanted to fly long-haul only to be made wet and seasick in the last few feet.

As outlined to the British government by Saunders-Roe in 1945, the Princess was the successor to the pre-war Empire flying boats. Powered by ten Bristol Proteus turboprops, eight of them linked in pairs, it offered a nostalgic return to the halcyon wickerwork-seat days, with 105 passengers able to stroll about the two decks. The British Overseas Airways Corporation (BOAC) showed interest in the aircraft, but by the time the prototype was launched, in 1952, BOAC had lost its fervour for the flying boat and had scrapped the last of its operations with them eighteen months before. Cancellation of the BOAC order, plus serious mechanical difficulties in the gearboxes connecting the paired engines, killed the Princess. Three prototypes were built; one continued to fly until 1953, when, like the others, it was beached and cocooned. (Gordon Swanborough Collection)

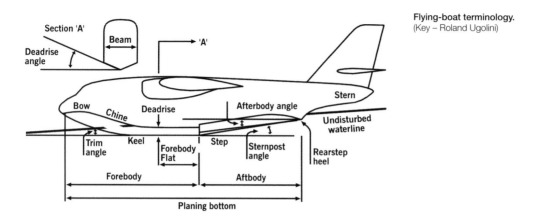

Flying-boat terminology.
(Key – Roland Ugolini)

Static stability. The forces acting on the hull and floats at rest are the weight acting through the CG and the buoyancy reacting it at the centre of buoyancy (CB). The static stability is measurable in terms of the distance between the metacentre (M) and the CG. The metacentre is the point of intersection of the line of action of the buoyancy. The distance between the metacentre and CG is called the metacentric height. If the CG lies below the metacentre when the aircraft is heeled, the flying-boat is statically stable (as shown). If the metacentre lies below the CG the aircraft is unstable, and will turn over at the slightest disturbance. It should be noted that a conventional hull such as shown is unstable by itself. Wingtip floats or sponsons (buoyant stub-wings from the hull sides) must be fitted.
(Key – Roland Ugolini)

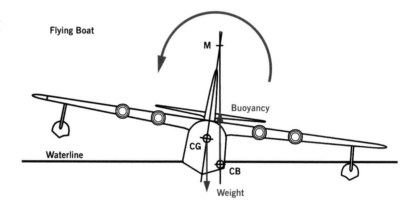

Design considerations

Flying boats had to satisfy the same requirements of safety, performance, efficiency, strength and reliability as land-planes, but had to posses some additional qualities. They had to be seaworthy, manoeuvrable and stable on the water, and have low water and air drag. The hull had to be designed and the aircraft configured in such a way that the amount of spray passing through the propellers, striking the tail and passing over the windscreen was minimized. Furthermore, it needed sufficient strength to withstand the loads imposed by rough water during alighting, take-off and taxying. All flying boats featured a high wing mounted atop a voluminous hull, a high tail, and stabilizing floats. The engines were mounted on the wings to minimize spray problems.

Buoyancy

The most noticeable differences between a flying-boat hull and an equivalent landplane fuselage are the depth and the shaped ventral surfaces that form the hull's planing bottom. The buoyancy of the hull is proportional to the volume displaced: the weight of the aircraft is equal to the weight of water displaced. The hull was usually designed with from 70–100 per cent reserve (or safety) buoyancy. When floating as a displacement boat, 100 per cent reserve buoyancy means that the hull will support twice the weight of the aircraft without sinking, and gives a safety margin for operations in rough seas.

The cross-sectional shape of the forward part of the hull is usually in the form of a modified 'vee'. The outside angle of the vee is called the deadrise angle. The larger this angle, the lower will be the impact loads imposed by operations in heavy seas. However, the water friction drag on the forward part of the hull increases with the deadrise angle, as does the spray problem. The intersections of the sides of the forward part of the hull with the vee bottom are called chines, and form a sharp angle, important in determining the hull's spray characteristics.

Stabilizing surfaces (wing floats or stub planes ('spon-sons')) are necessary because the narrow-beam hull, coupled with a high CG, make the flying boat laterally unstable on the water. They were usually designed so that the aircraft heels about 1 degree when one float touches the water. When the aircraft is laterally level, as in take-off from relatively smooth water, neither stabilizer touches the water. An important design criterion for wingtip floats and lateral stability is turning in a sidewind.

Early US and British practice was to provide small floats near the wingtips. As the safety of a flying boat depends largely on the tip floats it was necessary to make them and their attachments very strong. This was often advanced as a major criticism of the arrangement, but the perceived problem was not insurmountable as the wings could be specially strengthened to take abnormal loads. The size of the floats was determined by considerations of static stability and air drag, rather than by their efficiency on take-off, which resulted in them being smaller than if they had been designed purely under take-off constraints. As the float was equivalent to an overloaded hull, its efficiency in the water was compromized. The alternative, fitting stub planes or sponsons to the main hull, was much favoured in Germany, especially by Dornier. Not only did these greatly aid loading of passengers, but they could be used for fuel, keeping it as far away as possible from the engines for safety reasons. It also lowered the CG, giving added stability, and, in the case of a major repair, the tanks could be easily removed.

Dornier favoured fitting sponsons to the main hull, rather than floats to the wings. Not only did these greatly aid loading of passengers, but they could be used for fuel, keeping it as far away as possible from the engines for safety reasons. They also lowered the cg, giving added stability, and in the case of a major repair the tanks could be easily removed.
(Key Collection)

Hydrodynamic lift and drag

As with a landplane, a flying boat must accelerate to a speed sufficiently high, determined by the wing loading and maximum lift coefficient, for the wings to support the weight of the aircraft in flight. For a landplane its aerodynamic drag, together with the rolling friction of the wheels on the runway, gives the resistance to acceleration during the take-off run. In addition to aerodynamic drag, the flying boat must overcome the water drag associated with the hull. The manner in which this drag varies with speed makes the take-off problem of the flying boat uniquely different from that of the landplane.

The hull bottom is separated by a transverse step (or steps) into a forebody and aft body. At low speeds the hull operates as a displacement boat, with both forebody and aft body supporting the aircraft. Beyond a certain speed, called the hump speed, where the boat may be thought of as climbing over its bow wave and beginning operation as a planing hull, the hull planes only on the forebody. The step, the idea for which was first stumbled across by Glenn H. Curtiss, causes the flow to break away from the aft body (thereby breaking the suction that would otherwise glue the aircraft to the water), and allows the boat to transition into the planing regime. Because of this (and their higher wing loading) flying boats invariably required a considerably longer take-off run than a comparable landplane.

The more usual practice in later boats was to taper the aft body in planform to a point that effectively terminated the hull. The overall length/beam (l/b) ratio or fineness of the hull is an important design variable, as are the height and location of the step(s). At the hump speed the hydrodynamic lift and drag are centred well back, while the wing is not yet providing much aerodynamic lift and the drag is still too great to allow acceleration to flying speed, but it is an essential stage in getting the aircraft up and 'on to the step'.

The longer the hull, the higher will be both the hump speed and the corresponding wave drag. Using the principles of dynamic similarity, the values of speed and drag at and below the hump speed of one hull can be approximately translated to those of a similar hull of different length. By 1918 it had been definitely established that the quantitative results were virtually identical in model form and full-scale, and the measured resistance and trimming angles up to the hump

speed were very similar. However, qualitative results, such as the amount of water spray, were not similar (as may be familiar to moviegoers watching films in which models are used to simulate full-scale ship motion).

The achievement of hydrodynamic lift requires a steep rake to the bow, which means that the hull has to be fairly deep. Conversely, a shallow hull has to be compensated for buoyancy and lift with a long nose and/or broader beam. The water resistance depends to a large extent on the water loading of the hull bottom. It was demonstrated early on that the most efficient hull shape in this respect should have a maximum beam measured in inches of about four times the cube root of the displacement in pounds. For example, the Short Calcutta's actual beam was 120in versus 112in (3m versus 2.85m) by the simple rule. However, by the early 1930s it had appeared to Arthur Gouge, Short's chief designer, that it should be possible to built hulls with a much

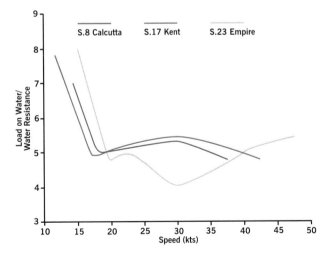

Water resistance versus speed. This graph shows the higher water resistance of the Short S.23 Empire hull at speeds greater than 20kt, compared with that of the S.8 Calcutta and S.17 Kent (due entirely to the S.23's narrower beam), and the higher take-off speed (because of its higher wing loading). Above 40kt the water efficiency (ratio of water load/resistance) of the Empire hull is better, and the narrower beam made the S.23 easier to alight and take off.
(Key – Ray Whitford)

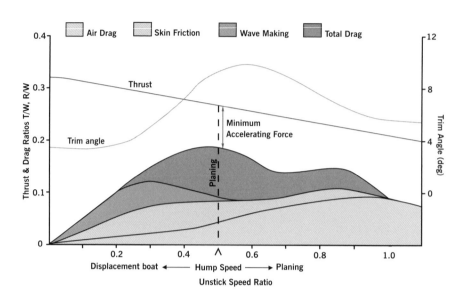

Variation of forces with speed. The figure shows the variation of drag/weight (R/W) and engine thrust/weight (T/W) with speed for a typical flying boat. All flying boats have had marginal performance in the vicinity of the hump speed, where (T/W-R/W) is least. At the hump the 'boat' may be thought of as climbing over its bow wave and operating as a planing hull. In this regime the weight of the boat is supported primarily by the reaction of the water against the forebody. Also shown is the variation of trim angle as the loads supporting the boat change with speed.
(Key – Ray Whitford)

narrower beam than the company's previous practice without incurring any loss in hydrodynamic efficiency.

Spray suppression

So-called blister spray, thrown upwards and rearwards by the chine, is heavy and damaging. The height to which it rises determines the vertical position of the wings, engines and tail surfaces. The engine is the most vulnerable component at low speed, when the spray is originating ahead of it, and the airflow through the propeller disc actually sucks spray into the blades. Spray is suppressed by hollowing the forebody from keel to chine, by increasing the forebody fineness and by attaching strips called spray dams to the forebody chine.

Dynamic stability on water

In addition to the high drag associated with passage through the hump speed, a longitudinal pitching instability can occur. This is characterized by a pitch oscillation in which the flying boat rocks back and forth between forebody and aftbody. A pitch attitude that is too high or too low can induce the onset of instability. The range of stable pitch attitudes varies with speed, and is a minimum in the region of the hump. Thus careful control of pitch attitude was required when traversing this critical speed range.

Manoeuvrability and control while taxying

Fine hulls (l/b around 10) have long forebodies and deep running keels that move the centre of the side area forward relative to CG, decreasing directional stability and making the hull prone to ground (water) looping. Directional instability could be cured by a small fin, protruding into the water from the aft body keel, but its effectiveness was limited by the range of trim angles at which it runs in the water. Directional control, in addition to the use of the engines, was by water rudder or by water flaps. A rudder usually formed part of the rear step heel, or the sternpost.

Effect of high engine position

The fundamental requirement of effective clearance of the engines from spray calls for a thrust line well above the CG.

At low speed, with a large part of the hull volume in the water, resistance to movement is very large and centred well below the engine thrust line. When the throttle is opened, a powerful nose-down moment tends to plunge the aircraft's nose into the water, causing enormous drag, heavy spray and the loss of directional control. The corrective parameters are the length and buoyancy of the nose and, as speed is gained, the upward slope of the forward hull bottom that produces much of the hydrodynamic lift. Nose buoyancy is improved by making the nose blunt and broad, or by extending it well forward of the engines.

Furthermore, large changes of trim were experienced between engines-off and engines-on, varying from zero in power-off/gliding flight to maximum at full power. In early flying boats this was uncorrected, and the aircraft were tail-heavy in gliding flight. By setting the tailplane in the slipstream with a negative angle relative to the chord of the mainplane, and by locating the CG well forward, the thrust moment could be almost balanced by the tail moment. For most of a flight the load on the tail was downward, so negatively cambered tailplanes were used on some flying boats.

Although the undercarriage of a landplane was dispensed with, bulk and weight were increased because of the need for a larger fuselage/hull to overcome the drag and suction effects when getting the aircraft airborne. Hence a greater overall size and a higher power/weight ratio were invariably required, although the extra power was not needed for the remainder of the flight. The twin-tandem (push/pull) engine layout was adopted for some early flying boats because of the lower drag, weight and interference compared with the twin outboard layout, and provided a good aerodynamic compromise, though the aft propeller had reduced efficiency if the front engine failed. This was avoided with the twin outboard installation, which also gave a higher degree of manoeuvrability on the water.

Aerodynamic drag

The water and air performance provided conflicting requirements, and a compromise was necessary. It has always been difficult to obtain an aerodynamically clean hull shape that also has good seaworthiness. The aerodynamic drag, critically important in determining the speed and range of a large bulky hull equipped with steps and sharp chines,

Aircraft	TOW (lb)	Span (ft)	Wing area (ft²)	Vmax (mph)	[M] C_{D_0}	(L/D)max (lb/ft²)	W/S (lb/hp)	W/P
O/400 (1918)	14,425	100	1,655	94	0.0427	9.7	8.7	20.4
F-5L (1919)	13,600	103.8	1,397	90	0.0694	8.2	9.7	16.9

tended to be higher than that of the fuselage of a well-streamlined landplane.

To put the characteristics of early flying-boats in context with contemporary multi-engine landplanes, the Curtiss F-5L (two Liberty engines) is compared in the table above with the Handley Page O/400 (two Rolls-Royce Eagle VIII). The two aircraft were roughly the same size and weight, but the landplane (O/400) was about 5 per cent faster on only 83 per cent of the power/weight ratio of the aerodynamically dirty flying boat, which had a 62 per cent higher zero lift drag coefficient.

Construction

The disadvantage of the original wooden types of construction was the large amount of water absorption, typically about 12 per cent of the bare weight of the hull within a few days from new. This led to consideration of metal hulls, but in the early 1920s steel was too heavy, the only alternative being duralumin. No insurmountable difficulties were found, and the alloy offered considerable potential for

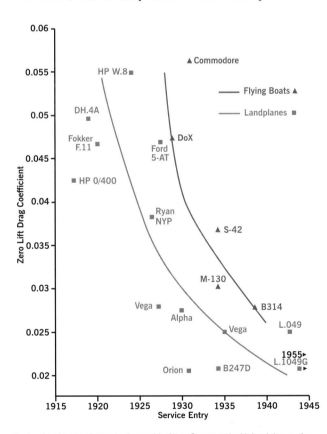

Reduction in aerodynamic drag with time. Compared with landplanes, the number of flying boats shown in the graph, albeit limited, have higher drag (due predominantly to the differences in hull versus fuselage shape). That said, the distinction appears to be reducing towards the end of the 1930s as flying boats become monoplanes and their hull shapes become more refined.
(Key – Ray Whitford)

straightforward and rapid production. Although duralumin was almost universally favoured, it was susceptible to corrosion. Various precautions were taken, probably the most satisfactory being the anodic oxidization process developed by RAE Farnborough.

The biggest problem was rivet heads on underwater surfaces, as although they were anodically treated before use, the action of forming the rivets destroyed the anodic film, resulting in rapid corrosion and water seepage. Chafing of the film on the planing surfaces could also cause early corrosion, so careful maintenance and frequent inspection was necessary. These troubles led to the use of stainless steel on the planing bottoms, both for the sheeting and rivets, which greatly increased life, but at the risk of failure due to the thin sections used to save weight.

Use of high-lift devices

It was the influence of a lecture on the Sikorsky S-42 flying boat, given by its designer to the Royal Aeronautical Society in 1934, that provided the impetus for British manufacturers to explore the use of higher wing loadings (W/S). Indeed, Oswald Short remarked that high W/S 'was a matter in which they in this country had been afraid to make explorations'. Arthur Gouge said that British engineers 'had to take a lesson from the Sikorsky paper and recast their ideas with particular reference to wing loading'. It was essential, though, that when high wing loading was used, some form of flap was used to assist take-off. In terms of the type of flap to be used (high- or low-drag), for a flying boat a steep angle of glide, when coming in to alight, was not of vital importance, and it was therefore better to fit a type of flap that as much as possible could be used for take-off.

Early use of flying boats

Throughout the 1920s British imperial air routes had been extended without serious competition from other national airlines, except on the high-prestige routes between London and Paris, and Brussels and Cologne. Direct rivalry was a question of political negotiation rather than technical superiority. Consequently, Imperial Airways, Britain's chosen instrument of commercial aviation, concentrated on developing larger aircraft suitable for the existing airfields along the routes to India and South Africa, making the most of comfort and safety rather than speed.

Four factors conspired to disturb this tranquillity. Firstly, US air transport operators, having built up a sound ground organization with the backing of the US Post Office, had progressed to the point where they could compete with surface transport for overland passengers, and were extending their services to overseas operations between offshore islands in the Caribbean. This enabled them to offer landplanes and flying boats to customers in Canada, South America and Europe. Secondly, the resurgence of German

Aircraft (first flight)	TOW (lb)	Wing area (ft²)	Maximum Power (hp)	W/S (lb/ft²)	W/P (lb/hp)	Maximum speed (mph)	Minimum flying speed (mph)
Short Calcutta (1928)	22,500	1,815	1,605	12.4	14.9	123	60
Short Kent (1931)	32,500	2,640	2,332	12.3	15.2	137	60
Consolidated Commodore (1931)	17,600	1,110	1,150	15.9	15.3	120	66
Sikorsky S-42 (1934)	38,000	1,340	2,800	28.4	13.6	170	70
Martin M-130 (1934)	52,000	2,170	3,800	24.1	13.8	163	80
Short S.23 Empire (1936)	40,500	1,500	3,180	27	13.7	164	71
Boeing 314 (1938)	82,300	2,867	6,400	29.3	13.1	184	70

Comparison of the major flying boats. The wing loadings for Calcutta and Kent are the same, whereas that of the S.23 Empire is doubled, though its minimum speed rose by less than 20 per cent. These results were achieved primarily by the use of flaps. Acceptable performance of the S.23 was thought to be a run of 1,500–1,800ft (460–550m) and take-off within 20–25sec. ICAN requirements stated that the take-off from calm water had to be less than 60sec with no wind. The S.23's W/S would have had to be increased to 34.3lb /ft² (considerably higher than most aircraft of the time), before it exceeded the requirement. Furthermore, the maximum speed was raised by over 30 per cent, again by the use of flaps to reduce wing area, slightly increased power/weight, variable-pitch propellers and moving to a monoplane configuration (greatly influenced by Gouge's examination of the Douglas DC-2 in 1934).

nationalism had strengthened its links with South America and South Africa. Thirdly, progress with RAF flying-boat operations had shown the value of deploying these aircraft at important Empire outposts such as Gibraltar, Aden, Basra and Singapore. Fourthly, airmail competition from KLM, which opened a regular service between Amsterdam and Batavia in 1931 with a journey time of ten days, was depriving Imperial Airways of revenue.

The new-generation flying boats

Today the name Igor Sikorsky is usually associated with his pioneering of the helicopter, but in earlier years he was known as the father of a number of multi-engine aircraft, including several flying boats. One of these, the S-38 amphibian, first appeared in 1928 and established the Russian designer in the USA. Serving a number of airline operations, notably PanAm, the aircraft was also used by various military services and in several exploratory operations. The first of the new-generation 'flying clippers' was the Sikorsky S-42, which made its first flight in March 1934 and began airline service between Miami and Rio de Janeiro less than five months later, an indication of the rapidity with which a transport aircraft could be flight-tested and certificated in a technically simpler age. It had the right combination of large span and aspect ratio, moderate power loading and, very importantly, a high wing loading, which, combined with flaps and variable-pitch propellers, produced the first really useable commercial flying boat. A higher cruising speed is a natural consequence of higher wing loading, and was essential if long flights were to be made. It turned out to be the right formula, and was copied and developed widely.

Transatlantic aspirations

It transpired that 1934 was a vintage year for Imperial Airways' Far Eastern route, and fulfilled the dream of an

UK–Australia service. Considering the area served, subject to rainy seasons, and the experience gained by military flying-boat operations through Central Africa to Durban and across India to Singapore and Australia, it was decided that Imperial Airways should re-equip with flying boats for all of its trunk routes. This avoided the need to transfer payload between flying boats and landplanes.

The North Atlantic seaway was the most lucrative in the world, and even in the 1920s it was thought that its airway would develop similarly. Its flying distances were considerable, but those over the Pacific were greater. Its weather was the worst, but the greatest complication was political. Questions of penury, politics and prestige frustrated operations over the North Atlantic from 1933 to 1939, and it was the last of the great transoceanic routes to be opened.

Although PanAm was organized only in 1927, and then with a Latin American orientation, by 1928 its management was already studying the Atlantic with an eye on a route via Newfoundland, Greenland and Iceland. The airline discussed transatlantic plans with Aeropostale (principal predecessor to Air France), which had a monopoly on landing rights in the Azores, and in 1929 PanAm broached the subject with Imperial Airways. This resulted in plans for a joint Baltimore–Bermuda route continuing through the Azores to Lisbon, provided France agreed. A year later a tripartite agreement was concluded towards a service over this mid-Atlantic route. All seemed well until 1931, when Aeropostale went bankrupt. The status of the Azores was in confusion, and PanAm began looking at the sub-Arctic route again.

In 1932 it opened an airmail route from Boston to Halifax, Nova Scotia, using a twin-engine Sikorsky S-41 amphibian, with the aim of extending the service to Newfoundland and beyond. At that time Newfoundland enjoyed dominion status similar to Canada, and could be dealt with separately. While PanAm was negotiating, surveys were made; a flying-boat base was recommended at Botwood, and a field for landplanes on the shore of Gander Lake.

Transpacific operations come first

In 1933 PanAm had ordered three Martin M-130 four-engine flying boats for transatlantic service, and commissioned Charles Lindbergh, then a PanAm technical advisor, to undertake a flying survey of the sub-Arctic and a route across the Greenland icecap. At the end of that year the British government was insisting upon concessions from PanAm that only the US government could grant. In an astute move PanAm revised the specifications for its transatlantic M-130s by asking for transpacific range. This was a significant change. The critical Atlantic distance was the 2,000-mile (3,200km) gap between Newfoundland and Ireland. Transpacific, between California and Hawaii, it was 2,400miles (3,860km), 20 per cent farther. Nevertheless, in 1934 PanAm announced it was aiming for a Pacific route across which the US government owned most of the vital real estate: Hawaii, Wake, Guam and the Philippines, so the project could proceed without foreign opposition.

Even though US aviation journals were received in Europe, there was a tendency to dismiss descriptions of new developments in the USA as 'American exaggeration', despite the remarkable performance of the Douglas DC-2 in the MacRobertson England–Australia air race of 1934. Until the M-130 demonstrated its capability in airline service its technical specification was regarded with widespread disbelief in Britain and Europe. By way of a routine exchange of information PanAm sent the M-130's performance estimates to Imperial Airways. Robert Mayo, the British airline's principal engineering consultant, dismissed them as hopelessly optimistic. He proved to his and his client's satisfaction that the claims for the M-130 'could not possibly be achieved', and that it would be 'quite incapable of operating on an Atlantic service over the Azores-Bermuda or Ireland-Newfoundland routes'. Mayo was among Britain's most respected aeronautical engineers; his report was circulated in the Air Ministry, and it was an important factor in nourishing British complacency with respect to the need of developing a transoceanic airliner.

Even after the M-130 was flying, the British aviation press treated its data with such non-sequesters as 'if the published figures are to be believed'. On the eve of the M-130's transoceanic operations the statistics were still doubted: 'It must be probably admitted that the Americans have more experience than we in getting their structure weight down, but it is difficult to believe the saving can be anything like as great as these figures indicate'. What made the numbers incredible was that they described a disposable load (fuel and payload) that was, at 49 per cent TOW, almost a ton more than the aircraft's structural weight. Although the M-130 had the range to fly California–Hawaii, it was not going to carry much payload. Nevertheless, the fact that any fully equipped airliner of 1934 could lift a ton of payload across 2,400 miles was full of portent. The world was to be almost girdled by commercial air services; only the Atlantic remained.

Transatlantic agreement

Negotiations for the North Atlantic were conducted between the British and US governments during 1935–37, with the UK government insisting, among other things, that the US service terminated in Montreal, but this the USA refused. However, the British succeeded in getting a clause that stated that the US service would not start before the British. Looking to the future, PanAm placed orders with Boeing in

1936 for six Model 314 flying boats and three Model 307 Stratoliner landplanes. However, with the political negotiations incomplete PanAm had to wait, though this may have been fortuitous, as Boeing was having trouble with its 314 and delivery dates were slipping.

With most of the political problems over the Atlantic resolved by 1937, arrangements were made for a series of reciprocal transatlantic survey flights. These operations showed how far ahead the USA was in terms of long-range airliner performance. It was now clear, even to Britain's Air Ministry, that 'no British flying boat had been designed to equal the Sikorsky and that we were even further behind the Martin'. The British had become intellectually trapped by their 'Empire Route' east of Suez, over which medium-range aircraft could operate with easy staging. When faced with the Atlantic they had to fall back on expedients. One was to delay the US operators, which proved less adequate than a good transatlantic aircraft. Others were the Short-Mayo composite aircraft (a variation on catapulting) and flight refuelling. Both would do for mail operations, but were too precarious for passenger service.

The battle for the Atlantic

It was hoped that the transatlantic services would begin in 1938, but Imperial Airways was not ready. The Short S.23 Empire flying boat it had ordered in 1935 had only very marginal transatlantic performance (even without a payload) and precious little growth potential. Two S.23s, *Caledonia* and *Cambria*, specially modified for experimental operations, made the first east–west airline flights across the Atlantic in 1937. Fuel capacity was increased from 650 Imp gal (2,955lit) to 2,320 gal (10,550ltr), their wing spars and planing bottoms were reinforced to carry the unusual load, and they were certificated to operate at 45,000lb (20,300kg) MTOW. The

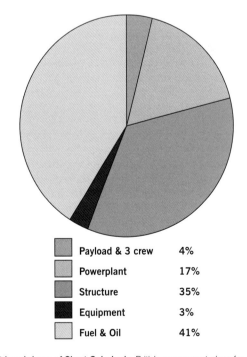

Payload & 3 crew	4%
Powerplant	17%
Structure	35%
Equipment	3%
Fuel & Oil	41%

Weight breakdown of Short *Caledonia*. British government plans for a transatlantic mail service led to the second S.23, *Caledonia*, being completed with long-range tanks and strengthened for an all-up weight of 45,000lb (20,400kg). Experimental non-stop 2,300-mile (3,700km) flights were made in 1937 from Britain to Egypt and back.
(Key – Ray Whitford)

A novel solution to long-range aviation, proposed by Robert Mayo, the bizarre Short-Mayo Composite consisted of a Short S.20 floatplane mounted atop a 'C-class' S.21 Empire flying boat. The composite was to take off under the power of all eight engines and fly as far as the carrier aircraft's fuel reserve allowed, whereupon they separated in the air, the upper component carrying the payload to its destination. This novel form of assisted take-off (essentially a flying catapult) was much ballyhooed at the time. However, the concept was short-lived, and was rendered obsolete by the introduction of superior landplanes.
(Gordon Swanborough Collection)

S.23s flew with a crew of four and as bare aircraft. Indeed, although the Empire flying boat continues to evoke warm memories and is often described as 'superb' and 'ahead of its time', these sentiments have been dismissed as the stuff of nostalgia by some writers, one of whom described it as 'an iron turkey with a paper bottom', referring to its propensity to hull failure. In the first two years of operation 28 per cent of Imperial Airways' fleet of S.23s was lost in fatal crashes, in some cases from incidents that would have been minor ones for landplanes. Four were lost due to planing-bottom failure.

In the spring of 1939 Imperial Airways announced that it expected to begin transatlantic operations by June, but if it did not, it would not delay PanAm's inevitable operations. However, the French had already granted PanAm access to Marseilles. The mid-Atlantic route was now open, except for Bermuda, but the Boeing 314 was capable of overflying this British obstacle. On 20 May 1939, the twelfth anniversary of Lindbergh's take-off from Roosevelt Field, the Boeing 314 *Yankee Clipper* took off with 1,314lb (590kg) of mail from the Port Washington base for Marseilles, via the Azores and Lisbon. This was the beginning of a service that has remained unbroken.

European operations across the Atlantic

Strictly in keeping with its commitment of providing Imperial connections between territories of the British Empire, Imperial Airways had ignored Latin America, leaving the South Atlantic route to Germany and France. Both countries tried landplanes and flying boats with ingenious methods of compensating for lack of range; and Germany persevered with airships long after the British abandoned them.

Germany made most of the running across the North Atlantic. While Britain and the USA were haggling during 1936, the airship *Hindenburg* cruised back and forth across the Atlantic with around 1,200 passengers, and Lufthansa initiated a series of survey flights with small twin-engine Dornier Do 18 flying boats. Based on the catapult ship *Schwabenland*, the Do 18s *Aeolus* and *Zephyr* flew surveys between the Azores and New York directly and via Bermuda. Lufthansa hoped to conclude its operations with flights from Nova Scotia to Ireland, but British pressure induced the Irish to refuse permission. So the Do 18s ended their brief season by flying to Lisbon via the Azores, and then back to Travemunde via Amsterdam.

In 1937 Lufthansa was back on the North Atlantic with two catapult ships, the *Schwabenland* in the Azores and the *Ostmark* in New York, and with two four-engine Blohm & Voss Ha 139 seaplanes, *Norwind* and *Nordmeer*. The assisted take-off, which allowed a 15 per cent overload, had prospects for mail-only operations, as it is difficult to imagine fare-paying passengers bracing themselves in their seats as they were 'shot' down the rails. Besides having a depot ship in New York, Lufthansa enjoyed use of PanAm's transatlantic base at Port Washington, as did Imperial Airways.

Design transformation, 1930–40

Operated by PanAm (with substantial support from the US Government) and Imperial Airways, four types of large four-engine flying boats pioneered long-range transoceanic commercial flights in the latter half of the 1930s. Their appearance suggests a technical era far in advance of that exemplified by earlier boats such as the Short Calcutta and Consolidated Commodore. Indeed, flying-boat technology had made significant advances by the mid-1930s, just as the Boeing 247 and DC-3 landplanes represented a higher level of technology than evidenced in the earlier Ford Trimotor.

Flying boats versus landplanes

Historical treatments of the dramatic changes in aircraft design and performance during the 1930s invariably focus on twin-engine aircraft of less than 30,000lb (13,500kg) that were used by domestic airlines, such as the Boeing 247 and Douglas DC-3. This has created a distorted impression that the four-engine long-range flying boats of the 1930s were perverse exceptions to the mainstream of development. An unfortunate consequence of this distortion is an almost universal assumption that the four-engine airliners of 50,000lb (22,500kg) or more that came into conspicuous usage during the 1940s and 1950s grew from the twin-engine experience alone, and it was a 'DC revolution'. This has tended to be the thrust of standard works on the subject. Nevertheless, if one chooses to treat flying boats as 'aircraft', which is what they are, and examine the aircraft of the 1930s in terms of their weight and long-range performance instead of what they look like, these developments become more dramatic than they are usually portrayed.

Aircraft	TOW (lb)	Vmax (mph)	C_{D_0}	(L/D)max	Useful load (% TOW)	Range (miles)
Short Calcutta (1928)	22,500	123			36	650
Dornier Do X (1929)	105,820	134	0.0472	7.7	27	1,740
Short Kent (1931)	32,500	137		10.2	36	450
Consolidated Commodore (1931)	17,600	120	0.0562	9.4	35	
Sikorsky S-42 (1934)	38,000	182	0.0362	12.2	37	2,900
Martin M-130 (1934)	52,252	180	0.0303	11.9	49	3,200
Short S.23 Empire C class (1936)	40,500	200		12.8	32	800
Boeing 314 (1938)	82,500	201	0.0274	13.0	39	3,500
Douglas DC-3 (1935)	25,000	226	0.0249	14.7	29	900
Boeing 307 (1938)	42,000	220		13	28	2,390

Major flying boats and comparable landplanes (Useful load: (payload + fuel); Cruise speed at 75 per cent power was in the range 75–82 per cent Vmax). The difference between the British and US flying boats of approximately the same dimensions, weight and power, but developed two years apart, is emphatic. The sleek S.23s, with their clean cantilever wings and commodious deep hulls, appeared far more modern than the cluttered S-42. Yet, except on the point of higher power loading, the Sikorsky was the superior aircraft. While PanAm's Sikorsky S-42Bs had slightly better than marginal capability, their payload was uneconomic.

Demise of the flying boat

The PanAm order for Boeing 307s, although for only three aircraft, is significant in that the airline was already (1936) moving from flying boats to landplanes for transoceanic service. The Boeing 307 (the first pressurized transport) and the early C-54 (DC-4) could cross the Atlantic quicker and more reliably than competing flying boats during the Second World War. Not only that, but PanAm also circulated to industry a specification for a transatlantic aircraft to carry 100 passengers (which led to the Lockheed L.049 Constellation). Landplanes were developing faster than flying boats.

Unfortunately this vision of the future was absent in Britain, with the result of two disastrous projects: the Bristol Brabazon and Saunders-Roe Princess. The Brabazon embraced the view that a small number of people would be carried in extreme comfort over long distances; the Princess repeated this idea, but added the second fallacy that water rather than land bases would be used. This was at that very moment when the USA was pressing ahead with the view that high-density seating, low fares and economy of operation were to be the new order in the coming era of civil aviation.

The flying boat was dead, essentially because it cost more to buy and operate: initial cost higher, insurance higher, maintenance higher and delays longer. In addition, because of their inferior aerodynamics, flying boats would have inevitably become progressively slower for a given power, or have a progressively shorter range for a given weight. Furthermore, flying boats were more restricted in their harbour requirements that had originally been thought. After the Second World War it became obvious that it was often more convenient and time-saving to fly direct to airports rather than to seaports, most of which were far from big cities.

The flying boat never made a post-war comeback. Too much reinforced concrete had been poured around the Atlantic's rim during the Second World War to make big flying-boat operations expedient any longer. The usual explanation of the flying-boat's demise is stated in terms of the

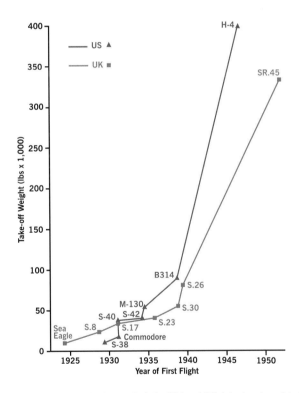

Increasing size of flying boats. Both the USA and Britain had protagonists for large flying-boats following the Second World War. The US aircraft was Howard Hughes' H-4 Hercules or 'Spruce Goose' (so called because it was made largely of wood to conserve strategically important aluminium alloys). On the other side of the Atlantic, BOAC was still mesmerized by pre-war memories, and showed enthusiasm for the Saunders-Roe SR.45 Princess. Remarkably, these two aircraft weighed over four times the heaviest flying boat each country had ever produced.
(Key – Ray Whitford)

landplane's superior characteristics, but this was as true in the heyday of the flying boat as it was in 1945. It is more correct to say that the flying boat was killed off by the bulldozer.

A light-hearted(?) proposal (*circa* 1995) for an ultra-large flying boat capable of carrying 1,250 passengers. It comprised three hulls, two of which are modified Boeing 747-400 fuselages, while the third is a triple-deck 747-400 extended to roughly twice the normal length. Such a craft, it was argued, could recapture the elegance and nostalgia of the flying boats and airships of the 1930s. Alternatively, it could form the mobile headquarters of a multinational corporation.
(Courtesy of Dr John McMasters of Boeing)

Designed as a light passenger/cargo aircraft, the Beriev Be-103 amphibian incorporates a low wing to give maximum air-cushion effect, and high-mounted piston engines to keep them and their propellers clear of water spray.
(Key Collection)

Beriev Be-200.
(Yefim Gordon)

Chapter 8

Passenger Cabins

In 1978 Jack Steiner, chief aerodynamicist on the Boeing Stratocruiser and 727, reviewing lessons learned with the 727, said: 'The most important single element to success is to listen closely to what the customer perceives as his requirements and to have the will and ability to respond'. This chapter examines the evolution of the passenger cabin, the introduction of pressurization, structural considerations, and the importance of getting the cabin size right.

By the late 1920s, airliners with enclosed cabins, such as the Fokker and Ford trimotors, had shown that the traveller preferred embarking upon his journey without having to put on helmet, goggles and flying suit. However, the aircraft were noisy. Reporting a flight in a 'Tin Goose' (a popular name for the Ford Trimotor), Arthur Raymond, designer for Douglas, said: 'They gave us cotton wool to stuff in our ears. The thing vibrated so much it shook the eyeglasses off your nose. In order to talk to the guy across the aisle, you had to shout. The higher we went, to get over the mountains, the colder it got in the cabin. My feet nearly froze. When the airplane landed on a puddle-splotched field, a spray of mud, sucked in by the cabin air vents, splattered everyone.' The Boeing 80A, introduced in 1928, carried eighteen passengers in a large cabin that had hot and cold running water, forced air ventilation and a flight attendant (all of whom were registered nurses employed by Boeing Air Transport). Public acceptance of these cabin aircraft gave manufacturers sufficient encouragement to go ahead with new designs.

In June 1933 United Airlines introduced a radical change; the Boeing Model 247 all-metal low-wing aircraft with a cruising speed of 185mph (300km/hr). The narrow fuselage had a rounded cross-section 5ft × 5ft (1.5m × 1.5m), though passengers had to clamber over a large obstruction on the floor where the two wing spars crossed. The ten passengers (each with an individual window) sat in single seats with a generous 40in (1.05m) pitch, arranged along each side of a soundproofed fuselage with a galley and toilet at the rear of the cabin. The 247 revolutionized transport by making possible 20hr coast-to-coast flights with only seven intermediate stops.

Douglas DC-1

On the face of it the 247 represented epochal gains for the airlines. It was 50mph (80km/h) faster than the aircraft it replaced, and its passenger appeal started to win much of the traffic. Furthermore, its operating costs proved to be 20 per cent lower per seat-mile than those of the Ford Trimotor. However, the 247 did not retain its superiority for long. Donald Douglas was encouraged by what he saw as obvious shortcomings in the 247, particularly its small size, and the more he looked at it the more he thought Boeing was selling its own concept short.

In response to interest shown in 1932 by Transcontinental and Western Air (TWA) for a twelve-passenger aircraft, Douglas proposed the DC-1. John Northrop evolved the 'cellular' wing, with two spars that passed under the cabin floor, making the cabin ceiling high enough to permit a normal-size person to walk without stooping. Coming from the world of naval aviation, Douglas designers had come to accept standards of amenities that cancelled out many of the supposed advantages of speed. If a passenger gained two days on a business trip from New York to Los Angeles only

Boeing's chief test pilot, Jack Waddell, was concerned about judging a landing from a flight deck so much higher off the ground than he was used to. Hence 'Waddell's Wagon', a mock-up of the 747's flight deck and part of the nose, was mounted at the appropriate height atop a rig that could be towed around Boeing Field by a truck, with a pilot sitting on the flight deck to get used to seeing the runway from that height. (Key – Steve Fletcher)

to lose it in recovering from the debilitation of the flight, there was no net gain. Passenger comfort was a high priority on the DC-1. If Douglas was to be successful in the commercial market it would need to 'build comfort and put wings on it'. A cabin mock-up was built; nowadays this is a routine step, but at the time it was a radical idea. An acoustical engineer was employed to soundproof the cabin. The bulkheads and fuselage were soundproofed with kapok, and thick carpets covered the floors so that passengers would not have to shout to carry on a conversation. Each of the DC-1's well-upholstered seats, mounted on rubber supports, had a reading lamp and footrest. At the rear was a galley with electric hotplates for coffee and soup, and a lavatory bigger than those on current aircraft. The cabin was heated to a toasty 21°C (70°F) when the outside temperature was well below freezing. Heating was provided by placing a boiler in the engine exhaust tailpipe to generate steam that was then piped to a radiator in the fuselage. Cold air ducted from the nose of the aircraft passed through this radiator to pick up heat and then flowed into the cabin, though the system was temperamental and sometimes iced up.

Douglas DC-2 and DC-3

Although the DC-1's superiority over the 247 was clear, the Douglas victory was not immediate, as TWA wanted more seats. This led to the DC-2, of which TWA ordered twenty. The DC-2's fuselage was 2ft (0.6m) longer than that of the DC-1, which, together with some rearrangement of the cabin layout, made possible the addition of another row of 19in (48cm)-wide seats, in a cabin 6in (15cm) wider and 3in (7.6cm) taller than that of the 247. By August 1934 TWA began advertising its Sky Chief service (an oblique reference to the Santa Fe Railroad's Super Chief), a Newark to Los Angeles run.

Among the airlines lining up for the DC-2 was the small and newly emerging American Airways, soon to become American Airlines. Its chairman, C.R. Smith, was pleased with its fifteen DC-2s but not content, believing that 18hr was a long time for any passenger to sit. The airline had obtained Curtiss Condor twin-engine biplanes to accommodate sleeping berths like those offered by railways. Although the Condor was slower, passengers apparently overlooked this if they got a good night's sleep. Nevertheless, the airline wanted to use something faster and more economical. It

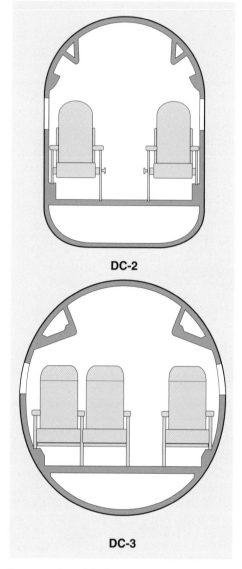

DC-2

DC-3

Cross-section comparison of the Douglas DC-2 and DC-3. The DC-2's cabin was not only 6in (15cm) wider and 3in (7.5cm) higher than that of the Boeing 247, but it was completely unobstructed because the wing spars passed through the fuselage beneath the floor. The DC-3's fuselage was over 2ft (0.6m) wider and, with that, three DC-2 seats could be installed in a row instead of two, with about the same aisle width. Soon after the DC-3 entered airline service it was apparent that the aircraft outclassed all others. (Key – Ray Whitford/Pete West)

Recognizing the advantages of cabin pressurization, Douglas followed its DC-4 with the DC-6. This and the Lockheed Constellation stimulated long-haul travel with a much higher degree of comfort because they could operate at altitudes of 15,000 to 20,000ft (4,500 to 6,000m), avoiding much of the turbulence prevalent at lower altitudes.
(Key – Tony Dixon)

wanted a revamp of the DC-2 with a fatter and longer fuselage to carry fourteen overnight sleeping berths. From this seemingly simple request the DC-2 grew remarkably. This Douglas Sleeper Transport (DST) meant a 90 per cent newer aircraft, so Donald Douglas was reluctant to retool his plant to build another aircraft when the DC-2 was selling so well. Smith was persistent, and finally convinced Douglas with an order for twenty of the as-yet-undesigned aircraft. Design work on the DC-3 began in late 1934. With twelve plush seats, 3ft (0.91m) wide in six compartments, each pair of seats could be folded down to form a bed. The widened and lengthened fuselage could accommodate twenty-one day passengers, arranged two-abreast on one side of a 19in (0.51m) aisle and in single seats on the other, in seats 21in (0.53m) wide. Even with two-and-one seating the passengers had more space than in the DC-2, the internal section of the cabin being 7ft 8in (2.36m) wide and 6ft 6in (1.98m) high. The result of these changes was the most economic and comfortable passenger carrier in existence.

Cabin size trend

The trend in essentially short-haul transport aircraft was for the capacity to increase from the twelve to fifteen passengers of the Fords, Fokkers and Condors, through the twenty-one seats of the DC-3 to the thirty-six to forty-four passengers of the post-war Martins and Convairs. This range of seating capacity parallels that of the autobus industry of the 1920s, when fifteen to twenty seats was the standard, rising to forty to fifty by the 1950s.

A level floor

Despite the DC-3's phenomenal success, passengers complained about its sloping floor. A level floor, however, required a tricycle undercarriage. For a low-wing monoplane this meant the cabin would be much higher off the ground, as would the fin. When Douglas designed its much bigger DC-4E in 1936, airlines became concerned over hangar-entry clearance and specified that the height of the tail should remain within the limits of existing doors. To accommodate this, Douglas spread the fin surfaces across the tailplane's span to get enough area, and the DC-4E became known as the 'five-tail monster'. The cabin could accommodate a crew of five and forty-two passengers, twice that of the DC-3. After initial flights by Douglas, each of the five sponsoring airlines operated the aircraft over its own routes to evaluate it and plan future route structures that the aircraft would make possible. The result of the evaluation was a new design concept. Cabin pressurization was needed to fly at high altitude without the use of oxygen masks, and the DC-4E's fuselage did not lend itself to this. The recommended changes were so numerous that it appeared futile to try to salvage the DC-4E. The limitation on tail height was dropped, so a single fin was now allowed; the result was the unpressurized DC-4 with a tricycle undercarriage. In the meantime Lockheed introduced the pressurized L.049 Constellation, forcing Douglas to design the pressurized DC-6.

Pressurization

The adoption of pressurization was an evolutionary step in the progress of safety and economy from low-altitude operations to medium altitudes. The custom of the early

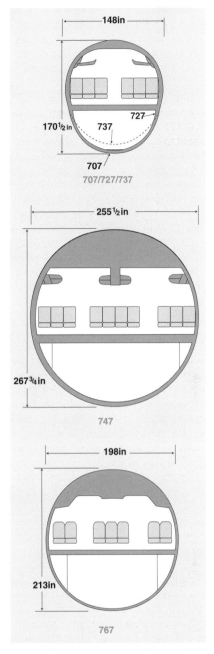

Cabin cross-sections. While a circular cross-section is ideal from a structural point of view, this has been compromised in a number of airliners for internal configuration (passenger seating) reasons. Typically, double-lobe cross-sections have been used for narrowbody (single-aisle) airliners such as the 727, 737, 757 and A320. Every frame in the fuselage is attached to the horizontal floor beam, which acts as a tension tie across the fuselage to resist the circularizing cabin pressure loads and to retain the double-lobe shape. The circular section is in common use for widebody types such as the A300, A310, DC-10, L.1011 and 777. For this the cabin pressure loads are carried by hoop tension in the skin, with no tendency to change shape or induce frame bending. (Key – Ray Whitford/Pete West)

years, with no blind-flying instrumentation, was hedge-hopping, which, under low-visibility conditions in mountainous country, resulted not only in unpleasant rides but also in many fatalities. Not until pilots abandoned the belief that their job was only to fly mail (passengers being regarded as a secondary and often undesirable cargo) and proceeded to seek higher altitudes for passenger comfort did the incidence of airsickness start to decline and flying become reasonably pleasant and safe. However, there was a reluctance to use oxygen because of numerous stories of its harmful effects.

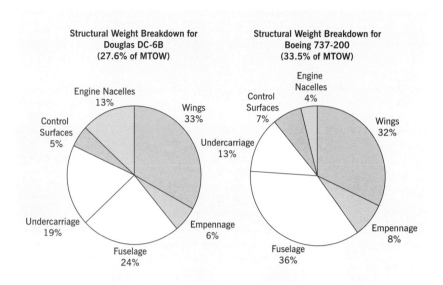

Structural Weight Breakdown for
Douglas DC-6B
(27.6% of MTOW)

Engine Nacelles
13%

Control
Surfaces
5%

Wings
33%

Undercarriage
13%

Undercarriage
19%

Empennage
6%

Fuselage
24%

Structural Weight Breakdown for
Boeing 737-200
(33.5% of MTOW)

Engine
Nacelles
4%

Control
Surfaces
7%

Wings
32%

Empennage
8%

Fuselage
36%

Structural weight breakdowns of Douglas DC-6B and Boeing 737-200. These two pie charts illustrate the rise in fuselage structure weight per passenger from 255lb (115kg) (for the DC-6, the first Douglas pressurized airliner, with a long-range cruise altitude of 22,000ft (6,700m)) to 360lb (164kg) (for the 737, with its much higher cabin differential pressure and designed for shorter flights at 35,000ft (10,700m)). (Key – Ray Whitford)

In the late 1930s power was available to lift aircraft out of the turbulent lower atmosphere, amid which the DC-3 cruised at 11,000ft (3,350m), into thin, calm, higher-altitude air where passengers would ride more smoothly. Furthermore, at 20,000ft (6,100m), aircraft could go straight over mountains instead of having to weave around them. Boeing, in particular, worked on the problems of high-altitude flight for the world's first pressurized airliner, the Model 307 Stratoliner, which entered service with TWA and PanAm in 1940. There was a touch of poetic licence in its name, because at best it could only get halfway to the stratosphere, but its four engines could lift thirty-three passengers to 20,000ft, a considerable feat at the time.

Pressurization operates on the constant-leak principle. Engine-driven pumps supply the cabin at the rate at which it leaks from the cabin due to minor gaps and imperfections in the hull. The original idea was to pump fresh air into the cabin to try to maintain the atmosphere as near as possible to that at sea level as the aircraft climbed into thinner air. However, the use of pressurization meant a great increase in weight, complexity and cost. Early pressurization systems worked at a maximum pressure differential of only about 2psi (0.14bar). From operational experience of the Boeing B-29 Superfortress with powerful and efficient cabin booster pumps, and with the ending of the Second World War, it was evident that pressurization was a must for passenger aircraft. The post-war generation, such as the Lockheed Constellation and Douglas DC-6, more than doubled the differential pressure. Since then the development of pressurization systems has continuously increased operational altitudes. Pressurization varies with altitude, and, sitting in an aircraft cruising at 32,000ft (9,760m), passengers would be breathing air at a pressure equivalent to an altitude of 8,000ft (2,440m), corresponding to a pressure differential of 8psi (0.54bar). With any physical exertion it would be quite difficult to breathe, but sitting relatively still while sipping a gin and tonic causes no discomfort at all. To reduce potential ear and sinus problems the cabin altitude is changed quite slowly, beginning long before 8,000ft is reached. Pressurization benefited the traveller in safety, comfort and speed of service, and brought substantial economies to the operator through more efficient performance.

Pressurization loads

The effect of cabin pressurization is to create loads to expand the cabin, which puts the skin in tension, acting in both directions parallel to the surface. As mentioned earlier, the tangential stress in the skin is twice the longitudinal stress; hence the need for heavy reinforcing frames along the length of the fuselage. Pressure loading and fatigue tend to dominate fuselage design, so stress levels and concentrations have to be watched. Skin thickness is around 0.04in (1mm), a fact of which most passengers are blissfully unaware when gazing through a window surrounded by substantial cosmetic trim. There is also a force stretching the fuselage along its length, which is equal to the pressure difference multiplied by the cross-sectional area of the fuselage. This load is felt by the fore and aft bulkheads, windscreen and associated structure.

The Comet 1 fatigue failures

In the case of early pressure cabins (Boeing Stratoliner, Lockheed Constellation), when the pressure differential was low at 4psi (0.27bar) the use of minimum practicable skin thickness ensured a low stress level. However, for a fuselage with a differential pressure of 8psi (0.55bar), a diameter of 10ft (3.05m) and a skin thickness of 0.028in (0.71mm), the hoop stress is 17,000psi (1.17MN/m^2). The stress at riveted seams away from a large cut-out might be 23,000psi (1.59MN/m^2), or 35 per cent of the ultimate static strength, giving a corresponding average life of 30,000 cycles or a safe life of 10,000 pressurizations. This suggests that there is no serious problem. However, there are inevitably cut-outs in the skin to accommodate windows and doors, and these, without reinforcement, can double, treble or quadruple the stresses. For instance, if stresses near a cut-out rise to as little as 50 per cent above the mean level, the mean life falls to about 5,000 cycles, or a safe life of 1,700 pressurizations.

With the growing use of pressure cabins following the Second World War, the need to make repeated loading tests on their structures became evident. It was clear from such testing that the rate of growth of cracks could be anything from very slow inspectable cracks, up to explosive tearing. Crucially, though, no specific attempt was made to relate the results to a safe fatigue life of the pressure cabin. At the time, expert opinion was that sufficient fatigue strength could

Among the notable features of the Sud-Aviation SE.210 Caravelle are its similar nose section to that of the de Havilland Comet, and its passenger windows, which are distinctly triangular with rounded vertices. The Caravelle was the second jet transport in service, and the first to have its turbojets mounted on the rear fuselage, a feature that proved popular with other manufacturers in the 1960s.
(Key Collection)

be gained by designing for twice the working pressure differential. This attitude persisted until 1954, when, following the two Comet accidents in January and April 1954, the RAE built a tank to accommodate an entire cabin with its wings attached. This permitted the simultaneous testing of a wing and cabin under repetitive flight loads and internal pressure. With the production Comet 1 that was tested (with riveted window reinforcement plates, rather than the de Havilland test sections, in which the plates were Reduxed (glued), a catastrophic failure occurred after the equivalent of only 9,000 flight hours. It originated in a tiny fatigue area (a rivet hole of $\frac{1}{8}$in (3mm) diameter) that explosively developed into a crack several feet long. An alarming feature of this test result was that the failure was not, in this case, an innocuous matter capable of inspection before reaching dangerous proportions. By the fluctuation of the circumferential tension in the cabin skin, pressurization, with change of altitude, had introduced a severe form of fatigue loading.

In the case of the Comet 1 the stress near the corners of the small radio-aerial windows on the top of the fuselage was reckoned to be over 40,000psi (2.76MN/m^2), significantly higher than had been previously believed. The public enquiry held that de Havilland could not be blamed for believing that the static tests it applied (at twice the working pressure differential) would give the necessary strength reserve and assurance against risk of fatigue failure during the life of the aircraft.

Cut-outs

Cut-outs for items such as doors, windows and inspection panels are a recurring headache for designers, for as soon as a hole is made in a load-bearing surface a reinforcing structure must be introduced to provide adequate load paths around that hole to carry the load. The stiffness of the reinforcement must be just right, as too stiff a reinforcement induces high stresses in the skin immediately adjacent to it. Although the ideal shape for a cut-out in a pressurized fuselage is a vertical ellipse, this is not practical for doors, which typically have a 0.6 aspect ratio with generously rounded corners, as sharp corners cause excessively high stress concentrations. For windows, quasi-elliptical shapes (height: 2 units; width: $\sqrt{2}$ units) give a roughly neutral effect on the overall tensile

stress concentration, in that the maximum principal stress in the vicinity of the hole is no greater than the hoop stress. Many windows are variants of the neutral hole, lying between that and the rectangular, the rounded corners being added to aid visibility. The windows are of fail-safe construction, with two panes, each sufficient to take the full pressure differential, and have an additional non-load-bearing pane so that the structural panes cannot be scratched.

Doors

Passenger doors may or may not carry some of the load of the fuselage structure, depending on their design, though they must be able to open easily and quickly on the ground in an emergency even when sealed by $\frac{1}{4}$in (6mm) of ice, and must not jam in a crash. Passenger aircraft have to have at least a minimum specified number and type of doors to allow rapid and safe evacuation when required. Aircraft doors that may open in flight represent a potential hazard and a classic problem of pressure-hull design.

Considerable ingenuity has gone into door design to ensure that doors do not come off. The structural integrity of the pressure cabin was greatly enhanced if the cabin doors, instead of closing in the old way, from the outside, closed from the inside and formed a plug-like seal. Along the door sides are metal projections, like widely-spaced square-cut teeth. On the doorframe are matching projections. As the door closes, the teeth on the door pass between the teeth on the frame, and, on closing, the spurs on the door fit over the pads on the frame. As the differential increases between the pressurized air inside the cabin and the air outside, the security of the door seal increases, like a bath plug. The problem was that, if the door closed from the inside, the movement of the swing ate up the equivalent cabin space of a row of seats. The prevailing wisdom in the 1950s was that it was impossible to design a plug door that did not cost seats. However, doors were designed that could be opened by pulling in and sliding upwards inside the fuselage. The most common arrangement is a door that is initially pulled inside the fuselage. The door is partly opened inward and then turned with a gymnastic, double-jointed movement to change its height and pass through the door aperture, so that in its fully open position it is outside. This was an effective plug door that did not take up seat space.

Cabin floor

The floor of the cabin is a long platform slung across the full width of the fuselage. It consists of a series of aluminium alloy (or CFC) beams running from side to side, with plates laid across and riveted to them. The trouble is that it is intrinsically harder to make a flat surface like this resistant to bending pressure than to make a tube resistant to internal pressure. No designer would delight at the prospect of making a 3,000ft^2 (280m^2) floor resistant to the pressure differential a fuselage wall has to withstand, and there would be a weight penalty of thousands of pounds. However, imagine the door blowing off a cargo hold. The floor above will collapse, certainly bending, if not rupturing, any hydraulic piping below (though the pipes have built-in hoops to allow for distortion). Since 1977 the floors of widebody airliners have been designed to withstand, without collapse, a depressurization of the underfloor cargo hold by tolerating a hole in the fuselage of 20ft^2 (1.85m^2) via extra sidewall/floor vents. This was prompted by the inadvertent opening of a cargo door on a Turkish Airlines Douglas DC-10 at approximately 13,000ft (4,000m) over France in March 1974. The floor collapsed and severed the controls to the number two engine, the elevators, the mechanically controlled trim and the rudder, resulting in the loss of the aircraft and the death of 346 people.

Cabin size matters

In 1953 Boeing decided to develop a large jet transport, hoping to design a basic dual-purpose fuselage that could serve both the military (as a tanker to replace the relatively slow KC-97) and the airlines (as a passenger and cargo transport). This was the Model 367-80, which proved very successful in its first flights in 1954 and made influential demonstrations to the airlines. It retained only a trace of Boeing's Stratocruiser: the 132in (3.35m) width of the passenger cabin, based on its comfortable two-plus-two seating. Gone was the two-deck cabin and downstairs cocktail lounge. Jets would slash travelling times, and there

was no need for elegant distractions. In its belly the jet transport would carry baggage and cargo. Boeing had taken to heart an airline dictum that 'payload' meant load that paid, and had already decided that the Dash 80 cabin was too narrow for its projected 707. To carry an effective payload the 707 needed three-plus-three seating. The KC-135 tanker being developed from the Model 80 already had a wider 144in (3.66m) cabin, which was considered wide enough since, at a pinch, it allowed six-abreast seating.

In Santa Monica Douglas had finally been forced to recognize the threat from Boeing. By comparison every piston-engine airliner Douglas was building was obsolete. Douglas faced up to the unpalatable prospect of having to spend hundreds of millions of dollars on its DC-8 to catch up. But Douglas still had one salient advantage over Boeing: the respect the company enjoyed among virtually all of the world's major airlines. While Douglas engineers would have to second-guess Boeing on wing design, they would, as they always did, let the airlines help them design the DC-8. With a cabin width of 147in (3.73m) the DC-8 could accommodate six-abreast seating, while the 707 could really only take five. The headroom in the cabin was somewhat better in the DC-8, as was the cargo space beneath the floor, because of the 707's double-bubble cross-section. To help decide between the two projects, United Airlines constructed plywood mock-ups of the two fuselage halves, abutted to each other. Then tests were carried out for cabin and cargo-handling duties.

The seemingly insignificant extra 3in (7.6cm) made an enormous difference. The geometry of the cabins, essentially a circle intersected by the floor, was critical at shoulder height. Douglas had set the cabin floor so that both shoulder room and headroom were strikingly superior to those in the Boeing layout. Ironically this had been decided partly by anachronistic reasoning, to allow space for upward folding sleeping berths, which were superfluous in view of the aircraft's speed. In the battle of inches, three was a decisive margin of victory in providing a cabin that the airlines would favour. Not only was the Boeing cabin demonstrably smaller but its floor was too high, restricting headroom and the space

Conceived for exactly the short/medium-range densely-travelled routes for which the Boeing 727 was sized, the Trident could have taken a large slice of the market. The aircraft that de Havilland first offered, the D.H.121, had a cabin roughly as wide as the 707's with six-abreast seating. However, British European Airways said this was too big, and insisted that the aircraft and its engines be shrunk. Only 117 Tridents were built, against 1,832 727s. (British Airways/Adrian Meredith)

for overhead bins. In cross-section the 707's fuselage was not circular. It retained the vestige of the Stratocruiser's 'double-bubble', being slightly nipped in at the waist, like an egg sitting high in an egg cup. The floor was set at the waistline, with the smaller lobe forming the cargo hold as well as accommodating parts of the aircraft's systems. Consequently United Airlines definitely preferred the DC-8. It was becoming clear that, though the airlines might concede that Boeing had defined the jet of the future on the outside, what happened on the inside was different. Boeing still had a lot to learn about seeing an aircraft in the same way as an airline manager.

Boeing's response

It was thought that Boeing would be convinced of the need for a larger-diameter fuselage, but this did not happen until United Airlines placed its initial order with Douglas for thirty DC-8s. Boeing then increased the diameter by 4in (10.2cm), which meant the 707 could no longer be built on the same lines as the KC-135. This was a costly penalty, but it saved the 707. The degree of disturbance to the structural design work already done, and, consequently, the cost of making the change, centred on one point, the crease between the upper and lower lobes of the body. A beam, called the crease beam, reinforced the integrity of the fuselage at this point. It was a delicate matter to change this without unravelling the fuselage, but it was successfully accomplished. Furthermore, Boeing, with its military jet experience, plus the information gained from the Model 80 prototype, was able to promise earlier deliveries.

Widebodies

In the 1960s international air travel grew by 15 per cent per year. If it continued at that rate the airlines would face problems of capacity. PanAm, for example, stressed that it did not have enough seats to meet the expected demand, and referred to an elongated airliner or a double-decker that would serve the needs of the 1970s until the much-vaunted SST arrived.

The double-deck configuration was the simplest way to more than double the passenger capacity of the 707, with six-abreast seating on both decks. Juan Trippe, the head of PanAm, had leapt at the very phrase 'double-decker', which he felt had the ring of a great marketing slogan. Douglas was also considering a double-decker. Indeed, the conventional

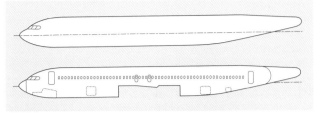

By the 1950s the pressure cabin had become commonplace. The most efficient shape has a cylindrical cross-section with spherical end caps. It is at this point that design compromises start. By the time aerodynamics, crew and passenger visibility, payload loading via doors and even more doors for emergency evacuation, and cavities for wing and undercarriage have received due attention, the only detail remaining of the original pressure vessel is the aft bulkhead.
(Key – Ray Whitford/Pete West)

wisdom never really considered anything else: engineers were inclined to see the six-abreast cabin as standard, and to add enough seats required a big stretch or putting another deck on top. If the aircraft's future after the advent of the SST was to be as a cargo carrier, getting the flight deck out of the way of the main cabin was an inspired stroke. Cargo could be front-loaded through a hinged nose. However, evacuating such an aircraft in an emergency would require escape chutes on two levels, and passengers on the upper deck, at 35–40ft (10.7–12.2m) above the runway, faced something resembling a bobsleigh run.

By this time a new international standard for freight containers had been arrived at, specifying a cross-section of 8ft × 8ft (2.44 × 2.44m). This was done to achieve commonality between road, rail and ship cargo. The containers could vary in length according to their conveyance, but not in width and height. Lightweight versions could be used for airfreight, cargo simply being switched from one container to another without being reconfigured. However, would this container fit into the cargo hold of an aircraft? The Head of Configuration at Boeing drew a circle outline for the belly of the projected aircraft around two side-by-side freight containers and calculated the required width of the cargo deck's floor. He then drew a circle to fit around the deck and the containers. It was a very wide fuselage, nearly twice as wide as a 707 cabin and more than 20ft (6.1m) across at the level of the passenger cabin above the cargo deck. By this means Boeing

This view of a 777 fuselage in assembly at Boeing's Everett plant illustrates the aircraft's circular cross-section, rather than the ovoid, or double-bubble, previously used by Boeing. Slightly wider than the 767, it is just under 1ft smaller than the 747. This allows twin-aisle seating, from six-abreast in first class to ten-abreast in economy class.
(Key – Tony Dixon)

Compared with its major competitors, the Boeing 737 and 757, the Airbus A320's cabin is 7.5in (19cm) wider. This allows the A320 to carry containerized cargo in the form of reduced-height containers.
(Key – Chris Penney)

had iterated its way to the most daring solution to the 747's configuration problems. It had not occurred to the company to start with a fuselage this wide for an airliner, although it had been used for the Lockheed C-5A Galaxy. It was the only viable form for the 747's fuselage; 'a brilliant decision based on damned few facts,' as Joe Sutter, head of 747 studies, commented. If a 707 was scaled up and superimposed on the new widebody it did not get out of scale; it looked right. One serious disadvantage did emerge, however. The single-deck fuselage was heavier by 12,000lb (5,400kg) than the double-decker because of the extra structure required to give it rigidity, but the widebody's virtues more than compensated for the weight penalty. The widebody also made the job of seating and evacuating so many passengers much easier. It was the combination of size and high-BPR turbofan engines that gave the 747 its 30 per cent reduction in DOC.

The three-seat units in the 707 (and therefore in its successors in body width, the 727 and 737) were 59.6in (1.51m) wide. The unit for the 747 needed to be 65in (1.65m) wide, allowing almost two more inches (5cm) for the average American, who had grown in height and width, and even this was a tight fit for some passengers. This provision was later sacrificed for payload in 747s that went to ten-abreast in economy class. Moreover, the cabin became an entertainment centre, since, for the first time, there was ample room for movie screens in all classes. All seats were to be equipped with headphones, music channels, and call and reading lights, which meant taking four or five wires to each seat's console and creating wiring trees that looked like a spaghetti mountain. Each stem of wires had to be bundled and then routed, and by the time they were all gathered for connection to the power sources they had become an

unfathomable maze, and far too heavy. A new system called 'multiplexing' enabled a single wire to time-share signals: in theory it could take as many as twenty separate signals by sending each one in increments. To use it for four or five signals for each 747 seat seemed well within technology. When every pound of the aircraft was reckoned to cost $100, multiplexing saved around 600lb (270kg). It took several years to debug the system; years in which passengers endured dying movies, overlapping music channels and imbecilic flashing lights.

Cabin air conditioning

Pressurized air for the cabin comes from the compressor stages of the engines, and as it is hot it has to be cooled by heat exchangers in the engine pylons, and by the main air-conditioning units under the cabin floor. The air is then mixed with an approximately equal amount of highly-filtered air from the passenger cabin. The filters are similar to those used to clean the air in hospitals, and are very effective at trapping microscopic particles. Older aircraft used only fresh air delivered by engine compressors, with only a modest impact on fuel economy. With the advent of high-BPR turbofans, which deliver most of their thrust from the front fan, air extracted from the engine core has an adverse effect on fan thrust, which seriously degrades fuel efficiency compared with older engines. By providing the cabin with the 50/50 mix a balance is achieved that maintains high-quality air (better than in most office buildings) and good fuel efficiency. Moreover, because cabin air is quite dry at cruise altitude, recirculation provides at least a modest level of humidity. Additionally, recirculation reduces the ingestion of exhaust and other pollutants during taxying.

Chapter 9

Supersonic Transports

This chapter looks at the evolution of SSTs. Essential to this daring venture was the development of a layout that would combine the features necessary for economic cruising and acceptable airfield performance. The crucial feature of the slender-delta wing was the revolutionary design for controlled separated flow, married to a structure that would resist high temperatures and an efficient propulsion system. The collaboration between France and Britain to produce the Concorde is contrasted with US efforts to leap ahead with a Mach 3 design, along with a look at environmental arguments and prospects for the future.

First thoughts from supersonic bombers in the 1950s

In the early 1950s supersonic bombers and fighters were being evolved, and industry wondered what civil spin-off could come from its deepening competence in high-speed design. In 1954 the RAE at Farnborough set up a discussion group to investigate the design, performance, economic and navigation aspects of an SST, with particular reference to the North Atlantic route.

The fashionable theme, evolved for supersonic bombers, was a slim cylindrical fuselage supported by very thin unswept wings. Thus the obvious starting point for an SST was to enlarge the fuselage to accommodate a reasonable number of passengers and then explore the sort of aircraft that resulted for a spread of ranges. Suitable take-off and landing constraints, to keep runway length within bounds, meant using trailing-edge flaps with flap blowing to generate an adequate maximum lift coefficient.

Some horribly large aircraft resulted for quite small passenger loads, even when pruning fuel reserves and using reheat (afterburning) for take-off. However, only silly aircraft emerged for the full non-stop London–New York range, with just fifteen passengers for a TOW of about 300,000lb (136,000kg) giving a DOC over five times that of contemporary aircraft. Even making an intermediate stop at Gander, and thereby losing much of the advantage of supersonic flight, did not give encouraging results. By 1955 the working group concluded that no thin, straight-winged layout could get passengers across the Atlantic with anything like competitive economics, and that a search should be made for more-attractive aerodynamic shapes, even though alternatives had already been examined without any showing promise.

Following BOAC's rejection of the Vickers VC7 (the commercial version of the V.1000 transport for the RAF), British industry felt that an entire generation of subsonic airliners was being handed to the USA on a plate. In an attempt to achieve a lead in SSTs the RAE was thus charged

Concorde's air conditioning was an example of complexity. In supersonic flight the external air at 100°C+ had to be reduced to 20°C before delivery to the cabin, while in subsonic flight it had to be raised from −55°C to 20°C. (BAE Systems/Geoff Lee)

with forming the Supersonic Transport Aircraft Committee (STAC) under its deputy director, Sir Morien Morgan. Very early on, the STAC rejected the concept of special 'beasts' that would demand a new approach to airfields and air traffic control (ATC). This meant accepting international runways as they were likely to be and fitting in with likely ATC patterns and procedures without the need for completely revamped ground systems to cope with SSTs.

Choice of speed

Potential prospects for favourable L/D ratios at supersonic speed were not promising, owing to the shock wave drag and the tendency for lift coefficient to fall with Mach number. Up to Mach 1.2 there was thought to be a chance of achieving shock-free flows by increasing sweep, carefully shaping (area-ruling) the body/engine-pod junctions and wingtips, and using judicious twist and camber. Swept-wing and slightly-alarming-looking 'M'-wing layouts were proposed that might postpone the fall in L/D. Economic aircraft, in effect fairly straightforward extensions of contemporary Mach 0.8 swept-wing transports, might result by cruising 50 per cent faster. However, the STAC considered the range Mach 1.2–1.8 unattractive, as it was difficult to evolve shapes that gave sufficiently high L/D to counterbalance the adverse effects on economy of low supersonic speed and lowish engine efficiency.

Apart from the fare, time of travel is what matters to passengers. On a transatlantic run, the dramatic jump and most of the advantage of supersonic speed is secured by cruising at Mach 2 and thereby reducing flying time from 7hr to 3hr. This saving of 4hr was highly saleable. With the 5hr time difference between New York and London, and the number of return trips per day being multiples of 0.5 (with adequate turnaround time), once Mach 1.8 is reached, the number of return trips per day is two, compared with one for subsonic aircraft. Further increase in speed does not affect the situation until Mach 3: at this speed 2½ round trips/day are possible, but only another 45min are saved.

The speed range Mach 1.8–3.0 was attractive. The fact that supersonic L/D ratios, albeit low, did not worsen with Mach number meant that the speed should be as high as possible. Long, slender shapes could produce good aerodynamic efficiency in the cruise, which, combined with confident predictions of greater engine efficiency, would yield acceptable productivity associated with the higher speed and gave encouraging cost figures. At the lower end of the range it was thought possible to evolve shapes compatible with reasonable landing performance. The optimum appeared to lie between Mach 2 and 2.5, and the choice within this band rested as much on structural and powerplant considerations as on aerodynamics, since kinetic heating difficulties mount very rapidly.

Furthermore, at speeds beyond Mach 2 much uncertainty existed on achievable values of the main parameters in the Breguet range equation:

$$\text{Range} = V \times \frac{L}{D} \times \frac{1}{\text{specific fuel consumption}} \times \log\left(\frac{W_{start}}{W_{end}}\right)$$

the L/D, the efficiency of the engine/intake combination, and structural weight fraction. The L/D value had to bear some relation to the trimmed configuration, not an idealistic model, and a shape that met sensible landing requirements. A

big difference arose if the airport approach speed was 160kt (300km/h), compared with 140kt (260km/h). The one real advantage of Mach 3 was that, while L/D hardly altered from about 7.5 (roughly half as good as a subsonic airliner), VL/D was increased and the greater intake compression increased the engine efficiency, both of which could mean greater range or more payload.

After prolonged study of several alternatives, the STAC Final Report of March 1959 recommended an SST to cruise at Mach 2.2 or 1,450mph (2,330km/h), with transatlantic range. Any speed higher than this would result in structural temperatures too high for long airframe life using well-tried aluminium alloys, the alternatives of steel and titanium posing great problems due to inexperience, cost, weight and, in all probability, a long and troublesome programme. Even so, some in the UK, mindful of US views, thought the STAC had not been adventurous enough. On balance, though, Mach 2.2 was all that the British industry dared attempt.

Evolution of the slender delta

Compared with skin friction and vortex drag due to lift, the major obstacle to economic supersonic flight is the large wave drag associated with lift and volume. Ever since supersonic flight was first seriously considered it had correctly been shown that wave drag could be kept low by using slender shapes. Elongating the fuselage was the obvious line to take, but elongation of the wing required much more careful consideration. It was sensible to keep the wing leading edge behind the Mach lines, and certainly to keep the whole aircraft well within the Mach cone from its nose, simultaneously distributing the volume and lift fairly evenly.

During the development of aircraft for high-speed flight after the Second World War, sweepback steadily increased, thickness ratios decreased and aspect ratio reduced, tending towards the delta planform. Supersonic aircraft demanded even thinner wings and more elongated fuselages, so greater extremes of aspect ratio and planform began to be explored. It appeared that, by pursuing minimum drag, long slender aerodynamic shapes, as advocated by Dietrich Küchemann at the RAE, promised to be serious contenders in generating an L/D of the right order for economical cruising at Mach 2. In addition to thickness ratio there are two other geometrical parameters which greatly influence supersonic drag: s/l (ratio of semi-span to total length of the

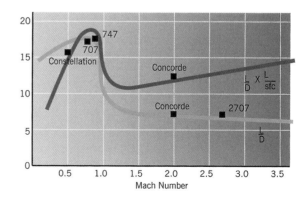

Lift/drag versus Mach number. This figure shows the drop in L/D near Mach 1.0 owing to the rapid rise in wave drag and reduction in lift with Mach number. However, the speed term in the range parameter compensates as Mach increases in the supersonic range.
(Key – Rolando Ugolini/Ray Whitford)

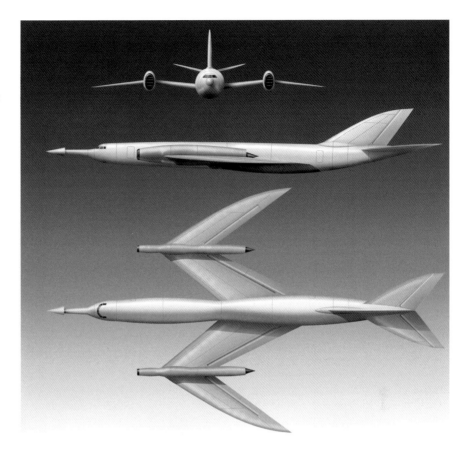

The 'M-wing'. In early 1956, based on work in the UK/USA on area-ruling, swept wing/body combinations began a swing towards Mach 1.2. Highly-swept, thin wings and a waisted fuselage were hallmarks of the theme, with the 'M-wing' as a variant. With the compensating effect of forward sweep over half the wing, the rolling effect of a crosswind at low speed would be sufficiently balanced and the sweep angle could be increased to 45 degrees, allowing low supersonic speed without producing a sonic boom. The idea was certainly novel, but there was no immediate burst of enthusiasm.
(Key – Rolando Ugolini/Ray Whitford)

aerodynamic shape) and the planform parameter p = S/2sl, where S is the gross planform area. For a lift coefficient of 0.1 at Mach 2 the drag is about a minimum when total span is 40 per cent of length (s/l = 0.2). This helps explain why slender-delta planforms emerged during the STAC work, although, at the time, the possibility of landing them satisfactorily seemed rather remote.

Uncontrolled flow separation

As with conventional subsonic aircraft, a slender-delta SST would have no difficulty in generating adequate lift in the cruise at reasonable AoA. The problem was producing enough lift for the approach and landing at low speed. The design requirements at each end of the speed range were in direct conflict.

For nearly all previous supersonic designs, wing sections had rounded leading edges, partly to discourage early flow separation, sharp leading edges being a recipe for premature stall. 'Flow separation' was, and still is, an emotive and ugly phrase. It denotes a stall, a breakaway of the airflow over the wing, almost invariably a nuisance, giving sharply increased drag, reduced lift, buffeting and vibration. However, flow separation is always present somewhere on a finite aerodynamic shape. The real issue was not *whether* separation occurred, but *where* it occurred, and the nature of the flowfield to which it gave rise. Unwanted separations appeared at quite modest AoA and spread in an unpredictable way, often causing havoc to longitudinal and lateral stability. The points of origin of these separations were difficult to tie down. The most troublesome of the separations originated from the swept leading edge, and took the form of vortex sheets springing from some point along the edge and then coiling up over the wing surface and

creating unwelcome changes in the distribution of lift. With such flow patterns, designers, in their ever-sharper quest for increased efficiency, were forced to skate aerodynamically on rather thin ice, and palliatives such as wing fences and notches were introduced.

Controlled separation

The flow pattern around a swept wing of very low aspect ratio (say a delta of aspect ratio 2.0) is very different to that for a high-aspect-ratio, moderately-swept wing. It is highly three-dimensional; 'all tip effect', is a graphic way of putting it. Work published by E.C. Maskell and Küchemann at the RAE in 1955–56 (and also research by the Office National d'Etudes et Recherches Aérospatiales (ONERA) in France and the NACA in the USA) spelled out the virtues of a

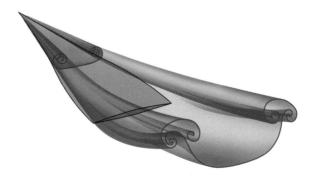

Slender-delta vortices. Vortices springing from the leading edge of a slender delta roll up smartly over the wing upper surface and dominate the overall flow. Moreover, such a wing could be made to exhibit essentially the same flow pattern over a wide range of AoA and Mach number.
(Key – Rolando Ugolini/Ray Whitford)

slender delta with *sharp* leading edges. It presented an alternative to the traditional approach of treating flow separation as a phenomenon to be suppressed. It suggested that one could positively stimulate a separation pattern that could be made to generate a stable system of vortices that would exhibit a regular growth with increasing AoA. The leading-edge vortices induce suction on the upper surface of the wing that remains constant along the chord, except in the region of the trailing edge.

As the vortices grow with AoA, the proportion of the total lift contributed in this way increases, with the lift curve being non-linear and steady throughout the range appropriate to practical flight. In effect, by living with leading-edge separation throughout the flight range one could eliminate the 'stall' as aircraft designers knew it. Corresponding tests confirmed that this vortex flow was maintained at supersonic speed, although the effects of the vortices became less marked with increase in Mach number.

Adequate lift?

As AoA increases, a slender delta produces lift only about half as vigorously as a modern swept-wing subsonic transport. The net result was that, just as cruise wave drag forced acceptance of much lower values of L/D than customary, take-off and landing of the slender delta would have to be made with small useable lift coefficients. Roughly speaking, subsonic transports could count on a useable lift coefficient of more than 2.0, whereas slender deltas could produce no more than 1.0. Even to generate such low lift, it looked as though a slender delta would have to be flown at AoAs approaching 20 degrees, very large by subsonic standards. Quite early on in the STAC deliberations it was firmly established that, at AoAs of this order, the lift was there and could be trimmed longitudinally.

The combination of large wing area and high engine thrust required for cruise led to lower wing loadings and higher thrust/weight ratios than those of subsonic transports. These features helped to promise a reasonable chance of the slender delta meeting take-off and landing requirements at field lengths similar to those of contemporary subsonic transports, in spite of the poor useable lift coefficient. For landing, the advantage of lower wing loading was further increased by an SST necessarily using a higher percentage of fuel during climb and cruise, and landing speeds only a little above those of subsonic transports seemed possible. On then current evidence it was felt, however, that lateral stability

considerations might ban use of AoA much greater than 5 degrees. Had this been the case, it would have stopped the evolution of a slender delta in its tracks.

Adequate control?

Confidence was boosted by evidence that a long slender shape necessary for Mach 2 cruise would have sufficiently good stability and control characteristics to be flown at AoA of 20 degrees or more, instead of being confined to the very restrictive useable AoA range imagined at the start of studies. However, it was by no means obvious that trailing-edge controls could operate with reasonable efficiency underneath a well-developed vortex, since the surface flow over most of the trailing edge was predominately spanwise. It was with some relief that wind tunnel testing revealed that fairly conventional ailerons and elevons were both effective and had reasonably linear characteristics. This removed a roadblock of some years' standing that had pushed supersonic bomber design in the direction of unswept wings, and which had made many advocates of the slender delta sympathetic to jet lift.

Structures and materials

The STAC recognized that the key to building a successful SST was intimate co-operation between the structures and aerodynamics teams, and a willingness for the structures specialists to shoulder extra burdens to retain aerodynamic efficiency without unduly sacrificing structural efficiency. While compromise was essential, it was thought that, until kinetic heating problems became acute (at Mach 2+), the structural problems of an SST could be handled with rather more certainty than the fundamental aerodynamic task. This implied that the aerodynamicists, in having to achieve the target L/D when trimmed for cruising and the desired approach speed on landing, should be allowed a little more room for manoeuvre and be shown some tolerance in playing safe. Ignoring, for the moment, kinetic heating problems and the use of novel materials, it was instinctively felt that the basic structural design for SSTs should be no more difficult than that of contemporary high-aspect-ratio subsonic military aircraft designed for long range (such as the Boeing B-47 and B-52), with their extreme aeroelastic problems and changing aerodynamics near the speed of sound. Ensuring pressure cabin integrity up to 70,000ft (21,300m) was essential, but it was not an insurmountable problem.

At a very early stage in the slender-delta research effort it was realized that rolling moment due to sideslip at high AoA might be very large, and that providing adequate rolling moment from elevons might be difficult because span is so small. To help prove the concept, Handley Page built the H.P.115, which showed that the handling qualities were a great deal better than anticipated. In particular, the lateral rocking motion proved to be easily controlled by the pilot. (Key Collection)

For high-speed flight research into the slender delta, Bristol Aircraft designed a new wing for the Fairey Delta 2, a 1956 holder of the world air speed record. At supersonic speed, BAC221 pilots found no problems, and control movements were progressive and instinctive. Not flying until 1964, it came too late to have much influence on the design of Concorde.
(Gordon Swanborough Collection)

Kinetic heating

With rising speed a complication to be faced is the rapidly increasing stagnation temperature. The forward motion of the aircraft compresses and heats the air, the areas most affected being leading edges and engine intakes. An additional effect is the exchange of heat from the boundary layer of air to which energy has been transferred through friction, by contact with the external surfaces.

Contemporary civil aircraft were operating with structural temperature differences of around 80°C (−50 to +30°C) and occasionally perhaps up to 90°C (structural temperatures of 75°C being reached on aircraft surfaces exposed to the tropical sun). Fuel could well be loaded at a temperature of 40°C, and a subsonic jet transport carrying fuel at this temperature is likely to have wing-skin temperatures at the end of the climb of about −35°C, allowing 25°C for kinetic rise above ambient. Thus there is a temperature difference of 75°C under such conditions. Similarly, on a long flight the structure may be soaked at −35°C, and at the end of the flight the aircraft may descend to conditions where temperatures of 40°C are reached on the aircraft skin. Temperature stresses due to these effects had not normally been regarded as significant.

At Mach 2.2, however, the stagnation temperature rises to 175°C in the boundary layer (modulated by the ambient temperature of −55°C at cruising altitude), so that the structure reaches a temperature of 120°C away from the leading edge. The Mach 2 proponents had based their case on involving only a 'reasonable degree of novelty' in materials usage. Modest development work on materials would be required, and skin temperatures would be below fuel-ignition points. In structural terms, the step from Mach 0.85 to 2.0 was less than Mach 2 to Mach 3. At the time, titanium (required for Mach 3) was approximately ten times as expensive as aluminium alloys, and at least 200 tons per year would be required to get that price. There was no point moaning about the advantages of titanium alloys when they were not going to be available. Thus the problem was to find a light alloy material that could provide the necessary integrity allied with long life. Only local areas subject to full stagnation conditions would require stainless steel or titanium.

Choice of materials

Structures subject to kinetic heating are affected in three ways, all of which had to be tackled together. Apart from reduced static strength and stiffness of metals exposed to elevated temperatures while under load, metals will creep, resulting in permanent deformation of the aircraft. This was a new problem for the structural designer, and the background provided by engine design was limited to what was regarded as short-term creep in the airframe context. As a basis for design it was accepted that the maximum permanent deformation should not be greater than that caused by a single application of proof load (that appropriate to 0.1 per

Typical skin temperatures of a Mach 2.2 SST. At Mach 2.2 the stagnation temperature rises to 175°C in the boundary layer (modulated by the ambient temperature of −57°C at cruising altitude), so that the structure reaches a temperature of 120°C away from leading edges. In cruise, the overall length of Concorde increased by 7in (18cm). Soaking with differential temperatures produces thermal stresses, and these could only be reproduced on test in real time. Hence the fatigue test rig built at RAE Farnborough was very complicated, and the testing covered years to establish fatigue life.
(Key – Rolando Ugolini/Ray Whitford)

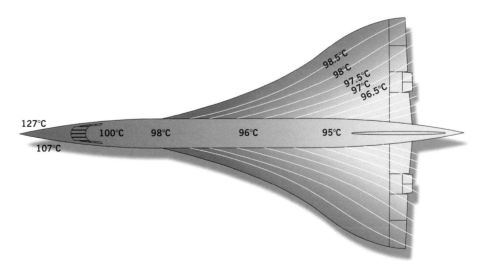

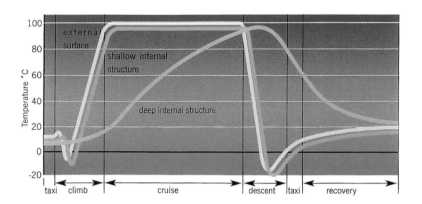

Temperatures on an SST. In the initial climb of an SST at subsonic speeds the external surfaces of the aircraft will cool a little and then heat up in the acceleration phase, reaching a temperature of about 100°C that will be maintained during the cruise. During deceleration and descent the external skin temperature will drop to about −10°C, rising to ambient temperatures after landing. (Key – Rolando Ugolini/Ray Whitford)

cent strain). With most heat-resistant materials this was not likely to impose a significant penalty, as fatigue considerations required similar stress limitations. Finally, internal stresses due to temperature gradients set up within the structure might well be significant. This aspect was the one about which least was known, and on which the greatest attention needed to be focused.

At the time there was a scarcity of specific design data that allowed assessment of the most suitable aluminium alloy for an SST, that would match temperatures between 100–200°C with a lifetime of 30,000hr. The problem was essentially due to the relatively low range of elevated temperatures of interest, coupled with the very long life requirements. The choice of materials for engines was not made on the basis of temperatures much below 200°C, and engine designers were satisfied if test periods were up to 1,000hr. By comparison, the designer of subsonic aircraft, for which there is no kinetic heating problem, is quite satisfied with knowledge of the room-temperature behaviour of various aluminium alloys.

In addition, any material for consideration had to be available at the time and in the form (sheet, extrusions, forgings) that the design needed. Furthermore, production facilities had to be able to handle the material, and could influence the designer in the choice of the type of structure that might entail fabrication processes requiring heavy capital expenditure on new plant.

The alloy finally chosen, known in the UK as Hiduminium RR 58, was selected because of its superior long-term creep strength, at around 120°C, of about 23,000psi (158MN/m^2) for 0.1 per cent total plastic deformation in 20,000hr. An aluminium-copper-magnesium-nickel-iron-titanium alloy (known in France as AU2GN, and similar to AA2168), it was evolved from an alloy originally developed to withstand the rigours of use in engines. It was specifically developed for gas turbine applications operating between 200° and 250°C, was available in many forms and had, by the late 1950s, given satisfactory service as the material for gas-turbine impellers, spacer rings and compressor blades, and for pistons for reciprocating aero engines. Although not the strongest aluminium alloy, it has superior strength at high temperatures, with good creep resistance.

Propulsion

Whereas, up to about Mach 2, a low-BPR turbofan might have a higher efficiency than a comparable turbojet, at higher speeds the advantage is reversed. It might be thought that the turbofan would offer some benefit in sfc at Mach 2.0, but although the sfc falls by 1 per cent or so as the BPR is

increased from 0 to 0.7, the specific thrust of the engine (thrust/air mass flow) drops dramatically. This requires an engine of perhaps 50 per cent higher mass flow to give the same thrust. This bigger turbofan would need a much longer and larger air intake in order to diffuse the airflow down from Mach 2.0 to the velocity required at the engine face. The weight penalty, perhaps 2,500lb (1,135kg), and extra drag of the bulkier engine would more than outweigh the reduced sfc. Moreover, the choice of a turbofan having slightly less cruise thrust than the turbojet would mean that the cruise altitude was slightly lower and the climb fractionally slower. With a large turbofan and accompanying higher installed weight and drag, the trends showed increasing operating costs. For a zero-wind sector distance of 3,000nm (5,570km), the best results showed that an equal quantity of fuel (37 per cent of TOW) was required by both turbofan and turbojet.

In cruising flight, air would arrive at the mouth of Concorde's inlet at Mach 2, or roughly 2,000ft/sec (600m/s). Yet on arrival at the first stage of the compressor the speed could not be allowed to exceed 500ft/sec (150m/s), to avoid shock losses at the tips of the rotating compressor blades. This was achieved by very carefully positioning the intake's shock waves by moveable ramps, whereby the velocity was reduced to below Mach 1 and the pressure increased accordingly, with minimum losses. (David Stephens Collection)

The poor L/D at supersonic speeds referred to above was only tolerable because its adverse effect on range, DOCs, or any parameter denoting efficiency, could be counterbalanced by the very marked increase in propulsive efficiency of jet engines at supersonic speed. This is greatly dependent on the design of the variable intake and exit nozzle. While engines themselves seemed to present no major difficulties, intakes and nozzles needed to be very carefully considered. As the range of operating conditions of an SST is very wide, this leads to complex arrangements. The intake has to control shock waves at its lips and throat, and pass appropriate mass flow through a long subsonic diffuser. The condition of the air in the intake closely approaches stagnation temperature and pressure. Because of this, much of the compressor blading of any contemporary engine would need to be changed from aluminium alloys to titanium, and the final compressor stages would have to be made of new high-temperature nickel alloys as, even before entering the combustor, the air temperature would reach 600°C.

The engine jetpipe had to house the afterburner (initially thought necessary only for transonic acceleration), primary nozzles, thrust reversers and variable final nozzles. In the case of turbojets the reheat solution had very limited scope, since the take-off noise limitations defined a minimum value of unreheated thrust. A greater advantage in this respect is available to turbofans, with their inherently higher thrust at low speeds. However, for an SST whose main function is to cruise continuously at Mach 2 it was found that straight turbojets of the Bristol Olympus or Pratt & Whitney J57 type would be most suitable.

Economics

By the beginning of the 1960s there was much criticism of the idea that the UK should be contemplating a supersonic airliner. On one side it was argued that development costs might reach £70–100 million (*see* later), and that it was an unjustifiable proportion of the total funds for technical development of all kinds. Furthermore, critics of the aircraft industry argued that a Mach 2 airliner would be unattractive to airlines confidently expecting a Mach 3 product from the USA.

From the airlines' viewpoint, nobody knew if the sonic boom would be tolerable, though there was general agreement that it had to be within the public's willingness to accept. Without that, there never would be an SST. Moreover, some airline executives warned that supersonic airliners could be a means of going bankrupt at supersonic speed, as governments were not going to undertake another round of heavy spending on supporting services such as the subsonic jets had required. In addition, the airlines felt that DOCs predicted by manufacturers were highly optimistic, and that the actual figures could be twice those of current aircraft. In

the past, passengers had paid less for a better service year by year. Could they be expected to pay more in 1970?

Between the years 1957 and 1960 ONERA in France was investigating very much the same kind of basic aerodynamic and structural problems as their British STAC counterparts. By 1960 the prospects looked sufficiently promising to launch a design competition for a medium-range SST (stage length 3,500km, 60–80 passengers) as a purely national project. The choice of speed was left to the manufacturers: Sud Aviation, Dassault and Nord Aviation. All three eventually chose a cruise Mach number between 2 and 2.2, and by late 1961 French officials concluded that the Sud design was the most promising.

In 1960 Bristol Aircraft was awarded a design contract for an SST with transatlantic range for 130 passengers. This led to some soul searching; allowing for the weight growth bound to occur, Britain was faced with a project more advanced than any hitherto. The study also asked for exploration of the possibility of collaboration with US and French manufacturers.

US views

The chances that a US partner could be found were extremely remote. The USA already had the Convair B-58 Hustler Mach 2 bomber flying, and a wave of optimism seemed to be sweeping the USA, with well-known authorities declaring that the initial design speed should be Mach 3. Indeed, this speed would have to be reached to achieve the range and efficiency factors to make an SST financially viable. The higher speed, it was argued, would involve little additional research for the same flying qualities as a Mach 2 aircraft, and there was more experience in the use of steel and titanium for Mach 3 than for aluminium at Mach 2.

The development of a Mach 3 aircraft was a certainty, and hence the active life of anything slower would be limited. A steel/titanium structure would be as good from a cost/weight viewpoint, if not better. The sonic boom might require the transonic acceleration to be above 40,000ft (12km), for which Mach 3 was more suitable. Given these US views, France was Britain's only potential collaborator, and Sud Aviation was the only company with significant airliner (Caravelle) experience.

Although the Tupolev Tu-144 (seen here at the Zhukovsky test centre in 1999) and Concorde had many similarities, they also had significant differences, such as the Tu-144's foreplanes, simpler wing design, closely-coupled engines and longer engine air inlets.
(Ray Whitford)

Joint Anglo-French project

Major advantages would accrue to both cross-Channel designs from comprehensive technical collaboration. But until a joint project was within sight, France and Britain understandably held their cards fairly close to their chests. In consequence there has subsequently been speculation, when discussing various novel features of the Concorde design, as to who first thought of what, and when. Sir Morien Morgan's impression was that France and Britain, largely independently, had evolved broadly the same approach to SST design. This proved fortunate, as it paved the way to a united effort that would benefit both parties.

With the BAC and Sud designs so similar, the stage was set for Anglo-French collaboration. November 1962 saw the French adhering adamantly to a short/medium-range SST of 220,000lb (100,000kg) TOW and BAC pushing a long-range (but not transatlantic) version at 262,000lb (120,000kg). Under the terms of the inter-governmental agreement, Bristol Engines would collaborate with Snecma. In contrast to the collaboration on the airframe, the engine companies got on well. With design definitions agreed, working arrangements were devised within the imposed conditions of equal national sharing of airframe-plus-engine development costs.

Within eighteen months of the start of work on the two versions, the medium-range version was cancelled. Sales missions visiting the major airlines of the world had failed to find any potential customers. None had believed that an overland sonic boom would be tolerated, a conclusion reached by IATA at its annual conference nearly a year previously. This enabled the design to go ahead, with Paris–New York range, payload increased to 130 passengers, and a TOW of 326,000lb (148,000kg).

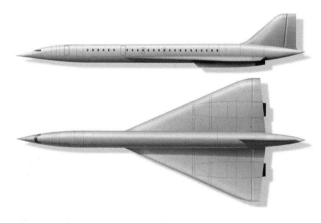

BAC 223 of 1960. This illustrates a British Aircraft Corporation proposal for an SST with a maximum take-off weight of 262,000lb (119,000kg), compared with Concorde's eventual MTOW of 408,000lb (185,000kg). The Type 223 followed the rejection of the BAC 198, having an estimated TOW of 380,000lb (172,000kg) with six Olympus turbojets.
(Key – Rolando Ugolini/Ray Whitford)

The US challenge

Wishing to be the first airline to 'go supersonic', PanAm was interested in Concorde and placed options to buy six aircraft. In the USA the decision to go ahead with an SST had not been made; no way had been found for supporting a civil venture with government funds, though there was emphasis on the prestige value of the most advanced airliner in the world. The head of the FAA had declared: 'It is a challenge to free enterprise American industry to show it can compete and

beat the nationalized efforts of the French, British and perhaps the Soviet Union'. PanAm's interest in Concorde had its desired effect. In mid-1963, at President Kennedy's suggestion, NASA started competitive studies of four fundamentally different configurations (canard delta, tailed delta, arrow wing and variable-sweep wing). A year later, after almost evangelistic support for an SST by William Allen and Juan Trippe (presidents of Boeing and PanAm respectively), the FAA was designated to conduct a design competition for a full-scale pre-production prototype programme. Financial support for the project was assured.

The USA thus declared its intentions: Boeing, Douglas and Lockheed were to design a transatlantic SST on the basis that the operating costs were no higher than those of contemporary subsonic types. Economics were based on the Boeing 707-320, which with 100,000lb (45,000kg) of fuel could carry 220 tourist passengers across the Atlantic. The demand for at least economic parity forced the SST design towards 700,000lb (318,000kg) TOW. At the time the DOCs of long-haul operations were in the region of 1.3–15 cent/mile. From a pure cost-per-seat-mile viewpoint it was necessary to consider carrying around 300 passengers. If comparison had been made with the expected operating costs of the forthcoming Boeing 747, an SST would have looked a lot less attractive, but the conventional wisdom was that the 747 might be relegated to the cargo role once the SST arrived.

Development problems could be solved for a 1970 aircraft, and it was believed that customers were willing to wait until then. To Europeans, even supposing that technical difficulties could be satisfactorily overcome, the advocates of the Mach 3 aircraft seemed to be confronted by a formidable array of self-imposed difficulties. Apart from the severe kinetic heating structural effects at Mach 3 (with temperatures up to 275°C), other problems included the cooling of hydraulic systems and electrical components. In cases where cooling was not possible, new materials needed to be developed for items such as radomes, body sealants, electrical insulation and lubricants. However, alarming technical difficulties have not usually deterred the aircraft industry, provided there is a strong possibility that eventual results will justify the effort.

Lockheed's ideas

The approach adopted by Lockheed was a double-delta configuration, the L-2000. The driving force behind this was to achieve a high supersonic L/D, minimum weight (by virtue of a low structural aspect ratio and wing loading), minimum sonic boom (conferred by the low wing loading), and the ability to fly at 70,000ft to minimize fuel burn. Being able to raise L/D from 7.0 to 8.0 could save around 80,000lb (36,000kg), or about the TOW of an early Lockheed Constellation! Improved L/D initiates a spiral having a big impact on DOC, as it reduces fuel burn, which in turn reduces aircraft size and weight, leading to reduced fuel burn, and so on. All of this promised to reduce the strength of the sonic boom.

Boeing's ideas

Boeing's SST effort began in 1957, at the conclusion of the North American XB-70 Valkyrie competition, at a time when its 707 was being readied for service. The excellent supersonic and high-lift characteristics of the very-low-aspect-ratio, highly-swept slender wing were becoming well

Concorde's design was optimized for supersonic flight. Its ogee wing planform, together with judicious use of camber and twist and CG variation by fuel pumping, gave low supersonic drag.
(BAE Systems/Geoffrey Lee)

understood. Such a low-drag wing at supersonic speed could generate high lift at low speed by creating strong vortices at its sharp leading edge. However, the growing concern over the noise generated by contemporary subsonic aircraft would make it difficult to achieve noise goals, and this loomed large in Boeing's thinking. At no time did Boeing consider using vortex lift on take-off (unlike Tupolev's Tu-144, Concorde and Lockheed's L-2000), because of the noise that resulted from the high climb-out thrust to offset the vortex drag. Full-span flaps on both the leading and trailing edges of the wing were needed to maximize both lift and L/D, so that low-power climb-outs could lessen noise. Furthermore, it had been assumed that the sonic boom would make supersonic overland flight undesirable, so the achievement of high subsonic aerodynamic efficiency, which dictated a large

span, became an important design goal. As far as Boeing was concerned this ruled out the low-aspect-ratio delta wing, and a search was made for other wing planforms, encompassing the arrow-wing and variable-sweep concepts, in early 1960.

For some years Boeing had proposed variable sweep to satisfy self-imposed criteria on both low-speed flight safety and performance. An early 1960 study suggested that, with variable sweep, landing speeds and field length would be considerably lower than those of contemporary fixed-wing aircraft, *provided* the weight penalty for the added wing complexity could be kept below approximately 4 per cent of TOW. Variable sweep offered these advantages, apparently with no penalty at supersonic speed, because the most efficient cambered and twisted arrow wing concept could be used. Both Boeing and NASA had demonstrated arrow-wing

Designed for a range of 4,000 miles (6,400km) with a 30,000lb (13,600kg) payload, the Lockheed Model L-2000-7, seen here in mock-up form, lost out to the Boeing 2707-200 in December 1966. The L-2000 was judged simpler to produce and less risky, but its performance was slightly lower and its noise levels were higher.
(Lockheed Martin)

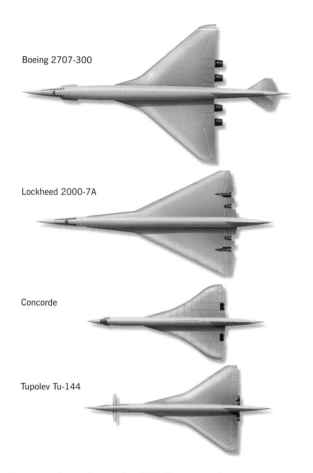

Boeing 2707-300

Lockheed 2000-7A

Concorde

Tupolev Tu-144

Size comparisons of competing SSTs. Contrary to other concepts, the final Boeing design had a high wing loading, moderate leading-edge sweep, large span and a horizontal tailplane. This configuration relied on obtaining lift at low speed through the use of flaps. In contrast, the tailless SSTs relied on low wing loading without flaps and required increased take-off and climb speeds to maintain high lift.
(Key – Rolando Ugolini/Ray Whitford)

L/D ≅ 9.0 with tailored wind tunnel models at Mach 3. It was hoped that the improved supersonic wing efficiency and the large span effects of variable sweep at subsonic speed would save sufficient fuel to offset the added wing weight.

With the emphasis on high-wing-loading variable-sweep configurations, titanium (Ti/6Al/4V) was introduced as the primary structural material to offset the otherwise 12 per cent weight penalty using high-temperature, high-strength steel alloys. It was used principally in conventional skin-stringer arrangements, though body sections used integrally machined components where there was a favourable weight trade. By 1964 Boeing had decided to reduce the cruising speed to the still formidable Mach 2.7, principally to avoid using heavy and costly superalloys, and to reduce basic systems and sealing costs. For a given percentage reduction in empty weight the payload increase of SSTs is nearly twice that of subsonic transports designed for the same range. Furthermore, by reducing the speed, the payload/TOW ratio improved, principally because the fuel burn is proportionally less at lower speed.

British views on variable sweep

One of the advantages claimed for variable sweep was that there will be occasions when the normal flight profile cannot be flown, because of overland sonic-boom restrictions or because diversions would be needed to alternative airports. If the subsonic part of the flight had thus to be lengthened, a variable-sweep design with its higher subsonic L/D in the unswept condition would have to pay less in fuel compared with a fixed delta. In the UK the RAE had looked at this, but to do it one had to start with a configuration quite different from the slender delta. Apart from leading-edge extensions, which are heavy and aimed at take-off and landing rather than subsonic L/D, there was little scope for varying the geometry of a slender delta. For a swing-wing aircraft the wing area is much smaller. The span is smaller in the fully-swept condition (to reduce the structural aspect ratio) but much greater in the unswept condition.

A tailplane, plus a fatter body, was needed to take fuel that would not go in the wing. For two Mach 2 designs the RAE found that the structural weight fraction, plus systems weight, had to be increased, from about 28 per cent for a fixed delta to 33.3 per cent for a variable-sweep layout. Of this, about 2 per cent was allowed for the pivot and jacks, and the rest was extra structure for the basic wing due to the different planform. This extra weight when compared with the fixed delta was something the RAE was unable to avoid, despite the reduced wing area and span. The span was low because of the high cost in weight of making it any bigger. It was apparent to the RAE that 'some people' (Boeing) thought that a wing of this sort could be built for less weight, and maybe it could for Mach 3 with extensive use of titanium. However, in 1964 the RAE could not see how, and this was one of the reasons why the British were never able to get very enthusiastic over the swing-wing compared with the slender delta.

Boeing's variable-sweep concept

Boeing, having been convinced by its studies for the Tactical Fighter Experimental programme (which led to the F-111) that variable sweep would work at low speed, favoured the highly-swept arrow wing for supersonic flight. For a given thickness and cruising speed, the higher the sweep, the lower the wave drag. Conversely, for a given cruise drag, the thickness of the wing could be greater, and it was hoped that this would offset the weight penalty and fuel volume limitations of variable sweep. Although thickness and sweep are important in determining wave drag, the distribution of thickness is also important. As it turned out, the features necessary to accommodate variable sweep in detail had a tendency to influence this effect adversely. Furthermore, with the sweep pivot in the wing, the loss of volume meant that additional thickness had to be provided. However, the weight penalty problem was the principal undoing of the subsequent Boeing effort.

In terms of supersonic drag, the ideal aircraft should not have a separate trimming surface such as a tailplane or foreplane. Trim at supersonic speed is then best achieved when the CG is near the aerodynamic centre, and when the lift distribution is such that what is best for low drag due to lift also satisfies the longitudinal balance. This had been achieved on the tailless Concorde by its ogee planform and judicious use of wing camber and twist, and CG variation by fuel pumping. Because of strict adherence to handling qualities and stability established by subsonic jet design practice, Boeing had found it impossible to avoid either a horizontal tail or a foreplane with the 300ft (91m)-long fuselage. Aeroelastic loss of stability at virtually all flight conditions had constantly plagued all its designs because of the aircraft's large size.

This computer-generated image shows the complex flow pattern over an arrow-wing SST design. The vortex pattern on the highly-swept inner wing can be clearly seen. (ONERA)

Propulsion

The Mach 2.7 cruising speed dictated mixed-compression intakes, delivering high efficiency but risking unstable operation. This entailed consideration of boundary layer ingestion, intake flow field distortion, and interference between inboard and outboard intakes, which could trigger an intake 'unstart'. Single pods with axisymmetric or rectangular intakes, and dual pods with rectangular intakes, were both considered. Dual pods were likely to suffer from sympathetic failure (if one engine failed, so would the other). Rectangular pods with mixed-compression inlets were abandoned as being too long and heavy. It would have been very difficult to install them without enlarging the wing area because of the strong shock-wave fields that occur near the wing leading edge. The single-pod axisymmetric type was selected. With the pods below the wing the intakes were subject to a complex flow field generated by the wing and body, which varied considerably with pitch and yaw in supersonic flight. Inboard pods were subject to large variations in boundary layer depth, while outboard pods had relatively large speed and flow direction gradients.

Initially there were a variety of engine offerings (dry and afterburning turbojets, and duct-heating turbofans). A remarkable complex variable-diameter centrebody intake was initially chosen for its ability to match the airflow of each engine. However, after extensive design and testing it was found that internal leakage and boundary layer bleed could not be reliably controlled, so a more conventional translating centrebody was adopted. By this time the General Electric GE4 afterburning turbojet had been selected as the project engine.

The integration of engines in the SST configuration constantly pressed technology limits. However, through proper monitoring of external pod geometry and tailoring of the wing, with consideration for area-rule principles, it was found that a pod/wing combination could be designed so that the incremental drag of the pod was equal to the wetted-area drag of the pod alone. Minimizing pod/wing interference drag and AoA effects on the intakes meant locating the engines near the rear of the wing, with the exhausts behind the trailing edge. Unfortunately, such an engine arrangement pushes the CG aft, compounding stability problems.

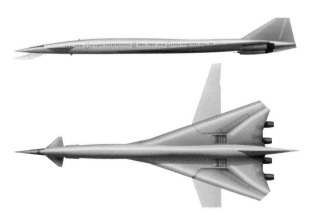

Boeing 2707-200. With its variable-sweep wing, maximum take-off weight of 675,000lb (306,000kg) and the predicted ability to fly at Mach 2.7 at 64,000ft (19,500m), the 2707-200 was the most ambitious of Boeing's SST proposals. Problems with aeroelasticity, weight and aft CG caused a total re-think in early 1969.
(Key – Rolando Ugolini/Ray Whitford)

Boeing's proposal

In late 1966 the variable-sweep configurations were narrowed down by Boeing to an integrated wing-tail layout, the 2707–100 (Model 733–467). This was based on several needs: to space the engines to prevent simultaneous unstarts of inlets; to avoid jet exhaust impingement on the tail at any AoA, altitude, or Mach number; to avoid tail suck-down at take-off; to alleviate the locked-in pitch-up experiences encountered with body- and wing-mounted engines on all previous configurations that used horizontal tails; and to improve the fuel volumetric efficiency of variable sweep. The integrated wing-tail allowed a deeper wing box for the same thickness ratio (giving an increase in fuel volume) than any of the separated wing-tail arrangements.

	Olympus 693 (Concorde)	NK 144 (Tu-144)	GE4 (B2707)
Max thrust (kN)	170	197	311
TET (K)	1,455	1,325	1,560
Mass flow (kg/s)	186	250	300
Bare mass (kg)	2,545	2,850	6,012

SST Engines

This most ambitious design from Boeing was additionally complicated by the only possible location for the engines, which was on the tailplane. This, giving an even further aft CG, exacerbated problems of stability and control. The fuselage was a departure from a straight tube, having much cross-sectional area variation to conform to the area rule. Nevertheless, with these complications Boeing had succeeded in raising the estimated payload fraction to 8.4 per cent, compared with Concorde's 6 per cent, but the fuel was also 50 per cent of TOW.

Boeing wins

Although the scope for problems seemed limitless, such was the confidence in Boeing's technical prowess that, at the end of 1966, its swing-wing design powered by General Electric engines was chosen by the FAA for national support over the two fixed-slender-delta rivals. It took another nine months of development to validate the concept before the design go-ahead occurred, involving testing of all critical areas including a full-scale fail-safe wing pivot.

The US government agreed to lend 90 per cent of the launch costs, with repayment via royalties from production aircraft, and the FAA placed a contract for two prototypes, which were expected to fly in 1970. Boeing had twenty-one airlines that had taken options on 115 aircraft (as well as some who had done the same for Concorde). The design weight was 720,000lb (327,000kg), with a payload of twenty-eight first-class and 260 tourist passengers and a design speed of Mach 2.7. In subsonic flight the outer part of the wing rotated about an inboard hinge to form a double delta with 70 degrees of sweep, and 20 degrees outboard with twice its fully-swept span. The leading and trailing edges carried the usual Boeing high-lift devices.

After the allotted nine months it became apparent that, even with the addition of a foreplane, introduced in late 1967, with its attendant weight, complexity and added body stiffness (to achieve reasonable elastic forgiveness), the weight of the 2707-100 was too high when compared with the original SST goals. It was decided to reopen the configuration

selection process for one year under rigid controls, and to separate the prototype and production programmes. This allowed the prototype design to proceed, albeit with added technical risk, to achieve performance objectives.

By early 1968 it became apparent that the promise of the integrated wing-tail, variable-sweep concept was not being realized. The layout suffered from poor mass distribution due to the aft engine arrangement. The close coupling of the control surfaces and the CG resulted in high trim drag and high pitching moment of inertia at low speed. The foreplane, added to offset these difficulties, complicated the longitudinal stability at all speeds. Considerable 'stiffness weight' was added to both the body and horizontal tail to control the aeroelastic deflections caused by the foreplane and engines. The low-speed operational goals of the arrow-wing concept, including noise, could not be realized, and the weight and aeroelastic properties of the large wing area resulted in an uncompetitive design even though its supersonic aerodynamics were the best of all the configurations.

Variable sweep's failure

The basic difficulties with the variable-sweep, integrated wing-tail design were:

1. It was impossible to configure an SST with a wing pivot sufficiently inboard to achieve the subsonic benefits of variable sweep and at the same time justify the added weight and complexity. Undercarriage installation further compounded the pivot design problem.
2. As the wing pivot was moved outboard to solve these problems, the resulting wing strake grew larger, which resulted in larger shifts in aerodynamic centre with speed and AoA.
3. The supersonic L/D of the arrow wing degenerated as a result of a less-than-ideal wing glove, and overlap at the wing pivot needing extra thickness of bump fairings to house the pivot. The subsonic L/D was decreased from the optimum because of the reduced span of the more outboard pivot, poor span load distribution with increased strake area, and bluff surfaces in the wing overlap area.

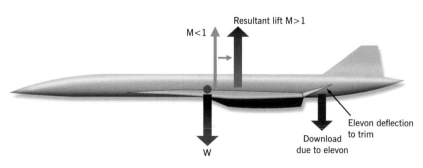

Trimming in supersonic flight. As any aircraft accelerates across the transonic region the lift centre moves aft. If elevons are used to trim out the nose-down moment, as shown, additional and unacceptable trim drag results. For Concorde the trim change was largely removed by carefully cambering the wing and by pumping fuel from a forward trim tank rearwards, to move the aircraft's CG roughly in step with the centre of lift movement. (Key – Rolando Ugolini/Ray Whitford)

4. The variable-sweep wing was always an inefficient fuel tank; it was necessary to oversize the wing to satisfy mission fuel requirements.

Thus, when attempts were made to maximize the range achievable with acceptable low-speed performance, the resulting weight for variable sweep was 6–7 per cent of the gross weight, instead of the 'just bearable' 4 per cent. As reported in an FAA review at the beginning of 1968: 'We had an aircraft that could cross the Atlantic empty, or fly halfway across full'. Six months later a new design was offered, with a fixed delta wing and a conventional tailplane.

1968 re-evaluation

In early 1968, just six months before the rollout of its 747, Boeing began an all-encompassing review of configuration possibilities. Carried out by competing design study teams, this included not only the integrated and non-integrated variable-sweep options, but also the whole spectrum of fixed-wing layouts. Both tailed and tailless fixed-wing designs that incorporated either subsonic or supersonic leading-edge wing planforms were examined. Finally, the competition narrowed down to a moderately-outboard-pivot, twin-pod design (Model 969-404) and a modified delta with separate pods (Model 969-302). Both configurations had artificial stability about all axes to maximize performance. In February 1969 Boeing decided on the Model 969-302, because no other could be found with better all-round performance and its development risks appeared to be far lower. Thus the fixed-wing tailed delta 2707-300 was born, approximately twelve years after the Boeing SST effort started.

There was prolonged controversy as to whether the project should continue. This only partly abated when, in 1969, it was decided to proceed with reduced funding. However, with the programme still in trouble in November 1970, the US Senate voted fifty-two versus forty-one against pumping another $290 million into the programme. Opponents of the funding expressed doubts as to the economic feasibility of the project, and many were deeply concerned about environmental issues such as the sonic boom and possible effects on the Earth's atmosphere. The death of the US SST was sealed by a vote in both houses in the spring of 1971.

The future

In the 1990s NASA resurrected the High Speed Commercial Transport, but abandoned the effort in 1999, having concluded that an SST would have to meet much tougher Stage 4 noise regulations. With twenty-first-century technology and what might be attainable in the next ten years there is the possibility to design a viable 300-passenger Mach 2.4 aircraft with 6,000nm (11,110km) range and operating economics 25–30 per cent higher than that of a Boeing 747-400. However, it would need to operate subsonically over land because the sonic boom remains a major problem for which only partial solutions exist. Noise and emissions are capable of being adequately addressed with advances in combustion technology and noise suppression, a variable-cycle engine being a possible route. The year 2030 is the very earliest introduction date for a second-generation SST. Even then, the market will only support one aircraft type, so a global alliance, with taxpayers' funding, will be necessary to launch such a project.

This artist's impression illustrates the ultimate fixed-delta-wing Boeing 2707-300, cancelled in 1971. Its fuselage diameter varied over the cabin section in accordance with area-ruling principles, to reduce interference wave drag between wing and fuselage. This was not done on Concorde because it was felt that the increase in production costs would be too high.
(Boeing)

Chapter 10

Flying-Wing Airliners

The concept of a flying-wing aircraft is not new, and designers have long been attracted by their intrinsic aerodynamic efficiency. With the largest current airliner, the Airbus 380, about to enter service, there are some highly imaginative and on-going flying-wing designs offering 1,000 seats for the year 2020 and beyond. However, as this chapter shows, there are some fundamental difficulties that require solutions.

The need for larger aircraft

Current forecasts predict that airline passenger traffic will double by the year 2010, even if growth is less than the air transport industry's average of 5.5 per cent over the last twenty years. This will lead to further increases in ATC-system and airport congestion, forcing airlines to use larger aircraft than hitherto.

On both sides of the Atlantic, design teams are working on concepts for very large aircraft (VLA) to satisfy the anticipated need. But larger aircraft present major problems: taxiway and runway width limits, gate limits, passenger handling, emergency evacuation, community noise and aircraft separation owing to wake vortices. A VLA must be designed with existing airport infrastructures in mind, the size constraint being an 80 × 80m (262ft) box. This is to ensure that they can operate from a large number of existing airports of interest (but by no means all) without the need to employ folding wingtips. These have been considered for some years, and were proposed as an option for the Boeing 777. Because of their high weight penalty and difficult certification failure case they have not been adopted.

The 'cookie-cutter' approach

Since the introduction of the jet engine for transport aircraft, considerable improvements have been made in subsonic aircraft aerodynamics, structures, propulsion and systems, but none could be regarded as a revolution. The classic Boeing 707/Douglas DC-8 configuration of the 1950s has remained essentially unchanged. Recent aerospace industry interest in developing a subsonic airliner with 50 per cent greater passenger capacity than the largest in-service airliner, the Boeing 747-400 (400–450 tri-seats), has generated a variety of proposals based on the proven configuration. Airlines additionally want a 20 per cent reduction in seat-mile costs, presenting a tall order for designers to meet. However, when aircraft grow big enough to become double-decked there is a jump in productivity. The floor area of the passenger cabin doubles with little increase in aircraft wetted area. So the operating cost per passenger gets more attractive as size increases, leading to the enlarged (600–800-seat) and refined double-deck 747 lookalike VLAs, such as the Boeing 747XX and Airbus A380.

Ultra-high-capacity aircraft

Looking well beyond the technically conventional A380 that may enter service in 2007, future commercial transports might have to embody radically innovative concepts. Indeed, much exploratory work was based on the assumption that, despite the increasing number of direct routes, major long-haul carriers will need to operate 800–1,000-seat transports. Moreover, sustained traffic growth will be tied to even lower fares, requiring further reduction in operating costs. Manufacturers will thus have to develop new concepts that will significantly lower airframe weight and reduce drag. Less thrust/seat-mile will be required, and fuel consumption per passenger will drop.

Despite the not unreasonable conservatism of manufacturers (even though Boeing, in the 1970s, backed 90 per cent of company worth on its 747), there is room for radical thinking. Several alternative and highly unconventional proposals have appeared that will potentially circumvent the

Aérospatiale's advanced study group has considered 1,000-seat flying-wing transports. Cruising speed would be Mach 0.85 and maximum range 7,400 miles (12,000km). This configuration would use four 445kN-thrust turbofans installed above the wing in staggered pods. To comply with airport constraints such as apron areas, folding wingtips would be required, with their resulting complexity and weight penalty.
(Aérospatiale)

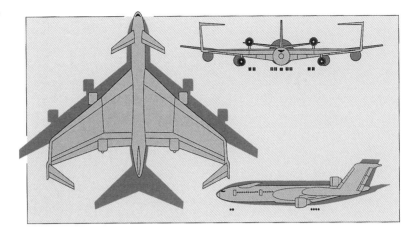

Boeing C-wing. This layout retains many of the features of a spanloader with the projected wingspan reduced to that of the Boeing 747XX and about the same induced drag. The price is the pair of winglets that are each roughly the size of the vertical fin on a 747, resulting in an aircraft with a height about 20ft (6m) less than the Boeing 747XX. The primary purpose in developing this new configuration was to address the problems of the 600–700-seat transport directly, rather than significantly improve aircraft performance.
(Pete West/*AIR International*)

practical operational and size limitations inherent in an enlarged VLA. It has been suggested that the standard configuration is nearing its full evolutionary potential, with 600-or-so passengers as a practical limit. Conceptual designers have sought new or dormant technologies that might be brought together to resolve ultra-high-capacity-aircraft (UHCA) problems. A departure in the form of the flying wing has been proposed.

Why flying wings?

An ideal cruising aircraft, from the aerodynamicist's view-point, at least, is a simple, elegant flying wing. Everything that does not contribute to the efficient generation of lift should be placed in or on the wing, provided that, in doing so, no significant penalties are incurred. The idea of a flying-wing airliner is not new, of course, but it has to be big enough to provide sufficient height within the passenger cabin. Moreover, not until the 1980s did the level of automation and reliability of flight control systems make it feasible to solve the problems of stability and control readily (as in the Northrop B-2).

The modern flying-wing concept applied to a UHCA of 800-plus seats could make an attractive alternative. The increased dimensions of the aircraft allow accommodation of the payload within and across the wing centre-section to produce a quasi-spanloader. The great allure of a span-distributed-loading design is that, by spreading the payload along the span, the wing bending moments arising from the aerodynamic lift are alleviated. Wing-mounted engines and fuel do this for conventional aircraft (*see* the figure on page 186). This allows reduced structure weight, leading to an improved payload/empty weight ratio. Since, very roughly, aircraft are bought by the pound (or kilogramme), lower weight means lower cost.

Furthermore, flying wings offer a major opportunity to benefit from laminar flow (*see* later), since a wing is easier to 'laminarize' than a fuselage. The spanloaded flying-wing configuration has an inherently large wing area, which means that the aerofoil's lift coefficient can be low. This allows aerofoil lift to be traded for thickness, while retaining an adequately high drag rise Mach number on a wing of acceptably low sweep, as needed for laminar flow. Because wing area is needed for good airfield performance (as well as fuel volume), high-lift system requirements are similarly reduced, at least in principle. Indeed, the high aspect ratio of the outer wing panels would not tolerate the high nose-down pitching moment of elaborate trailing-edge flaps, and current designs are limited to single-element Fowler trailing-edge flaps or leading-edge slats. This will reduce manufacturing and maintenance costs, as well as airframe noise.

Blended wing-bodies

In the past, fuselages have carried the payload and empennage but aerodynamically have produced little lift, contributing mostly to drag. Wing-body blending, as illustrated by the Aérospatiale Flying Wing, the McDonnell Douglas (now Boeing) BWB-1-1 and the TsAGI FW-900, gives a 'fuselage' cross-section that blends aerodynamically with the wing to contribute to lift. Assuming a typical passenger to be 1.8m (6ft) tall and current transonic-cruise aerofoils about 12 per cent thick, a wing having a chord exceeding about 21m (70ft) is thick enough to permit the passengers to be placed within the lift-producing wing (though with more profile drag), rather than on it, in a drag-and weight-producing fuselage.

The blended-wing structure could cut induced drag during high-altitude cruise by its relatively high structural efficiency, saving weight and therefore the lift required. This

Boeing C-wing. The initial configuration of the Boeing C-wing was developed around the fuselage of the Boeing 777, modified internally to allow seating for 600 passengers in the same three-class mix envisioned for the 747XX. This artists' impression shows the final preliminary configuration, powered by three 100,000lb (445kN)-thrust engines.
(Pete West/*AIR International*)

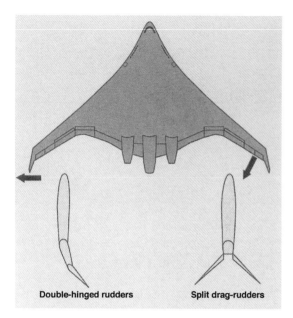

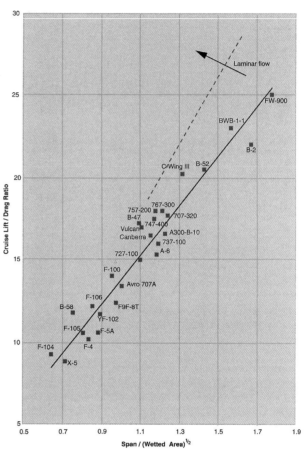

Boeing (Long Beach) BWB. On the BWB-1-1 the outboard elevons are the primary pitch and roll controls because they have the longest moment arms about the CG. The winglets (that increase the wing's effective aspect ratio) provide primary directional stability and control, but for low speed engine-out control drag rudders similar to those on the Northrop B-2 are used. The design features leading-edge slats as the only high-lift devices.
(Pete West/*AIR International*)

Lift/drag ratio increases with aircraft size. This is due primarily to boundary-layer effects, but also to the more efficient use of fuselage volume for double- and triple-deck arrangements, which tends to reduce the ratio of fuselage to wing wetted areas. This figure shows the increase in L/D and the importance of wingspan in the design of aircraft for high aerodynamic efficiency in the subsonic regime. All of the aircraft shown are turbulent-boundary-layer types. The beneficial influence of laminar flow is shown by the arrow.
(*AIR International* – Ray Whitford)

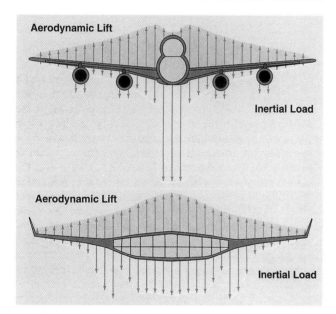

Spanloading. A key element in the flying-wing airliner is the extension of spanloading. In comparison with the conventional design (upper), in which the wing, fuel and engine weight offset the aerodynamic lift, the flying wing (lower) also distributes the payload (passengers plus cargo) weight across the wing. By itself this is structurally efficient and could reduce the weight of the structure. Compared with a conventional configuration, empty weight could be 12 per cent lower. That said, the beefing-up of the pressurized box (i.e. non-circular) cabin will offset this gain.
(Pete West/*AIR International*)

Structural considerations

A critical structural decision is cabin cross-section, as once this has been decided upon it is impossibly expensive to alter, requiring fundamental changes to production jigs and the rest of the design. A perfect 'O' is the most efficient pressurized cross-section, since it is in hoop tension with a minimum stress level that translates to low weight. A horizontal oval cross-section gives more usable volume and wider floors, and is structurally feasible. However, oval pressure vessels that are inflated and deflated several times a day, year after year, are always trying to become circular. They can suddenly develop alarmingly expensive fatigue cracks in middle age.

With the box-like passenger cabin of the flying wing giving a favourable contribution to overall lift, it will be heavier than the conventional circular-section structure. A horizontal bubble has not the same load-bearing depth as an upright (double-deck) bubble, and must be heavier to resist the bending loads. Moreover, the cabin, which is trying to inflate into a circular shape due to pressurization, has to be reinforced by a line of columns along its length. Because of this structural beefing-up, some, if not all, of the spanloader's crucial weight advantage may be negated.

will be further enhanced if sufficient confidence has been gained in the use of composite materials for primary structures in civil aircraft. As a final side benefit, when the wing section exceeds a given thickness the entire aft wing spar/pressure bulkhead becomes available as the location for emergency escape doors, thus potentially relieving a major problem with any large aircraft.

Parameter	Boeing BWB-1-1	Aérospatiale FW	TsAGI FW-900
Passengers	800	1,000	936
Span (ft)	280	315	348
Max. body depth (ft)	22	23	
Max. body t/c ratio (per cent)	16	14	16
Range (nm)	7,000	6,500	7,000
Take-off weight (lb)	823,000	1,322,000	1,234,000
Operating empty weight (lb)	412,000	727,000	666,000
Cruise L/D	23		25
Total thrust (lb)	3 x 62,000	4 x 100,000	4 x 77,000
Thrust/passenger (lb)	232	400	329
Thrust/weight	0.23	0.3	0.25

Nominal characteristics of projected flying-wing UHCAs
All (single-class) aircraft are designed for a cruise Mach number of 0.85.

There are basically two structural concepts for the pressure compartments for the flying wing, as shown in an adjacent figure. Both are based on the use of double skins: an exterior surface to maintain aerodynamic performance, with an inner, more flexible skin capable of sustaining fluctuating pressures. Currently there are no data available to establish the practicality of either concept, nor to enable assessment of the true weight penalty of such structures pivotal to the viability of the concept. If such flat pressure vessels could be developed, using lightweight composite materials together with sandwich skins, the overall benefits to be had by flying wings could be substantial.

Seating arrangement

Future generations of long-range airliners will have to offer unprecedented standards of comfort for passengers who want more space, so there is a need to get away from aluminium tubes, but barn-like cabins might be daunting. With the flying-wing layout, though, space may be available to provide passengers with bar and lounge facilities, as in the days of the downstairs Sky Dive of the 1950s Boeing 'Stratoboozer'.

The design must allow for fast and hassle-free boarding and disembarkation with a 105min turnaround time, and new methods of cabin cleaning, waste disposal and baggage handling. A revolution in thinking will be needed about the number of vehicles on the ramp if turnaround times equal to 747 operations are to be maintained, let alone shortened. Single-door loading will have to go, and two-level multi-door access must be realized without the need to tear terminals apart and rebuild them. Evacuating 800 passengers in 90sec will be even more difficult to achieve.

Passengers also prefer to feel more in control of their environment. With the no-window option and the use of closed-circuit TV cameras (primarily as a safety feature) and entertainment systems, passengers will be able to select a range of internal or external views. But (and this is a big caveat) passengers will have to be persuaded to accept a totally different cabin interior, with long seat rows and no windows. This may be the most difficult selling point of a flying-wing airliner.

Laminar flow

Central to the concept of the very-long-range airliner is the maintenance of a laminar flow over the aircraft. When air passes over a solid surface the fluid particles in contact with the surface are brought to rest. Moving away from the surface, successive layers of the air are slowed down by the viscous shearing of the layers beneath. The result is a thin layer of slower-moving air, the boundary layer, in which the speed of the air changes from zero at the surface to the full freestream value at its outer limit. Near the front of a wing the boundary layer is very thin and the flow steady. This is called laminar flow. As it moves downstream the boundary layer grows in thickness and becomes less steady. At some distance downstream, called the transition region, the boundary layer loses stability, becomes turbulent and jumps in thickness. Turbulent boundary layers can produce twice as much skin friction drag as laminar ones. Because of an airliner's size the normal state of the boundary layer is turbulent on the whole airframe. That said, the friction drag/wing area decreases with increasing size; a trend that is very favourable to large transport aircraft.

Laminar flow control

Laminar flow control (LFC) has been extensively researched on both sides of the Atlantic since the early 1930s. Even in those days it was well understood that slots in an aerofoil, to suck off the boundary layer, would stabilize it and prevent, or at least delay, the transition to turbulence and its accompanying higher drag. The greater the proportion of aircraft surface area occupied by the wing, the greater the effectiveness of LFC. In addition, reducing boundary layer thickness diminishes the associated pressure drag. There is no other way to achieve such large drag reductions, and it is the only technique already proven to work.

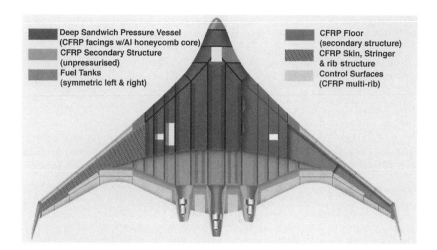

Structural layout and material usage. This is for the Boeing BWB airliner. The very-high-BPR engines are staggered so that, in the remote event of an uncontained disc burst, debris trajectories will minimize hazard to the structure, fuel tanks, control surfaces and pressurized cabin.
(Pete West/*AIR International*)

The turbulent skin friction of a typical airliner accounts for 45–50 per cent of total cruise drag. Elimination of, say, 70 per cent of this, after allowing for the equivalent drag of the suction system power, can lead to an overall drag reduction of 30 per cent and a corresponding increase in L/D. This could reduce the fuel consumption by 40 per cent on an 8,000nm (14,800km)-range conventional design, saving an airline hundreds of millions of pounds a year in fuel costs alone. However, LFC is very difficult to apply to a fuselage (which represents about half the wetted area on a widebody transport).

The large saving in fuel reduces the weight of the aircraft, further reducing drag, and allows corresponding reductions in the size of the wing and tail because of the lower weight. Moreover, with very low skin friction, the optimum aircraft design is significantly changed. It becomes profitable to use a lower wing loading (a feature of flying wings) because of the reduced wing profile drag.

Although LFC offers the greatest potential for drag reduction, it is at the same time the most difficult technique to achieve. The problem is the cost and difficulty of making wings with continuous suction capability, either through large numbers of fine holes or through spanwise slots every few inches along the chord, which are sufficiently smooth to enable laminar flow to be maintained. It also necessitates a very complex and heavy plumbing system. Even where this has been done experimentally there is concern about dirt and insects, the presence of which creates sufficient roughness to trip the laminar layer into a turbulent one. A high level of surface finish is relatively simple to achieve with careful

manufacture, but it inevitably deteriorates in service and needs regular cleaning. A possible solution to the insect problem may be a flow of de-icing fluid through orifices on the wing leading edge during take-off and low-altitude climb. One device that has been shown to work is the leading-edge 'Krueger flap/bug shield'.

Other factors adversely affecting the maintenance of laminar flow are wing-sweep effect (high is bad), aerofoil shape and engine noise. With extended amounts of natural laminar flow (of around 50 per cent chord), the boundary layer becomes very sensitive to pressure disturbances arising from the engines. All of the flying wings depicted exploit this by having aft-mounted engines (aimed primarily at airport noise shielding), though none are known to rely on LFC for their claimed performance.

An optimum wing design combining the advantages of LFC and natural laminar flow is the hybrid LFC wing. Such a wing has a porous skin (produced by laser drilling) with suction applied to the area forward of the wing's front spar, as well as natural laminar flow over the remaining wing chord.

Airline acceptance

The likelihood of the introduction of LFC into airline service depends on the construction and maintenance cost of the porous surfaces, system reliability in all weather conditions, and the solution of the insect and dirt problem. The concept is unusually risky because the optimum LFC wing area is much larger than that of a conventional design. If an LFC aircraft

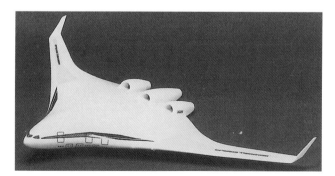

A configuration proposed by Boeing (Long Beach) for its BWB-1-1 incorporated a technologically risky, highly integrated propulsion system. The advanced ducted propeller engines are fed by inlets which swallow the wing boundary layer, which will be at least 0.3m (1ft) thick at this location. Compared with a conventional configuration, this design was reckoned to require 27 per cent less thrust, so reducing fuel burn by the same amount.
(Boeing)

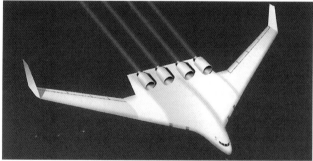

Russian flying-wing transport. The Russian Central Aerohydrodynamics Institute (TsAGI) proposed a series of flying-wing airliners, of which the FW-900 is shown. With a wing span of 348ft (106m) it would require folding wingtips. Aft mounting of the engines (common to all designs) is essential to balance the aft centre of lift and give an adequate CG range.
(Pete West/*AIR International*)

were to be operated without suction it would not just regress to a regular turbulent boundary layer aircraft, it would be a badly designed one and an economic disaster.

The conclusion is that laminarization could lead to huge savings in fuel and weight, in spite of the added weight of the boundary layer control system. However, a large bill for long-term R&D would have to be borne by the manufacturer before being passed on to the operator, along with the operational problems. At present, the practical achievement of laminar flow, though successfully tested, is a long way off, owing to its economic viability, and may remain so unless fuel prices rise markedly.

The C-wing

The designs mentioned so far have spans ranging between 280ft and 350ft (85m and 106m), which violate the 262ft (80m) airport constraint and would therefore need foldable wingtips. The quest for a solution to the wingspan problem led to the C-wing concept of Prof Ilan Kroo at Stanford University.

This novel layout, developed by Dr John McMasters of Boeing and Kroo under a NASA contract, retains many of the features of a spanloader, but with wingspan reduced to that of the conventional Boeing 747XX (for which it was an alternative) with its wingtips folded, and about the same induced drag. The configuration is a wing with very large vertical winglets, atop which are mounted horizontal winglets, all surfaces having 35 degrees of sweep. This arrangement puts the horizontal winglets in roughly the longitudinal location, relative to the wing, of a horizontal T-tail, operating with a download, as for conventional configurations during cruise. The forfeit is the pair of vertical winglets, each roughly the size of the fin on a 747, despite which the aircraft still has a height about 20ft (6m) less than the Boeing 747XX. The primary purpose in developing this new configuration was directly to address the problems of the 600–700-seater rather than significantly improve aircraft performance.

Adopting the C-wing configuration entails the judicious balancing of its characteristics as a means of reducing span while maintaining an acceptable level of lift-induced drag. Simultaneously, it will need to be an intrinsic part of the stability and control systems. Coincidentally, the C-wing may beneficially influence the wake vortex characteristics of the resulting design, a factor of particular concern for any large aircraft. Debatable as it is, the C-wing was stopped short of incorporating the technologically risky, highly integrated propulsion system proposed by Boeing (Long Beach) for its Blended Wing Body (BWB) approach to the UHCA.

Passenger accommodation in the C-wing

The double-deck passenger cabins of the various VLA designs work well enough until aircraft capacity (constrained by maximum body length) reaches the point at which the meeting of emergency evacuation requirements becomes overriding. Another objective in developing the alternative C-wing layout was to address this problem directly via a single-deck layout. By trading conventional fuselage wetted area for wing area, its increased chord length and thickness provide space for passengers seated laterally rather than vertically (multi-deck), which might make emergency evacuation easier.

Furthermore, It was also decided to develop the concept using a conventional single-deck cylindrical body, rather than adopt the fully blended wing-body approach. A significant portion of the passenger cabin thus remains independent of the inner-wing passenger cabin. This has the benefit that its weight can be estimated reliably using well-established data and methods. Additionally, much of the emergency evacuation and interior layout can be dealt with in a conventional manner. First-class and some business passengers can be provided with conventional windows. Moreover, growth can be provided by the simple expedient of adding fuselage plugs, without the very expensive necessity of a new wing.

Conclusions

The flying wings referred to have been extensively wind tunnel tested, and a 6 per cent-scale model of the Boeing (Long Beach) BWB was flown in the late 1990s. Despite its apparent attraction (not merely from an aesthetic viewpoint), the flying wing has some technologies critical to its success as a commercial transport:

- Stability, controllability and flight safety.
- Peculiarities of load distribution and weight efficiency of the integrated structure of the centre wing section.
- Interaction with airport infrastructure to allow taxying, parking, passenger loading and unloading, especially in emergencies.
- Passenger acceptance of windowless cabins.
- The efficient solution and airline acceptance of BLC systems and their maintenance.

Even if none of the above ideas proves viable, commercial aircraft design, though mature, is not a sunset industry (despite some sceptics), and designers still have the Joined (or Box) Wing concept up their sleeves.

The shape of things to come? This 16.9ft (5.18m) wingspan, 119.8lb (54.4kg) subscale aircraft was designed and built by Stanford University in co-operation with NASA and Boeing as part of a three-year $2.3 million NASA research contract on blended wing-body concepts.
(NASA)

Index